THE TRIUMPH OF
AMERICAN
CAPITALISM

The Development of Forces in
American History to the End
of the Nineteenth Century

BY

LOUIS M. HACKER

SIMON AND SCHUSTER

NEW YORK : MCMXL

MANUFACTURED IN THE UNITED STATES OF AMERICA
BY THE HADDON CRAFTSMEN, CAMDEN, N. J.

TO

LILLY

Contents

vii

Part II

THE VICTORY OF AMERICAN MERCANTILE CAPITALISM
IN THE REVOLUTION

Contents

Conclusion

END AND NEW BEGINNING?

Introduction

—

THE SETTING

CHAPTER ONE

The Climate of Capitalist
Development in America

IT IS A curious thing that American historians, when they have reflected on the distinctive part that the United States has played in the history of modern times, have given weight to considerations that almost entirely disregard our economic institutionalism. The doctrine of Frederick Jackson Turner and his disciples has been an attractive but only partial explanation: that American uniqueness has largely been caused by anthropogeographic conditions.

Isolated from the main currents of European development by three thousand miles of ocean, and largely preoccupied for the first three centuries of our history with the problems attending the conquest of a moving frontier made possible by the happy circumstance of an arable soil and rich timber and mineral resources, we have been able to build an American civilization to which, in the cultural-anthropological sense, most of the significant peoples of Europe have contributed.

Tried in and shaped by common experiences, and looking perforce inward rather than outward, this conglomeration of nationalities was able in time to take on distinctive qualities. The American, as a type, became an individualist, a democrat, an egalitarian, and a utilitarian; and he looked upon government only as an effective device for assuring his happiness and curbing the oppressive tactics of the monopolists.

Such an analysis, obviously, has real merits. It justifies a national pride; and it has the further effect of maintaining morale when times are out of joint. But it must be apparent, after some reflection, that a historical theory based almost exclusively upon increasingly remote pioneering experiences leaves out many facets.

3

There is the part played by organized religion in America, for example. Even before the writing of the First Amendment of the Constitution, forbidding "an establishment of religion" by Congress and guaranteeing freedom of worship, the American states had begun to dispense with the authority of an established church. Church and state were separated in America long before the move was attempted in France; in England, these two great conserving institutions are still linked. Now, freedom from an established church not only meant release from a single theological and educational authority (in England, for example, the principle of nonsectarian public education was not recognized until the 1870's, a whole century after the Americans had blazed the trails), but it also meant a fuller measure of political freedom.

There can be no question that established churches, as a rule, have buttressed the traditional institutions of the societies in which they have functioned. Developing a life and rhythm of their own, largely self-perpetuating, up to the nineteenth century finding it possible to receive and hold property without danger of alienation, established churches of necessity have been on the side of tradition.

One of the great consequences of the American Revolution, therefore, was the disestablishment of churches. It was no wonder that there existed a freer climate in which social experimentation—in the educational and political realms—could be pursued, unrestrained by appeals to an ecclesiastical authority whose origins were to be found in a remote and perhaps idealized past.

What has been said of established religion can be said with equal point about the principle of monarchy. A mystical concept in large measure, and today in actual practice having small validity, the idea of monarchy nevertheless has also been a powerful agent for the support of traditional as opposed to utilitarian or pragmatic attitudes. The American Revolution, here too, contributed vastly to release the American mind. Thus, the pattern of what we may call the American way of life has many strands and colors in it. And there can be no harm in submitting this many-hued Joseph's coat to a fresh examination. Particu-

tributed the possibilities of the realization of economic equality in America again to the existence of the moving frontier. Because there were present in America great reaches of arable land, virtually free for the asking and taking, the underprivileged in the more settled zones—the industrial workers, the unsuccessful small traders—could always pull up stakes and begin life anew as pioneering farmers. Free lands, in short, have made for a free and independent farming class: and this has served as the backbone of the American petty bourgeoisie.

Recent research has indicated that this analysis is not true in its literal sense. The free farmers of the American West, beginning with the 1820's, were not recruited from the industrial workers of the East, for these simply could not afford the costs of the long journey into the prairie states and the purchase and establishment of a family farm. The farms of the American West were settled by other farmers who came either from contiguous states for the greater part or direct from Europe; and such persons also were supplied with a capital fund adequate to pay the costs of transportation, the price of the land, and the charges required for the erection of the necessary improvements. There is another question that obtrudes at this point.

If the Turner theory of the moving frontier is true as an explanation of American development and the causative factor in the creation of a unique national psychology whose outstanding characteristic is the survival of petty-bourgeois traits and aspirations, then why is it inapplicable to the history of other new countries? For certainly, as regards Russian Siberia, Manchuria, Australia, and Canada, comparable cultural and economic patterns cannot be found.

That is not to say that the Turner theory is to be discarded entirely. For if industrial workers in America did not migrate westward to become free farmers, certainly *potential* workers did. In other words, these small farmers of New York, New England, the British Isles, Germany, and Scandinavia who began to fill up first the Old Northwest and then the prairie states would have been converted easily into industrial workers —as were the small farmers and agricultural laborers of England and Germany who stayed behind—if they had not had the opportunities to continue farming under more satisfactory conditions. These opportunities were to be found in the American West, certainly throughout the whole of the nineteenth century and, in considerable measure, up to the end of the World War.

But by 1920 an era was over: and then unsuccessful small farmers or their sons and sons-in-law had not two choices before them but only one. This was movement into the factories. The industrialization (or proletarianization) of our marginal farmers and of our surplus rural populations was delayed, therefore, for at least two generations.

What, then, shall we say about the actualities of opportunities of economic equality in America? They were real, certainly up to the end of the nineteenth century. In addition to the Turner explanation, as it applies to free farmers alone, the following other factors may be adduced in support of the assumption that America was the land where the petty bourgeoisie flourished.

First, it should be noted that thanks to the mercantilist system imposed by England upon the American colonies, opportunities for industrial production, except in limited fields, were closed to Americans during the seventeenth and eighteenth centuries. On the other hand, in England, industrial production had the direct support of the state—by bounties, tax remissions, the grants of monopolies, and crown subscriptions to joint-stock companies. The result was, as early as the sixteenth century, and certainly on a sizable scale by the seventeenth century, large-scale industrial enterprise was already flourishing in mining and in the manufacture of ironware, chemicals, glass, textiles, soap, foodstuffs, and the like. Production was still by hand, of course, and not by machinery; but the organization of production was already at many points on an industrial capitalist level, using workshops, division of labor, the wage system, and sizable capital funds collected by subscriptions to joint-stock companies.

This does not mean that all the industrial production in England, or indeed most of the production, was thus organized before the advent of automatic machinery. But it does mean that when mechanization came to supplant manufacture (in the literal sense) beginning with the third quarter of the eighteenth century, there already existed in England an enterpriser class which, while small, was schooled in the techniques of large-scale industry.

This class, as well, had already amassed a measurable capital fund. With its managerial skills and its capital, therefore, it was able to move easily into the widening field of industrial capitalism whose expansive opportunities became extraordinary as a result of the invention of the automatic spindle, the power loom, and the steam engine. Further, the capital accumulations from trade in England, because the mercantilist system was designed in the interests of English mercantile capitalism and her merchants had the whole world in which to range, and the capital wrested from the colonial possessions in the West Indies, Africa, and India made transfer into large-scale industrial production possible almost from the very start. In the early decades of the nineteenth century there already existed a powerful industrial capitalist class in England. The opportunities for the upward climb from humble beginnings were not nearly so frequent as is commonly assumed.

But this was not the case in America. After the American Revolution, all the industrial capitalists virtually started from scratch: for the advances onward and upward were not checked by the existence of privileged and already entrenched interests.

Second, in another great region for economic opportunities in America, that is to say in the exploitation of mineral lands, the doors were not closed to the little men. Thanks to the existence of a vast public domain sparsely settled by Indians and a generous land policy, it was possible for a fortunate prospector and a small capitalist to make a lucky strike and hit and work coal, iron, lead, copper, or oil deposits. Many early mining fortunes, in no way connected with special advantage, grew up in the pre-Civil War West out of modest beginnings in lead, iron, and copper. Notably in England and Germany exactly the reverse was the case; for the land had already been preempted by landlordism, and in England monopoly in coal production had been flourishing long before industrialism matured. Mining in Europe had always been a favored area of privilege; in the United States it was one of the regions in which free enterprise was able to flourish for a considerable length of time.

Third, Europe was not prepared to pour its accumulated capital into the United States to build up our industrial production (as it did later in Russia, Japan, and India, for example). Obviously it required its savings for capitalist construction at home. But a more important reason was that it could not obtain, and America would not give, the needed political guarantees that loans would be serviced and paid back.

European capital had helped in the original financing of public improvements (including railroads) in the United States before the panic of 1837 set in; but this was due to the fact that many of the securities launched in the English and Amsterdam money markets were state, or public, issues. But, as a result of his experiences with the depression of 1837-43, the European investor learned an important lesson; for many American states defaulted in interest payments and some repudiated their obligations altogether, leaving the foreign *rentier* without legal recourse. When the long depression terminated, European capital was coy.

The program of imperialism, as far as European capitalism was concerned, had therefore decided advantages. Either by outright conquest or by the establishment of spheres of influence or through the obtaining of government guarantees, European governments were expanding their area of political domination. And the enterprisers and their bankers who followed in the wake of missionaries, traders, and soldiers and who sank large sums in mines, plantations, railroads, and factories knew they were risking little; for economic and military sanctions could always be imposed on the subject peoples. At the very time, therefore, that America was presenting such golden opportunities for capitalist development, notably in the post-Civil War decades, the English and the French were turning their attention to Africa, India, China, and eastern Europe.

There is an illuminating passage in Trotsky's *History of the Russian Revolution* which reveals the extraordinary consequences, economically and politically, of imperialist penetration. He is talking of the Russia under Count Witte and later, when foreign capital was invited in to exploit the country's resources:

> The confluence of industrial with bank capital was also accomplished in Russia with a completeness you might not find in any other country. But the subjection of the industries to the banks meant, for the same reasons, their subjection to the western European money market. Heavy industry (metal, coal, oil) was almost wholly under the control of foreign finance capital, which had created for itself an auxiliary and intermediate system of banks in Russia. Light industry was following the same road. Foreigners owned in general about 40 per cent of all the stock capital of Russia, but in the leading branches of industry that percentage was still higher. We can say without exaggeration that the controlling shares of stock in the Russian banks, plants and factories were to be found abroad, the amount held in England, France and Belgium being almost double that in Germany.
>
> The social character of the Russian bourgeoisie and its political physiognomy were determined by the condition of origin and the structure of Russian industry. The extreme concentration of this industry alone meant that between the capitalist leaders and the popular masses there was no hierarchy of transitional layers. To this we must add that the proprietors of the principal industrial, banking, and transport enterprises were foreigners, who realized on their investment not only the profits drawn from Russia, but also a political influence in foreign parliaments, and so not only did not forward the struggle for Russian parliamentarism, but often opposed it. . . . Such are the elementary and irremovable causes of the political isolation and anti-popular character of the Russian bourgeoisie.

As in Russia, so in China, India, Japan, and many Latin-American countries. But not in the United States, because of the relatively minor role played by foreign capital (except in railroading). The upshot was, following the close of the American Civil War, it took a full generation before large-scale capitalist activities emerged in industrial production. I have said that foreign funds poured into the United States to help lay down our railroad net. But, what was even more significant than foreign capital assistance was the aid rendered by public authority. With huge land grants made from the public domain, with loans of funds by federal and state bodies, with stock subscrip-

tions, terminal sites, and special privileges made and freely
offered by local jurisdictions, our great trunk systems were really
made possible. Placing only a nominal value on the land grants
and adding in only the actual bond issues floated and stock
equities purchased, before the 1870's were over public authority
had advanced railroad promoters in the United States in excess
of one billion dollars. This situation explains clearly why the
first great post-Civil War fortunes in America were in railroading.

But in industrial production—because of the absence of foreign capital and direct public assistance—opportunities existed
for the small enterpriser. And if he were diligent, abstemious,
and shrewd (of course, knowing the right people often helped),
he could run up a small stake into a respectable and frequently
immense fortune. The annals of American enterprise, particularly in connection with industrial and smelting fortunes, have
been filled with the amazing histories of the Carnegies, Fricks,
Dodges, Rockefellers, Pratts, Gateses, and Reids, who, starting
obscurely—without links with either mercantile capitalism or
landlordism—made money, plowed profits back into capital
plant or bought out competitors, and ended by becoming modern Croesuses. Contrast the situation here with that in Russia
during the same period and the greater stability of our middle
class is revealed in a lightninglike flash. In the United States,
a home-grown capitalist class nursed its profits carefully, expanded its capital plant out of its own surpluses, maintained
owner management, rewarded the top layer of salaried employees by admitting them into its own ranks, and filled the
cities with evidences of its largess through the agency of phil-
anthropic giving: in short gave tangible proof of the reality
(as far as the lower middle class was concerned) of the American
dream that equality of economic opportunity existed. For the
middle class here life was rich with promise. In Russia, and
in all other countries under the sway of foreign, or imperialist,
capitalism, society was sharply polarized, with the small upper
class having a foreign, and not a native, allegiance. When economic and political shocks came, there were no middle layers
to cushion the blows for the regime.

Fourth, there was a constantly recurrent petty-bourgeois strain in our political life that gave aid and comfort to egalitarian aspirations. The leveling tendencies in America had their origins in England; and of course there continued to exist English counterparts. But while leveling doctrine became quickly submerged in the mother country, in America political leveling notions were constantly blooming. And they were effective, too. There is no country in modern times which can come near matching the successes achieved in the United States by the petty-bourgeois political ideas and leadership of Jeffersonianism, Jacksonianism, a part of original Radical Republicanism, Populism, and La Follette Progressivism.

Jeffersonian and Jacksonian states-rights doctrines kept financial monopoly in the federal sphere at arm's length and refused to countenance the use of the "law or the land" or "due process" clauses of state constitutions as devices to protect the property rights of corporations. The original or Old Radical Republicans sought to free the South's common man (Negro and white yeoman farmer) from his political and economic bondage at the hands of the large planters. Populism and La Follette Progressivism raised the battle cry once more against privilege and monopoly.

Thus, at any rate, into the greater part of the second half of the nineteenth century. And then, with the appearance of large-scale integrations in industry and with the growing significance of finance capital—as early as the end of the 1880's but more particularly during the years 1897-1904—the tradition of equal opportunity for men of small means became less and less an active and vital force and more and more a dream. We had come to the end of an epoch.

CHAPTER TWO

The Stages of Capitalism

I HAVE said that our American economic institutions have been developed wholly in a capitalist climate. A definition of capitalism is necessary at this point. Fundamentally, capitalism is an economic order based on the profit motive: therefore its leading characteristics are the private ownership of the means of production, their operation for pecuniary gain, their control by private enterprisers, and the use of credit and the wage system. This is capitalism in the pure form and it expresses the aspirations and program of a relatively brief era in its history. In other words, the capitalist system, as a program, held sway largely during the periods of the dominance of what we may call Industrial Capitalism and Finance Capitalism. Put chronologically, this era lay between the middle of the eighteenth century and the end of the 1920's in the histories of western European countries and the United States. Preceding the triumph of Industrial Capitalism and its development into Finance Capitalism, there was an antecedent stage, which we may call Mercantile Capitalism, and a subsequent stage, which we may call State Capitalism, in both of which the character of capitalism did not partake of the pure forms above described. That was due to the fact that the state, or public authority, played a part (not necessarily guided by the profit motive) in the determination of policies affecting production and trade. Nevertheless, whether the stage of capitalist development was mixed or pure, it may be said that production for profit set the tone, or represented the prevailing spirit, of producers and enterprisers over the epoch certainly from the sixteenth century to the present day. In the case of peripheral regions, as we shall see later, this capitalist spirit appeared even earlier.

Other manifestations of this capitalist order, or spirit, may now be detailed. It stands for the accumulation of money capital, over and above the satisfaction of the needs for current consumer goods, in order to convert these accumulations into more producer goods. It stands for the creation of a free working class divorced from ownership of the instruments of production —the land, the workshops, the machines; this working class, therefore, is compelled to sell its only commodity, its labor power, in the market. It stands for the establishment of large workshops, or factories, into which the working class is gathered for the purpose of producing goods; that is to say, labor is socialized and its functioning is continuous and under discipline. It stands for the creation of an ever-widening market which can absorb both the producer and consumer goods created in this fashion. And it is intimately linked with a commercial agriculture that is capable of feeding and clothing an industrial and urban population no longer self-sufficient. Finally, it requires a state, or public authority, to protect private property rights which articulates and encourages social and intellectual rationalization and explanation of the accumulative process. It may be said, therefore, that capitalism, operating on the basis of accumulation (the reverse of which is borrowed money) and utilizing a working class separated from the means of production and paid wages, produces goods for a market to enrich the private owners of the means of production. It is protected by the institutionalism of the state and by a large number of agencies for the dissemination of intelligence.

Subsidiary characteristics of the capitalist order may also be mentioned. It has rational organization. That is to say, its operations have been based on long-term and calculable planning. It has erected plants that may be expected to have a normal life and in the process of operation pay for themselves. It has produced goods as a rule in excess of current needs because of the existence of a widening market. It has been in a position to promise employment, at any rate with some degree of regularity, thus making possible the gathering of workers in large urban areas. And it has utilized a scientific system of accounts. It is not strange that double-entry bookkeeping, as we know it today, first appeared in the Italian cities in the thirteenth century, for it was exactly in the Italian peninsula that the original evidences of modern capitalism showed themselves. As Werner Sombart, the great German economic historian, has said: "Capitalism without double-entry bookkeeping is simply inconceivable."

Again, capitalism has perfected a financial mechanism as one of its most important tools. It utilizes bills of exchange. It employs negotiable securities. It has created banks for both savings and investment purposes. All this assures the universal recognition of counters, or symbols of capital, and permits a steady flow of savings into business enterprise for both long-term and short-term needs. As early as the end of the twelfth century bills of exchange were in common use in the commercial centers of Europe. Originating in Florence, in connection with its textile industries, bills on merchants in Germany, the Low Countries, and France were honored everywhere. Thus, even in the late Middle Ages, despite the chaos of languages and boundaries, capitalism had already learned to talk in a universal tongue.

Also, capitalism, in its modern sense, is based on machine production. It has applied the great lessons of physics, chemistry, and biology to the creation of technology; and technology has made possible mass production. With such methods, capitalism, holding out the promise of the achievement of a life of abundance, has populated, urbanized, and standardized the world. Indeed the application of technology to the production and exchange of goods has been capitalism's greatest functional achievement.

These attributes of capitalism, naturally, are not all unique to this particular system of production. Some were to be found under the slave economy of antiquity and the feudal economy of the Middle Ages; some exist today in the Soviet Union. However, if we were to seek a single distinguishing hallmark of the capitalist system, that one which could be truly denominated as setting it off from the orders that came before it, and that separates it from socialism, it would be the wage system. Under feudalism, the principle of the "just price" prevailed, and this was entirely an ethical concept. Under the plans for socialism, compensation is to be on the basis of need and not production, another ethical concept. But not so in the case of capitalism: for under its dispensation the free worker sells not the product of his labor but only his labor power; and he receives not the whole social value of the goods or services he creates but enough to sustain him and his family in terms of the prevailing standards of living. This is a market concept, divorced from ethics obviously, and based upon the automatic operations of supply and demand and the price system. Its rigors have been tempered a little bit, of course, over the past one hundred years, to prevent out-and-out distress; and today we are moving in the direction of social security. Nevertheless, for the working population, the wage system prevails.

I have said that there have been stages in capitalism's development, accounting for a movement from a mixed form to a pure form and again to a mixed form. This does not mean that our capitalist society has turned full circle and is, at the present day, back to the point from which it started as early as the eleventh and twelfth centuries. The discussion of the epochs in capitalism's history will illuminate what I have in mind.

1. *The stage of mercantile capitalism.* There are really two characteristics of this stage, the one economic and the other political; and they do not necessarily exist side by side. Economically, the hallmark of mercantile capitalism is the association of the capitalist or enterpriser with trade and banking rather than with industrial production. This stage started right within the Middle Ages and continued until the triumph of automatic production. Therefore, the *typical* capitalist (obviously there were always exceptions) in thirteenth-century Venice and Genoa, in fourteenth-century Barcelona and Bruges, in sixteenth-century London and Paris, in seventeenth-century Bristol and Liverpool, in eighteenth-century Boston, New York, and Philadelphia, indeed in mid-nineteenth-century New York, was a merchant capitalist rather than an industrial capitalist. He owned ships and warehouses, he operated in a counting-house or bank, he had agents and correspondents in different ports; and he did his business in the buying and selling of goods at wholesale and the lending out of money at interest. When he established links with production, it was again as a merchant

and banker rather than as an owner and operator of a workshop or mine.

In America, the first capitalists were such merchants who, creating the original urban communities of Boston, Philadelphia, New York, Newport, and Charleston, sent the produce of the New World to Europe and the West Indies and brought back the finished ware of textiles, iron goods, and notions. Indeed, mercantile capitalism continued to typify the activity of capitalists in America long after its leadership had been wrested away in England by industrial capitalism. In fact, we may say that in America the characteristic capitalist was a merchant or banker up to the middle 1840's; whereas in England the characteristic capitalist had become an industrial enterpriser by the end of the Napoleonic Wars.

The other side of this shield, that is, the political, was the doctrine of mercantilism. We shall have more to say later of this idea as a public policy; it is enough for our present purposes to indicate that the mercantilist conception of the state was very much like present-day totalitarianism. All the energies of the nation, and indeed of the empire, were to be bent toward the enrichment of the community as a whole: to make it more wealthy in this world's goods naturally but, even more important, perhaps, to make it more powerful. If the feudal economy was striving toward the achievement of plenty (which the Middle Ages never attained because of primitive organization and methods of production), the mercantile economy was striving toward the achievement of power (and for brief intervals met with success: witness the empires of Charles V and Louis XIV).

The significant thing about the mercantilist age was that economic power and political power were not necessarily conjoined. The merchant capitalists engaged in buying and selling and the lending of money capital; the control of the state, on the other hand, was in the grip of the royal dynasties. Hence, private fortunes did not have a long life, for at any moment the royal authority, which was absolute, by decree could snuff out a fortune or help in laying the basis for a new one. This was so, certainly, in Spain from the fifteenth right into the nineteenth century; it was also so in France up to the French Revolution. In England, as a result of the Puritan Revolution of the seventeenth century, state power fell increasingly into the hands of the merchant capitalists themselves. Nevertheless, the spheres of free economic activity continued circumscribed, by law at any rate, until the nineteenth century.

Mercantilism, in the interests of state power, therefore, stood for virtually complete control by public authority of economic activity. It was in such an environment that the American colonies were established and continued to grow during the first one hundred and fifty years of their history. The American Revolution cut the connection with English mercantilism once and for all, and by 1800, in the United States, the state was no longer an aggressive agency. The road was open for the development of industrial capitalism.

2. *The stage of industrial capitalism.* In this period, again, we are to note unique economic and political aspects. Under the dispensation of laissez-faire principles and the doctrines of utilitarianism, the enterpriser was encouraged to pursue his self-interest: and he had an extraordinary sphere of operations in industrial production. Capitalist activity now became associated largely with the ownership and management of factories, where, thanks to automatic devices, it was possible to turn out vast quantities of producer and consumer goods on a mass basis. The release of a rural peasantry from the land and its induction into urbanized communities were characteristics of this stage; as were also the widening of the market through railroad building and the opening up of backward economic regions of the world for the production of basic raw materials and the absorption of primary consumer goods.

Towering fortunes were built up in cotton textiles, ironware, steel, oil refining; and they were safe from the depredatory hands of the state because, politically, the state became a passive one. Side by side with the triumph of industrial capitalism went the dismantling of state power. Political authority was to be concerned only with the protection of the so-called natural rights of the individual—life, liberty, and property. So distrustful of the state was the average industrial capitalist (certainly this was so in England) that he was even willing to give up his claims to a protected national market. Laissez-faire, pushed to its obvious limits, meant also an international division of labor: an economic world, in short, based entirely upon the free exchange of goods and services without interference by any political authority.

This was an ideal, or the wishful thought, of English industrial capitalists; and for a short time, they, at any rate, were able to implement it. From the middle of the nineteenth century to the outbreak of the World War English capitalism lived in the uninhibited atmosphere of a free-trade economy. The United States threw up protecting tariff walls during the Civil War; France and Germany followed in the 1880's. But English capitalism, operating a rationalized plant and supported by great accumulations, was still prepared to sell its cheap goods in the world market in competition with all comers; and buy its basic raw materials wherever it could find them because it was ever ready to finance the primary producers.

3. *The stage of finance capitalism.* Even after controls over industrial enterprise began increasingly to fall under the sway of banking capital—as a result of the building up of giant integrations and the creation of combinations to check competition—capitalism was still free in the sense that it was not compelled to submit to political dictates. In the late 1870's in England, in the 1880's and 1890's in Germany, in the 1900's in the United States, the political program's emphasis increasingly was upon imperialist expansion. To find exploitable raw materials, to develop markets for finished goods, to open up areas into which capital accumulations could be moved, the state's assistance was necessary. This was the period when Europe advanced into and pacified the whole African continent as well as near, middle, and eastern Asia. This was the epoch of the conquest of backward peoples and establishment of colonies and protectorates.

Finance capital, piling up huge profits from monopoly and near-monopoly controls over industrial production at home, poured its savings into every economically backward region: to build railroads, establish plantations, work mines, construct and operate public utilities. The state's support was necessary to defend property rights in Africa, Syria, Persia, India, China; and it was freely given, but again under the rules of laissez-faire capitalism. In colonies and protectorates under imperialism foreign capital was not weighed down with disabilities or altogether banned. Indeed, the state made no effort to limit fields of capitalist enterprise so that in India and China quite often English and native capital was permitted to erect steel and textile works in competition with those in the United Kingdom.

4. *The stage of state capitalism.* The pendulum swung back once more, particularly after the World War. As a result of Europe's experience in that conflict, first in Italy and Germany, then in England, France, and the United States—with the overbuilding of plant, the opening up of new raw material resources, and the threat of social upheaval—capitalism was compelled to call upon the state for protection. The pressure of competition everywhere necessitated the erection of defenses for the safeguarding of the home market. And all over Europe, and in the United States, too, as a result, tariff walls were pushed up, quotas were imposed upon foreign producers, foreign exchange was regulated: to keep out the foreign trespasser. State power was being rehabilitated.

The onset of depression in 1930 further accelerated the process. The United States was not alone in experimenting with state capitalism, as a result of which the state not only became the defender of property rights but even began to initiate enterprise. For the danger of wholesale bankruptcy for producers of raw materials and fabricators of finished ware and the existence of vast numbers of persons without employment was more than a challenge: it was a threat to social stability. State intervention was necessary.

The political aspects of modern-day state capitalism more and more take on the features of mercantile capitalism. The hand of the state is to be found everywhere. It closely regulates industrial relations, of course; it limits production; it creates work. Indeed, in the totalitarian countries of Italy and Germany it moves toward the extinguishment of private-property rights and the supplanting of state capitalism by state socialism. In Russia, this step has already been achieved. Whatever the special condition, an outstanding attribute of state capitalism or state socialism, as was true under mercantilism, is the building up of a powerful bureaucracy whose members are the chief beneficiaries of the new dispensation.

This is the stage in which we now live. The freedom of capitalist enterprise is being severely contracted all over the world in varying degree. The freedom of the individual is constantly being submitted to attack. In the totalitarian countries the state has already conquered all zones, so that business enterprise and private conduct are the subjects of the bureaucracy's concern. In the United States, the role of state capitalism is becoming more pervasive, even if the bureaucracy is only partially formed and as yet is still responsive to the democratic processes.

I have said here that our present epoch begins to approximate the characteristics of the earlier one of mercantile capitalism. But only roughly, of course. Certain significant differences may be indicated.

First, the mercantile age never entertained the slightest hope of achieving plenty; indeed it forswore it, evolving an ethic of work and saving that frowned on the total use of income for consumer goods. In a sense, this sprang from the Protestant rejection of Catholicism's creedal system of salvation by good works. To the devout Protestant of the sixteenth and seventeenth centuries, salvation was by faith: a faith that took the form of application to a mundane "calling," so that the good man was not he who spent his substance and that of his children on pilgrimages, the erection of shrines, and the building up of the estates of the Church but in productive labor in this earth's vineyards. Again, the man of the mercantile age was appalled by the wasteful living of feudal landlordism. More particularly, perhaps, the rejection of plenty by mercantile capitalism simply flowed from necessity: for the productive processes were yet incapable of creating wealth for both immediate consumption and the erection of permanent additions to plant. The typical enterpriser of the sixteenth, seventeenth, and eighteenth centuries had to choose between eating his cake and having it. He picked the latter; with the result that the period saw the constant addition to national wealth, on the one hand, while the current rationalizations sang the praises of the frugal enterpriser. In this latter connection, I need refer only to Benjamin Franklin's *Advice to a Young Tradesman* and the guides to conduct and worldly success laid down in that amazing manual.

For we must not forget that the science of the sixteenth and seventeenth centuries was still largely preoccupied with the adumbration of a method. We stand in amazement before the overtowering achievements of the Cartesian and Newtonian revolutions; but sometimes we lose sight of the fact that it was not until the nineteenth century that the application of science to production really succeeded in devising a technology on a grand scale that made possible the harnessing of nature's forces in the interests of man. Then and only then did mechanics, chemistry, and biology begin their conquests of the zones of scarcity. Thus, the man of the mercantile age lived in a climate of want. One need hardly prove the point that we live today in a climate of potential abundance.

Second, the state power of mercantilism was used for aggression. Scarcity was real; there were no ideological curbs on the rapacities of absolutism; power was linked with personal and national physical might. The violence of the mercantile age flowed from natural necessity and the dominance of the principle of absolute monarchy buttressed by a court, that is to say, a parasitic, nobility. In modern democracies, at any rate, one can argue that state power in considerable measure is being employed for purposes of defense. I cannot lose sight of the facts, obviously, that many of these democracies are really sated imperialisms and that at home the state mechanism has as its prime function the protection of the property relation. But the modern state has been compelled to surrender many of the pretentions of its predecessor. It cannot cynically embark on a career of conquest or even warfare until it has proved at least to the satisfaction of its own people that its rights have been violated and its safety endangered. All wars today, the state can prove, are defensive.

More particularly, the modern state is compelled to concern itself with defense measures at home to prevent internal economic disturbance and social instability. The preoccupation with popular education, the creation of social-security codes, the acceptance of unemployment as a social challenge rather than as a proof of individual shiftlessness to be visited with savage penalties: these sharply differentiate the attitude of the modern state from its mercantile predecessor. On many important social questions the state has been compelled to move radically away from its earlier position where it commanded the loyalties of men without offering them any rights.

And that brings us to our third difference: our modern American state is still held in check by restraints imposed upon it by the doctrine of democracy. Our great heritages of the Enlightenment and the English, American, and French Revolutions are the flesh and blood of our institutionalism. How far we have traveled from the mercantile absolutist state we sometimes forget until we view the content of our political liberties. Thanks to the glorious concepts of the natural and inalienable rights of the individual to his life, liberty, and the private pursuit of his happiness; to the theory of popular sovereignty and the Lockian modification of the idea of the social contract; to the representative principle of republican government: the individual—that is, of course, the middle-class man—is free in an ideological sense.

In the foregoing pages I have presented the whole frame of reference into which my analysis of The Triumph of American Capitalism has been projected. But I have done this only to satisfy the very natural curiosity of the reader who, when he reads a work of history, particularly when it has to do with his own country, wants to have the narrative related to the problems and perplexities of his own day.

Here am I telling only part of the story, however. My leading preoccupations in this book will center in the following ideas. From the start of our development, our history was associated with Europe's progress. The discovery and settlement of America was an incident in Europe's growth. Our quick expansion in the nineteenth century in considerable measure was another chapter in that chronicle. At two stages in our history, revolutions took place to assure our steady march forward. At certain points, as I have been at pains to indicate, our development has followed unique patterns. But in the large, the growth of our economic institutionalism, that is to say, the various phases of capitalism, has been the growth of Europe's. Capitalism was a European phenomenon; and we inherited it. The history of America, therefore, begins in Europe's remote past. And to this subject we must now turn our attention.

Part I

—

EUROPEAN ANTECEDENTS

CHAPTER THREE

The Origins of Capitalism

1. EARLY TRADE AND EARLY CAPITAL ACCUMULATIONS

THE origins of capitalism are the subject of much learned debate. It is enough for our purposes to indicate the chief sources from which those accumulations came which finally succeeded in transforming the feudal system into the capitalist system. To a certain extent, early accumulations were formed from the rents of agricultural and, later, urban lands; and also from the sale of farm surpluses to the towns by lay and ecclesiastical lords and from the collections of the Catholic Church.

The returns derived from moneylending, despite the Church's condemnation of usury, were even more important. The Middle Ages was an era of dearth. In order to assure continuous production, funds had to be borrowed by all groups capable of pledging real or personal property. Upon this human necessity the moneylenders waxed and grew rich. In the later Middle Ages the moneylender performed other functions: he financed the struggle of the feudal lords against each other; he helped them embark on the Crusades; and he backed the ambitious dynastic princes in their wars of extermination of the feudal nobility and in the creation of the modern and nationalist states. The early monarchs of Spain, France, and England called upon the moneylenders to help in the financing of their military and civil establishments. Sometimes they paid interest; sometimes they granted monopoly privileges of one kind or another; sometimes they repudiated their indebtednesses. Thus usury capital played its part in furthering the processes of accumulation.

Most significant of all, however, were those accumulations that came from trade. It was no accident, then, that the first signs of the stirrings of capitalist enterprise were to be found

31

in those European centers (located outside the feudal system) in which trade began to flourish early. The Italian merchants succeeded in establishing outposts in the Near East; so did the north German merchants of the North Sea and Baltic Sea regions in Russia: and this was long before the First Crusade was preached. Penetrating with their Eastern wares into northern and western Europe—establishing entrepôts in the south German towns and in the towns of the Low Countries—these Italian and German merchants gave a mighty spur to the production of surplus commodities everywhere that they reached. It was in this east-west traffic that the Italian merchants and their allies grew rich, staked out imperial domains overseas, increased their argosies, bought mines in Hungary, the Tirol, and Spain, financed monarchs in their wars on the feudal nobility, and became patrons of the arts. The Renaissance flourished precisely in those regions where the merchant capitalists were most advanced.

With trade went hand in hand its twin sisters, joint-stock companies and banking institutions. Even as early as capitalism's infancy, finance began to play an important part in the shaping of the growing economy. The Bardi, the Peruzzi, and the Medici of Florence and the Fuggers and the Welsers of Augsburg, initially merchant families, became great bankers. In the late fifteenth century, Flemish speculators were already operating a bourse, or exchange, at Antwerp, where commodities were bought and sold and trading took place in the shares of joint-stock companies. The Bank of Amsterdam, the first great bank of modern times, appeared in the first decade of the seventeenth century.

It would be a mistake to assume that, while trade was the basis of the earliest form of capitalist economy, industrial enterprise was a later and successive stage. The fact is, industry— it is true, in a minor capacity—flourished in the very midst of mercantile capitalism. In the woolen, cotton, and silk textile industries, in Italy and the Low Countries as early as the thirteenth and fourteenth centuries, workers were already divorced from ownership of the means of production. They were collected in large workshops where they labored for wages on raw materials and with equipment furnished by the capitalist-employers of the day. The printing trades notably lent themselves to capitalist ownership and operation; and so did mining, the metal industries (particularly those engaged in the supplying of military equipment), and shipbuilding.

It was not until the middle of the eighteenth century—and largely in England at first—that trade definitely was superseded by industry as the chief form of activity of modern capitalist enterprise. The ever-constant growth of the proletarian populations of western Europe (the expropriation of the small yeomen from the land and the conversion of journeymen into hired hands as a result of the extending exclusiveness of the craft guilds were the chief reasons) furnished the labor supply. The improvement of agricultural techniques furnished the foodstuffs. The appearance of national states and oversea colonies and possessions furnished the market. Pacification at home and colonial conquest made possible orderly accumulation and furnished the capital funds. The invention and introduction of machinery took place and the factory system sprang up.

As has been said, therefore, industry had been in operation ever since the appearance of towns in the midst of the feudal economy. But industry had to pass through two transformations before it was ready to take on the forms of industrial capitalism. In the Middle Ages, under the guild system, the pivot of industrial activity was the guild artisan who was an independent producer owning both the raw materials that he fabricated into finished goods and the instruments of production with which he achieved these results. His shop was often his home as well as his workplace, his warehouse, and his store. Too, he produced largely for a local rather than for an export market.

In the period of the dominance of mercantile capitalism, the centers of production became more and more the workers' homes or cottages, which, for the most part, were located outside of the urban communities dominated by the guilds. Here, the raw materials were owned by the merchants who, after the processes of fabrication, disposed of the finished goods in the market. On the other hand, the artisan under this cottage, or domestic, or putting-out, system was in effect a wage earner:

with a difference. He received wages; but he labored in his own home, owned his own tools and other instruments of production, and was not completely cut off from the land. In short, he could still count upon subsistence if everything else failed him.

The industrial revolution, beginning in the middle of the eighteenth century, changed all this. For the merchant capitalist (sometimes he came to be called the merchant-manufacturer), there was substituted the industrial capitalist who bought the raw materials and sold the finished articles as before; but now he was chiefly interested in industrial production and not in trade. Thus, he began to erect large workshops, or factories, at a considerable outlay of capital. He installed machinery, requiring another capital expenditure. He went into the labor market to gather together and retain under the roof of the plant he owned a group of workers who were compelled to work for him exclusively, recognize his discipline, and bargain with him individually.

In return for their labor power the workers received wages; and upon these, now that they no longer were attached to the soil, they were entirely dependent for the support of themselves and their families. The modern age of industry had dawned.

2. THE FIRST STIRRINGS OF CAPITALISM

It has already been pointed out that mercantile capitalism made its first appearance in the Italian cities. Partly because the memories and habits of Roman economic life had never been extinguished completely in Italy, partly because of the propinquity of the Byzantine Empire, early ties were established between East and West around the borders of the eastern Mediterranean. "Syrians" (the name for all Easterners) from Constantinople, Asia Minor, and the Syrian coast made their way into the Italian cities bringing Eastern delicacies and finery with them and accepting in exchange wheat, wine, wood, salt, and slaves. Some of these traders remained abroad as resident agents of their houses, to introduce the financial practices and coinage of the East and to start local industries, particularly the manufacture of textiles.

Amalfi, Genoa, Venice, and other Italian cities became the

outposts of the Byzantine Empire across the sea. Indeed, so surely did Venice and its people thrive under this Eastern tutelage that by the end of the eleventh century its merchants were well known in the Eastern bazaars and became the recipients of a charter conferring upon them full trading privileges in Constantinople. When Pope Urban II preached the first crusade in 1095 the Italian merchants were already prepared to reap the full economic benefits from the expeditions.

The papacy was calling upon the faithful in Western Christendom to save the Holy Sepulcher from the infidel Moslems who were menacing the Near East. Behind the scenes, also, Rome was embarking upon an enterprise in power politics whose purpose was to link the Western and Eastern Churches under its undisputed headship now that the Byzantine Empire appeared to be slipping. Why did men, women, and children, knights, priests, traders, and moneylenders from every corner of Europe —throughout the twelfth and thirteenth centuries—leave their homes to endure dreadful hardships and to perish by the hundreds of thousands in the Alps and Carpathians and in the Syrian deserts? The reasons were various. Great numbers were true soldiers of the Cross. Many welcomed the opportunity to escape from the hard and humdrum round of the manor. Some were poor and landless knights who looked to the plunder of the rich East for their social rehabilitation. Some were merchants who anticipated swollen profits from trade, concessions, and colonies.

The papacy failed in its intention. Jerusalem and certain other cities of Palestine and Syria were taken and lost again. But the strong Moslem centers of Damascus, Aleppo, and Homs were never penetrated; and the Saracens remained true to their God Allah and to his prophet Mohammed. Indeed, the Crusades ended by weakening the last dike that stood in the way of the onsweep of Islam, for when Constantinople fell before the Turks in 1453 it was because the Christian traders of Italy had undermined its foundations a full two and a half centuries earlier. The Fourth Crusade, started in 1202, was turned into a Venetian military expedition against the Greek Catholic mentors and rivals of the Italians in the Near East.

First, the crusaders, who had hired the Italians to transport them to Egypt and who were unable to pay for their carriage, were compelled to despoil the Hungarian enemies of the Venetians on the other side of the Adriatic. Then they were moved on Constantinople, which they took and sacked, thus helping the Venetians set up a Latin empire on the Hellespont that lasted for more than a half century.

In other ways the crusaders called into play the customary functions of the merchant capitalist. Merchants and moneylenders equipped, transported, and supplied the Christian armies. When cities were seized, the merchants followed fast in the rear of the soldiery and founded trading quarters, or factories, in Acre, Antioch, and Tyre. The same persons established communications and commercial relations with the enemy even during those periods when the strife between Christian and Moslem was at its hottest. Thus, the Crusades failed as holy expeditions. But they did achieve another purpose: they piled up accumulations for the merchant princes of Italy, Spain, and France and in this way strengthened the hand of capitalism.

The history of Venice was typical of the rise of the Italian cities as a result of the commercial ties with the East. Starting as a humble fishing village, by the fourteenth century the Queen of the Adriatic was the seat of a vast empire. It had a population of almost 200,000 persons, a commercial fleet of 3000 ships under the single control of the city's council, and numerous trading stations along all the Levantine coasts, in Tripoli, Tyre, Salonika, Adrianople, Constantinople, and even in Trebizond on the Black Sea. Venetians proudly boasted that they ruled over "a half and a quarter of the Roman Empire"; in fact they did dominate the Adriatic, the Aegean, the Sea of Marmora, and the Black Sea. Unfree laborers worked the mines and tilled the soil in its oversea domains, while foreign subjects paid Venetian tax collectors for permission to operate their silk, cotton, glass, and pottery works.

The base of a great commercial empire, Venice was in a position to satisfy the newly acquired tastes of the returning crusaders for the luxuries of the East. The rich textiles and house furnishings, the spices, the personal adornments that the rough European knights had admired on the persons and in the homes of their Moslem foes, the Venetian traders poured into northern and western Europe. Venetian fleets regularly touched at Spanish, Portuguese, French, and Low Country ports; in time they reached England. German merchants, laden with the wares of the East that they obtained from Venice, traveled overland along well-trod routes into Germany and France—paying, it is true, the heavy exactions of tolls, tariffs, and marketing fees, risking the raids of the feudal robber barons, but making money. The accumulated profits of the Venetians were invested in home industries and workshops sprang up to weave woolen and cotton goods, make glass and manufacture brass and iron ware. Other accumulations went into the silver mines of Bohemia, Saxony, Alsace, and the Tirol and into the gold mines of the Carpathians, Carinthia, Bohemia, and Transylvania.

As in the case of the Venetians, so also in the case of the Genoese, Pisans, Luccans, Florentines. Argosies crossed the Mediterranean to the Eastern marts, then back home, and on outbound voyages carried rich cargoes of stuffs and spices into the western seas and out along the Atlantic coast. Itinerant merchants crossed mountains into the west European interior, by the twelfth century regularly pitching their tents in the fair towns of French Champagne, south Germany, and the Rhineland. Closer and closer the web of trade was spun over the face of Europe, so that Italians came to be familiar sights and welcome visitors in the Baltic Sea and North Sea ports, in England, in the Low Countries. Nor was their progress eastward checked. Notably in the fourteenth and fifteenth centuries, the Italian merchants penetrated into the deep interior of Asia, sometimes directly but more frequently through the agency of the Moslem traders who brought the wares from the Far East to the Italian factories on the Mediterranean and Black Seas. Thus, from Sumatra and Ceylon the Venetians and Genoese obtained pepper and cinnamon bark; from Arabia, India, and China, ginger; from the Spice Islands of the Malay Archipelago, nutmeg, cloves, and allspice; from Persia, precious stones; from India, sandalwood; from Sumatra and Borneo, camphor; from Arabia and

Persia, cane sugar; and glass, porcelains, silk, linens, rugs, and tapestries from a hundred Near and Far Eastern bazaars. And to the East the Italians sent out in return slaves, lumber, woolen goods, arsenic, antimony, coral, quicksilver, tin, copper, lead— and, above all, specie, obtained from the European mines that Italian and German mercantile capitalism had acquired.

What was taking place in the Italian principalities was being duplicated in varying degree in the Low Countries, Germany, France, and even in England. Great cities—the seats of trade, the home of foreign factories, the regular ports of call and depots for ships and overland caravans, centers for local manufacturing interests—were springing up. These made possible accumulations of wealth, built up a merchant-capitalist class, and furnished the power with which the feudal institutions were being weakened. The Hanse cities of Germany, grouped in the Hanseatic League, dominated the Baltic Sea as the Italian cities did the Mediterranean. The Hanse cities joined south and north, in one capacity acting as middlemen for the Italians and in another as the original developers of the north European countries. They bought and traded in furs, hides, leather, grains, and wax from Russia; in timber, iron, copper, furs, fish, meats, and grains from the Scandinavian countries; in wool, leather, hides, and tin from England. And they sold the wines, oils, salt, fruits, silk and cotton textiles, sugar, and Eastern spices and woods they had obtained at the Italian cities.

By the fifteenth century, the crisscrossing lines of European traffic were meeting in the towns of the Low Countries, and it was into Bruges, Antwerp, Ghent, Ypres, and Lille that were pouring the goods from the Baltic and the Mediterranean to be redistributed throughout England and France. Also, the Flemings became Europe's outstanding producers of woolen cloth. The result was that in many significant particulars the activities of the Low Country towns began to take on all the characteristics of modern metropolitan economy. The guilds were in decline. Great workshops existed, owned and operated by merchant-manufacturers. The wage system generally prevailed. A decided movement out of the incorporated towns—to escape the monopoly restrictions of the guilds—was in evidence on all sides. A money economy was in operation: for gold and silver coins were passed freely; so also were bills of exchange, checks, and letters of credit; while the sales of graded commodities on the basis of samples and for future delivery were becoming increasingly common.

Indeed, it was not strange that finance and trade should be thus intimately joined in the preindustrial era of capitalist development. The promotion of commercial enterprise, in all its ramifications, became the inevitable function of the Bardi, Peruzzi, Medici, Fugger, and Welser families, whose founders had started out by being traders themselves. Everywhere in the commercial centers these houses had their agents and branches. Soon, at Antwerp and Amsterdam, at La Rochelle, Bordeaux, and Paris, similar houses were to appear for the conduct of similar commercial ventures and to underwrite the independent trading expeditions of the western European countries into the Far East and the New World.

Such were some of the countless ways by which a commercial and banking middle class was growing to power during the four hundred years that preceded the sixteenth century. On innumerable small streams, from a hundred and one different sources were being carried the life-giving necessaries that were nourishing the new order. Italian ships and workshops; Baltic herring fleets; Low Country countinghouses; French moneylenders; Flemish artisans making cloth and glassware in England; German merchants and bankers owning and operating silver and copper mines in the Tirol and Hungary and silver and mercury mines in Spain; the cottages and workshops springing up in unincorporated boroughs and in the rural districts; the small yeomen and agricultural laborers being driven from the land as the enclosures turned the commons into sheep runs: this was the capitalist system on the make. And soon there was to appear an ethical code, linked with Protestantism, which was to teach that commercial and industrial enterprise, the accumulation of wealth, and the employment of the wage system were the true marks of the Christian and good life.

CHAPTER FOUR

The Bulwarks of Capitalism

1. THE ABSOLUTIST NATIONAL STATE

HAND in hand with the growth of the merchant-capitalist class went the development of the national monarchical state. The national monarchy, in the beginning, was clearly working in the interests of progress. Like capitalism, it was hostile to feudalism and suspicious and distrustful of the authoritarian power of the Church; it was quick to see that its survival depended upon its ability to break up the feudal bands and deprive ecclesiastical princes of their prerogatives. The ties of the early monarchies with the merchant capitalists were many and the connection strengthened both. The growth of administrative centralism, which the national monarchies represented, could not have been achieved had not the merchant capitalists been willing to finance the rising princes in their struggles against the feudal nobility, their wars with other dynastic houses, and the establishment of civil governments.

From the union, capitalism profited immensely. The establishment of national states widened the field of the domestic market obviously. Pacification at home—the initial task of the monarchies—made possible the safer movement of merchants and their goods. The royal courts dispensed justice by due process, in accordance with the law of the land rather than the earlier rule of the custom of the manor, so that rights of the person and of property could be protected. The monarchies built roads and bridges; sought to extinguish (in some cases with real success, as in England) provincial and local tolls and tariffs; moved to establish uniform weights and measures; tried, at any rate, to regularize the currency. Sometimes commercial agreements with other countries were entered upon. The kings granted to merchants, as rewards for their support or as security for money loans, important concessions and monopolies—to operate mines, to engage in exclusive fields in foreign trade, and to plant colonies in the opening oversea dominions.

As a result of the connection, the national monarchies in Europe rose in the fourteenth and fifteenth centuries and flourished mightily. There were other causes, as well. First, the change in the methods of warfare—the coming into use of gunpowder and firearms—literally blew the heavily accoutered feudal knights off the face of the earth. Also, the feudal armies were made up of knights exclusively; now the national monarchs could hire mercenaries who were kept loyal by being given the right of pillage in conquered regions. Second, the Crusades introduced Europeans to the monarchical states and the principle of absolute monarchy, which they found in the Near East. Also, the expeditions exacerbated national rivalries as a result of direct contacts. Third, the religious revolts and changes of the sixteenth century gave the national monarchs plausible reasons, in the countries which went Protestant, to enrich themselves through the confiscation of Catholic Church properties. In the Catholic countries, the monarchs demanded and obtained concessions from Rome, virtually leading to the nationalization of the Church, with the result that the national ecclesiastical organization was subordinated to the temporal power. The movement had extraordinary effects: as a result of confiscation and the filling of church offices, whether in Protestant or Catholic countries, with personal retainers, the monarchical princes were able to build up a court nobility whose loyalty was personal and direct.

During the fifteenth, sixteenth, and seventeenth centuries, therefore, there emerged great dynastic houses securely established. There were the royal families of Tudor and Stuart in England; of Valois and Bourbon in France; of Castile and Aragon and later Habsburg in Spain; of Habsburg in Austria. These, by pressing the work of national consolidation, became, in effect, powerful agencies to further the advance of capitalism. The European countries of the Atlantic seaboard were ready to challenge the supremacy of the Italian city-states—and to fight it out for leadership among themselves—when they had established at home peace, security, and a universally recognized civil government. From national unity flowed two great effects: the command over the tax resources of the nation and the ability to maintain mighty military and naval establishments. Oversea dominions and markets could now be established and, what is more important, held.

The word "progressive" has been employed in conjunction with the appearance of the national monarchies. This was true in the historical sense, for certainly the political stability that followed from the creation of nations was an advanced stage over the anarchy and disorganization of feudal society and the localism of the city communes. But the progressivism of the absolute monarchical principle quickly spent itself. The upshot was, monarchy increasingly began to prey on mercantile capitalism, its original ally. The absolute royal power, having become established, sought to dig itself in behind the barriers of privilege. To finance dynastic wars and to maintain royal courts, monarchy was compelled to live extravagantly. The merchant class began to feel the weight of the royal exactions: the judiciary began to operate in star-chamber proceedings, the tax collector and farmer began to be more oppressive, the royal monopolies began to cut down the areas of free commercial and productive enterprise. And to balance the growing numbers of the mercantile middle class the monarchy enlisted new friends. The monarchy, by the late sixteenth and early seventeenth centuries in England, for example, placed obstacles in the path of the enclosure movement, which was in the interest of the great commercial farmers, the wool merchants, and the woolen textile merchant-manufacturers. In this way, the monarchy sought to win the allegiance of the small yeoman class. Notably, the monarchy strengthened the numbers and position of the new court nobility. In England and France, these became the bureaucracy of absolutism. They controlled the national churches, sat on the bench, officered the armies and navies, received the most lucrative monopolies, acted (in France) as the farmers of taxes—in fact, directly and indirectly, were turned loose on the people for spoliation. The comparison with modern-day Fascism is remarkably apt, for the sixteenth- and seventeenth-century absolutist monarchies of England and France and the present-day Fascist states of Italy and Germany are alike in the building up of great companies of personal retainers which, in effect, become the controllers of the regimes.

By the seventeenth century in England and by the eighteenth century in France, the middle class began to sense that the individual enterpriser's chances for growth would forever remain stunted unless the areas of monarchical privilege were cut down. A government of laws had to be established to protect liberty and property against arbitrary procedure. These movements on the part of the middle classes culminated in the successful Puritan Revolution of the seventeenth century and the French Revolution of the eighteenth century.

2. MERCANTILISM AS THE PUBLIC POLICY OF ABSOLUTISM

In time, a public policy emerged that was to strengthen the hands of the rising national states and the emerging capitalist class. This we call today "the mercantilist system," although it must be understood that mercantilism was never consciously formulated as an economic doctrine or indeed as a set of rules for the guidance of the state. The term is convenient, however, for it does hit off the climate that prevailed in western Europe from the sixteenth to the end of the eighteenth centuries. Mercantilism can best be described in a series of contrasts, for it was the reverse of the laissez-faire liberalism which succeeded it. It was based upon the isolation of the national state—ringed about by jealous and hostile powers—instead of the internationalism that the nineteenth century preached. The colonial empires it sought to build up were to be the private preserves of the countries gaining them: to be exploited by their own nationals alone; to order their economic lives as the mother country directed; to operate within narrowly circumscribed limits. Mercantile states were much more interested in the making of money than in the production of goods. Further, all activities at home and in the colonial possessions were minutely regulated: high tariff walls kept out competing wares from abroad on the one hand and controlled closely the exportation of foodstuffs on the other lest prices at home be deranged; elaborate regulatory codes fixed

quality and fair weight of ware in the interests of the maintenance of foreign markets; wages were kept low to keep prices
down in the interests of the export trade; foreign artisans were
imported; monopolies were granted in the foreign trade and in
domestic production; and the state closely participated in the
economic life by itself investing in enterprise and through the
payment of bounties and the granting of tax remissions.

In short, the mercantile state was a totalitarian state interested
in the building up of state power. It sought to maintain the
dynasty, naturally, hence the unbroken record of dynastic wars
which were characteristic of the age; and to strengthen the economic resources of the nation so that rivals could be beaten off.
If a single idea may be employed to set off the concept of mercantilism it was this notion of the maintenance of state power, as
contrasted with the leading drive of the laissez-faire liberal state
of the nineteenth century, which was the production of wealth.
Certainly this intention, in the main, was in back of the policies
of Portugal, Spain, France, and England up to the Puritan
Revolution. And even in England, as we shall see, while the
middle class gained power after the overthrow of the absolutist
Stuarts, it continued to use the methods of mercantilism to keep
the American colonies in a state of subjection.

The program of mercantilism, therefore, was associated with
the following devices in order to achieve state power: national
unification; protectionism; bullionism; colonialism. In line with
the first—*national unification*—the dynastic houses broke down
the localism of the towns, sought to bring the guilds under national control, and labored—though not always with success—
to eliminate internal barriers to the conduct of trade, such as
tolls on highways and rivers and provincial tariff systems. In
line with the second—*protectionism*—the state sought to encourage the development of a favorable balance of trade by
stimulating the export industries, preventing the appearance
of foreign finished ware in the domestic markets, giving the
home merchant marine special advantages, and the like. Hence,
hand in hand with protection went state regulation, intervention, and participation. The state imported artisans, granted
bounties, staked out monopolies, invested itself in enterprise

and compelled private citizens to do similarly, sometimes erected state workshops; and on top of this structure imposed elaborate codes for the supervision of the home industries thus created. As in present-day Germany and Italy, not the private initiative of capitalism was at the controls of enterprise but an enormous and top-heavy bureaucracy.

In line with the third—*bullionism*—the state labored to increase the money stock of the nation. The attitude of mercantilism toward commodities was poles apart from that of the feudal age. The medieval world sought to attain plenty: hence it frowned on the export of goods while it tried to encourage imports. The mercantile world spoke slurringly of what it referred to as "a dead stock called plenty": hence it reversed the process and sought to stimulate the exports of goods and limit imports. Mercantile states, therefore, favored an increase in population, were not opposed to child labor, kept wages down (to give home producers a competitive advantage in foreign markets), and exploited the native populations of the colonial possessions overseas.

The measure of the success of this program was to be found in the increase of the money stock of the nation, that is to say, the excess represented by the greater outflow of exports at the expense of imports. It was no wonder that soldiers and adventurers scoured the four corners of the world for the precious metals; that sky-high barriers were erected against the outflow of gold and silver once they were brought home; that colonists were compelled to pay their adverse trade balances in specie. Notably in the seventeenth century, the apologists for mercantilism were bullionists; and while, in the eighteenth century, the theory was beginning to be looked at askance, there can be no question that the idea never was fully abandoned.

The national monarchs knew the uses of such a money stock. With liquid funds they could hire and outfit the mercenary armies by which the wars of the period were being fought, build great naval establishments, and keep a court nobility and bureaucracy with whose support their regimes were being maintained. The extravagances of the courts of Charles V, Philip II, Charles I, and Louis XIV (and paradoxically, their stability) were the other face of the shield of a mercantilist program based upon colonial spoliation, successful war, and the inflow of the precious metals.

In line with the fourth tactic of mercantilism—*colonial expansion*—the mercantile states chartered trading companies and gave them the right to erect colonies; sent armies overseas to pacify the native populations; and erected elaborate legal codes whose purpose was, generally, to compel colonial peoples to produce raw materials the mother country required and absorb finished goods the mother country produced in surplus. The colonials were to buy more from the mother country than they sold to her: and the balances were to be paid for in bullion. But where were the colonists to get specie? The thought was never articulated in so many words. Realistically, colonists got specie from the spoliation of the natives, their enslavement for work in the mines, piracy, illegal trade, the development of the Negro slave traffic. As far as the British mainland colonies in America were concerned, mercantilism by the eighteenth century had become a repressive device. To release the colonies from this leading string, which had become a fetter, became in effect the program of the American Revolution.

3. THE PROTESTANT ETHIC

Curiously enough, another important support for early capitalism came from the new Protestant churches. And yet, this should not be too surprising, for the middle classes needed spiritual comfort as they engaged on the rounds of trading, producing, and accumulating. The Catholic ethical system had served an earlier time's needs; it no longer could function in the rapidly changing world of bourgeois living. Upholding a slow and difficult progress toward not earthly but eternal salvation through sacraments and good works (the Church's doctrine of the dualism of man made imperative the utilization of a penitential system for the achievement of grace), the Catholic Church had impressed upon the humble the need for obedience and upon the great the sweet uses of charity. Upon the foundation of these principles was reared the great edifice of the Church itself. In every realm of human activity the Church's intervention therefore was real. Particularly was this true in the economic sphere. The doctrine of the "just price" called for the moderation of rewards—not equally, of course, but adequately and in accordance with the individual's station in life. Also, interest-taking and excessive profit-making (because money was sterile) were held to be usurious and therefore socially reprehensible.

To ambitious bourgeois, in the sixteenth century, the inadequacies of such guides to conduct—for the Catholic economics essentially was an ethic—became more and more apparent. The gap between the lives men were actually living and the moral standards recognized as valid was becoming wider and wider. Cynicism and a loss of faith were the reactions of the bolder spirits. The more timid were finding themselves becoming uncomfortable spiritually. The bourgeoisie, in short, was discovering it had lost its ethical mooring. This the Protestant Reformation and the Reformed churches which arose from it supplied.

For the bourgeoisies—of Holland, north Germany, France, Switzerland, England, Scotland—were developing new standards and new patterns of conduct. They were diligent, resourceful, solidly and stolidly respectable, abstemious in their personal living and in their pleasures. More often than not of lowly origins, they consciously resented the precept of humility and the notion that they were permanently fixed in a lower station. Looking about their expanding world, everywhere they saw openings for the attainment of wealth and personal aggrandizement: was it any wonder that they should be restive under the hobbles on enterprise put by the "just price" and the limitations on interest? They were hard-working and thrifty: why be content with the promise of a long-postponed reward in an afterlife? The adequate enjoyment of the fruits of their present toil seemed to them a not unreasonable demand. For such as these— and they represented, by and large, the middle class—the Catholic Church, with its old ethic, its monopoly over the sole means of salvation, and the growing monetary demands its representatives were making, was holding back the forces of progress.

Protestantism, on the other hand, released them. For the

Protestant creed freed the individual (that is to say, the economic man) from the authoritarianism of a powerful church mechanism, from dependence for salvation upon a constantly growing stream of good works, from the necessity for looking to the afterlife for his due. By giving the good middle-class Christian the doctrine of justification by faith, it permitted him to devote his energies to the present anticipation of future salvation. If men were truly glorifying God by application to their mundane affairs (once they had thrown themselves on His mercies) then, obviously, the godliest individual was the most diligent, the most enterprising, and the thriftiest. The good businessman was God's elect. An English Puritan divine of the seventeenth century thus phrased it: ". . . as Christ saith, to him that hath (using it well), shall be given. This riches is your strong tower." And because the Protestant churches (more particularly the Reformed churches) were to supply the needed ethic, it was natural that they should gain the adherence of the rising bourgeoisie. It thronged into the Reformed churches; and in one country, at any rate—in England—these churches became the rallying grounds for middle-class revolt against the privilege associated with the absolutist monarchy.

In a real sense, the upthrust in the ecclesiastical sphere dated not from the activities of the German Martin Luther, but of the French-born John Calvin. Luther, while still a priest, thundered against the mother church. And in so doing he won, in the beginning, at any rate, the adherence of the humblest and most oppressed in Germany (that is, the peasantry who were being ground down by the increasing exactions of their lords); and also that of the highest in station (that is, the ambitious local princes, who looked covetously on the rich lands of the Church). On the other hand, Luther was suspicious of the new bourgeoisie; he was complacent in the face of the prevailing unbridgeable class divisions; and he advocated the continuance of, or, rather, the reversion to, a static agricultural economy. In an age of great change, Luther, rather than face the realities of his time, particularly the demands of the bourgeoisie and peasantry for freedom, was prepared to return to feudalism.

Nevertheless, the Protestant Reformation did release a vast

number of forces which were to change profoundly the prevailing religious habits of thought—and in this way affect social and economic living. The most powerful of these was Calvinism. Calvin and the Swiss and French reformers who clustered about him, townsmen like the class their doctrines were reaching, were realists. They were aware of the mechanisms of daily commercial and financial enterprise and they set out to preach a religious creed and establish an ethical system which would be completely at home in this constantly evolving world. Calvinism and its offshoots, instead of commending humility and poverty, gave their approval to the economic virtues of work and thrift. The superstructure of the new Protestant ethic, therefore, came to be based on the objective conditions of bourgeois living. Personal responsibility for men's conduct was the clearly defined design; and it was to be a Christian conduct founded on those attributes which were everywhere meeting with victories in the daily battles of life. In the words of R. H. Tawney, this was the theology and ethic of the new system: "The rational order of the universe is the work of God, and its plan requires that the individual should labor for God's glory. There is a spiritual calling and a temporal calling. It is the first duty of the Christian to know and believe in God; it is by faith that he will be saved. . . . The only genuine faith is the faith which produces works. . . . The second duty of the Christian is to labor in the affairs of practical life, and this second duty is subordinate only to the first." Thrift, diligence, sobriety, industry; the application to a worldly "calling" and the attainment of success in it. Could the middle-class enterprisers of the sixteenth and seventeenth centuries have been more at home in Zion than when they had such a body of doctrine to comfort them?

Nowhere more clearly were the effects of the new creeds and their moral code to be revealed than in the changed attitude toward the indigent. If "industry" and "thrift" were the true characteristics of a state of grace, then the mendicant—that is to say, the slothful person—was irreligious and worthy of society's severest condemnation. This attitude became the rational basis of the English poor-law system, and it was as a result of the application of such touchstones that seventeenth- and eighteenth-century England came to look with approval upon the export into its colonies of the humble and the dependent as indentured servants. The reasons for the division of society into rich and poor have been clearly outlined by Tawney: "Convinced that character is all and circumstance nothing, he [the seventeenth-century English Puritan] sees in the poverty of those who fall by the way not a misfortune to be pitied and relieved, but a moral failing to be condemned, and in riches not an object of suspicion . . . but the blessing which rewards the triumph of energy and will. Tempered by self-examination, self-discipline, self-control, he [the Puritan] is the practical ascetic whose victories are won not in the cloister, but on the battle field, in the counting house, and in the market." Thus clothed in a righteous armor, the middle-class man of the seventeenth century could look calmly upon political revolution and civil war as devices in the attainment of his godly goal. And that was the free development of the individual through free business enterprise.

CHAPTER FIVE

The Discoveries and Their Effects

1. THE REASONS FOR THE DISCOVERIES

WHILE life was quickening in the Italian, north German, and Flemish cities and men were shaking off the restraints that for so long had hobbled their enterprise, the peoples of western Europe—of Portugal, Spain, France, and England—too were beginning to stir. In these countries a new merchant class was arising which was joining its destinies to those of the national princes and assisting in the work of national consolidation. But the merchants of the newer lands of the Atlantic seaboard were really performing the functions of middlemen. They acted as the go-betweens for the Italian and Flemish merchants and bankers in their various countries. They provided the raw materials (in England it was wool) that were fabricated into finished goods in the workshops of Bruges, Florence, and the other cities dominated by the older merchant capitalists. When they penetrated into the great market towns of Flanders, Tuscany, and the eastern Mediterranean, it was only with the consent of the groups who already possessed monopoly trading privileges in these centers.

By the fifteenth century, the merchants of western Europe were becoming restive. It is true they also were accumulating profits, buying mines, and becoming interested in the wholesale production of textile goods. But the chief source of wealth—direct participation in the rich trade with the Levant and the Orient—was closed to them. One of the most powerful impulses to discovery arose out of a desire on the part of the merchant capitalists of the countries of the Atlantic seaboard to slip free from the restraints imposed upon them by the Italians and to establish their own links with the crowded cities of India, the Spice Islands, and China.

51

There were other reasons that spurred men on. The hunt for precious metals had to be pursued ceaselessly—to add to the national store and to make possible the balancing of payments in the oriental trade. The Orient also was providing a steady market for slaves. Equally important was the growing necessity for finding an all-water route to the East as a result of the dislocations being effected by a powerful Islam.

It has commonly been supposed that the fall of Constantinople before the assault of the Turks in 1453 closed the door into the Near East to the Western traders. This was really not the case. In the first place, Constantinople's primacy had long before been destroyed as a result of its capture and subsequent loss by the Venetians in the thirteenth century. Again, the Turks did not gain control of Syria and Egypt and the important routes that led through these lands until a full quarter century after Columbus' first voyage. Finally, the Turks were as interested in keeping trade alive as were the Italians. But their reasons were different. The Turks afforded every encouragement to the merchants sending their ships and caravans into the Near East: for from this intercourse they hoped to derive revenue that would permit them to continue their task of empire-building. By controlling the sea and land approaches into the Eastern interior they could demand registration fees of the foreign merchants, impose tariffs, and collect tolls at ports, bridgeheads, and roads. It was, in short, the cupidity of the Turk and not his hostility that turned the thoughts of Westerners to the development of new trade routes into the East.

Also, there was the important consideration of high shipment costs. The journey into the East could not be made without breaking bulk many times. The Mediterranean Sea was the first to be crossed; then there was an overland route into either Egypt, Syria, or Asia Minor, with the shifting of cargoes to the backs of camels or horses; then once again goods had to be loaded on sea, lake, or river boats. This process was costly and frequently dangerous. Marauders and pirates might be encountered and had to be either fought or bought off. The upshot was that when the Eastern wares finally reached the hands of the middlemen in Portugal, Spain, France, and England they were burdened with excessive overhead costs. How much greater would the western European's profits be if he could reach the East directly —without the intervention of the Italians, the necessity for satisfying the demands of the Turks, and the need for paying fees, charges, and bribes to customhouse officials, ship captains, local chieftains, and roving freebooters!

Such were the hidden springs that nourished the hopes and ambitions of western Europeans throughout the fifteenth century. And as the years passed there was also being accumulated a body of knowledge that soon was to make possible the translation of dreams into reality. The wanderings of traders and priests into the distant places of the remote East—the travels of the Venetian Marco Polo has been the most important of these—had familiarized Europe with the geography of these far-away and rich lands. China lay on the edge of a great ocean; Japan and the Spice Islands were archipelagos and accessible to seagoing ships; there were populous cities spreading back from safe harbors. The revival of learning in the Moorish universities of Spain had its effects on the unlettered West: men were able to reason that if the earth were a sphere then the Far East could be reached by a number of all-sea routes. The aids to navigation afforded by the compass, the astrolabe, portolan charts, and improvements in naval architecture further laid the basis for maritime adventure. The final success of a group of national princes in Portugal, Spain, France, and England in their struggles with the feudal nobles and, therefore, their ability to place the resources of the new national states at the disposal of merchants—by financing and equipping expeditions and by protecting these against marauders—were all that were needed to launch the Atlantic countries on that astounding career of discovery, exploration, and settlement which linked the destinies of the Far East and Europe with that of the New World.

2. THE VOYAGES OF DISCOVERY

Portugal under the guidance of Prince Henry, son of its first national king, led the way. Slowly, intrepid Portuguese navigators inched their way around the African coast. In the 1460's they reached Sierre Leone, marking the capstone of Henry's career. The Portuguese found gold-dust, ivory tusks, and black slaves; and they therefore pressed on. The Congo was discovered in 1482; Bartholomew Diaz rounded the Cape of Good Hope in 1487; Vasco da Gama sailed into the Indian Ocean during 1497-98 and reached journey's end when he anchored in Calicut harbor. The West and the East were now linked. Before a half century was over, Portuguese merchants and sea captains, operating from the seatowns of India as their base, were reaching into every far corner of the East and were carrying on a regular intercourse with the Spice Islands, China, and even Japan.

Spain, united under the joint crowns of Castile and Aragon in the persons of Isabella and Ferdinand, and finally freed from the Moorish invaders, soon followed Portugal's example. It was only by chance that Spain established the first European foothold in the New World, however. For its initial adventurer when he sailed westward into the Atlantic Ocean was bound either for the cities of China or, as has been claimed by some modern scholars, was looking for new islands lying off Europe's and Africa's Atlantic shores. Christopher Columbus, a Genoese wool carder, trader, and sailor, had spent his early manhood in the ports of the Mediterranean and the Atlantic. Here he had acquired all there was to be learned of the then known mercantile and maritime knowledge. After unsuccessfully trying to reach the Portuguese king with a scheme for an expedition into the Atlantic, he finally got the ear of the Spanish queen. Isabella agreed to finance him. On August 3, 1492, Columbus, with a fleet of three tiny ships and a mixed company of eighty-seven men, sailed out of Palos, Spain, into the western seas. On October 12 he touched land—an island in the Bahamas in the Caribbean Sea. During the next decade Columbus made three subsequent voyages, in which, under the impression that he was cruising in Eastern waters, he actually explored portions of the coasts of Central and South America and penetrated into the mouth of the Orinoco. The standard of Spain was floating not over China and the Spice Islands but over the Spanish Indies (the Spanish designation for the new empire in the Western Hemisphere).

Other navigators, sailing under the flags of England and

France, followed fast on Columbus' heels and laid the bases for the subsequent claims of the English and French to empires in the New World. The Italian, John Cabot, in the employ of the English King Henry VII, reached Newfoundland in 1497. The Italian John Verrazano, in the hire of the French King Francis I, reached Cape Breton during 1524, and as he sailed southward entered New England harbors and probably put into New York Bay. Soon, the St. Lawrence River was entered, the northern coast of South America was explored, and Brazil was discovered. During 1519-22, Ferdinand Magellan's ships, sailing for Spain, entered the straits near the southernmost tip of South America, rounded into the Pacific Ocean, and discovered the Philippine Islands. The intrepid leader of the expedition was killed and most of the ships were scattered and lost; but one of them, navigated by its frightened crew, did succeed in making its way back to Spain, with positive proof that the earth was round and that a great land mass lay between Europe and the Far East.

3. THE TREASURE OF THE NEW WORLD

During the sixteenth century, the processes of discovery and exploration went on, with Portugal and Spain taking the lead. Aided by the papacy, which in 1493 had divided the "heathen lands" of the world, for purposes of exploitation, between the two monarchies—with Portugal established supreme in the eastern half and Spain in the western half—the two Iberian countries staked out vast empires in the Far East and the New World. Portuguese merchants located their trading stations, or factories, along both coasts of Africa and India, in the Persian Gulf, among the islands of the Malay Archipelago, and in the China Sea, where they carried on a rich trade in Negro slaves, spices, and textiles. They also settled in Brazil, which added its goods to the stream of profits pouring into the mother country.

The Spaniards, less hampered by the presence of large and well-organized native peoples, which the Portuguese encountered in the East, were not forced to deport themselves with the circumspection required of their Iberian neighbors. The result was that Spanish activities in the New World partook more of the nature of piratical expeditions and the lands that fell under

their sway were stripped of their wealth to enrich the grandees
and merchants at home. Settlers and priests, following in the
wake of the adventurers, established colonies, converted Indians
to Christianity, and introduced many of the higher domestic arts
of Europe into the New World. By the opening of the seventeenth century there were living in some two hundred Spanish
settlements upwards of 200,000 whites who had under their
domination at least 5,000,000 Indian subjects and some 40,000
Negro slaves.

Still, in spite of these great changes, the chief significance of
the new lands lay in the great stores of silver and gold treasure
they made available to the Spaniards. Hernando Cortez in 1519
had forced his way into the Aztec Empire of Mexico. Fifteen
years later his countryman Francisco Pizarro had laid low the
Inca Empire of Peru. In both these unhappy lands the local
rulers were stripped of their gold and silver plate and their subjects compelled to do forced labor in the silver mines. When the
Spanish King Philip II added the Portuguese crown to his own
in 1581, Spain was mistress over the great precious deposits of
the New World, the spice and textile trade of the East, and the
industrial and banking towns of the southern portion of the
Low Countries.

The opening of the New World had the curious and far-
reaching effects of some remote disturbance which puts into
motion tidal waves all over the face of the earth. It reintroduced
Europeans to the institution of human slavery. It revitalized the
West-East trade. It hastened the processes of enclosure. It
strengthened English mercantile capitalism. And it helped to
lay the foundations of our modern world.

The Negro slave trade. The Portuguese had first learned of
the advantages to be derived from selling black slaves in the
East. More important to the development of the traffic was the
fact that the Spaniards and Portuguese, requiring a cheap labor
supply for the operations of the mines and plantations of the
New World, and meeting with no success in their initial efforts
to enslave the native Indians, turned to the African Negroes.
Soon, Dutch and Italian slave runners, in the employ of Spanish
merchants, were making regular calls at West African ports,

taking on cargoes of blacks, and carrying them to the plantations
of the West Indies and the mines of Spanish America. In 1619
a Dutch privateer brought the first boatload of Negro slaves to
the new Jamestown settlement of Virginia. Later in the same
century Englishmen became interested in the traffic and they,
subsequently joined by American merchants, became the chief
sources of supply of slaves for the sugar, coffee, tobacco, and rice
fields, and the silver mines of the Western Hemisphere. French-
men, too, participated in the traffic. In the eighteenth century,
Bristol and Liverpool in England, Nantes in France, and Newport and Charleston on the American mainland became the
great entrepôts of the trade. Here was a point at which many
significant merchant-capital fortunes were built.

The flow of the precious metals. The successful exploitation
of the precious metal deposits of the New World—largely the
silver mines—had equally portentous results. Europe's trade
with the East essentially was based upon the ability of European
merchants to ship silver to India, the Spice Islands, and China;
for the East did not buy as much goods from the West as it sold,
with the result that Western merchants were required to pay
their balances in specie. But the mines of Europe were proving
unequal to the task of supplying both the needs of the East-West
trade and the demands of Europeans themselves for currency.
The fifteenth century, therefore, had witnessed a slowing up of
the new processes of expansion. The Eastern trade was dropping
off, prices were falling, and mercantile capitalism was confronted by serious hindrances to its continued advance.

The opening of the great silver mines of Mexico and Peru and
the perfection of a process for extracting silver by amalgamation
with mercury changed all this. From the 1530's on, mercantile
capitalism in Europe had a new lease of life; and for some three
quarters of a century a flood of silver (and gold to a lesser extent) tumbled into Europe. During this century alone, Europe's
gold stock probably doubled and its silver stock more than
trebled. By the time this original flow from the Spanish Indies
had largely ceased, that is, by 1660, some 18,000 tons of silver
(present value about $200,000,000) and 200 tons of gold (present
value $170,000,000) had passed into the hands of the officials in

Spain. Indeed, it has been estimated that during the three hundred years of the sixteenth, seventeenth, and eighteenth centuries Europe received from Mexico and South America a total of 2,500,000 kilograms of gold (to be compared with the 550,000 kilograms it possessed in 1500) and from 90,000,000 to 100,000,000 kilograms of silver (to be compared with its 7,000,000 kilograms in 1500). This precious stream flowed through the veins of Europe's business enterprise, reaching even the most remote villages and hamlets. Generally, the grand effect was that it put Europe definitely on a money economy.

The treasure moved first largely to Spain, although some of it was smuggled out of the Spanish possessions into other European countries. Why didn't it stay in Spain, to make that land the first great capitalist nation of Europe? The reasons were various. The Habsburgs helped to run through the Midas hoard rapidly to support their extravagant royal household and to finance their disastrous military adventures in France and in the Low Countries. The tax system of Spain rested heavily on merchants and industrial producers, while the tax farmers, in control of the mechanism, were inefficient and corrupt. The new court nobility built up a nonbourgeois psychology: it frowned on productive labors and looked to its aggrandizement through the control of the land, the army, and the Church. The Church's economic power continued to grow, thanks to the maintenance of the institution of the "mortmain" (inalienability of land acquired by the Church), with the result that a good deal of the wealth of the nation came to rest in the hands of the ecclesiastics, who were content to live off land rent rather than by the profits of industrial enterprise. The upshot was, the Spaniards spent, squandered, or lost a good deal of the treasure of the New World; and it came to rest in France, the Low Countries, and England.

Some of the effects of the inflow of the New World treasure into Europe may be indicated.

Revitalization of the trade with the East. Now European merchants could again pay their unfavorable balances with specie. The trade became so great that during the first half of the seventeenth century Europeans sent as much as £1,000,000 in silver eastward every year. And how did they benefit in return? It is enough to cite the example of the Dutch East India Company which, during this period, was able to pay annual dividends ranging from 12½ per cent to 50 per cent; and of the English East India Company, which was able to pay as high as 334 per cent on single voyages.

The resulting price revolution. The flow of treasure (supplemented, it is true, by debasement of the currency) encouraged an extraordinary rise in prices, giving further stimulus to commercial and industrial activity. In Spain, during the decade 1601-10, prices stood at 3.4 times the level of those of 1501-10. In England, over the one hundred and fifty years 1500-1650, the prices of 1642-48 were in the ratio of 3.5 to 1 to those of 1501-10. Wages, on the other hand, lagged behind. In Spain, in time, they caught up. In France, the spread between prices and wages gradually narrowed, although the workers continued to occupy an underprivileged position for two centuries. But it was in England that the disparity was most apparent and by the end of the sixteenth century the purchasing power of wages was only half what it had been at the beginning of the century.

Here was a gap at which accumulation was occurring. In J. M. Keynes' phrase, a "profit inflation" was taking place that permitted enterprisers to embark on new ventures, take new risks, and expand capital plant in manufactures and mining. The following figures show the *ratio of commodity prices to costs of production* in England for the one hundred and fifty years and indicate clearly the advantaged position of the new middle class over the laborers. (In his calculations, Mr. Keynes assumes that money wages accounted for half the costs of production.)

Period	Prices Received to Costs Paid
1500–1550	100
1550–1560	116
1560–1570	112
1570–1580	116
1580–1590	120
1590–1600	137
1600–1610	139
1610–1620	135
1620–1630	141
1630–1640	134
1640–1650	133

There were other points at which accumulation was appearing. For one, there was a spread between prices in the West and those in the East, for the East hoarded and hence sterilized its bullion with the result that *its* prices were lower for its wares. Merchants in the Eastern trade therefore were able to take extraordinary profits. Again, another area of costs at home did not increase spectacularly, that is to say land rents, due to the continuance in England of copyhold tenure as a result of which rents were based on the custom of the manor. From this situation enterprisers were also able to benefit. They profited from the low rents, of course. Of equal significance was the fact that many landlords became embarrassed as a result of declines in revenues and were compelled to sell out to the rising bourgeois. It should be had in mind that rents notably in England were being affected at this time also by the expropriation of the monasteries being carried on by Henry VIII.

The process spread in widening circles. Treasure raised prices but wages lagged. The "profit inflation" led to accumulation and the piling up of liquid capital for investment in heavy industry. New mines in coal and iron were opened up, new technological processes were developed, large-scale industry in metals, glass, and textiles began to emerge in the sixteenth and seventeenth centuries. Thanks to the recent researches of John U. Nef we know that England was experiencing the first years of its industrial revolution in that early epoch; and as a result of further lowering of costs under workshop organization and the introduction of mechanization, more profits were being made. In this fashion the capitalist class was growing to maturity.

The enclosure movement. Hand in hand with this development went the processes of enclosure. A widening market for woolens necessitated the production of more wool, so that the sheep runs began to encroach upon the arable and the common lands. Landlords (frequently merchant princes who had picked up estates at bargain prices) raised rents in disregard of the rights of the copyholders (the so-called process of rack-renting) and succeeded in driving many of these customary tenants off the land. The consolidation of properties then took place. At the same time the common lands were being enclosed, also in violation of the traditional rights of the villagers. On the one hand, the new landlords gave their estates over to sheep raising, although in the seventeenth century the more forward began to experiment with the intensive raising of cereal and animal feed crops. On the other, the small farmers were expropriated so that they became either agricultural laborers or uprooted peasants who took to the highways and byways. These swelled the growing army of "vagabonds and sturdy beggars" whose presence alarmed the gentry of Tudor England so much.

As a result, customary social relations were dissolved as ownership in land was transformed and the middle class expanded. A new yeomanry appeared, allied with the merchant capitalists of the towns. The merchant capitalists grew in power, proliferating into all regions of the economic life. They were to be found not only in the foreign trade and increasingly in mining and manufacture; they also entered into and took over the guilds which became centers of the wholesale trade and privileged areas of local production. The gulf between the lordly masters and the humble artisans widened. And finally, the enclosing of the demesne lands, arable, and common created a free labor force. These persons drifted into the workshops of the new urban communities, where they entered the ranks of the wage laborers in industry; or they reached the large towns where they helped to augment the numbers of the underprivileged artisans and mechanics in the guilds; or they shipped before the mast as sailors on the merchant marine; or they embarked for or were transferred to America in the capacity of indentured servants.

Indeed, while new opportunities for commercial and industrial enterprise were appearing in so many bewildering forms, notably in England, during the sixteenth and seventeenth centuries, the lot of the humble was steadily worsening. The decline in real wages; the increase in the available labor force; the spreading monopoly control over the guilds by the old merchants; the growth of central workshops: all helped to contribute to the same general effect. And that was a widening fault in the structure of society which was sharply dividing off the groups that owned the instruments of production from those who had only their labor power to sell. It was this latter class that thronged into Cromwell's Model Army in England and assured the successful outcome of the Puritan Revolution. It was this same class that furnished the tens of thousands of men, women, and children, who, quitting the country lanes and obscure city streets of England, Scotland, Ulster (and west Germany, too), braved the hazards and cruelties of the Atlantic crossing so that they could start life anew in the continental colonies of British America.

CHAPTER SIX

The English Background

1. THE CROWN AIDS THE EARLY CAPITALISTS

CURIOUSLY enough, England lagged behind in the race of capitalist expansion and oversea development. And yet, it was England that was in the van of all the European powers by the time the eighteenth century opened. What were the reasons for English supremacy? They were various. The maintenance of civil peace permitted the monarchy to establish itself and business enterprise to extend its horizons. The sequestration of the monasteries, as we have seen, furnished capital (as well as a new nobility) for new adventure in mining and manufacturing. The overthrow of the Church and the acceptance of the Protestant ethic helped to bourgeoisify the ruling class. Also, the country was fortunately dowered with metals and coal, both important for the advance of technological production and the fabrication of iron ware.

There was a chain of political events equally significant in the upward climb of the English nation. The English were the first to clear away the remnants of medievalism that came to take their final stand in the absolutist national state. The Puritan Revolution not only led to the overthrow of the absolute monarchy and the establishment of a government responsible to the English middle class. Out of this event also came the establishment of a system of national taxation and the creation of the national debt: both designed to protect the wealth of the producer and the saver.

Up to the fifteenth century, English economic life lay in a backwater. Its habits were for the most part local and agrarian, although the feudal land relations had already largely disappeared. What commercial intercourse existed with the outside world was controlled by the Italians, the Flemish, and the north

Germans. While producing small surpluses of tin, lead, and grains, England was primarily important to Europe because of its wool, which Italian and Flemish merchants bought to be manufactured into woolen cloth. In the late Middle Ages, England regarded its wool stocks as its "Golden Fleece" and wool came to be called "The Goddess of Merchants"; for wool was the main source of revenue and the staple of commerce. Not until the fifteenth century did an independent woolen-cloth industry appear in the country. This was made possible in considerable measure by the arrival of Flemish refugees in England who, because of the fact that they were skilled artisans, furnished the wool merchants the opportunity to invest their mounting profits in woolen manufactures.

With woolen cloth of their own to sell, the English were ready to challenge the Italian and Flemish merchants. At the beginning of the sixteenth century there began to flourish a regulated company of individual English merchants, the so-called Merchant Adventurers. These persons were aided by the state, which gave them monopoly trading rights in many of the north European markets; and the result was, they were soon maintaining their own trading stations in European ports and reaching European markets directly. By the seventeenth century, because of the decline of the Flemish merchants growing out of their struggles with Spain, England was dominating the European woolen-cloth market.

The Tudor monarchy, established securely as a result of the extermination of the feudal nobles in the Wars of the Roses and the confiscation of the Church properties, was able to give yeoman aid to the rising merchant capitalists. It could assure them of their wool supply by stopping the export of wool stocks. It could protect them against the authoritarianism of the old guilds by permitting settlement outside of towns and the manufacture of woolens through the domestic, or putting-out, system. It could make available more lands for sheep runs by winking at the processes of enclosure. All this the Tudor monarchy did, though not without occasional hesitancies. The result was a great capitalist advance during the sixteenth and seventeenth centuries and the building up of new families whose power was based on manufacture and trade. In addition to woolen cloth, works appeared given over to the production of alum, sugar, and saltpeter; most significant were the changes effected in the production of coal, ores, and metalware. John U. Nef has pointed out: "Large-scale industry was becoming the normal form of enterprise both in mining and metallurgy. . . . During the century preceding the Civil War, thousands of men, whose ancestors had labored on the land or as small craftsmen in their own homes, were drawn into large-scale enterprise in mining and in converting ore into a form of metal suitable for craftsmen to fashion into anchors, tools, machine parts, wool combs and cards, and household utensils."

There were other ways by which the absolute monarchy was of great help. It protected those bold marauders who sailed the seven seas to prey on the Spanish plate, or treasure, ships and the Dutch argosies heavily laden with Eastern textiles and spices. It chartered trading companies, both of the regulated and joint-stock varieties, and gave them exclusive mercantile privileges all over the world. And it fostered the organization of merchant groups for the exploitation and settlement of the New World.

Those picturesque Elizabethan heroes, John Hawkins and Francis Drake, did much to pave the way for the establishment of English oversea greatness and the rise to power of English mercantile capitalism. Typical seafarers of the period, they ran slaves from the African coast to the Spanish colonies, carried on an illicit trade with the Spanish islands in violation of Spanish law, despoiled Spanish ships, and sacked Spanish settlements. During Elizabeth's reign, pirates such as these brought in (it is estimated) as much as £12,000,000 from the scuttled ships and the gutted towns of a nation with which England, for a considerable part of the time, was officially at peace.

It was the second of Drake's three expeditions that was the most startlingly successful. Financed by a joint-stock company (today we would call the association a syndicate), of which the Queen herself was a member, Drake left England in 1577 and returned in 1580. In those three years this captain, with the blessings of his sovereign, harassed the Spanish settlements along the coast of South America, captured and rifled the stores of the treasure ships, took on a load of pepper at the Spice Islands, and reached home to report to his backers that he had realized for them a profit of £600,000 on an original investment of £5000! With her share, Elizabeth paid off the crown's indebtedness. Her noble partners invested theirs in a new company to tap the Near East trade; and when this was successful they founded the East India Company in 1600. It might almost be said that Drake's *Golden Hind,* in that one piratical voyage around the globe, had laid the basis of England's imperial might in India.

Whatever the chain of circumstances, there was no question that the crown looked with favor on the extension of oversea enterprising and aided the process by chartering companies for this purpose. The development of joint-stock companies, in which independent investors were invited to buy shares much as they do today in corporate organizations (without, however, having limited liability), was of prime assistance. The result was the collection of liquid capital first for trade and then later for industry and the expansion of English commercial venturing into the four corners of the earth. It has been estimated that capital investments in this type of economic enterprise grew from £50,000 at the accession of Elizabeth to £4,000,000 in 1695 and £50,000,000 in 1720.

The first joint-stock company to appear, with exclusive trading privileges, was the Muscovy, or Russian, Company, chartered in 1555 to tap the markets of eastern Europe and to seek a northeast passage to China and the Spice Islands. Soon, English traders were appearing in the fair towns of the Muscovites and shipping back to England furs, hides, tallow, wax, flax, and hemp. The Eastland Company, chartered in 1579, was given a monopoly of the Baltic trade. The Levant Company, chartered in 1581, received similar privileges in the Near East. Most important of these companies was the East India Company which was established in 1600 for the purpose of exploiting the vast Far Eastern market lying between the Cape of Good Hope and the China Sea. With its private armies, civil bureaucracy, and treaty-making powers, the company fought and overawed the Portuguese, the Dutch, and finally the French in the contest for supremacy in the lands fringing the Indian Ocean and the China

Sea. It survived long after other trading companies had disappeared, and it was not until 1813 that its monopoly of trade with India was ended and not until 1833 that its primacy in China had to be surrendered.

Also, there were joint-stock groups chartered to develop the gold-dust, ivory, dyewoods, and slave trades of Africa; the fisheries of North America; the fur trade of Hudson's Bay; and the minerals, furs, and fine woods of the lands and islands of the South Sea. In fact, the first abortive colonization projects in America grew out of the enterprising of such joint-stock companies. Humphrey Gilbert, when he sought to plant a colony in Newfoundland in 1583, was acting as the agent of such a chartered company. So was Walter Raleigh, when he made three successive attempts, during 1584-87, to found settlements in Virginia. Finally, the first successful English colonies on the North American mainland grew out of the efforts of such trading companies, for Virginia was settled by the Virginia Company, organized in 1606 as a joint-stock group. The voyage of the Pilgrims was financed by a company of merchants gathered together as a limited joint-stock. Massachusetts Bay Colony, the seat of the Puritans, was founded by a similar company in which many of the settlers held stock and which was different from the others only in that the company and its charter were moved over to the New World. Very truthfully has it been observed that this combination of private venturing and state supervision and control "has been the greatest of all factors in the making of the British Empire."

2. THE GROWTH OF ENGLISH CAPITALISM

Thus the splendor and the might of England grew. Merchant capitalists, basking in the royal favor, piled up accumulations in trade. Profits were invested in great landed properties by some, in mining and manufacturing enterprises by others. The middle of the seventeenth century saw manufacturing making such giant strides that the value of woolen textiles alone was put at £8,000,000 yearly as compared with £9,000,000 obtained from agricultural products and £7,750,000 from agricultural rents. The base of the great cotton manufacturing industry had al-

ready been laid; and, unhampered by the existence of backward
guild relations which kept the woolen industry in check, it was
growing rapidly, organized on capitalist lines and with the
merchant-manufacturer in complete control. The coal and iron
industries were making rapid strides. The London money market, at last freed of Italian dominance, was being operated in
the interests of English trade, industry, and finance. Opportunities for investment and speculation arose on every side, and with
each fortunate coup a new group of merchant capitalists sprang
up to challenge the supremacy of the older families.

The national wealth and income mounted by leaps and
bounds. According to an eighteenth-century estimate, the national wealth stood at £17,000,000 in 1600 and £88,000,000 in
1688. At the end of the seventeenth century the annual national income was £43,000,000. This new ebullience made its
influence felt everywhere. In agriculture, the great landlords, no
longer feudal nobles but money princes, leased their lands to
commercial farmers; and these experimented with root crops,
manured their fields, bred blooded livestock, and grew foods and
fibers for an expanding commercial market. In industry, the
hold of the guilds, particularly in the provinces, was being
shaken off increasingly. Merchant-manufacturers moved out
into the countryside to extend the putting-out system or, if they
remained in the towns, captured the organizations of the guilds,
restricted the entrance of journeymen, and virtually converted
most of the artisans into wage laborers.

Such were some of the many extraordinary changes that were
taking place in the English economy. England was rapidly developing the mechanisms of expanding capitalist enterprise in
trade, mining, and manufactures. It possessed liquid capital, a
working class released from feudal and to some extent guild
authority, a commercial agriculture, oversea markets; and yet,
it did not have the free and complete use of these agencies. Authoritarianism, making its last stand in the crown and the established church and supported by the great landlords—many of
whom had originated in the merchant families and were now
seeking to consolidate their power by alliances with royal privilege—stood in the way.

The forward march of enterprising traders and merchant-manufacturers coming up from the ranks (significantly, they were called "interlopers" by their already-arrived brethren) was being slowed down. Why? Because of the existence of the royal prerogative, which was pushing the common law farther and farther into the background. Because of the arbitrary use of the tax power. Because of the constant interference of the national church in lay concerns. Because of the crown's efforts to face both ways, now looking to the past and now into the future.

What had happened was that the seventeenth-century crown, in order to entrench itself, had built up a corporate polity and economy in which the individual's rights were completely subordinated to those of the state. Archbishop Laud, that great spokesman for Stuart absolutism, plainly presented the ideology of what we must today recognize as the totalitarian state as early as 1621. In a sermon he said: "If any man be so addicted to his private interest that he neglects the common State, he is void of the sense of piety, and wishes peace and happiness for himself in vain. For whoever he be, he must live in the body of the commonwealth and in the body of the church."

3. THE CROWN BECOMES REACTIONARY

The absolute monarchy sought, by playing off authoritarian institutions against capitalist hopes, to maintain itself in power as a kind of third estate. It encouraged, it is true, the progressive tendencies of commercial and industrial enterprise. At the same time, it refused to extirpate all the feudal remnants. Thus the crown compromised on the question of enclosure; for here it permitted the Privy Council to interfere with the wiping out of commons and small properties. The crown maintained the laws of apprenticeship. The crown adopted and indeed expanded into a great system the medieval conception of the poor, under which society assumed full responsibility toward both unemployables and unemployed. The crown also moved to build up a group loyal to itself alone, by using the prerogative of granting charters in order to create a growing number of monopolies in domestic trade and manufactures.

The crown, exactly because it hoped to balance one great

interest against another, was getting more and more into difficulties. And when, under Charles I, it threw in its lot definitely
with those groups that sought to take their stand on authoritarian privilege—the great landlords, the older merchant classes
entrenched in the guilds and livery companies, the monopolists, the established church—it first aroused the discontent of
and then forced into revolt all those elements who were finding
their progress checked as a result of the arbitrary exercise of the
royal authority.

4. THE ROLE PLAYED BY THE NATIONAL CHURCH

The Puritan Revolution was a religious uprising only in the
sense that its participants were also identified with the Reformed
Protestant churches. The humble, obscure, underprivileged
town artisans, the struggling, ambitious interloping traders, the
small independent yeomen, all those who dreamed of attaining
economic and civil liberty, were precisely the ones who were
likely to listen eagerly to the preachments of Puritan divines
and Independent ministers. New doctrines were arousing men's
hopes: that of salvation by faith and not through the intervention of a great ecclesiastical authority; that of the priesthood of
all believers; and that of the divineness of a mundane "calling,"
of the ability of every man to rise above his station. And when
the established Anglican Church began to be employed as a
direct agency of oppression—to break up the meetings of Puritans and Independents, to try offenders in church courts, to attack moneylenders, and the like—it was not difficult for Puritans,
Pilgrims, and Quakers to see epitomized in the national church
all those evil tendencies that were successfully hampering the individual's advance.

The national church exerted a pervasive influence over both
ecclesiastical and economic matters through, in particular, the
civil and religious Courts of Special Instance. The outstanding
civil courts of this kind were the Star Chamber and the Privy
Council. The outstanding ecclesiastical court was the Court of
High Commission. And in both of these the church hierarchy
was firmly established. These courts, naturally, were employed
to hunt down and punish severely religious dissent. The meas-

ures and penalties the courts used, however, had the direct effect of stultifying industry and trade. Thus, the Courts of Special Instance imposed heavy fines upon dissenters. They hounded foreign dissenters resident in England and, in view of the fact that most of these were highly skilled artisans from France and the Low Countries, the English industrial arts which these persons were serving suffered. They used the device of excommunication, and in this way drove many dissenters—again largely from the artisan class—into exile. They protected the special privileges of monopolists and this in the face of the opposition of the common law and special parliamentary enactment.

It was not difficult for those who felt the hostility of church authority, therefore, to couple the struggle for religious and economic freedom. The result was, what had started out by being a movement against the national church on religious grounds (at least, in terms of the articulation of grievances) turned into a general demand for the severance of the corporate unity of church and state in the interests of the liberty of the person in every realm.

5. BARRIERS PLACED IN THE WAY OF ECONOMIC ENTERPRISE

In purely lay concerns, the crown introduced all sorts of rigidities into a system that could hope to move ahead only by granting the individual enterpriser more and more freedom of action. In the first place, commercial agriculture could expand if the enclosing of the demesne and common lands continued unhindered. But enclosing necessitated the eviction of peasants. A crown that meant to look both ways could be prevailed upon, by great landlords who sought to continue the old land system and who therefore needed agricultural laborers, to stop the progress of consolidating large estates. In the second place, dispossessed peasants gravitated toward the newer urban settlements where they expected to find employment in the cottage industries and the workshops of the rising merchant-manufacturer class. But this tended to break down the monopoly of the guilds as regards employer-employee (and therefore wage) relations. A compromising crown could be persuaded to check such a development. In the third place, "sturdy beggars" roamed the high-

ways until they were absorbed into industry or driven into emigration. Why not compel them to stay in the neighborhoods in
which they originated and make their upkeep a charge upon
their parishes? In line with this policy, local communities were
called upon to provide work for the unemployed at prevailing
wages.

All these purposes—in the interests of the maintenance of an
authoritarian (we would call it today, totalitarian) state—the
crown, particularly under Elizabeth and the Stuarts, sought to
achieve over the protests of the newer, the more progressive, and
the "interloping" groups in the English merchant-capitalist
class. Statutes were passed, variously called Statutes of Laborers
and Statutes of Artificers, whose intention it was to check the
social and economic instabilities of an age characterized by
changes in the prevailing property relations. The great codifica-
tion of these laws under the Elizabethan Statute of 1563 was a
dike to hold back the waters of progress. In order to establish
a regular and controlled supply of labor for the great landlords
and the guild masters, this code ordered that labor contracts run
for at least a year; it fastened a compulsory seven-year apprenticeship law upon most of the industries; it gave the local justices
of the peace power to fix wages; and it provided for a parish
poor-relief system based on taxation. As a result, merchant-
manufacturers (as opposed to guild masters), seeking to get
workers from the countryside, were told by the courts that the
only apprentices they might acquire had to be the sons of freeholders: in short, the industrial life of the country was to be
organized on a class basis. Similarly, enterprisers, trying to establish themselves outside of the cities (where the guilds reigned
supreme), were confronted by the extension of the guild hierarchical system of journeymen and apprentices to their shops
and by restrictions imposed on cloth manufacture in the interests of the older merchants. Increasingly the Privy Council—the
agency of the crown—began to intervene in wage questions, thus
striking at the very basis of a free labor supply; to fix the price
of corn, thus hitting at a free agriculture; and to enforce the
collection of taxes for the support of the parish poor, thus bur-

dening with fixed charges industrial enterprisers and commercial farmers alike.

These were some of the reasons why the decades following the death of Elizabeth were years of such great uncertainty. This was the time when the lowly Pilgrims, finding life growing harder and harder, quit England for new chances in Holland. When middle-class yeomen, confronted by rising prices for the things they bought and by managed prices for grain, and with financial disaster staring them in the face, left their broad acres and followed John Winthrop into the wilderness of the Massachusetts Bay Colony. When John Pym, John Eliot, John Hampden, and Oliver Cromwell, respectable, well-to-do citizens, no longer able to bear the exactions of a grasping crown, a vindictive church, and a compliant judiciary, began to entertain thoughts of resistance.

6. THE ROLE OF THE ROYAL MONOPOLIES

This turbulent host was strengthened by the addition of the city burghers, who found opportunities for economic advancement more and more blocked because of the creation of monopolies. James I and particularly his successor Charles I, seeking to build up sources of revenue that would make the crown independent of Parliament, and at the same time hoping to create a court nobility that would be loyal to the crown directly, used this expedient more and more. The refinements became more subtle. Initially the crown charged fixed annual rents for the monopoly privileges it granted. Then it imposed a royalty fee on each item of sale. Monopolies were also knocked down to the highest bidders. They covered virtually every aspect of economic enterprise. There were monopolies in the export trade, in the import trade, in the domestic trade, and in many fields of manufacture. In this last region the monopolies were particularly oppressive because they, unlike the monopolies of the corporate guilds, were established on a national scale. Sometimes the holders of these monopoly patents or licenses were the livery companies, or guilds; sometimes they were joint-stock companies specifically organized to exploit such a privilege; very frequently they were the courtiers who thronged the royal court.

There were monopolies imposed upon the soap, salt, glass, starch, vinegar, wine, alum, cloth-finishing, gold- and silver-thread manufacture, and the pin industries; upon the selling of playing cards and dice; upon the importation of tobacco; upon the issuance of licenses for the keeping of taverns, the engrossing of wills, and the printing of linens. The principle of the "mines royal"—under which the mining of all gold and silver in the kingdom was a royal prerogative—was extended to metal mining generally, so that the crown felt free to grant monopolies for the mining of tin, lead, copper, and iron in disregard of the property rights of landowners. No project was too vast or too small for the royal attention. Country granaries were established which yeomen were compelled to use. The exchange business was made a royal monopoly and the city goldsmith or banker found his trade as a dealer in the precious metals curtailed by the re-establishment of the ancient office of the Royal Exchequer. There was a grant for the weighing of hay and straw in London and Westminster. Another patent was given for the gauging of red herrings. There was one for the marking of iron, another for the marking and gauging of butter casks, still another for the gathering of rags.

The judicial authority became the particular instrument of royal oppression. Moneylenders were hounded by the Court of High Commission; while the Star Chamber was permitted to arrogate to itself jurisdiction over patents and monopolies, on the ground that infringement constituted a contempt of the royal prerogative. How profitable to the crown were the rents and royalties from these patents is indicated by Price, who estimates that in 1639 Charles I was getting £30,000 from wine licenses, £13,050 from tobacco licenses, £30,825 from soap licenses, and £750 from playing-card and dice licenses.

Nor was this all. At every turn the rights of petition, assembly, and protest were being curbed. The press was rigorously supervised; trials were held *in camera* and penalties were severe; the free gathering of religious assemblies—where the underprivileged might also discuss their civil and economic disabilities—was sternly checked. So serious did the situation become that in 1640 the exactions of the monopolists could be described in the following bitter terms:

Like the frogs of Egypt they [the monopolists] have gotten possession of our dwellings, and we have scarcely a room free of them. They sip in our cup; they dip in our dish; they sit by our fire. We find them in the dye-vat, the washing-bowl, and the powdering-tub. They share with the butler in his bar. They have marked and sealed us from head to foot. They will not bate us a pin.

The imposition of the ships' money levies, as an arbitrary device for further augmenting the royal revenues without parliamentary sanction, was simply the last straw. It is not difficult to understand why the Long Parliament, once it had been summoned in 1640 by the hard-pressed Charles I, should be converted into a revolutionary convention. The Long Parliament at once struck out against the monopolies, expelling their holders from its councils and canceling a large number of the grants: the royal prerogative, in open defiance of judicial authority, was thus flatly challenged. This Long Parliament articulated the discontents of the English middle class—the country squires and yeomanry, the country clothiers, the city burghers. Supporting this class—indeed, often pushing it into advanced positions—was the great mass of the disfranchised small farmers and humble mechanics and artisans, who had felt the weight of monopoly prices and had everywhere encountered the restrictions of the older guilds, bolstered up and encouraged by the crown. Thus the revolution had a mass base; and after the Civil War broke out in 1642 these were the Englishmen who thronged into Cromwell's Model Army and made possible the successful overthrow of the absolutist crown and the authoritarian state.

ᴼᴼ

The Puritan Revolution

1. THE PERIODS OF THE REVOLUTION

THE Puritan Revolution may be divided, roughly, into five periods. First, from 1642 to 1647, there was the period of Civil War, during which all the revolutionary elements joined forces to rout the royal armies. Second, from 1647 to 1649, there was the period of struggle between the left and right wings of the revolutionary host, ending in the victory of the less radical, that is to say, the large-propertied, interests. Third, from 1649 to 1660, there was the period of consolidation, under the rules of Cromwell and his son, in the interests of the newer merchant capitalists, the merchant-manufacturers, and the commercial farmers. Many vestigial feudal rights were abolished; monopolies in the domestic sphere were suppressed; enclosing was resumed—and on a much larger scale than the sixteenth century had witnessed; and the Mercantile System was converted from an instrument of royal power into one of middle-class power. Fourth, from 1660 to 1688, there was the period of "restoration" under the Stuart Kings Charles II and James II. Only superficially could these twenty-eight years be called a restoration, however. For the old state, based upon the corporate unity of crown and national church, had been torn up root and branch. The revolution, indeed, went on, marked by the termination of the few remaining feudal rights; the establishment of a free judicial system through the passage of the Habeas Corpus Act (1679); the continuance of the processes of enclosing; and the extension and strengthening of the Mercantile System, particularly in its imperial-colonial relations.

But the efforts of the Stuarts to revive a personal government, their subservience to the French crown, and their encouragement of Catholicism were increasingly becoming intolerable.

Finally, the overthrow of James II and the establishment of a constitutional monarchy, in 1689, marked the culmination of the fifth and last period of the Puritan Revolution. The passage of the Bill of Rights in that year and its acceptance by the crown made parliamentary authority and the rule of the common law once and for all supreme. All the vestiges of irresponsible absolutism, linked with the medieval remnants, had been cut away. England was now, at last, facing in a single direction— that of capitalist advance. It was no accident that from this point on the preoccupation with the British colonies in America should be constant and undivided: for the ruling middle class in England saw in the colonies a fertile region for its own aggrandizement.

Thus, the successful conclusion of the Puritan Revolution created those objective conditions that were to lead to the American Revolution a century later. In another sense, the influence of the events of the 1640's upon America was immense.

It has been said that the success of the Puritan Revolution had been made possible because the English dispossessed had flocked into the Model Army. During the first revolutionary period (1642-1647) all the energies of England's little men— her small yeomen, agricultural laborers, city artisans, and mechanics—had been united to those of the city burghers, the commercial farmers, and the country merchant-manufacturers in the common cause. In 1647 the King had been captured and was Parliament's prisoner. The Revolution was over, at least as far as the large-propertied and moneyed classes were concerned.

But the four years of campaigning, of long nights around campfires, of weeks of enforced inactivity, had converted many of the common soldiers of the Model Army into a radical revolutionary host. The Army had brought together men from all sections of the country. It had fused them into a united fighting force. It had given them leaders. And it had offered them the opportunity of comparing and clearly defining their grievances. Parliament's waning interest in the common soldiers and its refusal to raise the funds with which to meet their arrears in pay fed the flames of discontent. The humbler members of the

Model Army gathered about the banners of the Levelers, a left-wing, Separatist group among the Independents. The Levelers furnished the leadership for radical disaffection and produced the written programs out of which were formulated the demands of the rank and file of the Model Army.

In 1647, the soldiers of the Model Army separated themselves from their upper middle-class allies who made up the officer corps, formed councils within their regiments, and, assisted by the Levelers, drew up a manifesto which later, in its amplified form, came to be called the "Agreement of the People." This they succeeded in laying before Parliament in 1649.

The "Agreement of the People" has had a profound influence over the centuries. Its ideas are to be found deeply embedded in the *Two Treatises of Civil Government*, published in 1690 by the great English libertarian John Locke, which was the theoretical justification of the Revolution. From Locke, its principles came into our own Declaration of Independence. It was at the basis of the Declaration of the Rights of Man and of the Citizen issued in 1789 by the French Revolution; and of the People's Charter, promulgated by the English Chartists in 1838. For the "Agreement of the People" articulated the protest of the lower middle classes—the men of small property, the independent small farmers and traders, the skilled workers struggling to maintain their economic independence—in the face of threatened submergence at the hands of large-propertied groups.

These were the political tenets set down in the "Agreement of the People." First, the individual derives from nature certain inalienable, or natural, rights which neither state nor church can abridge or jeopardize. In line with this, the soldiers of the Model Army called upon Parliament to respect freedom of religion and sought to obtain guarantees that no individuals would ever be exempted from the operations of laws duly passed. And second, all the powers of government are derived by delegation from the people alone. This was the famous principle of popular sovereignty. In this connection, the soldiers of the Model Army insisted upon a wider extension of the suffrage, a written constitution, and biennial Parliaments. The

Army's spokesmen also presented demands for a greater dif-
fusion of property and civil rights. They called for the end of all
monopolies as well as termination of imprisonment for debt,
capital punishment (except in the case of murder), primogeniture, and all feudal tenures and feudal courts. Excise and customs taxes were condemned as weighing heavily upon the poor.
The rights to the use of the commons were to be restored.

But Parliament never was compelled to act on the "Agreement of the People." The strength of the Levelers was divided
by the appearance within them of another group, known as the
"True Levelers," or Diggers, who demanded the establishment
of a kind of primitive communism based on the collective cultivation of the soil. The Diggers were suppressed in 1649. Also,
the outstanding leader of the Levelers, John Lilburne, was imprisoned; while Cromwell himself marched against and put
down the disaffected groups in the Army. The left wing was
crushed; and now the work of consolidating the gains of the
Revolution, in the interests of large property, could go ahead.

2. THE RESULTS OF THE REVOLUTION

It is not necessary here to enumerate in detail all the great
ideological and institutional triumphs of the Revolution. It is
enough to say that the basic cause for which it had been waged
—the freedom of the individual, particularly in the economic
sphere—was in considerable measure achieved. Hermann Levy
has characterized this victory in the following terms:

The modern "economic man" was born. The new spirit exalted
work into the chief moral aim of life. It had unlimited confidence in
the self-regulation of industry by free competition and in the free
and untrammelled evolution of the individual. It rejected any and
every kind of interference on the part of temporal or ecclesiastical
authority in individual economic behavior and demanded the complete concentration of individual capacity on industrial success.

In the field of constitutional law, the royal prerogative was
abolished: Parliament, as the representative of the middle class,
now ruled the land. In the field of civil law, the special courts,
with arbitrary powers, were wiped out: the common law was

now enthroned. The bishops were shorn of their temporal power. Toleration for dissenters was assured. Freedom of speech and the press was proclaimed. Bans against aliens were relaxed; and the Dutch, the Huguenots, and the Jews were invited to settle in England.

It was in the domain of private enterprise, naturally, that the greatest gains were achieved. The patents of monopoly were abolished; and their suppression was nothing less than a revolution in the national economic life. In the words of W. R. Scott, the following was the result:

> The whole tendency, both of legislation and parliamentary practice, was to afford stringent protection to infant industries by prohibiting competitive imports from abroad, and at the same time to trust that the founding of several factories of the same kind would provide sufficient safeguards for the consumer by keeping prices low through the resulting competition.

Further, the principle of the "mines royal" was sharply abridged so that mining rights in the base metals were taken away from the crown and assured to the landowner. Quite as significant were the modifications of the Statutes of Laborers and the poor laws. No longer, the state indicated, was there to be any public concern over the right of merchant-manufacturers to hire and fire when they pleased, to pay what wages they pleased, or to establish their industries whenever they pleased, whether in town or country. The labor supply, henceforth, was to be "free." In keeping with this policy, the state released employers of all responsibility toward the poor and there was written into the new poor law an antisocial bias which came to look upon unemployment as a choice freely elected by the shiftless and lazy. By 1704, Daniel Defoe, who was one of the most enthusiastic defenders of the triumphant middle class, could write: " 'Tis the man who will not work, not the man who can get no work, which makes the numbers of our poor."

In the field of agriculture, the legal and institutional obstacles to free commercial farming were largely wiped out. Christopher Hill has summarized the achievement in the following words:

> Feudal tenures, the court of wards, the prerogative courts, were abolished, and local government left in the hands of landowners,

to the advantage of those who wished to enclose; the sale of church and crown and many royalist estates to speculators, even though most of them were restored in 1660, led to a rapid jerking up of conditions of landholding on the lands to the market level (copyhold to leasehold, shorter leases) by absentee landlords who had no patriarchal ties to their tenants and looked on their purchases simply as an investment; in any event much of the land restored in 1660 had been sold again by 1688. Taxation, finally, came under parliamentary control. . . . After 1660 legal technique was steadily adapted to facilitate commercial transactions in land. The settlement laws guaranteed a steady supply of cheap and docile agricultural labor; free export of corn, with bounties from 1673, enormously stimulated its production.

The capstone of the whole structure was the new political organism that appeared: in short, the Civil War and the "Glorious Revolution" changed completely the character of the state. To quote Professor Levy again:

The new state which they created was not merely the negative antithesis to the old organization it had shattered. It was something essentially novel, a new political and social structure systematically evolved out of the revolutionary movement. The democratic constitution, the same law for all, toleration, capitalist competition, and the other liberal "triumphs" were in part the reaffirmation of old popular liberties temporarily suppressed, and in part new conquests made in the War by the downtrodden subjects.

How sharply the philosophical conception of the role of the state had changed in not more than half a century—it was but fifty years from Laud to Locke!—one may note from the following from Locke's *A Letter Concerning Toleration*:

The Commonwealth seems to me to be a Society of Men constituted only for the procuring and preserving and advancing of their own civil interest. Civil interest I call Life, Liberty, Inviolability of Body, and the possession of outward things such as Money, Lands, Houses, Furniture, and the Like.

3. ENGLISH MERCANTILISM AND THE IMPERIAL-COLONIAL RELATIONS

The Puritan Revolution, it must be apparent, was linked with the American tradition at a number of important points.

The Puritan Revolution cut the bonds that hampered individual enterprising and it was in this free environment that our American economic institutionalism developed. So, feudal land tenure, communal village agricultural organization, and the monopolistic guilds never took root in American soil. The Puritan Revolution broadcast the idea of individual political liberty, at any rate as far as men of property were concerned. The doctrines of natural rights and popular sovereignty—those great slogans of the Revolution—became as much the heritage of American colonists as they were of native Englishmen. Finally, the Puritan Revolution, by giving control over the state to the middle class, permitted the utilization of the instrumentalities of power to bring the colonies in a subservient economic relationship to the mother country.

Mercantilism, as we have seen, was not born in the Puritan Revolution, nor was it unfamiliar to absolutist states; indeed, it was one of their main props. As a public policy, associated with state power, it was of particular significance in England after the Puritan Revolution because it was really under the control of the now triumphant middle class. That is to say, in England, after the middle of the seventeenth century and notably after 1689, state power and middle-class power were closely joined. And the ascendant middle class directed state policy into the following channels.

First, the agency of the state was to be employed to make the national economy as nearly as possible independent of other countries. Second, Englishmen were to produce all their own foodstuffs and manufactured articles. Third, they were to control their carrying trade, that is to say, the merchant marine. Fourth, the oversea possessions were to be made integral parts of the system, being utilized to develop those raw materials England herself could not produce and to absorb her surpluses of manufactured goods. Thus, English mercantilism after the Puritan Revolution had two faces: at home, it employed the agency of the state to strengthen the position of the commercial enterprisers in trade, agriculture, and manufactures; and abroad, particularly in the colonial relations, it attached the colonies in a subordinate capacity to the economy of the mother country.

We shall not understand the character of the American crisis of 1763-75 unless we are prepared to hold ever in mind the fact that every imperial administrative program, whether in the economic or political realms, was designed to further this end: to utilize the colonies as an economic appanage of the mother country. That the English from the very beginning were fully conscious of the nature of this relationship, there is ample evidence. Thus, as early as 1726, a member of the Board of Trade wrote:

Every act of a dependent provincial government ought therefore to terminate in the advantage of the mother state unto whom it owes its being and protection in all its valuable privileges. Hence it follows that all advantageous projects or commercial gains in any colony which are truly prejudicial to and inconsistent with the interests of the mother state must be understood to be illegal and the practice of them unwarrantable, because they contradict the end for which the colony had a being and are incompatible with the terms on which the people claim both privileges and protection. . . . For such is the end of the colonies, and if this use cannot be made of them it will be much better for the state to be without them.

Under mercantilism, therefore, English merchant capitalists shipped bullion to the East and they invested capital in the oversea colonial establishments. The point about mercantilism was this, however: the balances and surpluses in the colonial trade that were not brought home were utilized to produce colonial raw materials needed by the home manufacturing interest and to free it of dependence upon foreign supplies. Under this system of imperial-colonial relations there took place a constant flow of English capital into the staple-producing colonies of America, that is to say, the sugar islands and the southern plantation colonies. Where mercantilism broke down as far as America was concerned was in the fact that these investments were made only in land and in the products of the land and not in manufacturing. Had the policy permitted the expansion of English capitalist enterprise into colonial large-scale manufacturing, the colonial tie with America would not have been broken, at any rate not in 1776.

At home, in England, the mercantilist policy was developed along the following lines. In the interests of commercial agriculture, on the one hand, enclosing was renewed; and, on the other. the Corn Laws were revived and strengthened to assure the mother country of an adequate fiber and food supply and to protect landlordism's control of the home market for food-stuffs. In the interests of manufacturing, the state exerted every effort to make certain of a steady flow of raw materials, to protect the domestic market against foreign competition, and to prescribe standards of quality so that competition in oversea markets with foreign producers could be overcome successfully. In the interests of commerce, the carrying trade was made a national monopoly through the agency of the Navigation Acts.

Agriculture. With the overthrow of the absolutist monarchy, the program of converting the arable into sheep runs was renewed with increasing vigor. Indeed, the eighteenth century saw an extraordinary extension of wool raising as a result of this benevolent attitude on the part of the state. But a balance between food and fiber lands was imperative in view of the growing needs of the domestic market as a result of the expansion of industrial populations. Hence, every encouragement was given to commercial farmers to grow more grains; and, in this case, the strengthened Corn Laws and the great advances made in scientific techniques in the late seventeenth and the whole of the eighteenth centuries went hand in hand. It was the function of agriculture to feed the English people, as well as to furnish the wool needed for the great primary industry, woolen manufacture. Through the agency of the Corn Laws, landlords were protected by prohibitions placed on the importation of grains (even colonial foodstuffs were barred from the home market), by the payment of bounties for the production of surpluses for export, and by the regulation of prices. By these means new lands came to be put under the plow and incentives were created for the development of progressive methods in land use, cultivation, and animal husbandry. Up to the middle of the nineteenth century England continued this protection of its domestic growers of grain in order to assure its self-sufficiency of food supply.

Manufactures. Throughout the whole period in which the mercantilist theory was the guide to state conduct, Parliament was constantly exercising itself on behalf of the home manufacturing interest. It discouraged the importation of foreign finished goods through the imposition of high duties and embargoes. It removed duties on foreign raw materials. It forbade the exportation of wool. It controlled standards of quality as regards articles entering into the foreign trade, so that, for example, in the case of the woolen industry there were by the end of the eighteenth century some three hundred pieces of legislation on the statute books which laid down rules for the maintenance of the fineness of the cloth, its dimensions, the composition of the raw materials entering into fabrics, and the like. But even more important, Parliament and its administrative agencies granted enterprisers fiscal immunities and paid them bounties; prevented the emigration of skilled workers; placed embargoes on the exportation of tools; compelled by statute and under penalty the wearing of home-fabricated textiles; and, finally, seriously circumscribed the processes by which English capital might be exported out of the country into any field of investment or production other than land and the creating of raw materials that the home economy required.

Commerce. The most significant additions made to the policy of English mercantilism, as a result of the capture of the state by the middle class, were in the fields of foreign trade and the colonial relations. The instrumentality employed here was that series of enactments called the Acts of Trade and Navigation. The Navigation System, reinaugurated in 1651 under Cromwell, had as its initial purpose the wresting of sea power from the Dutch. But its subsequent extensions were designed openly to close English ports to foreign ships. The intentions behind the policy were many: the building up of the English merchant marine, the development of new sources of customs revenue, the guarantee of a constant supply of raw materials needed by English industry, and the creation of England as the chief source for goods required by the establishments overseas.

The Navigation Act of 1660, therefore, contained the following provisions, chiefly for the purpose of assuring a national
monopoly of the carrying trade. Only English vessels (which
were built in England and its plantations, manned largely by
English crews, and captained by an English subject) could engage in trade with the English oversea possessions or import
any colonial products into England. All commodities grown or
manufactured in Asia, Africa, or America could be imported
into England or the plantations only in English- (or colonial-)
owned and manned ships. Certain specified commodities produced in Europe could be imported into England only in
English ships or in ships of the countries of origin. The Act of
1663 more specifically was intended to bring the colonies into
the orbit controlled by English mercantile capitalism; or, in the
words of Professor Andrews, "the making of England the staple
for all European goods imported into the colonies, that is, the
imposing of the requirement that all commodities from other
countries which were wanted in the plantations should pass
through England as the sole exporting center before shipment overseas to America." Therefore, all the commodities
grown, produced, or manufactured in Europe could not be sent
to the colonies unless transshipment had been effected first at
English ports. The carriage to England had to be in "lawful
shipping, lawfully manned." And transshipment meant, of
course, export duties and additional handling charges, all of
which increased the cost of European goods for the colonists.
Subsequent acts were designed to strengthen the administrative
regulations of enforcement, notably through the agency of vice-
admiralty courts.

Also written into the Navigation System was a significant device for the buttressing of English industry and commerce; and
this was through the so-called "enumerated lists" in the various
Acts of Trade and Navigation. This meant, simply, that certain
listed commodities produced in the plantations overseas (and
they were as a rule the outstanding colonial raw materials,
always excepting northern foodstuffs) were to be exported to
England alone, either for use there or for transshipment to
Europe. In this way, freights were furnished for English ship-

ping, raw materials were assured for English industry, and sources for the customs revenue of the mother country were extended. Accordingly, the Acts of 1660 and 1663 placed the following colonial commodities on such an "enumerated list": sugar, cotton, tobacco, ginger, indigo, and various dyewoods. In 1704 and 1705, the list was expanded to include rice, molasses, naval stores, hemp, and masts and yards. In 1721, copper ore and beaver and other furs were listed. And as late as 1764 there were enumerated whale fins, hides, iron, lumber, raw silk, and pot and pearl ashes.

Professor Andrews summarizes in this fashion the thought of the English lawmakers:

> To allow the colonies to buy elsewhere than in England their woolens and the finished products of other countries and to carry them from the place of purchase directly to their own ports, passing by the merchants and manufacturers of England and taking advantage of the lower French and Dutch prices, to their own profit but to the injury of English trade and customs revenue . . . such a policy was inconceivable. . . . Trade was becoming essential to the attainment of prosperity and the value of commerce and the colonies, as means whereby this result was to be attained, was recognized by all responsible men during the first years of the Restoration when the Acts of Navigation and Trade were passed.

In the interests of English mercantile capitalism, control over the economic life of the colonies was even more closely supervised. It has frequently been assumed that English colonial policy underwent a marked transformation in the middle of the eighteenth century and that this change was responsible for the hastening of the crisis of 1763-75 which preceded the American War of Independence. According to this theory, so persuasively presented by the American historian George Louis Beer, Englishmen up to the 1760's looked upon the colonies merely as sources for the production of raw materials. After the end of the Seven Years' War they came to regard their colonies chiefly as buying markets for finished goods.

A moment's reflection must indicate the inadequacy of this viewpoint. Commercial intercourse between the home country and colonies was possible only on the basis of the steady flow of goods and services between the two. In other words, if the colonies were to be encouraged to sell their raw materials to the home country it was imperative that they be created into open markets for the absorption of English finished goods and the services of English shipowners, merchants, and financiers. The balance of payments was largely to be maintained by the colonial export of sugar, tobacco, indigo, dyewoods and logwoods, and naval stores to England, and the colonial import from England of drygoods, hardware, notions, and house furnishings. These were the visible items of international trade of the seventeenth and eighteenth centuries. Invisible items—of which England had a favorable balance—were freights, brokerage, insurance, commissions, profits, and interest on borrowings. But what if the flow of goods and services from the colonies did not equal each year the flow of goods and services to the colonies? What then was to be the utilization of the surpluses to the credit of the mother country? For sooner or later, in most imperial-colonial relations, the tendency is for the colonial debits to outstrip colonial credits. This was particularly true under English mercantilism, where the mother country was virtually the only source of finished goods and the principal outlet for raw materials.

The outstanding factor that distinguished English mercantilist relations from modern imperialist relations was the way in which these capital surpluses were utilized. Under mercantilism, the colonies were pressed to make returns on unfavorable balances in specie (gold and silver coin) and when specie was not constantly available—as it usually was not—the creditor home country was compelled to invest its surpluses in the colonies in land and in land operations. Under present-day imperialism, the investment of such surpluses is in all types of capital goods: in land, of course, but with an accelerating tempo in factories, public utilities, means of transportation, and the like. In other words, under mercantilism, the colonies could never look forward to duplicating the advancing industrial economy of the mother country. And the reason was plain: colonial capital accumulations, or savings, and English capital surpluses, or favorable balances, were not permitted to enter into manufacturing or, for that matter, commercial banking, but were compelled to stay always in agriculture, trade, and such mining activities that did not compete with home interests.

The American mainland colonies from the beginning, therefore, were attached to the English leading string. It was their economic function to produce the raw materials that England needed and to consume (but not manufacture themselves) English finished goods. The development of forms of enterprise calculated to enter into competition with English capitalism was seriously frowned upon; efforts were made to check them; and, when everything failed, rigorous measures aiming at suppression were adopted. Just as the discovery of America, on the one hand, grew out of and, on the other, strengthened the growing European capitalism's needs, so English policy as regards the colonies at once buttressed the triumphant home capitalism while it produced those conditions in the colonies that led to the American revolutionary crisis of 1763-75.

Part II

—

THE VICTORY OF AMERICAN MERCANTILE CAPITALISM IN THE REVOLUTION

The Settlement of the English Colonies in America

1. WHO WAS RESPONSIBLE FOR SETTLEMENT

U P TO the time that the Mercantile System was fully launched, England had no clearly indicated policy of colonial settlement in the New World. The fact is, the only colony that was initiated directly by the crown was that of Georgia; and Georgia was not planted until the eighteenth century, to serve as a buffer province against the Spanish in Florida and as a kind of mercantilist semitropical paradise in which the mulberry tree and the vine could be cultivated. The crown also had seized and retained certain other settlements through war: Jamaica, an original Spanish enterprise; New York, founded by the Dutch; and Nova Scotia, the work of the French. All the others sprang up as a result of the initiative of private individuals who were largely motivated by private gain. The chartered companies and the proprieties (i.e., the proprietors of Maryland, the Carolinas, Pennsylvania, and New Jersey) were the chief agencies of this advance into the lands beyond the sea. On the mainland, Virginia, Plymouth, and Massachusetts were planted by English companies specifically formed for that purpose; at New Amsterdam first sprang up a Dutch settlement financed by the Dutch West India Company; Delaware was the work of a Swedish trading company; while Maryland, the Carolinas, New Jersey, and Pennsylvania were founded by proprieties.

Certain portions of New England were settled by brave individuals who pushed on into the wildernesses because of the restrictive theocratic rule—at once authoritarian politically and ecclesiastically and monopolistic economically—of the original

Massachusetts Bay founders. Seeking opportunities to worship
God in their own ways—and to carve out for themselves more
generous farming properties than the old settlers were willing
to permit—Roger Williams and Anne Hutchinson and their
followers settled the Rhode Island plantations; John Wheel-
wright and John Underhill helped in the early colonizing of
New Hampshire; and Thomas Hooker was the spiritual and
lay leader of the first English settlements in the Connecticut
Valley. The Rhode Island experiment, notably, was the first
triumph for petty-bourgeois democracy in America: for Roger
Williams, steeped in the leveling doctrines of English Inde-
pendency, set up a commonwealth that was responsive to the
political and economic needs of small-propertied men. The
principles of natural rights and popular sovereignty—those very
principles that were expressed in the "Agreement of the People"—first took firm root in the backwoods of early Rhode
Island.

2. WHY PROMOTERS WERE INTERESTED

Oversea adventure, very clearly, represented an aspect of
developing mercantile capital at home. Enterprisers, confronted
by accumulated savings which had piled up in the textile and
mining industries and in trade, sought new outlets for their
capital surpluses. Virginia and Massachusetts Bay, notably, were
founded and settled because all manner of moneyed people were
prepared to invest their funds in such expeditions and because
they had made profits from previous ones. The Virginia Company gathered together and spent at least £100,000 in the pushing of its unsuccessful schemes. The expenses incurred in
building up the Massachusetts Bay Colony cost its promoters
and original settlers close to £200,000. Even humble Plymouth
would have been impossible had not a group of merchant
capitalists been willing to stake the Pilgrims (who, in return,
bound themselves to put aside all the surplus goods they produced in a common storehouse for the benefit of their backers).

The proprietary colonies sprang from the desire of their
owners to build up fortunes through land-promotion schemes,
the collection of rents, and the cultivation of their own private

estates in the New World by agricultural laborers and tenants. The Baltimores, the Penns, and the proprietors of the Carolinas and New Jersey were not feudal lords but capitalist land speculators and landlords who sought money profits and rents from the sale of land, the operation of their own farms, and the collection of annual charges levied on tenants. Only the quitrent was a feudal hang-over and this in reality very often was employed in place of a general property tax. How profitable these landed possessions were to their proprietors may be noted from the fact that the Baltimores, exclusive of their own estate rents and profits from land sales, were deriving £10,000 annually out of Maryland.

The financiers of colonial expeditions, whether joint-stock companies or proprietors, initially hoped to equal the remarkable exploits of the Spanish in opening up new gold and silver deposits. This failing, they turned to the more prosaic, but in the long run more profitable, development of the natural resources of the new country. In this way, England in time was able to free itself of its dependence upon foreign lands for many of its raw material requirements. The forests of the New World furnished masts and naval stores, so important to the home shipbuilding industry. The island colonies began to grow coffee, oranges and lemons, and, to a lesser extent, pepper and ginger. They also produced dyewoods and hardwoods. The mainland colonies yielded whale products, fish, furs, skins, and a variety of minerals like pot ashes, pearl ashes, and saltpeter, necessary for the manufacture of soap and the maintenance of the textile industries. They produced iron and indigo and rice. Most important of all, the island colonies grew sugar and the mainland colonies tobacco on a great commercial basis, so that these two staples in time became the centers of a ramified commercial system which affected large numbers of English ship-owners, brokers, commission men, merchants, financiers, and processors.

The colonies, as outlets for England's finished goods—for her drygoods, hardware, and notions, her house furnishings and luxury wares—were never lost sight of. At the outbreak of the revolutionary crisis, in the 1770's, the English possessions in

America were absorbing one third of all the English goods entering into foreign trade.

3. WHY IMMIGRANTS CAME

The schemes of enterprisers and the plans of statesmen were not enough to build up a new colonial establishment. There had to exist objective factors in England, and elsewhere also, to make possible successful settlement. The dislocations and confusions in the mother country, as a result of the forming capitalist economy, provided the human resources so necessary to the creation of America. Demesne and common lands were being enclosed, resulting in the uprooting of great numbers of agricultural laborers and small independent farmers. The compromising attitude of the crown made difficult the absorption of these people into manufacturing enterprise, leaving them the stranded beneficiaries of an uncertain local parish relief. This was the great rural reservoir that could be tapped to settle a wilderness overseas. Many from this class of lowly and dispossessed voluntarily bound themselves out for a term of years as so-called indentured servants, in order to pay for their transportation overseas. Many became the victims of kidnaping gangs. Dependent children were virtually deported because overseers of the poor wanted to terminate the costs of their care. Others drifted into petty crime or were jailed for vagabondage. These, too, were shipped overseas as indentured servants. Even political prisoners and prisoners of war fed the insatiable thirst of the planting colonies for unfree labor.

The ranks of this truly forced emigration from the English countryside were swelled by others who were finding economic adjustments in a transitional age difficult. Apprentices and journeymen, in many of the craft guilds, realizing the futility of hoping to become independent artisans, were not averse to emigration. Many yeomen, or independent small farmers, who were being oppressed by high taxes and high prices for their necessaries, while the prices of grain were being maintained at lower levels, and many small tradesmen who were being declassed as a result of the growing extension of monopoly privileges under the Stuarts: these too turned their eyes westward to seek new chances and new fortunes. The same shaping crisis that provoked the parliamentary revolution against the crown in the 1640's drove thousands of petty-bourgeois families into flight overseas. Between 1607 and 1640 from 50,000 to 70,000 Englishmen, giving up the unequal struggle, transported themselves, or were transported, to the colonies.

Economic necessity and religious oppression were closely linked. The Pilgrims, Quakers, Puritans, Huguenots, Moravians, Mennonites, Mystics, and Pietists, coming from England, France, Germany, and Austria, risked the perils of the seas to set up their tabernacles in the wild lands of America; and to find those opportunities for material advancement that were denied them in the older civilizations of Europe.

4. THE UNFREE WHITE LABOR SUPPLY OF THE COLONIES

Colonial America was built upon the unfree labor of whites and blacks. Fully 250,000 white men, women, and children and another 250,000 black persons—constituting in all at least one half of the original immigrants to the mainland colonies by 1770 —had come in this way. During the seventeenth century, these unfree white laborers—the indentured servants—had made possible the firm establishment of the plantation system of the southern colonies; and from its founding until the outbreak of the American Revolution, Pennsylvania continued to employ them as field hands on her great wheat farms to create those breadstuffs that were to link together so closely the mainland settlements and the West Indian sugar colonies.

The indentured servants were brought over largely to labor as field hands. When they completed their terms, which ran from three to seven years (with four years as the most common), some were able to set themselves up as independent small farmers. A few, as a result of ingenuity and enterprise, became prominent landlords. Many drifted to the towns and became the artisans and mechanics of colonial America. The less hardy, the more quickly dispirited, fell behind in the race and neither pressed on into the still-ungranted lands nor sought opportunities for employment among the many handicrafts where skill could be employed. They remained locally in those areas into which they had first been taken, settled on small patches of sandy or wooded soil, and engaged in a meager self-sufficiency whose standards of living constantly declined. These were the forebears of those poor whites whose wretched settlements, in the heart of plantation areas, have continued into our own day.

The traffic in white servants was organized at both ends. In the British Isles and in Germany, regular agents circulated through the countryside and in the poorer urban districts and periodically made up groups of servants who were turned over to sea captains for transportation. Many came involuntarily. Vagabonds and persons on local parish relief were in effect deported. Kidnaping was openly practiced and in England in particular this kind of unholy traffic thrived with official connivance until the 1670's. Many of the servants were felons: that is, common criminals, debtors, and unfortunates arrested on suspicion alone and kept imprisoned because of their inability to pay the high jail fees. During the first three quarters of the seventeenth century as many as 50,000 men, women, and children were taken from the jails of England and sold as indentured servants for seven-year terms. Political prisoners and prisoners of war also were transported into involuntary servitude overseas. Thus Cromwell, after putting down with great cruelty the revolt of the Irish, turned over his foes (one estimate has placed their number at 100,000) to the British sugar planters of Barbados, where they were used as unfree field hands.

Upon arrival in the New World, the indentured servants either were received by contractors who had been responsible for their importation or were auctioned off to the highest bidder in regular markets set up for that purpose. In sections of the South the servant trade was largely controlled by a class of middlemen called "soul drivers," who were described by a contemporary as follows: "[These are] men who make it their business to go on board all ships who have in either servants or convicts and buy sometimes the whole and sometimes a parcell of them as they can agree, and then they drive them through the country like a parcell of sheep until they can sell them to advantage."

During the seventeenth century, in the South, the costs of

transportation and middlemen commissions for an indentured servant came to from £10 to £12. The cost of freedom dues— that is to say, the food, clothing, seed, tools, arms, and sometimes a cow, that every landlord was called upon to equip his servant with upon release—came to another £10. In the beginning, the freedom dues had also included a small tract of land; but very little land actually was transferred in this way. The result was, for not much more than £20 to £22, a planter or large farmer was able to secure the services of a farm laborer, who sometimes was a skilled artisan, as well, for from three to seven years. The only regular charge upon him was cost of food and shelter.

Thus the poor, toiling men, women, and children who settled so much of colonial America streamed into the country. They came from the English and Scottish countrysides where enclosing was driving them off the land; from the cities' tenements, from which they were being snatched by kidnapers and contractors; from the foul jails; from the war-ravished Rhineland and from famine-stricken Ulster. They were despoiled of their few possessions before embarking to their new homes and often robbed of what little was left when they arrived. They were crowded into horrible, reeking ships called gruesomely "white Guinea-men"; many died of starvation and disease en route; families were cruelly separated, often never to be reunited.

Once the servant had entered the status of servitude, he remained a virtual slave in the eyes of the law. He might not marry without his master's consent; his master might transfer his services to another at will; he could be flogged without a trial; if he ran away and was caught, two days of extra service might be added for each one that he was missing. Arbitrarily his term might be extended if he violated his contract, was away without leave, or struck his master or overseer.

Throughout the greater part of the seventeenth century this flow of unfree white labor kept pouring into the southern colonies. Toward the end of the century it ceased, partly by the choice of the planters who were paying transportation costs, partly because the servants themselves refused to be carried to the Southland because of their realization that land engrossment prevented the possibility of obtaining freeholds. The traffic continued into the eighteenth century, but Pennsylvania became its principal focus. It was not until the end of the Revolution that England moved definitely to terminate transportation of unfree white labor in the interests of the maintenance of her own growing factory system.

5. NEGRO SLAVES

The reasons southern planters themselves began to shift from white servant labor to black slave labor are not difficult to seek. The short term of the white indenture militated against the building up of a permanent labor force. The whites (or so it appeared at first) were not as tractable as the blacks and less willing to submit to the arduous rounds of field labor; nor could the white women be utilized as field hands. Because their white skins did not allow for easy and complete differentiation from free workers, escape was relatively easy. And, it may be noted, havens for runaway servants were not very distant— the upcountry of North Carolina, for example, serving as a refuge for many of the escaping servants from Virginia and South Carolina. Although initial costs were greater, the final cost of the black slave was much less than that of the indentured servant. Most significant for the development of Negro slavery was the regularization of the slave traffic.

Negro slaves first appeared at Jamestown in 1619 when a Dutch privateer sold a cargo of twenty blacks to a group of settlers. But their numbers increased slowly during the seventeenth century, and in the 1670's in Virginia, for example, there were not more than 2000 slaves. With the opening up of the Carolinas to settlement and notably with the appearance of Barbados sugar planters in South Carolina, who brought their slaves with them, the Negro population began to grow.

Originally the colonial slave market had been supplied by occasional Dutch traders. The tightening of the Mercantile System, during and after the Cromwellian period, had made it increasingly difficult for these ships to deal with the mainland colonies. The supply had never been a steady one; now it was ceasing. But the appearance of the Royal African Company on the scene, in 1672, well financed by English merchant capitalists (the joint stock was £111,000) and invested with a monopoly charter; and the defeat of the Spanish in 1713, as a result of which England obtained the right to the exclusive transport of Negro slaves to the Spanish American possessions for thirty years: these put the traffic definitely on a sound, business basis. Capital poured into it for the outfitting of the ships engaged in the trade; regular stations were established on the west African coast; and an elaborate chain of middlemen was devised. Notably, independent traders, operating out of Bristol and Liverpool in England and Newport in America, appeared in the early eighteenth century; and these exploited all the potentialities of the trade with amazing success.

The African source of supply steadied, also, because local chieftains became parts of the slave system. Either acting as dealers and enslaving their own tribesmen or selling their defeated foes to the carriers, the chieftains established regular channels of communications with the coast stations. Of course, as demand increased the price of a prime field hand mounted. In Virginia, before the turn of the century, such a young slave was selling for £18 to £25; by 1770 he was bringing £50 to £80. The trade was a highly speculative one. The slavers ran the gamut of coast marauders; sometimes they encountered insurrection on board their ships; and not infrequently the filth, inhuman crowding, and wretched sanitary conditions swept the whole ship and wiped out the white crews along with the black men and women in the holds. Nevertheless, so great were the profits on a single voyage—often they ran to 1000 per cent—that the risks of the traffic were easily overcome in time. And on these profits the English ports of Bristol and Liverpool were able to found some of the great English middle-class families of the eighteenth and nineteenth centuries. It has been estimated that in 1750, English slave traders were getting an annual return of £1,200,000 on £800,000 invested in the traffic.

In addition, as we shall have occasion to see, the slave trade made possible the expansion of the mercantile economy of the New England and middle-colony ports. In exchange for the foodstuffs, lumber, and live animals shipped to the West Indian sugar colonies, American ship captains brought back sugar and molasses; these were converted into rum and carried to the African coast where the liquor was bartered for slaves; and finally the slaves were loaded on ships and sold in the sugar islands. Thus there developed a triangular trade that was immensely profitable to all concerned.

By the eighteenth century planters were beginning to see that the Negro slave had decided economic, as well as social, advantages over the white servant. The planter was able to appropriate all the surplus value, above the cost of subsistence, produced by the labor power of the black. This was not true in the case of the indentured servant who tended to produce in value of goods not much more than the costs of his transportation, profit for the middleman, upkeep, and freedom. Had the planter been able to exact more labor out of his servants, their prices would have risen on the one hand and their terms shortened on the other; thus quickly bringing about equilibrium. The final cost of Negroes was considerably lower. At the beginning of the eighteenth century, a servant for a four-year term could be obtained for £10 to £15; an adult Negro could be had for £18 to £25. But the Negro did not have to be paid a freedom due and not only did his owner acquire his services for life but he also had those of all children born to his slaves. It might take a little longer to train a black for field work but, once taught his simple functions, he was likely to be more obedient than the white servant. Women slaves also worked in the fields, so that they were sought after not only as breeders of children but as laborers. And finally, the cost of the upkeep of blacks was less than in the case of the whites.

It has been estimated that during the century 1686-1786, more than 2,000,000 Negroes were transported overseas to be sold into slavery to the planters of the West Indies and the American continental colonies. Of this number, probably more than 250,-000 black men, women, and children were brought over to the American mainland colonies; and it may be said, roughly, that this number approximated that of the indentured white servants. At the opening of the Revolution, there were fully 500,000 blacks (as against 2,240,000 whites) in the colonies, with the concentration, of course, in the South. Indeed, in Virginia, the blacks were almost as numerous as the whites, while in South Carolina they actually doubled the number of whites. In the whole North, there were not more than 75,000 blacks, of whom 20,000 were to be found in New York and about 11,000 in Pennsylvania. Except in Rhode Island, where a plantation system producing cereals and cattle flourished for a short time, northern slaves were employed as house servants and town laborers.

Particularly in the South, as the slave population grew, a slave code began to make its appearance on the statute books; and this code became more detailed and harsher in its requirements as the result of occasional black revolts. By the second decade of the eighteenth century every device had been perfected for the perpetuation of the servile relationship upon which slavery was founded. The code ran as follows.

The Negro was a slave for life. Children born to him were the property of the owner of their mother. He was forbidden to own or carry arms. He could not assemble with his fellows at any time or in any place. No black might leave his owner's plantation without written permission. If a black struck a white, the black was to receive forty lashes, no matter who was at fault. It was no crime for a master to kill a slave. No blacks were to be freed in the South, and such masters that freed their slaves were required to pay the costs of their transportation back to Africa.

In this fashion Negro slavery made possible the continuance of the plantation system and the production of staples. And the southern staples furnished that firm base for the erection of the Mercantile System within whose limits colonial mercantile capitalism was able to operate for such a long time.

6. SIZE OF POPULATION

Thus they came. White and black. The enterprisers, the adventurers, the underprivileged, the dispossessed, and the forced. At the end of the seventeenth century there were 275,000 whites in the English mainland colonies in America; by 1776, as has been said, the host had grown to number 2,240,000, with an additional 500,000 blacks. The flood poured in, notably during the eighteenth century, not only from England but also, although in a smaller stream, from the German Rhineland, the Scotch-Irish plantation of Ulster in Ireland, and the Scottish Highlands. Everywhere the humble annals of the poor were the same: the victims of oppression—whether war in the Rhineland, high rents and mercantilist restrictions against the woolen industry in Ulster, the breakup of the clan system and the enclosing of the lands in the Scottish Highlands—they sold themselves to ship proprietors and captains and voyaged to America.

The great majority entered into the forced labor of the indenture system so that, when free, they might aspire to become owners of farming properties. The economy of America was largely agrarian: indeed, by 1770, there were only five places with populations in excess of 8000; and these among them had 84,000 inhabitants, or 3.8 per cent of the total. These seats of urban civilization in the New World were Boston, Philadelphia, New York, Newport, and Charleston. Coastal America presented all the aspects of a well-established and secure society. The British controlled the seaboard region in an unbroken stretch from Maine through Georgia and in it improved areas were virtually continuous; the line of the wilderness was steadily being pushed back to the crest of the Appalachians. There were adequate facilities for communication and intelligence. The countryside, in every section of the domain, was dotted with pleasant farmhouses whose occupants had long ago learned to enjoy many of the amenities of a settled civilization.

CHAPTER NINE

The Building of a Class Society

1. STRUGGLE FOR THE LAND

THESE throngs of eager immigrants sought land. Torn up from their moorings by enclosing and rack-renting, displaced by the raisers of sheep and despoiled by landlords, the humble men and women from the British Isles and from western Europe risked the hazards of the Atlantic passage in order to become freehold farmers in the New World. The land, in colonial America, produced the people's wealth; and upon the fruits of the land was erected the mercantile enterprise that made possible the establishment of economic relations with the outside world. In continental America farmers grew tobacco and rice for sale in the English and south European markets, wheat for sale as flour as well as beef cattle and meats in the expanding West Indian market. As supplementary activities, they engaged in the raising of work animals, the cutting of timber, the catching of fish, and the trapping and hunting of wild animals. It was to be expected, therefore, that at the outbreak of the Revolution nine tenths of the colonial population should be associated with agriculture.

But the immigrants were to be disappointed. Land was not to be obtained easily. The ownership of the land continued, even long after the Revolution in many of the original colonies, in the hands of a small group of persons. Some of these were European landlords, while some were American landlords. Indeed, it may be said that one of the results of the mercantilist policy was the establishment and recognition of monopoly in both trade and land ownership. Hence, the lower middle classes of the colonies—the small farmers, traders, and artisans—who were the victims of monopoly, were in frequent opposition to the engrossing landlords and merchant capitalists. We shall have occasion to see, later, how desire to overthrow monopoly was among the causes for the entrance of these same lower middle classes into the American Revolution.

The systems of land settlement and land tenure prevailing in colonial America were of various types. In New England, settlement was on a community basis and freehold tenure—that is to say, outright ownership—prevailed. In the southern and middle colonies, settlement usually was on an individual farm basis but, while the lands were held as freeholds or leaseholds, quit-rents had to be paid to the absentee proprietors. In the South for the most part and in the middle colonies to a somewhat lesser extent, large holdings operated as plantations or great estates were the rule. These were worked either by unfree labor—indentured servants or Negro slaves—or were operated by tenants, each family being seated on its own small leasehold. It is to be noted that in portions of the middle colonies there was also to be found a sizable group of small owner-farmers.

2. THE NEW ENGLAND LAND SYSTEM

In New England, the original land grants were made by the general courts, or representative assemblies, of Massachusetts, Connecticut, and Rhode Island. These grants, as a rule, were in the form of towns and were deeded to companies of men acting together. Such lands were held as freeholds; the payment of quitrents was not required; and the towns and colonial governments derived their revenues from taxation. The company of original settlers proceeded to divide up the towns granted to them in the following fashion. A village was laid out at the center and in it the house lots of the settlers were located. Then the arable lands and meadows were distributed, the grantees receiving holdings in various sections so that, somewhat as in the feudal system, a settler might have many scattered fields. However, these individually owned fields had around them a common fence which permitted all the animals to be pastured on the stubble after the harvesting seasons. This device lasted through most of the seventeenth century and consolidation and enclosing did not set in until the eighteenth century was well advanced. Finally, all the lands of the town were not immediately divided up. The unassigned lands were held in common, not by the town itself, however, but by the company of original, or old, settlers and their heirs. Also, the privilege to purchase already assigned lots and farms (with, of course, rights to the undistributed common lands) was vested first in the original settlers. These constituted, therefore, a monopoly group called the commoners, or proprietors.

It should be noted that from the very beginning equality in land ownership did not prevail, even among the old settlers. The magistrates and ministers, as a rule, received the choicest village lots and farms; and sometimes, as well, they were given individual holdings apart from those located in the towns. Furthermore, the New England colonies employed the land as a means of paying bounties to encourage the setting up of sawmills, saltworks, and iron furnaces and forges.

Causes for disaffection and hostility began to appear quite early in New England for two reasons. The most desirable lands in the eastern sections of the colonies were quickly pre-empted by such companies of proprietors. Also, a small group in each town began to accumulate the rights in the common, through either direct inheritance, marriage, or purchase. The result was, later comers were compelled to buy land or lease it—without any rights, however, in the common lands. In other words, possession of freeholds, as a result of grants, became increasingly difficult. The upshot was, as the eighteenth century progressed, a sharp cleavage manifested itself between these two groups. On one side were the descendants of the old settlers, who, although in a numerical minority, were in control of the land policies and therefore of the economic resources of the New England towns. On the other side were the numerous little farmers—either small owners or tenants—who had no real opportunities for advancement because the common lands, which were constantly mounting in value as settlement became denser, were engrossed by the proprietors. Between the two classes bitter controversy raged. Recourse was had to the courts and assemblies but, more frequently than not, this was without avail, and the proprietors continued in possession of the common lands until the Revolution broke out, and even afterward.

In the frontier western and northern sections of New England, the establishment of a freehold met with equal difficulties, although for other reasons. In these frontier areas, during the eighteenth century, the general courts took to making town grants not to companies of settlers but to land speculators. Eastern merchants, accumulating profits from successful trading ventures, turned to the wild lands as investment outlets; and without difficulty they were able to buy whole towns from the general courts of Massachusetts and Connecticut. The farmer who sought a freehold was compelled to purchase from these land speculators; or, if he was without capital, he moved into the area as a squatter, running the risks of lawful eviction without any compensation for the improvements he erected.

Thus, the acquisition of land in colonial New England was difficult and its monopoly by town proprietors, or absentee landlords and speculators, was at the basis of the discontent of the lower middle classes.

3. THE LAND SYSTEM IN THE SOUTHERN COLONIES

In the southern colonies, where land was more plentiful, monopoly also sprang up. Powerful landlords quickly appeared, either as proprieties or as the recipients of the bounty of the proprieties or the crown directly. And these were able to establish their position economically by selling or leasing out lands. Tenure was on a freehold basis but quitrents had to be paid— a system that did not exist in the New England region.

Grants of land were made to individuals originally through the so-called headright and, later, by sale. In order to attract persons of means into the southern colonies, the Virginia Company and, later, the proprieties of Maryland and the Carolinas offered a sizable grant to such individuals as were able to pay their own passageway. Additional grants were made to these adventurers for members of their families and servants who were also brought over. The land grants could be patented after an improvement had been erected and the soil prepared for use. The only charge upon the grantee was the payment of the annual quitrent. So, in early Maryland, for example, the headright came to 100 acres for each free immigrant, 50 additional

acres for each child under 16 years, and as much as an extra
1000 acres for every five laborers brought over. The headright
method of land grants, however, was accompanied by so much
fraud that beginning with the eighteenth century the southern
colonies abandoned it and began to dispose of their unassigned
lands by outright sale.

The adoption of a policy of easy grant and sale did not prevent efforts at the establishment of great estates and the limitation of the available supply of land. In Maryland and South
Carolina, in particular, great landlords sought to monopolize
the areas into which an agricultural population might flow. In
Maryland the Baltimores granted tracts of from 1000 to 3000
acres for the erection of estates. The proprieties were to receive
quitrents; the landlords, in turn, were given permission to
seat both copyholders and leaseholders on as much as five sixths
of their domain. In fact, in order to encourage the maintenance
of such estates intact the proprieties demanded the payment of
alienation fines for those portions that were sold.

In the beginning, of course, due to the scarcity of labor, it
was impossible to find enough tenants to cultivate such large
holdings. Squatters and stockmen freely invaded the areas. But
as available land became scarcer, during the eighteenth century,
tenants became more numerous and these estates not infrequently were operated by landlords who were not working
farmers themselves. The early feudal institutions introduced
could not take firm root in the American soil and in time were
abandoned; so that the courts-leet and courts-baron, which were
the centers of privilege, disappeared. But of course privilege
continued, firmly entrenched in land ownership. The Carolinas repeated the same tale.

Particularly under the headright system and also as a result
of the attempt to build up large manorial estates, the engrossing, or monopoly, of the land became inevitable. The following factors contributed. 1. Grants under headrights were very
loosely administered so that fraud was not unusual. 2. Prices for
land were low, so that the few who were supplied with liquid
funds could quickly amass great tracts. 3. Only nominal requirements were imposed as regards the improvement and use

of headrights. 4. There was an extraordinary amount of favoritism openly employed by crown, proprieties, and colonial administrative agencies in the disposition of the unassigned areas. 5. In the southern colonies, laws imposing entail and protecting primogeniture were conducive to the same end.

The result was, as William E. Dodd has said: "A landed aristocracy was built up, social inequality was promoted, the advance of settlement was to an extent hindered, and a sinister and corrupt influence was continually exerted on the political and social life of these provinces."

Examples of land engrossing were common. In early eighteenth-century Virginia, for example, William Byrd, 2nd, owned as much as 100,000 acres, and Robert Carter when he died left 300,000 acres of land. In South Carolina, at the outbreak of the Revolution, there were many holdings existing that ranged from 20,000 to 100,000 acres. It was next to impossible for small farmers to acquire farms in the eastern sections of the colonies; and such small farms as were sold commanded much higher prices per acre than did the great holdings. It was inevitable that the little men of property should look with resentment upon the large estates on which much of the land remained unimproved. Movement westward offered only a temporary escape: for most of the pioneers had no cash with which to purchase and were compelled to run all the risks that squatters had to suffer.

4. THE LAND SYSTEM IN THE MIDDLE COLONIES

In the middle colonies the processes of settlement, the system of land tenure, and the building up of large properties were somewhat similar to those in the provinces to the south. Headrights were granted in New Jersey. In Pennsylvania, lands were sold at low prices initially, with grants to masters transporting groups of laborers. But prices soon were raised with the result that before fifty years were over fully two thirds of the settlers were squatters without legal titles. In the Dutch New Netherlands, outside of Manhattan Island itself, the basis of settlement and tenure was the patroonship. Under this dispensation a number of great estates were carved out, one of them, Rensselaers-wyck on the Hudson, including 700,000 acres.

The English, after they possessed New Netherlands, did not disturb the Dutch titles and proceeded to use the patroonship as a model for the disposition of unassigned lands. In the 1690's, one governor made six grants which varied in size from 50 to 840 square miles. Indeed, during the period 1700-75, at least 60 per cent of the more important patents of land ran from 1000 to 10,000 acres each. In Westchester County, for example, six manors covered one half of the area of the whole region; and a not dissimilar situation existed in the counties extending along the Hudson River up to Albany. These estates used the tenancy system when tenants were available; otherwise, the lands were kept unimproved. So loosely defined were the boundaries of the great patents that small farmers settled in the areas at their peril; for the erection of an improvement might tempt a landlord to claim the land as his own. Many did so, and through expensive litigation they succeeded in driving the small farmers out of the area or converting them into tenants.

Of course, small holdings persisted in the middle colonies, notably on Long Island in New York, in New Jersey, and in Delaware. But the presence of the great estates prevented the easy increase of the small-farmer class, and, to a very considerable extent, was at the basis of much of the hostility that ran like a swift current beneath the surface of things.

5. THE QUITRENTS

It has been said that except in New England all holders of land in the colonies, whether they were freeholders or lease-holders, were required to pay a quitrent, or money due, either to the proprieties or to the crown where it succeeded the proprieties. The totals received from the quitrents were quite large. It has been estimated that at the outbreak of the Revolution the rent rolls of the crown and the proprieties amounted to £37,500 annually, of which fully half was being collected. The burden of such charges, of course, was not a light one; in addition, the imposition of the quitrents brought in its train a whole series of irritations that could not be lightly dismissed.

1. Often the rent collectors demanded that the rents be paid in currency, and in a land where hard money was scarce this requirement was an onerous one. 2. When payments were made in kind—tobacco or wheat or rice—acrimonious discussions were bound to develop over such matters as the value of the commodities, how they were to be graded, who was to pay transportation costs, and the like. 3. In the frontier areas, where surpluses were few, the demands of the collectors for rent payments were resented and often resisted. 4. Land owners had to be on their guard constantly against the raising of the rents to what they regarded as "selfish and grasping" levels. 5. When rents fell into arrears, not infrequently legal means were resorted to with threats of seizure of properties and forced sales. The upshot was, small farmers in particular regarded the quit-rent as an oppressive device of absentee landlordism; in hard times they resisted collections; and occasionally they even clashed with law officers when resort was had to compulsion.

6. THE ESTABLISHMENT OF A CLASS SOCIETY

Thus, based on the unequal holding of and access to landed property, a class society sprang up in colonial America. At its head were the great landlords, who, linked to the crown and the proprieties, were in possession of the instruments of government. Allied with these were the big merchants. Indeed, as in England itself, landlords and merchants were often one and the same: so that the typical man of property—whether he was William Byrd of Westover at the beginning of the eighteenth century or George Washington in the third quarter of the same century—was a plantation lord, a speculator in wild lands, a fur-trade promoter, a dealer in grain, a wholesale merchant, and a moneylender.

The broad lower middle class was made up of the small farmers: whether as independent owners, tenants, or squatters. Small traders, fur trappers, and the urban mechanics and artisans were also members of this class: and, like the yeomen-farmers, they resented and resisted the disabilities the rich and powerful sought to impose upon them. And at the bottom of the social scale were the white and black unfree laborers: for free laborers, other than seamen and shipyard workers, in the essentially agricultural and commercial economy of the colonies were few. These were the various social groupings which built colonial America; and, in the War of Independence, they also made it free.

The annals of colonial America were filled with dissension as the upper and lower middle classes fought each other, sometimes silently, sometimes legally, sometimes in open clashes. Long before the Revolution, there broke out two serious risings of the underprivileged in colonial America; and these presaged the bitter antagonisms that were to divide the two wings of the revolutionary host in the years 1776-89.

The first of these risings occurred in Virginia. As the seventeenth century progressed, the structure of the colony's economy and the well-being of its ruling class came increasingly to be founded on land engrossment, tobacco cultivation, a large capital investment in the unfree labor force, and the fur trade.

It is not difficult to see how the form of government and the early struggles within the colony inevitably stemmed from such a scheme. The affairs of the colony were controlled by the governor and a council appointed by the king, both of whom represented the great landlords; the assembly, to a considerable extent speaking for the small farmers of the regions beyond the tidewater and for the few craftsmen of the towns, found itself relegated to a minor sphere. Under the arbitrary rule of Sir William Berkeley, who was at the head of the colony from 1641 to 1652 and from 1660 to 1677, the governor might determine all matters affecting either war or peace, maintain an established church, summon the general assembly, appoint all officials, dispose of the ungranted lands, prevent foreign vessels from trading with the colony, and compel all tobacco to be shipped to England exclusively.

The period of the Commonwealth afforded a brief breathing space from official tyranny. But when Berkeley returned in 1660 and re-established his personal sway, oppression weighed down the lower orders more heavily than ever before. Berkeley refused to call new elections, he harried Quakers and Baptists out of the colony, he increased the tax burden of the small farmers, he monopolized the beaver trade, he limited the franchise to freeholders, and he rigorously enforced the Acts of Trade and Navigation. The small farmers found themselves without markets for their grain and meatstuffs and at the mercy of the English tobacco monopolists and the London merchants. The fall in the price of tobacco, as a result of the elimination of the Dutch traders, brought hard times, particularly to the debt-ridden interior planters. And to their economic distress was added the physical danger of Indian uprisings as a result of the governor's refusal to safeguard the frontiers, a policy in the interests of the fur trade—a lucrative business that the pacification of the frontier and removal of the Indians would have destroyed.

In 1676 the upcountry settlements rose in revolt, collected an armed force, and under the leadership of the youthful Nathaniel Bacon compelled the summoning of a new assembly which not only repealed the repressive legislation of the previous decades but enacted a series of laws definitely in the interests of the small landed proprietors. This was the first stirrings of that Populist, or lower middle-class agrarian, discontent which was to have such a profound influence on the shaping of American affairs during the next two centuries. Bacon deported himself like a revolutionary captain out of Cromwell's Model Army. He issued proclamations in the name of the "Commons of Virginia." He signed himself "Gen'l. By the Consent of ye People." He confiscated the property of the governor's supporters. And he set up a system of committees to take the place of the council. To his banner flocked, as a hostile contemporary described them, all the "tag, rag, and bobtail" of the colony; and with such an army Bacon first moved against the Indians and then on Jamestown, which he burned.

Unfortunately for the group he represented, Bacon fell ill and died on October 18, 1676, and the uprising collapsed. Berkeley took a cruel revenge: he hanged thirty-seven of Bacon's lieutenants, forced many others into flight, confiscated the property of those involved, and summoned at once another assembly which proceeded to rescind the leveling legislation that the House of Burgesses had passed under Bacon's direction.

But Bacon's struggle was not forgotten; for a century later two other spokesmen for the small farmers of Virginia, Thomas Jefferson and Patrick Henry, again raised their voices against oppression.

A somewhat similar outbreak occurred in the New York colony in the last decade of the seventeenth century. As a part of the deadly commercial war waged between the English and the Dutch, the English had seized the Dutch settlement on the Hudson River in 1664 and attached it to their imperial establishment.

The naval expedition had been sent out by Charles II's brother, the Duke of York, who later was to succeed to the throne as James II. As a reward for his triumph, the Duke was granted a charter, and made sole proprietor, over the Dutch lands lying between the Connecticut and Delaware Rivers. Here he proceeded to set up an absolutist government in no particulars unlike that of the Dutch company. Local pleas for a popular assembly were unavailing for almost two decades, and it was not until 1683 that the Duke finally bowed before the general demand. A decree was issued: an assembly might meet; but it might not pass tax bills without the Duke's consent. The body functioned for two years and then, with the Duke's accession to the throne, it was abolished. New York, now a royal province, was placed under the complete charge of a governor and council.

Under the propriety, the demands of the small men of property for economic relief fared poorly. As a result of the English Acts of Trade and Navigation, many merchants and artisans, who, under the Dutch, had established close trading links with Europe, soon saw continued opportunities for their financial advancement being sharply curtailed. Too, the large merchants of New York City obtained monopoly control over the trading activities of the colony when the government, for tax purposes, ordered that all the wares bought and sold in the colony pass through the port of New York. One such law required that all the flour exported from the colony be processed and packed only in the city, thus placing all the wheat growers and small flour traders at the mercy of the New York monopolists. James, also, not only had not molested the Dutch patroonships but he had utilized the device to divide up the ungranted lands among English landlords who were given estates running from 50,000 to 1,000,000 acres. These payed small quitrents; and in return they obtained great revenues from rents and the activities of agricultural laborers.

Thus, the population of the colony was sharply divided into two classes. The lower class, which was largely disfranchised, consisted of the small farmers, small traders, fisherfolk, and mechanics and artisans who suffered from the economic disabilities imposed by the engrossing landlords and great merchants. The upper class, who held the reins of government, were the favorites and friends of the proprietor and they monopolized the land, the commerce, as well as the fur trade of the Albany district.

By 1689 New York was seething with discontent. When word of James II's overthrow reached the colony, disaffection flamed into open rebellion. The uprising originated in the militia of the city and was led by Jacob Leisler, a German merchant who had come to the settlement originally as a soldier in the service of the Dutch West India Company. In June, 1689, a convention of delegates of the whole province met at Leisler's summons and erected a revolutionary committee of safety with Leisler as its chief. Supported by the small traders, artisans, and farmers of the city, Long Island, and the southern counties, Leisler put the province into a state of defense against possible attack by the French, captained his forces with men from among the lower middle classes, and issued a call for the election of a popular assembly. This met, authorized Leisler to carry on the war against the French and their Indian allies, and enacted a measure for the destruction of the trade monopolies of the large New York merchants. An important passage of this law ran: "All towns and places shall have equal freedom to bolt [flour] and bake and to transport where they please directly to what place or country they think fit, anything their places afford, and that the one place shall have no more privileges than the other." So widely did the revolt spread that Leisler in time was controlling even Ulster and Albany Counties.

But the English Privy Council, alarmed by Leisler's leveling notions, had decided that his government had to be put down, by force if necessary. The royal governor, dispatched to New York in 1691, was ordered not to recognize Leisler's party in the composition of the council and to demand the disarming of the militia bands. Fighting broke out between the militia and the royal forces but when a naval expedition arrived in New York Harbor, early in 1691, and threatened to bombard the city, resistance appeared useless. Leisler surrendered, was tried for treason, and was put to death. To still the popular clamor, however, the governor was compelled to issue writs for the election of a representative assembly, and on April 9, 1691, this body formally met. Thus, Leisler's work had not been completely in vain, although the men of large property continued in control of the economic and political life of the province into the whole of the eighteenth century and a considerable part of the nineteenth.

CHAPTER TEN

The Economy of Colonial America

1. THE FARMER IN THE AMERICAN TRADITION

AT THE outbreak of the American Revolution, the great majority of the American population—perhaps nine tenths of it—was engaged on the land. It is a mistake to assume, as has so frequently been done, that the colonial farmer in most areas operated a self-sufficient farm. Indeed, virtually from the first years of settlement, colonial agriculture to a great extent was conducted in a commercial environment and the American farmer either produced surpluses for sale in a market or sought to develop subsidiary activities that would net him a cash return. Self-sufficiency is usually impossible under capitalist organization. Ready cash is required for taxes, mortgage payments, the improvement of wild and wet lands; and also for those necessaries which no self-sufficing unit, no matter how completely equipped, can hope to produce. Even the frontiersman needs cash and therefore must produce goods or services that possess value in the market; for the frontiersman must buy salt, rum, iron, and a gun and its ammunition. And even the most primitive farm plant occasionally will require agricultural implements, farm buildings, paint and glass for its houses, chinaware and iron utensils for its table and kitchen, and sometimes feed for its animals. This position the humblest backwoodsman and small farmer of the colonial period frequently occupied.

A brief digression is required here. The figure of the American farmer has been bathed in a soft glow of romance. It has been generally assumed that as a freeholder from the beginning and concerned quite completely with the feeding and sheltering of himself and his family, he has been impervious to the pullings and haulings of the market place. The freehold was an isle of safety and sanity distantly removed from the turbulences of the capitalist world. The American farmer and his numerous and sturdy sons, despite the alarms and excursions of the outside, occupied themselves exclusively with their simple and self-contained affairs: they plowed and harvested their broad acres for their own breadstuffs and the feed of their own herds and flocks; when they required timber for fencing and construction they repaired to the home wood lots; they dipped their own candles, tanned their own leather, made their own harness and even their work clothes. And the womenfolk delved and spun and wove; and churned and baked and sewed. Thus it continued until the free lands of the public domain were exhausted and the evil genius of capitalism came pounding on the door of the American freehold. It was not until the late 1880's—so runs the legend—that the American farmer fell on evil times: and then the conspiratorial railroads, the engrossing land companies, the monopolist industrialists, and the usurious bankers began to demand their pound of flesh. The farmer was caught in the capitalist relationship; and he had to become commercial in his attitudes in order to survive—or perish at the hands of his oppressors.

I believe that this analysis is a fiction in very considerable measure. I have said that the American farmer—not simply the grower of wheat or tobacco or cotton, but even the general farmer—virtually from the beginning could not escape the necessity for creating cash. This does not mean that he produced with an eye to making profits, as an ever-conscious process. Nor does it mean, on the other hand, that he became enmeshed in the tangled skein of the market relationship only when he sold a calf or a ham, a cheese or a bag of seed. He was an enterpriser in the real sense: for he labored to add to his capital plant (draining his wet meadows, buying the adjoining farm, erecting barns and silos), to fill his pastures with herds and flocks, and, later, to acquire machinery to increase the productivity of his own toil. To do so, he produced surpluses over and above his own home and farm needs; not, necessarily, single crops, but surpluses nevertheless that he sold in order to meet his debts and expanding requirements.

Some American farmers—but a smaller proportion than we

have been led to assume—did obtain freeholds for the asking and taking or for the payment of nominal sums (under the later pre-emption system). Nevertheless, even these could never avoid debt. The moneylender was always to be found in the American Arcadia: and a monetary obligation perforce made even the humblest producer aware of the existence—and uncertainties—of the capitalist relationship. Even in early colonial times the American backcountry was preoccupied with the money question and the ever-existing presence of the mortgagee. And again, in the 1780's, the late 1830's, the late 1860's, the 1870's, the backcountry farming communities rang with the clamor of restless agrarians. At least these two staples: currency inflation and mortgage stay laws: have always been found at the center of farmer agitation. Under such banners, could one possibly see the farmer as a simple Arcadian?

The American farmer was aware of the pressures of his financial obligations: and that made his psychology essentially a capitalist one. He therefore produced agricultural surpluses or, what came to the same thing, he tried to find employment among a number of occupations that did not interfere with his agricultural activities. The colonial farmer, for example, was a trapper and a hunter; or he worked in logging camps; or he shipped with a fishing fleet. After the Revolution, when the English mercantilist ban was lifted off manufacturing, he and his family engaged in home industry: in the farmhouse, under the orders of the merchant-manufacturer, shoes were made, woolen cloth was woven, straw hats were plaited, brooms were fabricated. When railroads came, the farmer and his son worked on the maintenance and repair gangs.

Always, and this factor helps to explain why the agricultural community in America continued to be so large despite the fact that many farmers were never more than marginal producers, the American farmer was a land speculator. That is to say, because land values in the United States continued to mount, the farmer always could—and often did—sell his improved holding at a profit and buy a cheaper farm in the frontier areas: where the round of conquering the wilderness could be started once more. Thus, the American farmer was a dealer in land from the very dawn of settlement until 1920, a period of three centuries. The decline of land values after 1921 began to shake the basis of American agricultural well-being to its foundations. Now, for the first time, the marginal American farmer (and he was a vast company) began to approximate the position of the agriculturist of Europe and Asia: and there seemed small likelihood of real and lasting improvement in his economic status. Decline had set in.

2. AGRICULTURE IN THE NORTHERN COLONIES

The colonial farmer, then, was trying to develop a cash crop, something he could sell in the market. By the eighteenth century, even in rocky New England, staples had appeared: beef cattle and hogs, work animals, corn to be used for stall feeding. And a considerable portion of these products moved into the hands of Connecticut Valley merchants who shipped them directly to the West Indies. The middle colonies were the great granary where wheat was grown to be converted into flour for sale to the towns and also to the faraway West Indies. In the southern colonies, of course, commercial agriculture was the keystone of the whole economic structure. Virginia and Maryland planters grew tobacco for sale in England and Scotland. Interior farmers grew grains and raised cattle to be used in the West Indian trade. The tidewater planters of the Carolinas and Georgia cultivated and harvested rice, indigo, and some cotton. These crops were sent to seaports, sometimes processed, particularly in the case of cereals and meats, and then put on ships to be carried to distant places where they furnished those funds which were the basis of the commercial enterprise of the day.

Of the three regions, New England was able to develop agriculture least successfully. The reasons for this are not far to seek. The colonies, as we have seen, had been founded and were being maintained as commercial ventures within the framework of the Mercantile System. The export of goods and services to England, or the development of other commercial goods or services acceptable to England, was the key to the whole plan. England did not require foodstuffs; but it did need furs, the products of the forest, and iron. Occasionally it bought fish.

Nor did it frown upon the establishment of a triangular trade with its own West Indian colonies as a result of which New Englanders might sell to the sugar planters of Barbados and Jamaica fish, lumber, and work animals, import sugar and molasses for manufacture into rum, and trade the heady liquor for Negro slaves on the African coast. The requirements of the Mercantile System, therefore, compelled New Englanders to create those goods and services with which they could pay most quickly their English balances—incurred by purchasing English manufactured goods. This meant they resorted to lumbering, fishing, trapping, shipbuilding, and the West Indian traffic.

The character of the New England soil and climate made the establishment of an intensive commercial agriculture difficult unless farmers were prepared to invest a heavy capital fund in it. Thus, it was not ignorance that prevented New England farmers from applying the lessons of scientific agriculture: they knew of the work of the English agriculturists Tull, Bakewell, Coke, and Townshend, who had demonstrated how easily animal stocks could be improved, forage crops raised, and the fertility of the soil renewed by rotation and natural and artificial manuring. It was simply that returns on investments could be obtained more readily from shipbuilding, the rum and slave trades, and from land speculation. When the West Indian market began to expand and opportunities for sizable profits began to present themselves in the production of beef cattle and work horses and oxen, many New England farmers turned to these activities. They could not, however, raise sheep because mercantilist bans on colonial manufactures prevented the growth of a market for wool. It is enough to note, in this connection, that New England today is a great agricultural region producing tobacco, dairy cattle, and a large variety of fruit and vegetable crops; and this indicates that no soil or climate is so stubborn or inhospitable that the enterprise of man cannot tame it.

New England farmers, therefore, grew for the market—largely the West Indian market—provisions and live animals. Complementary to their agriculture they also produced for the same market fish and lumbering goods. They caught and shot the wild creatures of the forest and sold the skins and peltries.

And to a very considerable degree the smaller farmers of the interior valleys fed, clothed, and housed themselves. They produced their own flour, meatstuffs, lard, and maple sugar, sirup, and honey. But they had to buy, of course, salt, rum, and tea. They produced their own wool and woolcloth, flax and linen and leather. But they had to buy broadcloth when the goodman wanted a fine coat for prayer meetings. They produced their own dairy products. But they had to buy pedigreed cattle to improve and maintain the quality of their own herds. They made their own woodwork for the farm carts, plows, yokes, and tool handles. But they had to buy iron for the plowshares, chains, axes, billhooks, scythes, hoes, forks, and pitchforks; and they had to buy nails. In short, they never achieved complete self-sufficiency.

The middle colonies developed commercial agriculture on a more significant scale than did New England. Farms were greater in size; soil and climatic conditions were more favorable. The presence of a large landlord class and the existence of tenancy made necessary the development of cash crops. The local markets of New York, Philadelphia, and Baltimore gave spur to the production of foodstuffs. There existed a cheap and constantly renewable farm labor supply in the shape of the indentured servants; in Pennsylvania, notably, such servants were being employed as farmers and husbandmen. And proximity to the many excellent seaports encouraged the growth of agricultural products for the West Indian trade. As a result, during the eighteenth century, the middle colonies were producing large quantities of surplus grains which were being milled into flour and packed for export to New England, the West Indies, and occasionally to Great Britain and southern Europe. The middle colonies, like New England, also were raising beef and dairy cattle, hogs and work animals and entering them and their products into the foreign trade.

The importance of the West Indian sugar islands to the establishment and maintenance of a commercial agriculture in the mainland colonies has been commented on. In the year 1770 the following quantities of agricultural wares were shipped from the mainland to the sugar islands, chiefly from the middle

colonies, though to a lesser extent New England also participated in the traffic: 559,000 bushels of Indian corn; 230,000
barrels of flour; 28,200 barrels of beef and pork; 55,400 pounds
of cheese; 172,600 pounds of lard and tallow; 6000 horses; 3300
live oxen; and 18,500 hogs and sheep.

3. THE PLANTATION SYSTEM OF THE SOUTHERN COLONIES

In the South, agriculture from the beginning operated on a
commercial basis. The plantation form of economy prevailed,
although many small independent farmers inhabited the interior. On the plantations, tobacco, rice, and indigo were being
grown; in the backcountry the chief crops were tobacco, cereals,
and cattle, which also by the eighteenth century were reaching
markets. Tobacco was the great cash crop of colonial America
just as cotton was to become that of the Middle Period. And
because the economic fortunes of early America were so closely
linked with the tobacco plant, it is important to examine closely
all questions associated with its cultivation.

At the center of the tobacco cultivation stood the plantation
—the customary farming organization. The plantation is not
unique to colonial and slave America; it still exists as a significant form of agricultural economic organization and many of
its characteristics remain today. What are these characteristics?
Generally, they have been the following. The plantation is a
large operating farm plant under unified direction and control.
It produces staple crops for sale in a market and for this reason
it is at the mercy of the price system and similar capitalist
relations. It utilizes an unfree labor supply. The capital resources of the planter are not invested so much in the land and
the improvement of its techniques (machine planting, cultivation and harvesting, irrigation, conservation of the soil) as they
are in the maintenance of a permanent labor force. From this
there flows either the institution of indenture or slavery or
peonage or share cropping, and the distinguishing hallmark of
all these systems is the fact that the capital fund is used to keep
the agricultural laborer more or less permanently attached to
the plantation.

Therefore, the plantation economy will spring up and flourish in those regions where land is relatively plentiful and cheap, where extensive rather than intensive operations can be carried on, and where a permanent labor supply can be collected and retained. There is nothing inherent in the crops themselves that accounts for the appearance of the system; tobacco and cotton can be grown successfully by small independent farmers. Nor have climate and the racial composition of the farm laborers anything to do with it. Plantation agriculture, essentially, is an exploitative activity that will appear in new countries where land is not restricted, where liquid funds are relatively scarce, and where surpluses can be invested in a growing laboring group.

It is not hard to see why the plantation system should take root almost immediately in colonial Virginia and Maryland. It furnished opportunities for the investment of capital in land, in the transportation of the labor supply, and in the carriage, financing, and processing of the crop. It worked in closely with the theory of mercantilism, for England looked to the southern colonies to produce many of those necessaries for which it was dependent upon the Near and Far East. Sugar and indigo were two products the New World grew for England; and when it also produced tobacco this gave additional cause for public encouragement. For as the taste for tobacco developed and began to spread into the European continent, England possessed a natural monopoly. Tobacco furnished an export in return for which large English stores of finished goods might be sent to the southern colonies. These colonies also provided an outlet to which might be sent, at the expense of the planter, those uprooted populations whose idleness at home was such a source of concern to seventeenth- and early eighteenth-century England. These persons became the indentured servants of the plantations.

Thus all the English mainland southern colonies and the British West Indies established the plantation system as a form of capitalist enterprise. And, as a rule, the planter-landlord came over to the mainland to manage personally his own undertaking. Because he was supplied with a capital fund, he quite frequently became interested at once also in furs, the raising of livestock, and the carrying on of a considerable trade with the Indians. Later, it was equally natural for the planter to utilize his capital fund and his surplus to enter into mercantile and financial activities and to buy up the wild lands of the western zones. In the eighteenth century, the southern planter was likely to be tobacco grower, retail storekeeper, merchant, Indian trader, banker, and land speculator all rolled into one. But the basis of his economic position was the fact that he grew a staple crop for sale in a market and had the greater part of his capital invested in his unfree labor supply, whether it happened to be indentured servants or Negro slaves.

4. TOBACCO

Tobacco was the first and for almost two centuries the most important cash crop of the southern plantation economy. Made known to Europeans when Columbus discovered its cultivation by Indians in the West Indies, the tobacco plant was being grown in England in the middle of the sixteenth century and in the English colonies overseas at the beginning of the seventeenth century. Disappointed in their hopes that gold would be found to bring returns on their investments, the Virginia Company ordered the cultivation of the plant in Virginia. So quickly did the agents of the company and the first adventurers adapt themselves to its culture that in 1628 a crop of 500,000 pounds was harvested. Tobacco also became the foundation of Maryland's well-being. The result was, at the end of the seventeenth century, these two colonies were exporting 35,000,000 pounds to the mother country; and in 1763, the export to England and Scotland was close to 100,000,000 pounds. In England, the leaves were processed and sold in the home market or re-exported to the Continent. Indeed, in the eighteenth century from three fourths to seven eighths of the annual importation was sent out to France, Spain, the Low Countries, and the like.

In line with the mercantilist tradition, the Virginia and Maryland governments did everything in their power to protect the tobacco crop. Legislation was passed setting up inspection systems and public warehouses to assure standard quality, grading, and fair weights. Negotiable receipts were issued against warehouse tobacco and accepted as public money for the payment of debts and taxes. And from time to time public authorities were prevailed upon to limit the crop or wink at the destruction of surpluses when their presence seemed to threaten the price structure. England, in its turn, exercised itself on behalf of the tobacco growers. It suppressed growing in England and seemed to offer colonial planters a monopoly of the English market by virtually excluding foreign-grown tobacco through a system of heavy taxes and licensing restrictions.

The Mercantile System was not, however, altogether a blessing. Colonial planters did not have to meet the competition of other growers in the English market; but because they themselves, as a result of the "enumeration" of tobacco, were limited to the English market, they became the victims of English mercantile capitalism. In search of revenue, the English imposed high sumptuary taxes on tobacco (in the shape of import duties). This not only restricted English consumption of the weed but the heavy load of taxation kept the prices the planters could command at a low figure. Thus, during 1685-1703, the English duty on colonial tobacco was from four to six times its selling price in America; and by 1760 the ratio of duty to price was as high as fifteen to one. It is true that the English remitted a part, and later the whole, of the import duty upon re-export; but the only group to profit were the English merchants and bankers handling the crop.

It is a truism that commercial agriculture, because its capital fund is invested in its operations, cannot adjust production swiftly to counteract a fall in prices. This was the tobacco planter's dilemma. Prices received were controlled in very considerable measure at London. In addition, capital costs of plantation operation continued to mount: due to the high cost of labor (the price of indentured servants and, more particularly, that of slaves went up while their productivity remained constant); the exhaustion of the soil in older regions; and the necessity on the part of the planters to buy new lands to which they could be ready to transfer their activities. The other charges on operations—freight costs, insurance, merchants' commissions and profits, interest on borrowings—hung like millstones about the necks of the encumbered planters.

The planters sought to escape from this unfortunate situation by extending their cultivated holdings. To overcome price drops their only reply could be an increase in production in an effort to lower the unit costs. Forced to send their supplies to England only and at the mercy of the English tax system, colonial growers were helpless in the face of falling prices. Almost every twenty years saw a sharp depression in tobacco as planters grew blindly for an uncertain market. Not infrequently prices fell below normal costs.

Why did tobacco cultivation continue, then? From time to time encouraged by a rising market, the grower acquired more land and invested his liquid funds in his labor supply. When the market was falling, liquidation was out of the question, for who would buy his Negro slaves? Losses were met from those other commercial and financial enterprises that most planters engaged in: the fur trade, land speculation, the stocking of inland peddlers, and the financing of trading voyages. Probably tobacco cultivation, most of the time, was not conducted at a profit at all. The plantation system had certain social attractions: its expansiveness, its prestige value, its outdoor living. And these help to account for its continuance for such a long time.

5. OTHER SOUTHERN CROPS

Rice and indigo also were grown on the plantation and, hence, were important southern cash crops. Rice first made its appearance at the end of the seventeenth century in the neighborhood of Charleston, and before long was being planted in the low swampy tidewater regions along the coast from the Cape Fear River in North Carolina south into Georgia. Like tobacco, rice received the attention of the Mercantile System. It was an "enumerated" article; by the 1730's, however, this restriction was relaxed so that rice planters, after first paying export duties, might ship direct to any part of Europe south of Cape Finisterre (in northwestern Spain). With such an extending market, plantations grew, lands jumped in value, slave imports into

South Carolina and Georgia increased manyfold, and there sprang up a rich and aristocratic planter class seated on wide acres and lording it over charming manor houses.

Indigo, although grown early in South Carolina, did not enter into commercial production until the 1740's. Necessary to furnish dyes for the expanding home woolen industry, indigo growing was encouraged by English bounties and duty remissions. Another series of southern products to receive English support, largely for the purpose of terminating England's dependence upon the Baltic countries of Europe, had to do with the shipbuilding industry. Chief among these products were the naval stores of tar, pitch, and resin; hemp, which was converted into rope; and flax, out of which sailcloth was manufactured. At the beginning of the eighteenth century, the home government began to offer bounties and duty remissions for the colonial production of these articles and their shipment to England. In New England, the mercantile traffic was too profitable to tempt capital into the production of naval stores and hemp. But in the South, where the forests were so much greater and the production of naval stores and hemp could be linked as a subsidiary enterprise with commercial agriculture, the English met with a substantial success. In both North Carolina and South Carolina the naval-stores industry flourished; while hemp and flax were being grown widely in the southern colonies, in a short time penetrating even into the backcountry.

6. THE PLANTATION SYSTEM BASED ON CREDIT

Southern commercial agriculture, like every capitalist operation, depended upon credit. Credit was required to assist in the acquisition of the labor force, to market the cash crop, to buy necessary equipment, and to finance the purchase of consumer goods. Because plantations and slaves (to a lesser extent) could be mortgaged and because tobacco enjoyed a steady market, a basis for credit existed, so that English money flowed into the southern colonies. The movement of English funds across the ocean was facilitated by the higher interest rates prevalent in the colonies. Thus, when the Revolution broke out, money was bringing only 5 per cent in England and from 8 to 10 per cent in the southern areas. In time, almost all the mercantile-financial operations of the South came to be controlled by English capitalists because their funds made possible the day-to-day continuance of the planting economy. Adam Smith, writing in 1776, was able to declare:

The greater part both of the exportation and coasting trade of America is carried on by the capitals of merchants who reside in Great Britain. Even the stores and warehouses from which goods are retailed in some provinces, particularly in Virginia and Maryland, belong many of them to merchants who reside in the mother country.

With credit playing the important role it did, it was inevitable that the financier should loom large in the capitalist relations in which the planter was involved. The financier was not a banker, pure and simple, in the colonial period; he was rather a merchant who also engaged in private banking. These were some of the activities of the English merchant. He bought goods in England which he sent to the colonies to be traded in, or he deposited them in a colonial warehouse from which they were withdrawn at the order of one of his local correspondents. Frequently he bought special wares at the direct orders of his correspondents. He was the banker for his correspondents: acting as their depository, accepting their bills of exchange, collecting their bills drawn on persons in England, and advancing them credit. Also, he bought colonial staples when they arrived in England or he sold on commission such staples as his correspondents shipped to him personally. Not infrequently, the English merchant operated through a representative in the colonies. This person was known as a factor. Sometimes the factor was a regular employee of the merchant; at other times he was likely to be a colonial merchant or planter who, for a commission, worked for his English principals.

There were a number of points at which irritations inevitably appeared. The dependence of the planters upon book credit and the high interest charges they were forced to pay made the southern landlords constantly chafe under the controls imposed upon them by the English merchant capitalists. As we shall see, demands for the widening of the credit base and for inflation became increasingly common and were among the important causes why planters entered into the Revolution. Southern planters entertained strong suspicions, which frequently were confirmed, that English merchants were combining to control prices. Often the rigid prices of tobacco, rice, and indigo in the English market, despite fluctuations in the crop, and the high prices of the necessaries which colonials were compelled to buy, pointed to monopoly control. Constantly weighed down by debt, it was small wonder that the planters of colonial America increasingly sought to expand their activities, by extending their tobacco lands and engaging in the more speculative aspects of land dealings. And that they turned to thoughts of inflation as relief from debt oppression was also to be expected.

Thus, virtually from the beginning, the plantation system was conducted on a narrow margin of profit which, by the middle of the eighteenth century, probably had contracted almost to the vanishing point. What sustained the southern plantation economy? It was nothing else than the presence of easily preempted lands in the wilderness areas west of the cultivated regions, and these lands the planters could buy up for speculative purposes. The ability of planters to make a profit (not on the cultivation of their staples but in their role as speculative landlords) furnished the incentive for the flow of short-term capital from England into the southern colonies for the financing of the planting, cultivating, harvesting, and shipping of their crops, the purchase of their servants and slaves, and the satisfaction of their personal and household needs. And short-term borrowings were converted into long-term indebtednesses by the placing of mortgages on plantations. When these profits from speculative land operations threatened to disappear the flow of English credit ceased, and southern planters were confronted by wholesale bankruptcy.

Because the wild lands of the frontier areas were so important to the maintenance of the stability of the southern planting economy, southern planter capitalism was ever preoccupied with them. The West was not opened up by the hardy frontiersman; it was opened up by the land speculator who preceded even the

Daniel Boones into the wilderness. When the young Washington surveyed the lands around the waters of the upper Potomac in 1748 he was doing so as the representative of a great colonial landlord and as the scion of a rich landowning family; and when he bought up soldier-bounty claims in the decade following he was only pursuing the same line of interest already marked out by the Fairfaxes, the Lees, and the Mercers.

But the English (and the Scotch, in this case) had also learned to regard with more than a curious interest these wild lands of the West: they saw in them opportunities for profits from the fur trade and from the speculative exploitation of the region by their own capitalist enterprise. It was at this point that English and American mercantile capitalism came into conflict. When, as a result of the promulgation of the Proclamation Line of 1763 and the Quebec Act of 1774, the western lands were virtually closed to colonial enterprising, southern planter capitalism began to totter on its throne. Without the subsidiary activity of land speculation, the planting economy could not continue solvent; there is no cause for wonder therefore that southern planters were among the first to swell the ranks of the colonial revolutionary host in 1775.

Nothing indicates more completely the debtor position of southern commercial agriculture than the mounting burden of debt and the almost continuous attention devoted by southern assemblies to cheap-money measures. At the outbreak of the Revolution it was not unlikely that the American colonies were indebted to English merchant capitalists to the extent of fully £5,000,000, of which at least five sixths had been incurred by the southern planters. These loans bore heavy interest charges, and funds for short-term operations and for long-term renewals were becoming increasingly difficult to obtain as English creditors took alarm after 1763. I. S. Harrell, whose excellent monograph plainly reveals the economic basis of revolutionary crisis and struggle in the most important southern colony, Virginia, sums up the situation in these words: "With their plantations, slaves, and sometimes household furniture hypothecated, the planters were in an almost inextricable position in 1775."

7. OTHER FIELDS OF PRODUCTION

Colonial producers and enterprisers engaged in all those other activities that are associated with a newly settled region. The trapping and slaying of the wild animals of the forests early attracted pioneers and promoters; and the prevalence of the beaver, otter, mink, bear, raccoon, and fox in the New England and middle colonies and of the deer, raccoon, fox, and beaver in the southern colonies led to the creation of a thriving peltry-and-hide industry and trade. The English demand for furs and skins was constant, profits were great, and capitalism quickly became interested and sought to monopolize the field. This it was not difficult to do, particularly when the lines of the traffic lengthened as the wild lands kept on receding beyond the tide-water settlements. English merchants and the great southern and northern landlords financed the individual hunters, trappers, and traders, or employed them as their agents, and furnished the truck and firearms which served as the basis for the Indian barter. As the extermination of wild life went on, the colonial economy had to keep open an ever-extending frontier zone. The struggle over the fur trade had involved England and France in a long series of colonial wars in America, and the desire to continue the fur traffic was one of the reasons for colonial interest in the wild lands beyond the crest of the Appalachians—and, hence, collision with the mother country.

Lumbering and the production of forest products offered further opportunities for colonial capitalist enterprise. The abundance of stands of white pine and oak in the North and of yellow pine in the South, the great need for timber and naval stores as the basis of shipbuilding industry, and the wide uses to which wood was put for construction and cooperage made lumbering an obvious field of interest for many elements of the colonial population. The lumbering camps that sprang up near the many rivers of seaboard America offered winter employment to farmers and their sons. And in the erection of sawmills and the carriage of the cut timber to markets, merchants invested their funds and, indeed, by expanding their operations very quickly succeeded in driving small competitors out of business. On a modest scale, obviously, the sawmill industry in many regions began to acquire monopolist characteristics. These lumbering products were important articles of commerce, the chief outlet being the sugar islands, Spain, and Portugal.

Utilizing the products of the forest and in response to the needs of fishermen and merchants, a thriving colonial ship-building industry sprang up. Mercantile capital was closely joined to the carrying trade; and the expansion of trading relations on the part of England with the Orient and Africa and on the part of the mainland colonies with Newfoundland, the West Indies, the wine islands (Madeira, the Azores, and the Canaries), and the Guinea coast gave spur to the building of ships at every coast town easily accessible to a timber supply. Shipyards, encouraged by the mother country, which exported the needed ironware and shipwrights, arose on the Massachu-setts shore and at Philadelphia and New York. Financed early with British capital, they were turning out, by the opening of the Revolution, all the ships the American carrying trade needed and a large part of those employed by the British. The building of ships was one of the great outlets for New England, and, later, for Pennsylvania capital accumulations. Massachusetts alone between 1696 and 1713 produced at least 1118 vessels of 69,468 tons; during the second quarter of the century Phila-delphia became the chief shipbuilding center of the colonies. So pressing was this colonial competition that the English in-dustry exhorted Parliament to prohibit American shipbuilding, but without avail, so that by 1775, it has been estimated, 30 per cent of the ships flying the British flag were built in American yards. American ships served another important eco-nomic function: they were a significant item in the balance of international payments. Ship captains, after having sold their freights in England, the wine islands, or the sugar islands, also disposed of the ships themselves at handsome profits and re-turned as supercargoes on the vessels that were carrying back to America the hardware and drygoods or rum, wine, or hardwoods they had bought.

Not least among the fields cultivated by American enterprise were the fisheries. Starting originally and modestly as inshore fishermen, the New England colonists were able to supplement their meager diets with the catches of cod, mackerel, haddock, and halibut they found in such great quantities in the waters around Massachusetts. Operations were on a small scale and seamen participating in the industry shared with the owners of vessels in the profits of the catches. But as the New England fishermen were able to shake off the competition of the English in home waters and as they extended their activities farther and farther northward to the Newfoundland banks, the Nova Scotia coast, and the St. Lawrence Gulf, the industry more and more began to attract a large capitalist interest. The outfitting of ships and the curing and sale of the fish demanded liquid funds. Also, the supply of the growing market—to southern Europe, Ireland, and the wine islands which bought good fish, and to the sugar islands which bought the so-called refuse for their slaves—made links with big merchants imperative. These functions only a well-developed mercantile capitalism could perform; so that consolidation and control began to appear in the fisheries as they did in the fur industry. In 1765 more than 31,000 men were engaged on the New England fishery fleets; and more than 350 ships carried fish to the markets of southern Europe and the West Indies.

Whaling, by the opening of the eighteenth century, also began to take on significant proportions. Whales—particularly important for their blubber whose oil was the chief source of illuminants and lubricants—were hunted far out into the North Atlantic; and by 1770, 4000 tons of whale oil were being exported after local needs had been filled.

The mining and production of crude iron—of pigs and bars—appeared early in colonial America, when enterprisers in Massachusetts took to working bog deposits. Starting with the second decade of the eighteenth century, the industry took on new life; and using English capital and slave labor, American owners of iron-ore lands began to erect blast furnaces and forges in western Virginia and Maryland. The Principio Company, organized in Maryland in 1724, in time acquired 30,000 acres of ore lands and numerous plants; at the outbreak of the Revolution, its properties were worth at least $500,000. Spreading into Pennsylvania and New Jersey, in the 1770's the colonial industry could claim more operating blast furnaces and forges and the production of more pigs and bars than could that of the mother country. Foreign capital began to appear in this field, although without real success, at the end of the colonial period. When Baron Stiegel erected iron- and glassworks in Pennsylvania he did so with funds from Germany; and when Peter Hasenclever built iron furnaces and forges and other plants in New Jersey and New York in the 1760's he was sinking more than £50,000 belonging to English investors.

The production of crude iron by the colonies England encouraged; but when colonials, instead of shipping their pigs and bars to the mother country, took to erecting rolling and slitting mills and plating forges—in short, began turning the crude iron into nails and sheets—then the heavy hand of the Mercantile System descended on this young industry. The Iron Act of 1750 put crude iron on a free list and denied to colonists the right to extend the manufacture of wrought iron, by forbidding them to erect new slitting and rolling mills, plating forges, and steel furnaces. In 1764 iron was included among the "enumerated" articles.

8. MANUFACTURING

Colonial America possessed no manufacturing, in the commercial or industrial sense: and in this fact we are to find one of the important keys to the outbreak of the American Revolution. Household manufacturing there was: many of the colonial farming households and some of the great plantation establishments supplied part of their own needs. Food was prepared for home consumption: bread was baked, butter was churned, shoulders and hams were salted and smoked, fruits were dried, beer was brewed. Wool, flax, hemp, and, in the South, cotton for clothing and home uses were carded, spun, woven, and sometimes even rudely dyed. Leather was tanned and made into shoes, caps, gloves, and rough workclothes. The wood lot furnished the timber for house and barn, shingles, furniture, carts, implement handles, casks, and staves. Ashes were leached, soap was boiled, candles were molded, and kitchen utensils of wood, horn, and gourd were devised. Sometimes working with his family, sometimes assisted by traveling artisans, the colonial farmer was able to fabricate many crude articles for his daily needs out of those raw materials that he had at hand. Occasionally a surplus of cloth, linen, butter, or honey was taken to the local village and sold or exchanged for the salt, iron, paint, and tools that were essential to the conduct of the household: for self-sufficiency, of course, was never fully attained.

This was not manufacturing in the capitalist sense. The conversion of raw materials into finished goods and their sale in large and distant markets, in modern times, have gone forward under the supervision of two different types of organization. Sometimes found side by side but in the broad and abstract sense existing in a sequential relationship, these have been domestic manufacturing, or the putting-out system, and industrial manufacturing, or the factory system. Stated simply, the putting-out system was that type of manufacture under which an intermediary, the merchant-manufacturer, who was more interested in commerce than in production, supplied the raw materials to independent artisans who, laboring in their own homes and possessing their own equipment, performed the processes of production. The finished goods were then taken over by the merchant-manufacturer who transported and sold them in the markets he had developed. Associated more particularly with the manufacture of woolens, although it was to be found in many other industries, even in metal mining, the putting-out system flourished generally in western Europe in the period between the decline of the guilds and the appearance of the factory. It was controlled by the merchant capitalist: he it was who had the liquid funds that made possible the financing of the various transactions involved in the gathering together of the raw materials, their manufacture, and their sale. The producer, on the other hand, was not a wage laborer primarily. He owned his own workshop, which was his home; his loom, frames, and tools, as the case might be; and his kitchen garden. When, in addition to owning the wool, yarn, stuff, and the shop in which it was sold, the merchant-manufacturer came also to possess the looms and frames, then the transition was complete.

In the words of the French historian Paul Mantoux: "Thus the producer, gradually deprived of all rights of ownership over the instruments of production, had in the end only his labor to sell and his wages to live on." The movement of the expropriated producers into unified workshops, where they worked under discipline and engaged in social rather than individual production, and the more intensive division of labor completed the process.

The factory system was now in operation. Not necessarily associated with automatic machinery—for central workshops existed in Florence in the thirteenth century and in England as early as the sixteenth century—industrial manufacture was chiefly characterized by the complete separation of the laborer from the instruments of production and by the sale of his labor power for wages. The private and concentrated ownership of the fixed capital—workshop, equipment, tools—the hiring of wage labor, gathered together in factories and working under discipline, and the division of labor were its primary and unique attributes. In a secondary sense, it was distinguished by owner management, rationalization of production, the greater circulation of capital, the more intensive organization of the market, and, later, the introduction of power. Such was the factory system that began to supplant the putting-out system in England in the middle of the eighteenth century and that became the distinguishing mark of industrial capitalism.

Neither of these types of manufacturing organization was to be found in colonial America. Why was this? Colonial America did not want for liquid capital. Witness the extraordinary extension of capitalist enterprise, the work of both English and American capitalists, in trade, shipbuilding, land speculation, the financing of the plantation system, and crude-iron production. Colonial America had its fair share of wealthy men: as early as 1680, there were said to be at least thirty merchants in Massachusetts alone who were worth between $50,000 and $100,000. Thomas Amory, one of the greatest early colonial merchants, left an estate worth $100,000; Peter Faneuil, who died in the 1740's, left many times that amount. Every colony could boast of its big merchants, who were, in fact, capitalists; indeed, George Washington, the greatest of these, in the 1770's was calling himself not "planter" but "merchant." Colonial America did not want for the means of creating a free labor supply: the engrossing of the lands in the settled areas had compelled small farmers either to become tenants or to move westward where they squatted on the wild lands held by absentee landlords. The frontier had not been made secure against the Indians because of the fur trade and the necessity for supporting tidewater land values; but, had the owners of the wild lands so desired it, the pacification of the western areas would have driven the landless into domestic manufacturing or workshops. Also, indentured servants and slaves (as they were, indeed, used in the colonial heavy iron industry) could have been employed in industrial production. Colonial America did not want for a market: by 1770, concentrated in a relatively small area and excellently served by harbors and rivers, lived a population at least one fourth as great as England's; in addition, the very rich market for finished goods of the sugar islands could have been exploited. Colonial America did not want for raw materials: never was a land endowed with richer natural resources. Manufacturing did not appear in colonial America because the very nature of the Mercantile System prohibited it.

9. THE PROHIBITION OF MANUFACTURES

In describing the Mercantile System, in its imperial-colonial relations, I said that following the triumph of English mercantile capitalism in the Puritan Revolution the policy of England was based on the economic subservience of the colonies. This was so from the very beginning—certainly, at any rate, from the turn of the eighteenth century when mercantile capitalism was fully installed in the economy of the empire and in possession of its prerogative power. And a governmental apparatus was set up whose purpose it was consciously and constantly to maintain the imperial-colonial connection in this relationship. The real significance of all those imperial administrative agencies—the Privy Council, the Board of Trade, the Secretary of State in charge of Colonial Affairs, the Commissioners of Customs, the Treasury, the Admiralty, and the royal governors—lay in the fact not that they created political or constitutional ties to unite colonies to the mother country but that they forged the fetters that bound the colonial mercantile and planter capitalism to that of England.

An examination of the activities of the imperial administrative agencies will plainly indicate that such an economic policy was consistently pursued: the period after 1763 merely marked its intensification as a result of the sharpening of the contradictions that appeared in mercantilism itself. The Board of Trade had been established in 1696, as O. M. Dickerson points out, largely "to make the colonies commercially profitable to the mother country." And this it sought to do, over a period of more than three quarters of a century, with a devotion and singleness of purpose that left small room for complaint. The commissioners, of course, made it their business to keep the Privy Council and Parliament informed as to the progress of the oversea possessions; but their powers were more than reportorial, for through a number of specific devices they were able to direct and supervise closely the economic development of the colonies. The Board of Trade was more or less in charge of preparing the colonial civil list; and it was also its function to supervise the activities of the colonial judiciary: by control over personnel its influence therefore was measurable. But it had other and still more important functions. It had the right to deny charters, or patents, to English-financed companies seeking to invest in enterprises in the colonies which were inimical to the interests of home merchant capitalists, particularly those engaged in manufacturing. It had the power to review colonial legislation and, if the purposes of provincial statutes ran counter to the welfare of the mother country, recommend their disallowance (or veto) by the Privy Council. And finally, it had the power to prepare specific instructions to the governors for their guidance in the exercise of the veto over colonial encroachments on the privileges and prerogatives of English citizens.

At at least a dozen points the Board of Trade (representing English mercantile capitalism) and the colonial legislatures (representing colonial mercantile and planter capitalism) came into constant conflict, exactly because of the clash of economic interests. The outstanding of these were: colonial interference with the mother country's hold on foreign trade and shipping; attempts by the colonies to control the traffic in convicts and slaves; and colonial efforts to permit the payment of quitrents in paper money, to lower interest rates, to ease the judicial burdens imposed on debtors, and to monopolize the Indian trade for colonials. Even more important were the stern checks imposed by the Board of Trade on attempts by the colonial assemblies to encourage native manufacturing and to relieve the oppression of debts (because every section of colonial America was in a debtor relationship toward England) through the increase of the money supply of the colonies.

In order to maintain the English control over trade and commerce, the Board of Trade recommended and obtained the disallowance by the Privy Council of legislation placing export duties on colonial raw materials needed by English enterprise. It was equally successful in outlawing acts whose purpose it was, through the grant of exemptions, to favor colonial shipowners in the carrying trade. It ceaselessly moved against measures placing import duties on foreign wines and liquors and on English merchandise. Finally, when this last threatened to become a general practice, the Board issued blanket instructions to the governors ordering them to veto laws placing duties on European goods imported in English vessels (1724) and on the produce or manufactures of Great Britain (1732), and all those laws under which the natives of a province were given preferential treatment over those of Great Britain (1732).

The Privy Council repeatedly was called upon to disallow legislation laying high or prohibitive duties upon the importation of Negro slaves and interfering with the free transport of convicted felons overseas. The colonies for the most part were moving to protect themselves against the growth of undesirable elements in their population; although the motives of revenue and the protection of the quality of the slaves also were present. But the Board and the Privy Council were not unmindful of the great English slave-carrying trade that was bound to be affected by such legislation: its solicitude therefore was plain.

Finally in 1731, when the colonies persisted in their efforts to pass such bills, circular instructions were sent to the governors ordering them to veto legislation interfering with the free importation of Negroes and felons.

When colonies sought to foster local manufacturing enterprise, the Board of Trade could be expected to exercise an unceasing vigilance. Partly due to the abundance of raw materials and the constantly growing market but largely because of the accumulation of capital surpluses won in trade, colonial merchant capitalists always were pressing for the passage of laws to help the development of native industries. They obtained them; and colonial statute books, therefore, were filled with legislation that was, in effect, only modeled after those acts Parliament itself was passing: measures calling for the payment of bounties to private enterprisers and the extension of public credit to them, for exemptions from taxation, for easy access to raw materials, for the maintenance of standards of quality, and for the encouragement of the location of new towns and of the settling of artisans in new and old urban communities.

Against such legislation the Board of Trade regularly moved. On important matters, appeal was had to Parliament and general statutes were passed, notably the Woolen Act of 1699, which barred colonial wool, woolen yarn, and woolen manufactures from intercolonial and foreign commerce; the Hat Act of 1732, which prevented the exportation of hats out of the separate colonies, excluded Negroes from the industry, fixed a seven-year apprenticeship, and restricted colonial hatmakers to two apprentices; and the Iron Act of 1750. In addition, the ax of disallowance descended regularly. Thus, in 1705, a Pennsylvania law for building up the shoemaking industry was disallowed on the ground that, as the Board said: "It cannot be expected that encouragement should be given by law to the making any manufactures made in England . . . it being against the advantage of England." And in 1706, a New York law for developing the sailcloth industry was disallowed because, said the Board, it would be "more advantageous to England that all hemp and flax of the growth of the plantations should be imported hither, in order to manufacturing of it here." And in 1756, a

Massachusetts law for encouraging the production of linen was disallowed on the general ground that "the passing of laws in the plantations for encouraging manufactures, which any ways interfere with the manufacture of this kingdom, has always been thought improper, and has ever been discouraged." Nothing was too minute to escape the Board's attention in its zeal to protect English mercantile capitalism. So, in 1706, 1707, and 1708, it went so far as to call for the rejection of laws passed in Virginia and Maryland providing for the establishment of new towns, on the grounds that such new communities must invariably lead to a desire to found manufacturing industries and that their existence would draw off persons from the countryside where they were engaged in the production of tobacco. To cap it all, the governors were closely instructed to veto all legislation designed to assist the development of such manufactures as might compete with those of England. This had its effect, so that E. B. Russell, the outstanding authority upon the subject, has been led to conclude: "Largely as a result of the government's determined attitude in the matter, comparatively few laws for this purpose were enacted in the plantations."

In no small measure, the general result was heightened by the limitations imposed on English capital seeking investments in the colonies. English balances in the colonies and English new capital were kept away from manufactures; and they might be placed only in land and land operations. The overextension of sugar planting, in the West Indies, and of tobacco planting, in the mainland colonies, undoubtedly was due to this restriction and therefore helped in the shaping of the crisis in the imperial-colonial relations which set in in the 1760's.

That such was the design of the Mercantile System was not unfamiliar to Englishmen of the period. J. M. Swank, the author of that curious work, *The History of the Manufacture of Iron in All Ages,* comments as follows on the position of English defenders of the system:

The first Lord Sheffield declared that "the only use and advantage of American colonies or West Indies islands is the monopoly of their consumption and the carriage of their produce." McCulloch, in his

Commercial Dictionary, admits that it was "a leading principle in the system of colonial policy, adopted as well by England as by other European nations, to discourage all attempts to manufacture such articles in the colonies as could be provided for them by the mother country." Dr. William Elder, in his *Questions of the Day*, says: "The colonies were held under restraint so absolute that, beyond the common domestic industries and the most ordinary mechanical employments, no kind of manufactures was permitted."

Thus, at the very time when the putting-out system in England was rapidly being converted into the factory system and great advances were being made in the perfection of machinery exactly because the existence of a growing market was demanding more efficient methods of production, in the colonies methods of production remained at a hopelessly backward level because English and colonial capital could not enter manufacturing. An important outlet for accumulated funds was barred. The colonial capitalist economy, therefore, was closely restricted to land speculation, the dealing in furs, and the carrying trade. When English mercantilism, for the protection of its home mercantile capital, began to narrow these spheres, then catastrophe threatened. The American Revolution can be understood largely in terms of the necessity for colonial mercantile and planter capitalism to escape from the contracting prison walls of the English Mercantile System.

CHAPTER ELEVEN

The Pressures on Colonial Mercantile Capitalism

1. COLONIAL COMMERCE

IN A functioning imperial economy, the capitalist relationships between mother country and colonies as a rule lead to a colonial unfavorable balance of payments. The colonies buy the goods and services of the mother country and are encouraged to develop those raw materials the home capitalists require. In this they are aided by the investment of the mother country's balances and by new capital. Thus, in the southern colonies, tobacco largely was being produced to furnish returns for the English goods and services the plantation lords required; but, because the exchange left England with a favorable balance, by the 1770's its capitalists had more than £4,000,000 invested in southern planting operations. To meet the charges on this debt, southern planters were compelled constantly to expand their agricultural operations and to engage in the subsidiary activities of land speculation and the fur trade.

The northern colonies were less fortunately placed. The northern colonies directly produced little of those staples necessary to the maintenance of the English economy: the grains, provisions, and work animals of New England, New York, and Pennsylvania could not be permitted to enter England lest they disorganize the home commercial agricultural industry; and the fishing catches of the New England fishing fleets competed with the English fishery industry operating in the North Sea and off the Newfoundland banks. The northern colonies, of course, were a source for lumber, naval stores, furs, whale products, and iron, and these England sorely needed to maintain her independence of European supplies. By bounties, the relaxing of trade restrictions, and the granting of favored positions in the home market, England sought to encourage these industries, partly because it required these staples and partly to divert northern capital from expanding further into shipbuilding, shipping, and manufacturing. But the policy yielded no really successful results. The advance of population into frontier zones cut down the field of operations of the fur trade. The northern merchants found more profitable outlets for their lumber in the West Indian sugar islands and in the Spanish and Portuguese wine islands off the African and European coasts. Although the production of crude iron received a stimulus due to English encouragement, most of the pigs and bars came to be absorbed in the colonies themselves so that the export of iron to England was disappointing; while the production of naval stores, despite a consistent program of bounties launched upon by England as early as 1705, never took hold in the northern colonies and therefore the plan of the Board of Trade to keep northern mercantile capitalism entirely dependent upon England completely failed.

The northern colonies, therefore, produced little for direct export to England to permit them to pay their balances; for balances there were to be paid despite the household manufacturing of textiles and the fabrication of iron goods. They were buying increasing quantities of English drygoods, hardware, notions, and house furnishings, and were thus heavy debtors on visible account (and even on invisible items, although they were using their own services of shipping, commercial exchanges, and the like) in the direct trade. Also—and this is an economic factor of the utmost significance—the northern colonies never, to any appreciable extent, presented important opportunities for English capital investment. As we have seen, the English capital stake was largely in the South: only to a very slight degree was any of it to be found in the North. The result was the imperative necessity for the northern colonies to develop returns in order to obtain specie and bills of exchange with which to balance payments in England.

The most important of these was trade (and the subsidiary industries growing out of trade) with areas outside of England. Northern merchants and shipowners opened up regular markets in Newfoundland and Nova Scotia for their fishing tackle, salt, provisions, and rum. They established a constant and ever-growing commercial intercourse with the wine islands from which they bought their light and fortified wines direct instead of by way of England and to which they sold barrel staves, foodstuffs, and live animals. They sold fish to Spain, Portugal, and Italy. Their ports to a measurable extent during the eighteenth century (and in this way they competed directly with the English shipping fleets plying between England and the southern colonies) acted as entrepôts for the transshipment of southern staples—tobacco, hardwoods and dyewoods, indigo—to England and of rice to southern Europe.

The trade with the West Indian sugar islands—as well as the traffic in Negro slaves and the manufacture of rum, which grew out of it—became the cornerstone of the northern colonies' capitalist economy. Northern merchants, loading their small swift ships with all those necessaries the sugar planters of the West Indies were economically unable to produce—work animals for their mills; lumber for houses and outbuildings; staves, heads, and hoops for barrels; flour and salted provisions for their tables; and low-grade fish for their slaves—made regular runs from Salem, Boston, Bristol, Newport, New York, and Philadelphia originally to the British islands of Barbados, the Leeward Islands, and Jamaica, and then increasingly to the French, Spanish, Dutch, and Danish islands and settlements dotting the Caribbean. Here they acquired in return specie for the payment of their English balances, indigo, cotton, ginger, allspice, and dyewoods for transshipment to England, and, above all, sugar and molasses for conversion into rum in the distilleries of Massachusetts and Rhode Island. It was this wondrous alcoholic beverage that served as the basis of the intercourse between the northern colonies and the African coast: and in return the northern traders picked up ivory, gums, and beeswax and, most important of all, Negro slaves which were again carried to the sugar islands on that famous Middle Passage to furnish the labor supply without which the sugar-plantation economy could not survive.

The freights, commissions, and profits earned as a result of the successful conduct of trading enterprise thus furnished important sources of return through which northern merchant capitalists obtained specie and foreign bills of exchange with which to pay English balances. Shipbuilding, with New England and, later, Philadelphia as the leading centers, was another source. Northern ships were sold for use in the intercolonial trade and in the local trade of the West Indies and the wine islands; also ships were frequently sold in England and southern Europe after the completion of voyages. Still another source of return was the colonial fisheries. Northern fishermen, operating in fishing craft and whalers owned by colonial merchant capitalists, fished and hunted the waters off the New England coast and increasingly penetrated northward into the Newfoundland banks.

Apparently, however, despite the complexity of all this activity still other means of obtaining remittances and finding outlets for northern mercantile capitalist accumulations had to be developed. For those already mentioned were not enough with which to pay all the English bills and to absorb all the mounting funds of the Amorys, Faneuils, and Hancocks of Boston, the Whartons, Willings, and Morrises of Philadelphia, the Livingstons and Lows of New York, the Wantons and Lopezes of Newport, and the Browns of Providence. In three illegal forms of enterprise—piracy, smuggling generally, and particularly the illicit sugar and molasses trade with the foreign West Indian islands—northern merchants found opportunities for the necessary expansion.

It is not generally appreciated to what extent piracy—at least up to the end of the seventeenth century—played a significant role in maintaining the mercantile capitalism of the northern colonies. English and colonial pirates, fitted out in the ports of Boston, Newport, New York, and Philadelphia and backed financially by reputable merchants, preyed on the Spanish fleets of the Caribbean and even boldly fared out into the Red Sea and the Indian Ocean to terrorize ships engaged in the East Indies trade; and with their ships heavily laden with plate, drygoods, and spices, they put back into colonial ports where they sold their loot and divided their profits with the merchants who had financed them. It is impossible, of course, to estimate the size of this traffic; that it was great every evidence indicates. Curtis P. Nettels, in his outstanding monograph *The Money Supply of the American Colonies Before 1720*, cites reports that single pirate ships frequently brought in cargoes valued at between £50,000 and £200,000; that New York province alone obtained £100,000 in treasure yearly from the illicit traffic; and that the greater supply of specie in the colonies before 1700 than after (after that date England began its successful war of extermination against the seafaring marauders) undoubtedly was due to the open support of piratical expeditions and the gains obtained thereby by some of the wisest mercantile heads in the northern towns.

Smuggling also contributed its share to swell the remittances the northern merchants so badly needed. Smuggling traffic could be carried on in a number of directions. In the first place, there was the illegal direct intercourse between the colonies and European countries in the expanding list of "enumerated" articles. And in the second place, ships on the homebound voyages from Europe or from the West Indies brought large supplies of drygoods, silk, cocoa, and brandies into the American colonies without having declared them at English ports and paid the duties. Most important of all, of course, was the trade with the foreign West Indian sugar islands which was rendered illegal, after 1733, as a result of the imposition by the Molasses Act of prohibitive duties on the importation into the colonies of foreign sugar, molasses, and rum. It is imperative that something be said of the productive system and the social and economic relations prevailing in the sugar islands, for just as the western lands constituted the Achilles heel of southern planter capitalism so the trade with the sugar islands—and notably that with the foreign islands—was the highly vulnerable point of northern mercantile capitalism. When England, beginning with 1763, struck at these two vital and exposed centers, it immediately threatened the very existence of free colonial enterprise.

2. THE WEST INDIAN TRADE

By the opening of the second third of the eighteenth century, the English sugar planters of the West Indies were beginning to find themselves hard pressed, in the great colonial sugar market, by the steadily growing competition of the foreign sugar planters in the islands and settlements owned by the French, Spanish, Dutch, and Danes. The British sugar planters occupied a unique position in the imperial-colonial sphere. Favored from the very beginning by the tender solicitude of English imperial officialdom, supported in all their extravagant demands for protection by the great English merchant-capitalist interest allied with and dependent upon them, in time represented in Parliament itself by what today we would call a sugar bloc, the plantation lords of Barbados, the Leeward Islands, and Jamaica exerted an influence on British colonial policy that, in the words of Professor Andrews, "was probably greater than even that of politics, war, and religion." The reasons for this are not difficult to find. Sugar, even more than tobacco, was the great oversea staple of the eighteenth-century world. It was a household necessary, it had a constant and growing market everywhere in western Europe, it was the basis for the flourishing of a ramified English commercial industry made up of carriers, commission men, factors, financiers, processors, and distributors. Also, sugar was converted into molasses which in turn was distilled into rum; and it was rum that was the very heart of the unholy slave traffic and the unsavory Indian trade. Small wonder, therefore, that sugar cultivation attracted at once the concentrated attention of English mercantile capitalism: and by the time Adam Smith was writing English capitalism had succeeded in building up in the islands plantations with a capital worth of fully £60,000,000—a gigantic sum even in our modern imperialist age. Of this amount at least half continued to remain the stake of home English investors in long-term (land titles and mortgages) and short-term investments. When it is recalled that in the whole of the North American continental colonies the English capitalist stake at most was only one sixth as great, the reason for the favoring of the sugar colonies as against the northern commercial colonies, after 1763, is revealed in a single illuminating flash.

By the second third of the eighteenth century it was everywhere being admitted that the English sugar-planting economy was being uneconomically operated. Plantations were large and were worked by inefficient slave labor and primitive methods. Affairs of business were in the hands of paid clerks. No attention was paid to the restoration of the soil's fertility. The single crop was planted year in and year out without thought to the state of the market and mounting operating costs. The whole system was stripped of its productive capital to sustain in idleness and luxury an absentee owning class. It was the dream of every British West Indian to flee from his tropical estate and settle in England, where he could buy a country property and a seat in Parliament and play the English country gentleman. This was generally realized: by the early 1770's more than seventy plantations lords sat for country boroughs in the English Parliament and were therefore in a position to fight savagely all efforts at survival on the part of northern colonial mercantile capitalism.

This was all very well as long as nothing appeared to endanger the sugar monopoly of the English planters. But with the third decade of the eighteenth century, following the establishment of peace, such rivals appeared in the shape of foreign planters, notably the French; and the British planting interest was being threatened. The foreign planters clearly were at an advantage: their lands were newer and therefore more productive; ownership operation, on the basis of small holdings, was the rule, with therefore more efficient methods and lower operating and capital costs; they practiced diversification, and the coffee crop of some of the islands often exceeded the sugar crop. These factors, growing out of their superior economy, permitted the French and other foreign sugar planters to undersell the British. There were other reasons, implicit in the English mercantilist scheme, which strengthened further their command of the market: British sugar was compelled to pay a heavy export tax (4½ per cent) at the island ports; also, it was an "enumerated" commodity and could be sold only to England or its colonies; on the other hand, foreign sugar was free of imposts and enjoyed lower marketing costs because it reached oversea markets directly.

All this Englishmen and colonials saw. Adam Smith referred to the "superiority" of the French planters; while John Dickinson spoke of the British in the following slurring terms: "By a very singular disposition of affairs, the colonies of an absolute monarchy [France] are settled on a republican principle; while those of a kingdom in many respects resembling a commonwealth [England] are cantoned out among a few lords vested with despotic power over myriads of vassals and supported in the pomp of Baggas by their slavery."

In short, foreign sugar and molasses could be had for 25 to 40 per cent cheaper: it is not hard to see, therefore, why northern colonial ship captains bought more and more of their sugar at the foreign islands. They found it possible also to develop new markets here for their flour, provisions, lumber, work animals, and fish, thus obtaining another source from which specie and bills of exchange could be derived. So great had this traffic become by the 1720's that the British planter interest took alarm and began to appeal to Parliament for succor. In 1733 Parliament yielded to pressure and passed the Molasses Act, which sought to outlaw the colonial-foreign island trade by placing prohibitive import duties on sugar, molasses, and rum. But the act did not have the desired effect because it could not be adequately enforced: the British customs machinery in the colonies was weak and venal and the naval patrols that could be allocated to this duty were inadequate because England, from 1740, engaged in foreign wars almost continuously for twenty years. Within these twenty years the illicit intercourse with the foreign West Indies took on such great proportions that it virtually became the foundation of northern colonial mercantile capitalism. By the late 1750's, when the traffic was at its height, at least 11,500 hogsheads of molasses reached Rhode Island annually from the foreign islands, as against 2500 from the British; in Massachusetts the ratio was 14,500 to 500. In Massachusetts alone there were some sixty-three distilleries by 1750 and perhaps half that number existed in Rhode Island: the manufacture of rum undoubtedly was the most important single industrial enterprise existing in New England in the second quarter of the eighteenth century. Rum was a magical as well as a heady distillation: its fluid stream reached far Guinea, distant Newfoundland, remote Indian trading posts; and it joined slaves, gold-dust, the mackerel and cod, and peltries with the fortunes of the New England trading enterprisers.

Peter Faneuil, regular church attendant, kindly, charitably disposed bachelor, was one of the greatest of these. He traded all over the world, paying English duties on his cargoes when he had to, avoiding them when he could. He was interested, of course, in rum and slaves. The distinguished historian of New England, Weeden, speaks in the following bitter terms of one of Faneuil's ships, the *Jolly Bachelor*: "Did Peter slap his fair round belly and chuckle when he named the snow *Jolly Bachelor*?—or was it the sad irony of fate that the craft deliberately destined to be packed with human pains and to echo with human groans should in its very name bear the fantastic image of the luxury-loving chief owner? If these be the sources of profit and property, where is the liberty of Faneuil Hall, where the charity of good Peter's alms?"

It is not to be wondered, therefore, that British planters kept up a constant clamor for the enforcement of the laws and the total stoppage of the foreign island trade. In this they were joined by the merchants and manufacturers whose fortunes were linked with theirs, and the bankers and *rentiers* who saw their great capital investment in the British islands threatened with destruction unless the British West Indians once more obtained a monopoly of the production of sugar and molasses. The northern colonial merchant capitalists were the foes of British prosperity. The very reasonable exposition of the situation coming from Rhode Island's governor attracted no sympathy; apparently, it was to be the British West Indies or the northern colonies, and the stake involved in the former, as far as England was concerned, was far, far greater.

Wrote Governor Stephen Hopkins to England:

By the best computation I have seen, the quantity of flour made in these colonies yearly is such, that after all the English inhabitants, as well of the continent as of the islands, are fully supplied, with as much as they can consume with the year, there remains a surplusage of at least one hundred thousand barrels. The quantity of beef and pork remaining after the English are in like manner supplied is very large. The fish, not fit for the European market, and the lumber produced in the northern colonies, so much exceed the market found for them in the English West Indies, that a vast surplusage remains that cannot be used. . . . From the money and goods produced by the sale of the surplusages, with many others of less consequence, sold by one means or other to the Spaniards, French, and Dutch in America, the merchants of those northern colonies are principally enabled to make their remittances to the mother country for the British manufactures consumed in them. . . .

Supposing this intercourse of the colonies with the Spanish, French, and Dutch entirely stopped, the persons concerned in producing the surplusages will of course change the manner of their industry, and improvement and, compelled by necessity, must set about making those things they cannot live without, and now rendered unable to purchase from their mother country [i.e., manufactures].

When, during the Seven Years' War, the colonial "Smuggling Interest" extended the bounds of its activities and openly set about supplying the French enemy of the mother country with provisions, lumber, drygoods, and the like, British sugar planters in Parliament, confronted by bankruptcy, found ready allies in outraged patriotic statesmen. Then it was that Pitt, deeply angered by knowledge of the open sale by colonial officials of commissions for flags of truce and the winking at the whole illegal practice by vice-admiralty courts, bitterly wrote to America that it was "an illegal and most pernicious trade . . . by which the enemy is, to the greatest reproach and detriment of government, supplied with provisions and other necessaries, whereby they are principally, if not alone, enabled to sustain and protract this long and expensive war." The process of repression began in 1760 with the stricter enforcement of the Acts of Trade and Navigation; from then on, particularly after the last imperial rival, France, had been disposed of and the country at last was at peace, the screws came to be applied tighter and tighter. Soon, northern merchant capitalists, aware that every avenue of continued activity was being blocked to them, moved into the colonial revolutionary host.

3. THE CONTROL OF THE COLONIAL CURRENCY

At still another point the Mercantile System brought an unendurable pressure: this was in its control of the colonial currency. The colonies, it has been pointed out, found themselves constantly in a debtor status within the imperial-colonial relations; and their plight was accentuated by the insistence upon the payment of colonial balances in specie and the absence of easy credit facilities. It has also been indicated how illegal activities—piracy, smuggling, trade with the foreign sugar islands— were compulsory precisely because of these unrelaxing pressures. The heavy burden of debts, therefore, the paucity of specie, and the absence of commercial banking made all the colonies steadily preoccupy themselves with the money question. Efforts to debase the currency, on the part of the colonies and, contrariwise, efforts to maintain it at a high value, on the part of England, were symptomatic of the disharmony that existed within the mercantilist framework. When, in 1764, all the devices at the service of the Board of Trade having failed, Parliament passed its act (the so-called Currency Act) outlawing the use of legal-tender paper money in all the colonies, it was apparent that the crisis had been reached: whether it meant universal breakdown for the colonial economic life or not, England was going to insist that debts be paid in pounds sterling in order to protect English mercantile capitalism.

The colonies resorted to innumerable means to expand their available money supply. They employed commodity money, the assemblies fixing the value; but Parliament warned the colonists that they could not impair contracts by fixing rates for commodities contrary to those stipulated in agreements. They tried to mint their own money; but in 1684 colonial mints were forbidden. They sought to place embargoes on the exportation of coin; but beginning with 1697 the Privy Council regularly disallowed such laws. They tried, by statute, to raise the legal value of foreign coins in circulation, particularly the Spanish pieces of eight; such acts in Maryland and Virginia (and in Barbados and Jamaica) were disallowed. And when, as a result, the tobacco and sugar colonies were drained entirely of coin, in 1704 Parliament proceeded to fix a uniform value for pieces of eight in all the plantations and in 1708 prescribed prison sentences for those failing to observe the regulations.

Beginning as early as 1690, in Massachusetts, the colonies turned to the emission of paper money. This currency started out by being short-term bills of credit issued in anticipation of taxes (and therefore retirable at fixed dates after the taxes had been collected) and to be employed only for public purposes. The enactments specifically declared that the bills were not to be held as lawfully current money and could be submitted only in payment of public obligations. Within the first third of the eighteenth century, all of New England, as well as New York, New Jersey, the two Carolinas, Pennsylvania, and Maryland had emitted such bills. It was an inevitable corollary that the bills of credit next be declared legal tender not only for public but for all private transactions: the intention was a sorely needed currency expansion, to be pursued by the road of a paper inflation. The steps by which the various colonies sought to attain this end may be briefly indicated. Some tried to issue bills based not only on tax anticipations but on private land securities (utilizing the agency of public and private mortgage banks). Some pushed the dates of collection of taxes on which the bills were based so far ahead that the issues virtually became permanent paper currency. Some failed to provide adequate taxes from which bills were to be redeemed. And some colonies openly embarked on a course of repudiation, merely reissuing bills when the dates set for cancellation had arrived. Also, steps were taken to compel the acceptance of these bills as legal tender by fixing penalties to be imposed on those individuals refusing to honor them in private transactions.

The establishment of so-called public banks, which really were agencies for the issuance of notes against the security of land mortgages, was particularly common. The first such provincial institution was set up in South Carolina, and before 1750 every colony except Georgia had followed its example. Massachusetts went a step further when it permitted a group of private individuals to organize a "Land and Manufactures Bank" in 1740. This society, capitalized at £150,000, was to accept land as security for its stock and against this real estate it was to print notes to be used for lending purposes. Stockholders were to pay 3 per cent interest for the privilege of putting up their land as security, to be paid either in bills of the company or in nonperishable raw materials or rough manufactures (hence the use of the term "manufactures" in the title); also, every year 5 per cent of the principle of the subscription was to be amortized in the same way. Loans, too, could be paid off in bills or in the same commodities. The purpose here, obviously, was the expansion of credit through the utilization of nonperishable commodities as a base for currency issue; and within the single year of its operation the bank succeeded in lending out and therefore issuing notes to the extent of £40,000. But Parliament insisted upon regarding the bank as a dangerous speculative enterprise and descended on it at once; it extended to it the terms of the Bubble Act of 1720 and the bank was outlawed with the ensuing ruin of many of its backers, the father of Samuel Adams among them.

A notion of the mounting size of the paper currency in circulation may be gained from the experiences of Massachusetts. When this province emitted its first bills in 1690, it was ordered that the issues should not exceed £40,000; by 1750, however, some £4,630,000 in bills had been released, of which fully half still remained outstanding. Depreciation was inevitable. In Massachusetts the value of sterling to paper money reached a maximum ratio of 11 to 1; in Connecticut it was 8 to 1; in New Hampshire it got to 24 to 1, and by 1771 sterling had vanished altogether; in Rhode Island it was 26 to 1; in North Carolina it was 10 to 1; in South Carolina it was 7 to 1. Only in New York and Pennsylvania was there some effort made to check the downward career of the bills, the depreciation here never reaching more than 25 per cent.

It was the steadfast English policy to maintain a sound (that is to say, a contracted) currency in the colonies; and provincial acts were closely scrutinized from this point of view. Acts were disallowed and instructions issued, as affecting the bills of credit, therefore, on the basis of the following general principles: that the amount of bills to be issued was to be limited to the minimum requirements necessary for the legitimate needs of the colonies; that there be created adequate provisions for refunding; that the term of issues be fixed and no reissues be permitted; and that the bills could not be made legal tender for the payment of private debts. Finally, when these methods seemed to be without avail, Parliament intervened. It has already been pointed out with what swiftness Parliament acted in the case of the Massachusetts land bank. A decade later, in 1751, an act was passed forbidding the New England colonies to make any further issues of legal-tender bills of credit or bank notes; the only exceptions permitted were in the cases of issues to cover current expenses and to finance war costs. And in 1764 the Currency Act extended the prohibition to include all the colonies, even rescinding the exception in the case of military financing; further, provision was to be made for the retirement of all outstanding bills. The currency immediately began to contract until by 1774 there was not much more than £2,400,000 in the colonies available for exchange and for financing the credit operations of colonial enterprise. John Dickinson was scarcely exaggerating the plight of colonial mercantile capitalism when in 1765 he wrote:

Trade is decaying and all credit is expiring. Money is becoming so extremely scarce that reputable freeholders find it impossible to pay debts which are trifling in comparison to their estates. If creditors sue, and take out executions, the lands and personal estates, as the sale must be for ready money, are sold for a small part of what they were worth when the debts were contracted. The debtors are ruined. The creditors get back but part of their debt and that ruins them. Thus the consumers break the shopkeepers; they break the merchants; and the shock must be felt as far as London.

CHAPTER TWELVE

The Revolutionary Crisis

1. ENGLAND TIGHTENS THE SCREWS

SUCH was the pattern of imperial-colonial relations which makes the events of 1763-75 intelligible. Not human stupidity, not dreams of new splendor for the empire, not a growing dissimilarity of psychological attitudes, but economic breakdown in the Mercantile System: the inability of both English mercantile capitalism and colonial mercantile and planter capitalism to operate within a contracting sphere in which clashes of interest were becoming sharper and sharper: this was the basic reason for the onset of crisis and the outbreak of revolutionary struggle. The mother country had bound the colonies to itself in an economic vassalage: opportunities for colonial enterprise were possible only in commercial agriculture (supported by land speculation) and in trade. But when the expanding commercial activities of northern merchant capitalists came into conflict with the great capitalist interest of British West Indian sugar and the related merchant and banking groups dependent upon it; when the southern tobacco and rice planters, in their role of land speculators, collided with English land speculators and the mighty fur interest; and when the colonial need to move into manufacturing and to develop adequate credit facilities for its growing enterprises threatened the very existence of English mercantile capitalism in all its ramifications: then repression, coercion, even the violence of economic extinction (as in the case of the Boston Port Bill) had to follow. There could be no accommodation possible when English statesmen were compelled to choose between supporting English mercantile capitalism and supporting colonial mercantile and planter capitalism.

As Curtis P. Nettels has so justly insisted, American scholars for more than a generation have been led astray by George Louis Beer's erroneous interpretation of the motives that prompted Pitt in 1763 to demand Canada instead of the sugar islands, Guadeloupe and Martinique, from vanquished France. The Beer argument runs as follows.

Pitt had great visions of empire; this dream and the imperial policies that stemmed from it prepared the way for conflict between colonies and mother country. For a mighty western empire, based as yet on a wilderness, demanded the formulation of a wise program with regard to the Indian problem—hence the shutting off of the lands beyond the crest of the Alleghenies to further settlement and the checks placed on the exploitation of the Indians by colonial traders. It demanded a system of defense—hence the dispatching of a British army to the colonies and provisions for its quartering and maintenance. It demanded a revenue—hence all those methods used by a hard-pressed home government to develop new sources of financing. Thus the chain of circumstances was complete; it had to snap at its weakest link—the raising of funds through tax measures among a liberty-loving and individualistic colonial people which too long had been permitted to go its own way. So Mr. Beer, and after him virtually every American colonial scholar.

The events of 1763-75 can have no meaning unless we understand that the character of English imperial policy never really changed: that Pitt and his successors at Whitehall were following exactly the same line that Cromwell had laid down more than a century before. The purpose of their general program was to protect the English capitalist interests which now were being jeopardized as a result of the intensification of colonial capitalist competition, and English statesmen yielded quickly when no fundamental principle was at stake but became insistent only when one was being threatened. If in the raising of a colonial revenue lay the heart of the difficulty, how are we to account for the quick repeal of the Stamp Tax and the Townshend Acts and the lowering of the molasses duty? And, on the other hand, how are we to account for the tightening of enforcement of the Acts of Trade and Navigation at a dozen and one different points, the passage of the Currency Act, the placing of iron on the "enumerated" list, English seizure of control of the wine trade, and the attempt to give the East India Company a monopoly over the colonial tea business? The struggle was not over high-sounding political and constitutional concepts: over the power of taxation or even, in the final analysis, over natural rights. It was over colonial manufacturing, wild lands and furs, sugar, wine, tea, and currency, all of which meant, simply, the survival or collapse of English mercantile capitalism within the imperial-colonial framework of the mercantilist system.

2. THE ACTS OF TRADE RIGOROUSLY ENFORCED

Even before Pitt gave up the French sugar islands in 1763 because of the insistence of the British sugar interest in Parliament, he had already moved to protect the same monopoly group through his orders to the navy to stamp out colonial smugglers operating in the illicit foreign West Indian trade. The colonial courts were directed to issue and recognize the doubtfully legal writs of assistance (general search warrants), as early as 1761. Two years later, the peacetime navy was converted into a patrol fleet with powers of search even on the high seas. In the same year, absentee officials in the customs service were ordered to their colonial posts. A vice-admiralty court was set up for all America in 1764 and the number of local admiralty courts (sitting without juries) was increased. In 1768 a new board of five customs commissioners, resident in America, was created. Statutes, orders, instructions—every conceivable weapon was employed to break up a traffic and therefore to weaken a group so dangerous to English capitalist interests. Spying was encouraged by offers to share with informers the sequestered cargoes. Customs officials were protected from damage suits for unwarranted seizures when they were declared nonliable personally and when the burden of proof was placed on the owners of vessels and goods. The stricter registration and inspection of vessels were ordered. To protect informers and make possible the easier obtaining of verdicts, it was provided that suits for the seizure of cargoes might be tried directly in the vice-admiralty court and that revenue cases might be heard in the admiralty instead of the local courts. And further to free the courts from local pressure, the payment of the judges' salaries was to be made out of customs revenues.

The revenue acts of 1764 and later were used as a screen to conceal the work of compressing the economy of colonial mercantile capitalism within even narrower limits and reducing it to an even more dependent status. The Act of 1764 and the Stamp Act of 1765 called for the payment of duties and taxes in specie, thus further draining the colonies of currency and contracting the credit base. To divert colonial capital into raw materials, the first measure increased the bounties paid for the colonial production of hemp and flax, placed high duties on the colonial importation of foreign indigo, and removed the English import duties on colonial whale fins. To cripple the trade with the foreign West Indies a high duty was fixed on refined sugar and the importation of foreign rum was forbidden altogether. Lumber was put on the "enumerated" list. To give English manufacturers a firmer grip on their raw materials, hides and skins (needed for the boot-and-shoe industry), pig and bar iron (needed in the wrought-iron industry), and potash and pearl ashes (used for bleaching cloth and soapmaking) were placed on the "enumerated" list. To maintain the English monopoly of the colonial finished-goods market in 1764 certain kinds of French and oriental drygoods were taxed for the first time at the point of entry; in 1765, the importation of foreign silk stockings, gloves, and mitts was altogether forbidden; also the drawbacks of duties paid on foreign goods landed in England and re-exported to the colonies were rescinded. To extend the market of English merchants in Europe, in 1766 Parliament ordered that all remaining "nonenumerated" articles (largely flour, provisions, and fish) bound for European ports north of Cape Finisterre be landed first in England. And to weaken further colonial commercial activity, in 1764 high duties were placed on wines from the wine islands and wine, fruits, and oil from Spain and Portugal brought directly to America (in American ships, as a rule), while such articles brought over from England were to pay only nominal duties.

As has been said, the revenue features of these acts were

quickly abandoned; the Stamp Act was repealed; and in 1770, three years after their passage, the Townshend duties on paper, paint, and glass were lifted. Only the slight tax on tea remained and even this was lightened in 1773 when the new Tea Act provided for a full drawback of English import duties on British tea shipped to the American colonies.

But it was exactly this new Tea Act which clearly revealed the intention of London: that not only was the economic vassalage of the American colonies to be continued but the interest of colonial enterprisers was to be subordinated to every British capitalist group that could gain the ear of Parliament. For, to save the East India Company from collapse, that influential organization was to be permitted to ship in its own vessels and dispose of, through its own merchandising agencies, a surplus stock of 17,000,000 pounds of tea in America, and in this way drive out of business those Americans who carried, imported, and sold into retail channels British tea (and indeed, foreign tea, for the British tea could be sold cheaper even than the smuggled Holland article).

The merchants all over America were not slow to read the correct significance of this measure. Their spokesmen sounded the alarm. As Arthur M. Schlesinger has put it, pamphleteers set out to show "that the present project of the East India Company was the entering wedge for larger and more ambitious undertakings calculated to undermine the colonial mercantile world. Their opinion was based on the fact that, in addition to the article of tea, the East India Company imported into England vast quantities of silks, calicos and other fabrics, spices, drugs, and chinaware, all commodities of staple demand; and on their fear that the success of the present venture would result in an extension of the same principle to the sale of the other articles." The result would be, as a Philadelphia pamphleteer signing himself "A Mechanic" warned:

They will send their own factors and creatures, establish houses among us, ship us all other East India goods; and in order to full freight their ships, take in other kind of goods at under freight, or (more probably) ship them on their own accounts to their own factors, and undersell our merchants, till they monopolize the whole trade. Thus our merchants are ruined, ship building ceases. They will then sell goods at any exorbitant price. Our artificers will be unemployed, and every tradesman will groan under dire oppression.

3. THE CLOSING OFF OF THE WEST

The southern landlords did not escape. The Proclamation Line of 1763, for the purpose of setting up temporary governments in the far western lands wrested from France after the Seven Years' War, in effect shut off the whole area beyond the crest of the Appalachians to colonial fur traders and land dealers. By taking control of the region out of the hands of the colonial governors, putting it in charge of imperial agents, and ordering the abandonment of the settlements already planted, the British looked forward to the maintenance of a great Indian reservation in which the fur trade—in the interests of British concessionaires—would continue to flourish. A few years later these rigorous regulations were relaxed somewhat. But the designs of English land speculators on the area, the prohibition of free land grants, the ordering of land sales at auctions only, and the imposition of high quitrents hardly improved matters.

By 1774 the final English land policy emerged: it meant no less than the complete exclusion of colonial capital from the newly gained western domain. In the words of Professor Nettels, this program

closed to [colonial] speculators and settlers the territories north of the Ohio and south of Virginia, it opened only a small tract in western Virginia, it subjected all ungranted lands in the east to rigorous and hampering conditions of purchase and it deprived the landed colonies of their claims to the interior. Even the Vandalia speculators had not gained approval for their project, and despite the powerful forces making for westward expansion in Virginia that colony was denied independent access to the West. The restrictive policy applied to the thirteen colonies did not mean, however, that British investors and speculators were being ignored. After 1763 the crown conferred numerous large tracts upon merchants, army officers, and wealthy landowners (all residents of Britain), such tracts being located in Canada, Nova Scotia, Florida, and Prince Edward Island—regions accessible to British trade and not likely to produce commodities that would compete with the products of industries in which British investors had a large stake. By opening these areas Britain created speculative opportunities for her own investors while opposing the schemes of colonial promoters to develop the trans-Allegheny West.

The fur trade was similarly monopolized in the interest of British capital. The English conquest of Canada had resulted in the ousting of French merchants at Montreal, who controlled this lucrative traffic in the North, and their replacement by the agents of British companies. By the Quebec Act of 1774, with an eye to diverting the movement of western peltries from Philadelphia and New York to Montreal, the British provided for the regulation of traders by the governor of the province of Quebec. The intention was simple: colonial dealers in furs were to be driven out of the area north of the Ohio just as colonial land speculators (often the same persons) were to be barred from exploiting the wild lands of the West. By such restrictive and arbitrary acts the southern large planters were lost to the English cause. Their situation, already made perilous by the manipulation of the tobacco market in England and the passage of the Currency Act of 1764, was now hopeless.

Thus, colonial capitalists—whether planters, land speculators, fur dealers, or merchants—were converted from contented and loyal subjects into rebellious enemies of the crown. Tea was destroyed in Boston harbor, turned back unloaded from New York and Philadelphia, and landed but not sold in Charleston. In 1774 the First Continental Congress, to which came delegates from all the colonies, met and wrote the Continental Association, an embargo agreement, which was so successfully enforced that imports from England virtually disappeared in 1775.

4. THE RISING OF THE LOWER MIDDLE CLASSES

The discontents of planters and merchants were not enough, in themselves, to hasten the releasing process. To be successful, assistance was required from the more numerous lower middle-class small farmers, traders, shopkeepers, artisans, and mechanics, and the working-class seamen, fishermen, and laborers. This was not difficult: for the material well-being of the lower classes was tied to the successful enterprising of the upper.

The colonies had enjoyed a period of unprecedented prosperity during the years of the war with France. The expanding market in the West Indies, the great expenditures of the British quartermasters, the illegal and contraband trade with the enemy forces—all these had furnished steady employment for workers on the fleets and in the shipyards and ports as well as lucrative outlets for the produce of small farmers. But with the end of the war and the passage of the restrictive legislation of 1763 and after, depression had set in to last until 1770. Stringency and bankruptcy everywhere confronted the merchants and big farmers. At the same time, seamen and laborers were thrown out of work; small tradesmen were compelled to close their shops; and small farmers faced ruin because of their expanded acreage, a diminished market, and heavy fixed charges made particularly onerous as a result of currency contraction. Into the bargain, escape into the frontier zones—always the last refuge of the dispossessed—was shut off as a result of the Proclamation of 1763 and the land policy of 1774. The lower middle classes and workers of the towns in almost all the colonies, beginning in 1765, organized themselves into secret societies called the "Sons of Liberty" and demonstrated and moved against the colonial agents of the crown. In these acts they were encouraged by the merchants and landlords.

It would be a mistake to assume, however, that the lower middle-class and working-class groups operated only at the behest of the colonial merchant capitalists. Under the direction of their own leaders, of whom Samuel Adams of Massachusetts was the outstanding—although some of the leaders came from the merchant class, too (Christopher Gadsden of South Carolina, John Lamb of New York, Stephen Hopkins of Rhode Island)—they perfected a powerful revolutionary weapon they sought to wield in their own interest. In 1772, at first in Massachusetts and then in all the other colonies, there began to appear the Committees of Correspondence: these conspiratorial clubs kept in constant touch with one another, intimidated royal officials and colonial placemen, and with all the devices of terror and violence on the one hand and popular appeal on the other crushed opposition and added to and solidified their ranks. They were the ones who moved against the Tea Act, who were instrumental in summoning the First Continental Congress, and who saw that the agreed-on boycott of English goods was enforced. In 1775, beginning to call themselves Committees of Safety, they mobilized the people for defense and carried on a systematic, vindicative, and successful civil war against those who remained loyal to the crown.

In effect, the committees were undermining the authority of the crown in the colonies and setting up, step by step, first in the localities and then in the provinces, revolutionary extralegal governments. The old state was disintegrating; a new revolutionary one was replacing it.

These clubs, too, were beginning to articulate those demands which later gave the lower middle classes and workers their basis for participating in the Revolution. The merchants and landlords regarded the methods of the radicals with misgivings and dread; but they dared not interfere lest, in alienating the underprivileged farmers, tradesmen, and laborers, they lose that mass support upon which their own destiny so completely was dependent.

The lower classes began to look upon the Revolution as the instrument for attaining their *own* freedom. In the *political* sphere, they wanted release from the civil disabilities of almost universal disfranchisement, unequal legislative representation for the newer areas, and an absence of local government. In colonial America, only men of sizable properties could vote and hold office; indeed, before the Revolution, the proportion of potential voters varied from one sixth to one fiftieth of the male population in the different colonies. In the *economic* sphere, the constricting hand of monopoly everywhere was to be found. On the *land*, the legal institutions of entail and primogeniture checked opportunity for younger sons. Engrossing landlords and land speculators (whether they were the crown, the proprieties, absentee owners, or the New England "common" land proprietors) prevented the settlement and improvement of small properties. In the South, the tidewater lords would not erect warehouses to encourage tobacco cultivation among the farmers of the upcountry. And in New York, inadequate boundary surveys furnished the big manor lords with an easy instrument to oppress their smaller neighbors. Everywhere, the threat of Indian risings, because a wild frontier was in the interests of the fur trade and the maintenance of land values in the settled regions, filled the days and nights of pioneers with dread.

In the *towns,* newcomers, seeking to become small tradesmen and mechanics and artisans, had been compelled to struggle against the early and established shopkeepers and craftsmen. For the old artisans and shopkeepers, not unmindful of the special positions of their fellow craftsmen in England whose privileges were protected by the livery companies and guilds, had sought to introduce guild regulations in America. In Philadelphia, Newport, and Boston, early in the eighteenth century, such enabling statutes had been passed by city councils: but they had been unsuccessful. The guild system did not take root in America. But that did not prevent the older craftsmen and shopkeepers from burdening with disabilities the later arrivals.

In all the chartered urban communities, the privilege of obtaining the "freedom of the town"—which meant the right to engage in free enterprise, whether as tradesman or artificer—was severely limited. The devices were many: sometimes being the payment of high fees, sometimes the posting of a large bond, sometimes the possession of a property qualification. There were other oppressions from which the lower middle classes suffered. Peddlers were submitted to close regulation and forced to pay sizable license fees. It was impossible to maintain city markets, for long, because small merchants here tended to compete successfully with the big ones. In New England, a small company of chandlers had got the whole whaling industry in its grip and not only choked off the competition of the lesser manufacturers but fixed the prices for the basic raw material.

Men of little property were weighed down by debts and oppressed by an inadequate currency; they were forced to support, in many of the colonies, an established church; and they were at the mercy of arbitrary executive and judicial authority. On many sides, too, they saw looming larger and larger the threat of a slave economy to the free institutions of small properties and independent craftsmen. Such were the persons who constituted the left, or radical, wing of the colonial revolutionary host.

From 1774 until the creation of new governments in the American states these radicals were in control everywhere. Joining hands across the boundaries of the provinces, they effected united action. They set up extralegal provincial congresses to supersede the assemblies; they boycotted the English military in Massachusetts when it sent out a call for mechanics; and they began secretly to form popular militias and to store up military equipment.

Upon these maneuvers the big landlords and merchants looked with alarm. Gouverneur Morris, later to become one of the patriots of the right, thus wrote to John Penn on May 20, 1774, of a New York meeting:

Yesterday I was present at a grand division of the city, and there . . . my fellow citizens . . . fairly contended the future forms of our government, whether it should be founded upon aristocratic or democratic principles. I stood in the balcony, and on my right were ranged all the people of property, with some few poor dependents, and on the other all the tradesmen. . . . The spirit of the English Constitution has yet a little influence left, and but a little. The remains of it, however, will give the wealthy people a superiority this time, but the mob begin to think and to reason. Poor reptiles! It is with them a vernal morning; they are struggling to cast off their winter's slough, they bask in the sunshine, and ere noon they will bite, depend upon it. The gentry begin to fear this. Their committee will be appointed, they will deceive the people, and again forfeit a share of their confidence. And if these instances of what with one side is policy, and with the other perfidy, shall continue to increase, and become more frequent, farewell aristocracy.

The English government met the resistance to the Tea Act and to the other oppressive British measures with what was tantamount to the imposition of an economic death sentence on the colonies. In 1774 and 1775, Parliament passed first the so-called Coercive and then the Restraining Acts: they were nothing less than the opening of hostilities. One of the laws passed in 1774 closed the port of Boston; another reduced the government of Massachusetts to the status of a crown colony; another called for the furnishing of ample barracks for His Majesty's troops within twenty-four hours after they were ordered; and another, through the Quebec Act, made permanent the Proclamation Line of 1763 by putting all the far western lands north of the Ohio under the administration of Quebec Province. The Restraining Acts of 1775 cut almost all the colonies off from the northern fisheries and limited their trade entirely to Great Britain, Ireland, and the British West Indies.

The revolutionary ferment began its work. In almost all the colonies illegal congresses were called; the Second Continental Congress met; military stores were collected; and Thomas Paine wrote his stirring pamphlet *Common Sense,* to whip all those who still faltered into revolutionary enthusiasm. The Second Continental Congress struck off two declarations of freedom. The first, naturally representing the dominant interest of colonial mercantile capitalism, was embodied in a series of resolutions passed on April 6, 1776. These resolves nullified the Acts of Trade and Navigation and put an end to the colonial slave trade: and with this single blow the colonial merchants and landlords smashed the hampering chains of the imperial-colonial relations. The second, adopted by the Congress on July 4, 1776, was the Declaration of Independence: written by the radicals, this was a political manifesto which called upon the masses to defend the Revolution. The American Revolution then moved fully into the stage of armed resistance.

5. THE POLITICAL DEFENSE OF THE REVOLUTION

By 1774, the die had been cast: reconciliation was out of the question. And the same year saw the radical lawyers completing their formulation of the Revolution's defense—a defense that stood on shaky ground constitutionally but made an overpowering emotional appeal. Their brief ran somewhat as follows. Disregarding the fact that the events of the English "Glorious Revolution" had established a constitutional monarchy once and for all and that therefore sovereignty really rested in Parliament, men like Franklin, Jefferson, and John Adams argued that the colonies owed fealty to the crown alone. The crown had founded them; it had granted them their charters; it had appointed their officials. It naturally followed that the colonies were now occupying the status of virtually independent states.

From such a situation there flowed two results. Since authority vested in the king and not in Parliament, Parliament did not possess the unlimited power of taxation. This argument was buttressed by the fact that before the 1760's Parliament had imposed no taxes on the colonies without their assent. The passage of the Stamp Tax in 1765 and the voting of the Townshend duties in 1767 therefore violated precedent and constitutional law. In the second place, if colonial allegiance was to the crown alone, and if the crown deported itself tyrannically, then the colonies were "and of right ought to be, free and independent states."

It was at this point that the Revolution's defenders leaned heavily on Lockian doctrine. A state—civil authority—had been established for purposes of maintaining order and guaranteeing the natural rights (life, liberty, property) of the citizens. A contract had been entered into between the citizenry and the sovereign to maintain those natural rights and to assure the continuance of the sovereign's powers. But the contract was not inalienable: its life was to continue as long as both parties were prepared to act in good faith. The sovereign was to safeguard the natural rights of his subjects; the subjects were to render up loyalty to the sovereign.

Now, by 1776, said the colonial lawyers in the Declaration of Independence, the contract had been made void. The English crown, whose sovereignty the colonies recognized, by "abuses and usurpations" had oppressed its subjects; and it was their right, nay "their duty, to throw off such government, and to provide new guards for their future security." It was for this reason that the Declaration of Independence entered into its long catalogue of the "injuries and usurpations" of the crown, which stemmed from George III's desire to impose "an absolute tyranny over these states." And here was the basis of the sacred character of the Revolution.

CHAPTER THIRTEEN

The Triumph of the First American Revolution

1. RADICALISM IN THE SADDLE

THE Revolution, on its military side, of course represented an heroic effort to defeat the foe on the field; and thanks to the courage and devotion of the commander in chief, George Washington, plus the financial assistance of France, Holland, and Spain and subsequently the naval and military assistance of France, the war was pursued to a successful close. An equally significant aspect was the creation of an adequate civil power to meet the threat of disloyalty, to unite all the forces necessary to carry on the military struggle, to build up a functioning economy, and to make sure that the Revolution would achieve the purposes for which it was being waged. In one sense, therefore, the Revolution resolved itself into a civil war between patriots and loyalists. In another, it became a struggle for power between the right and left wings of the revolutionary host.

The crown was not wanting for defenders: placemen, the Anglican clergy, great landlords in the middle colonies, and merchants in the southern colonies were actively prepared—indeed, these represented perhaps one third of the population—through subversive activities and frequently by resort to arms to challenge the desperate pretensions of the patriots. They were put down with fire and the sword. At first operating locally through the Committees of Safety and without any pretense of legality, patriots carried on a savage war of extermination against their domestic enemies. Making no effort to stay mob violence, the Committees seized and physically mistreated loyalists, incarcerated many in concentration camps, killed not a few, burned down their homes, confiscated their belongings, and drove fully 100,000 into flight. When more systematic agencies, under state direction, were erected, the sequestration of loyalist properties took place universally and on a wholesale scale. According to Sydney George Fisher: ". . . the patriotic organization for holding in check and destroying loyalism was fully as systematic, elaborate, and far-reaching as the military establishment which Washington and his generals directed against the British regular army."

In the beginning in all the states, and in some throughout the whole period of revolutionary struggle, this dictatorship by Committees, operating often without legal warrant at all and certainly under no judicial restraints, was in the saddle. In all the states the structure of dictatorship came to be headed up by supreme State Committees of Safety invested with executive and judicial power. These Committees of Safety as a rule preceded the creation of new governments; and even when such were already established they continued to function as the executive of the legislatures when these bodies were not sitting, and sometimes when they were. Indeed, in the case of New Hampshire, for example, which had adopted a new state constitution in 1776, the State Committee of Safety sat during the recesses of the legislature from 1775 to 1777, and was in continuous session from 1778 to 1784. In those states overrun by British armies the Committees of Safety combined all the agencies of government. Thus, the State Committees were terminated early in Massachusetts and Virginia; but they continued to operate until 1777 in Pennsylvania, until 1778 in New York and New Jersey, and as late as 1783 in Connecticut.

The State Committees of Safety, functioning through their vast network of local committees, set themselves the customary wartime tasks of a revolutionary epoch. They gathered arms together. They kept the forces in the field supplied with clothing, blankets, horses, wagons, and munitions. They sequestered property, when it was needed for war purposes. They issued bills of credit on dubious or nonexistent security. They fought the enemy, the loyalists, at home. Frequently, their activities took on wider and decidedly extralegal forms: for they fixed prices; punished monopolists and profiteers; sat as courts in both civil and military cases; granted letters of marque and reprisal to privateers; and even sought to stimulate home manufactures through the payment of bounties and the extension of other privileges. Systematically, these revolutionary organizations applied themselves to the task of sequestering the estates of crown, proprieties, and loyalists and the sale or grant of these properties to Americans who were devoted to the cause of independence. That many of the new beneficiaries turned out to be great landlords, so that free access to the land in the settled areas continued to be as difficult as before, was an incident of the struggle that became apparent only later. In all, loyalist property losses were put at $40,000,000.

At the same time, the contest between the left and right revolutionary forces in each state was raging. In some, notably in Pennsylvania, North Carolina, Delaware, New Hampshire, and Georgia, the radicals were in the majority and they were able to assume power quickly and write state constitutions in their own class interest. A new frame of government was not erected in Rhode Island or in Connecticut; in the former, however, the radicals were in control. Thus, the Pennsylvania Constitution of 1776 was a characteristic leveling document. It granted the franchise to all freemen who were paying taxes. It included a bill of rights. It erected a single-chambered house in which was deposited even the choice of state civil and judicial officers. And it was so fearful of any encroachments on the rights of the people that it provided for a multiple executive and a council of censors, meeting every seven years, to make inquiries as to whether justice and liberty had been preserved inviolate. In those states where the radicals captured power, qualifications for voting were eased. Equal representation for all districts in the legislature, both the backcountry as well as the more settled tidewater regions, was provided. The powers of the lower legislative house were increased, notably through the right granted it of originating money bills. The executive prerogative was ringed about with all manner of restrictions and the judicial function was severely limited. Thus, the governor's veto was abolished, and he was to be elected either popularly or by the all-powerful legislatures and for only brief terms; as for the judiciary, it was to be elected by the voters or chosen by the legislatures and it might be freely removed.

In another sphere, as well, the radicals took the bit in their teeth, and that was in the passage of fiat-money and price-fixing laws. In the interests of debtors, legislatures in all the states authorized the issuance of bills of credit and treasury notes, until their total came to the gigantic sum of $250,000,000 and depreciation everywhere took place. It is doubtful whether the debtors were benefited in the long run by this paper inflation; at any rate, by 1782, all the states had repealed their legal-tender laws. Price fixing was ordered by statute in a number of states—in Pennsylvania, Connecticut, Massachusetts, New York, and New Jersey. Indeed, even interstate conventions were resorted to. One such, held at New Haven in January, 1778, advocated a price-control system permitting an advance in prices of only 75 per cent over those prevailing in 1774. Another such convention met in 1779. But the Continental Congress refused to support the radicals; while the conservatives were slowly but steadily gaining back power in the states. By 1780, price-regulating laws were gone from the statute books.

It is a little difficult to determine exactly why the strength of the radicals spent itself. There was no open struggle during the revolutionary period itself. It may be that the radicals, who were younger men, gave of themselves unstintingly to the services of the Continental Army, so that the conservatives quietly were able to take over administrative power at home. It may be that some of their outstanding leaders lost their zeal for egalitarianism as they found opportunities for personal aggrandizement in the new manufactures, in supply contracts, in the partition of loyalist estates, and in western land speculation. It may be that the desertion of some of their outstanding spokesmen left them leaderless: for certainly, Samuel Adams, John Adams, and Patrick Henry moved farther and farther to the right as the war progressed.

The upshot was, the conservative faction, by the early 1780's, was recapturing the instrumentalities of political power. Certainly the conservatives knew what they wanted. Robert A. East, following the lead of Charles A. Beard's path-blazing *An Eco-*

nomic Interpretation of the Constitution of the United States, has summarized their position very well. The conservatives, speaking for the large-propertied interests of trade, land speculation, manufactures, and landlordism, were hostile to legal-tender laws and price-fixing legislation. They sought bank charters. They wanted contracts protected. They looked forward to shifting the burden of taxation from industry and trade onto the land. They were suspicious of the democratic town meeting and hoped to see more incorporated towns. Notably, they were interested in the pre-empting of the lands seized as a result of the Revolution.

The first significant triumph of the conservatives occurred at Philadelphia. The Articles of Confederation did not mean a powerful central government; but they were a definite advance over the shadowy rule of the Continental Congress. The final ratification of the Articles in 1781 strengthened the hand of the conservatives, so that, about this time, Arthur Lee could write: "Toryism is triumphant here. They have displaced every Whig but the President." The appointment of Robert Morris to the all-powerful post of Congressional Financier, in 1781, was another gain for business and political caution. Morris opposed the paper inflation and state embargoes. In the words of Dr. East: "Perfectly free trade and the sanctity of private property were his guiding principles, and political and economic freedom were closely associated in his mind."

What was true of Philadelphia was true of the states. In Massachusetts, the conservatives were able to hold the radicals at bay until 1780, when they wrote an antileveling constitution. In 1784, the conservatives rewrote New Hampshire's constitution, and in 1790, Pennsylvania's. There can be no question that by the end of the struggle with England the radicals were clearly on the defensive.

2. THE VICTORY OF THE REVOLUTION

It would be a mistake to assume that the purposes for which the Revolution was being waged were lost sight of, while the operations against the loyalists, on the one hand, and the struggles between the radicals and conservatives, on the other, were taking place. In fact, quite generally, the Revolution was being employed as an instrument to crush economic and social oppression.

As regards the land. The broom swept clean here. The chief area of land engrossment, the ungranted lands of crown and proprieties, was wiped out and the states and Congress took possession. The parliamentary acts against movement into the trans-Appalachian West were disregarded, and immediately land speculators and pioneers began to push across the mountains, so that by 1790, 221,000 persons were settled in a widely sprawling area. The quitrent was abolished. The movement for outlawing entails and primogeniture was begun. The institution of the King's Woods—under which the crown claimed the fairest stands of timber for the royal navy—was terminated.

As regards manufactures. By bounties and prizes, by the establishment of societies and the raising of protective tariff walls, the new states did everything in their power to encourage the manufacture not only of the wartime guns and powder but also of peacetime textiles, ironware, pottery, paper, glass, and leather goods. In this sphere, successes were measurable.

As regards trade. The war years saw a vast extension of American enterprising as the termination of the Mercantile System threw open the ports of Holland, France, and Spain and those of their colonies to American ships.

Also, the Anglican Church was disestablished in Maryland, North Carolina, and Virginia, while the constitutions of New York, Georgia, and South Carolina guaranteed freedom of worship to Christians of all sects. The importation of Negro slaves was stopped by nearly all the southern states, and many of the northern states began to provide for gradual abolition. Serious efforts were made to put an end to the savage penal code the colonists had brought over from England. And provisions for the inauguration of programs of popular education appeared in a number of early state constitutions.

In 1783, with the Revolution victorious, the American states were free, politically and economically, of the leading strings that had bound them to the British imperial power. And American mercantile capitalism had the whole world, productively and geographically (except, of course, for the British Isles and the British colonies), over which to range.

CHAPTER FOURTEEN

The Establishment of a National Union

1. "THE CRITICAL PERIOD"

DESPITE their growing economic and political successes, men of large property continued to pretend—particularly after peace had been formally established in 1783—that their newly gained liberties were in danger. Peace did not bring in its wake economic chaos, as so frequently has been maintained; but it did threaten to slacken the advance that had been begun so signally during the years of the war's conduct.

Indeed, it may be argued plausibly, as Robert A. East does, that the depression of 1785-86 was not due to a breakdown of the economic processes, but to the fact that merchants—particularly in the import trade—and land speculators—in western land deals—had overreached themselves. One might also make the point that the large-propertied interests took advantage of the revival of radical agitation in 1785-86 to insist that the failure of leveling government was at the heart of their distress; and, using temporary financial and business recession as a pretext and political uncertainty as a weapon, sought to entrench themselves once and for all in the seats of government through the establishment of a powerful national union.

Certainly, business was anything but languishing in the years immediately after the end of war. To·quote Dr. East:

High rentals, building activity, and luxurious living actually impressed Franklin on his return to America in 1785. Stage coach routes and facilities were steadily being increased in various regions. The paper industry continued to grow, and important companies were organized for iron and woolen manufactures in 1786 and 1788. Above all, it is significant that capital was much sought after everywhere during "the critical" years. Interest rates were high in 1784. New York merchant capitalists were even invited to New Jersey and

Connecticut, being promised liberal treatment. . . . And if it be argued that all this merely emphasized a great lack of capital, rather than a general demand for it, it can be pointed out in reply that there was no difficulty in securing subscriptions of specie value for large amounts of bank stock in 1784 in Philadelphia, Boston, and New York.

On every hand there were evidences of an expanding capitalist interest. Land companies for the exploitation of the new western territories were being organized and bands of pioneers were being sent out. Groups of capitalists were pooling their funds, seeking company charters, and establishing joint stocks. England had frowned on company organization during the colonial period and notably had refused to tolerate the formation of commercial banks. In fact, there were not more than five or six business charters granted during the whole period of imperial rule. But, once released from the confines of the Mercantile System, American capitalism rushed to organize. Eleven charters were requested and issued by state legislatures between 1781 and 1785; twenty-two between 1786 and 1790; and one hundred and fourteen between 1791 and 1795. The companies thus provided were to perform the characteristic functions of the mercantile capitalism of the period: build and maintain turnpikes, canals, bridges, and river-improvement projects; manufacture wrought iron, woolens, sailcloth, and glass; buy up and develop the wild lands; and establish commercial banks.

In this last field of activity, there was particular interest—and notable success. The Bank of North America was established at Philadelphia in 1781; the Bank of New York began to function in 1784; so did the Massachusetts Bank, at Boston, in the same year. Taking advantage of the high premium on English bills of exchange, these banks, through their discounting functions, were able to furnish invaluable assistance to merchants in the foreign trade—and of course, in the process, enriched their promoters. The banks also helped in the financing of company enterprise.

Nor was foreign trade stagnant. It is true there was a falling off in the export trade to England and the British West Indian islands, although in the latter case not nearly as much as has been generally assumed. Nevertheless, the years 1784 to 1788 saw a steady return to the volume of the prewar years. On the other hand, there were compensations from other quarters. The direct trade with France, started during the Revolution, continued to flourish so that Americans actually enjoyed a favorable balance during the 1780's. The commercial relations with Holland were particularly happy. The Dutch began to absorb more and more of those raw materials that, in the colonial period, could be moved, by the Acts of Trade and Navigation, to England alone. So, as Dr. East points out, the end of the so-called "critical period" saw the Dutch-American export trade fully half as great as the English-American trade; the balance of payments was in favor of the Americans; prices of commodities for foreign shipment were good, except for 1785 and 1786; and Dutch merchant bankers freely extended commercial credits to their American customers.

Further, the foreign West Indian trade was expanding. New direct commercial relations were being opened up with Scandinavia, Russia, and the Near East, and the great India and China trades were being tapped, thanks to the smashing of the English mercantilist restrictions. Certainly, in connection with this last, new chapters were being written in the history of American commerce.

The Empress of China sailed from New York in 1784 bound for the China Sea and Canton; the *Grand Turk* left Salem the next year for the same destination; in 1787 Boston merchants, operating on a joint-stock basis, fitted out a ship to tap the North-west-China trade. Soon, American masters were as familiar with the ports of the Indian Ocean as they were with those of the Caribbean. American ships carried mixed cargoes to Europe; there they picked up consignments for Madagascar, Aden, Muscat, Madras, Calcutta, and the islands of the Eastern archipelagoes; and they traded in coffee, sugar, pepper, allspice, textiles, and chinaware. The Northwest-China trade was to become a rich source of profits for Yankee merchantmen. Otter and seal furs were acquired in the Northwest and carried to

China and there exchanged for tea, fine textiles, and chinaware. Notably, Boston and New York merchants waxed rich on this traffic.

One cannot deny the commercial letdown of 1785-86. Prices for many staples at home—tobacco, lumber, flour—dropped; the merchants in the import trade, being largely concerned with domestic distribution, were therefore hard hit too. But this situation points to overexpansion of domestic production of raw materials and excess inventories rather than to a complete destruction of confidence at home and a drying up of markets at home and abroad. The fact is, the interstate barriers to trade, of which much has been made in justifying the thesis of collapse during this period, really played only a negligible role. After 1783, the restrictive state laws were really not functioning as far as domestic commerce was concerned, since products grown in the United States were being exempted from state import duties while American-owned vessels of sister states were often receiving preferential tonnage rates over those of foreign registry.

The point has been made: there must have been motives, other than the threat of complete business disorganization as a result of political decentralization, that prompted men of large property to agitate for a powerful national union from 1786 on. To quote Dr. East in conclusion:

The Revolution was immediately followed by several years of confused readjustment; but some economic life was vigorous, at least until a sharp decline in prices for American produce took place in 1785; and even then it did not cease, though agriculture was particularly hard hit. Commerce had suffered even earlier, however, simply because the merchants had long been indulging in excessive importations at falling prices, and they thus helped to pave their own way to hard times. Their recovery led to the development of a new world-wide commerce which the Revolution had legalized, and this frequently promoted longer cooperatively financed voyages. The tendency of the hard times was to weed out the smaller business men to the eventual benefit of the larger, and to evolve more highly organized business communities; all of which cleared the way for greater business activity in the later years.

2. THE MOTIVES OF THE MAKERS OF THE CONSTITUTION

There had been a runaway paper inflation during the period of the war, with the inevitable partial repudiation of both these Continental and state bills of credit. While small businessmen, farmers, and soldiers had suffered particularly, it is doubtful whether the men of large property had been seriously affected. As Professor Nettels points out:

Realizing that the currency bubble would one day burst, the shrewdest investors converted their paper profits [derived from wartime contracting and profiteering] into some durable form—into land, commodities, mortgage loans, capital goods, and the securities of the state and federal governments, thereby acquiring claims to future incomes to be realized in a better currency. At the end of the war, the investments of the creditor class (as expressed in dollars) greatly exceeded their prewar investments, and the burden of debt, both public and private, was correspondingly increased.

Notably, a speculative interest appeared that obviously was concerned over political stability. This speculative interest had invested heavily in lands and public securities—the first acquired with cheap money and often as a result of favoritism, the second bought up at large discounts running from 50 per cent to 90 per cent of the original face values. With the outbreak of the war, the states, as has been pointed out, seized the ungranted lands of the crown and the proprieties, the estates of the proprietors, and the real possessions of loyalists. These were quickly sold by the states, hard pressed for funds, as a rule at not much more than nominal prices, and more frequently than not to men of large property. Similarly, companies for the development of the trans-Appalachian country made their appearance and these obtained charters and titles with little cash outlays. The end of the war saw land speculators also doing a heavy business in the purchase of soldiers' land warrants.

The quick depreciation of bills of credit compelled the Continental Congress and the states to turn to the floating of long-term securities. After 1777, a market for these was established as a result of French borrowings, which permitted the meeting of interest charges on loans, and the willingness to accept bills of credit in payment for bonds. The states pursued a somewhat similar course, except that here a market for the public issues was maintained by the sale of land. Speculators, in time, succeeded in rounding up a large part of the Continental and state issues: here, therefore, was to be found a real vested interest which looked, by one device or another, to eventual redemption at face value and in specie.

In brief, it may be said that special groups, associated with the large property rights of land speculation, security investment, banking, manufactures, the fur trade, and foreign commerce (and these large property interests had taken the conservative position during the Revolution), wanted a greater measure of political stability than either the Articles of Confederation or the really sovereign states afforded. A more powerful national union, in the economic realm, would have the following obvious advantages. It would permit the land speculators to realize on their paper investments. It would help in the pacification of the West, thus putting the fur trade on a firm foundation. It would pay interest and principal on the public securities of the central and perhaps even the state governments. It would write commercial treaties with foreign powers for the protection of mercantile capitalism abroad. It would create a single tariff system, for revenue and protection. It would establish a navy to hunt down piracy. It would expand the horizons of business on a national scale by the granting of national charters to manufacturing, banking, and transportation companies.

Whether articulated or not, these considerations must have been appreciated and their importance weighed by men of affairs and their legal representatives as the inadequacies of the Confederation became apparent. The Confederation was an advance over the *de facto* Continental Congress; but it had fatal shortcomings. It could command no revenues; it could not regulate trade; it was incapable of assuring the fulfillment of contracts; it had no military force with which to maintain domestic peace or pacify the frontiers. The legislature was supreme: it was hampered by neither an executive nor a judiciary.

As regards the sovereign states, the increasing power of the conservatives permitted the elimination of wartime excesses. Men of large property, as they took over the instrumentalities of government, began to adumbrate and indeed in many states carry out the following program. They put a stop to the emission of legal-tender bills of credit, and their liquidation (at discounts, of course) was commenced. They gave thought to the refunding of the revolutionary long-term debt. They laid plans to survey and settle confiscated wild lands. Courts were supported in vigorous action against debtors, in order to establish once and for all the sanctity of contracts. But this was a slow and tortuous journey, exactly because it had to be started and pursued in thirteen different commonwealths and because there existed a no man's land of interstate relations where neither an executive nor a judicial authority existed.

Into the bargain, in the thirteen sovereign states, as James Madison so clearly understood, there always threatened the likelihood of successful legislative attacks by egalitarians on big property: for state paper money and the inadequate judicial safeguarding of contracts were the deadly enemies of capitalist enterprise. How more surely and rapidly could the advance be pushed if it were done with the encouragement and blessing of a single centralized government! Particularly one in which the legislative power was *not* supreme!

The threat of the recapture of power by radicals during 1785-86 and the disorders of the same years pointed to the necessity for immediate action. For the dangerous leveling spirit of the early war years was once more raising its head: a leveling spirit that was fed by the hard times and that especially hit small producers, farmers, and traders. The evidence existed on every side. Within a short time at least seven legislatures emitted new paper currency. Judges, foreclosing properties and jailing debtors, were being bitterly denounced and even threatened with physical violence in New York, New Jersey, and North Carolina. Levelers in legislatures were drawing up programs to abolish imprisonment for debt, to enact stay, or mortgage-moratorium, laws and to write down the face values of mortgages themselves. In Rhode Island, the agrarian host, holding the seats of authority, openly flouted the claims and protests of merchants and moneylenders.

When small-propertied men rose once more, notably in Massachusetts and New Hampshire, and took up arms to combat judicial tyranny, the time for decisive action had come. After writing conservative constitutions, the governments of Massachusetts and New Hampshire announced their intentions of stabilizing public and private financial policies: the revolutionary debt was to be paid off, taxes were to be increased, paper money was to be contracted, debts were to be paid or properties foreclosed. Small farmers of interior counties took alarm and began to clamor for stay laws, for the scaling down of debts, for the passage once more of legal-tender acts, and for the closing of courts to put a stop to the mounting toll taken by foreclosures. Where legislatures and courts were unheeding, revolutionary soldiers took down their muskets and began to march. General Knox, writing to George Washington in 1786 of the once more embattled small farmers, said: "Their creed is 'That the property of the United States has been protected from the confiscations of Britain by the joint exertions of all, and therefore ought to be the common property of all. And he that attempts opposition to this creed is an enemy to equity and justice, and ought to be swept from off the face of the earth.' In a word, they are determined to annihilate all debts, public and private, and have agrarian laws, which are easily effected by means of unfunded paper money which shall be a tender in all cases whatever."

The appearance of a troop of armed men, under the leadership of Captain Daniel Shays, in central Massachusetts in 1786, their threat to shut down the courts entirely, and their move to seize arms and munitions from government stores alarmed the seaboard. A militia force, financed from private subscriptions made by seaboard merchants and capitalists, hastily assembled and moved against Shays' insurrectionists, who were quickly disbanded.

3. THE WRITING AND RATIFICATION OF THE CONSTITUTION

This armed challenge to authority had a profound effect. There can be no question that Shays' Rebellion strengthened the determination of large-propertied men to see established a powerful national union. As General Knox expressed it: "Our government must be braced, changed, or altered to secure our lives and property." In February, 1787, Congress issued a call for a national convention to revise the Articles of Confederation. Fifty-five representatives from all the states but Rhode Island assembled at Philadelphia. Clearly, in terms of their personal interests and class loyalties, they spoke not for the under-privileged and oppressed, as did so many in the First and Second Continental Congresses, but only for the high-born and the affluent; not for small farmers and traders and for town mechanics and laborers, but for security speculation, commerce, manufacturing, slave planting, land jobbing, and moneylending. Indeed, of the fifty-five, only two may be said to have had any sympathy with the aspirations of small-propertied men: the aged Benjamin Franklin of Pennsylvania and Luther Martin of Maryland. Jefferson at this time was in France. George Washington presided over the proceedings; but if the thought of any single individual dominated them, it was Alexander Hamilton's.

Sitting in secret session and laboring with a skill and singleness of purpose truly unique in legislative annals, the Founding Fathers devised a new frame of government for a centralized national state.

Not a federal but a national union was created; and in its agencies were vested those powers necessary to assure the unhindered progress of commerce, manufacturing, land speculation, and finance. In two simple clauses, the Constitution effectively tied the hands of agrarian state legislators: the states might not emit legal-tender paper money nor might they impair the obligation of contract. And the national government was given the right to lay and collect taxes; impose duties on foreign imports; regulate interstate and foreign commerce; borrow and coin money; provide for patents and copyrights; lay down rules for proceedings in bankruptcy; raise and support armies; dispose of the public lands; guarantee to every state a republican form of government and protect it—on its application—against domestic violence (the echoes of Shays' Rebellion were still being heard); and pay all revolutionary debts contracted by the Continental Congress and the several states.

The numerous majority—"the turbulence and follies of democracy" of which Edmund Randolph spoke—was to be curbed at all costs. It was difficult to deny it representation altogether. But it was imperative to furnish within the instrument, against the day when the people might seek to control the national government, adequate checks and balances—through the indirect choice of an upper house and the presidency, the grant of a veto to the President, executive appointment and life tenure for a Supreme Court and its supremacy over Congress, and through well-nigh insuperable barriers to the amendment of the Constitution. While the right of judicial review was not written into the Constitution, contemporaries understood that the Court was to have this power.

Madison issued this solemn warning:

The landed interest, at present, is prevalent, but in process of time . . . when the number of landholders shall be comparatively small . . . will not the landed interests be overbalanced in future elections? And, unless wisely provided against, what will become of our government? In England, at this day, if elections were open to all classes of people, the property of landed proprietors would be unsure. An agrarian law would take place. If these observations be just, our government ought to secure the permanent interests of the country against innovation. Landholders ought to have a share in the government, to support these invaluable interests, and to balance and check the other. They ought to be so constituted as to protect the minority of the opulent against the majority.

And later on, he said:

An increase of population will of necessity increase the proportion of those who will labor under all the hardships of life and secretly sigh for a more equal distribution of its blessings. These may in time outnumber those who are placed above the feelings of indigence. According to the equal law of suffrage, the power will slide into the hands of the former. No agrarian attempts have yet been made in this country, but symptoms of a leveling spirit, as we have understood, have sufficiently appeared, in a certain quarter, to give notice of the future danger.

The Constitutional Convention labored well. With equal skill its participants achieved ratification of the instrument. They had provided that not the legislatures of the states but special conventions elected for the purpose were to pass on the document; and that acceptance by nine states alone was needed for adoption despite the requirement in the Articles of Confederation of amendment by unanimous consent. With not more than perhaps one fourth of the adult males in the population voting in the convention elections, and with certainly majority delegates in New York, Massachusetts, and New Hampshire committed to an adverse vote—in short, constituting a small minority, but well organized, amazingly earnest, and literate—the managers of the campaign for ratification, using unseemly haste in some states and calculated dilatory tactics in others, and not above the employment of what looked very much like irregularities in some, finally obtained the consent of the ninth state in June, 1788.

The supporters of the Constitution—the Federalists—quickly obtained ratification in Delaware, Connecticut, New Jersey, and Georgia. They forced a recalcitrant legislature in Pennsylvania to summon an election and here they triumphed. Where the conventions were hostile, as they were in Massachusetts, New York, and New Hampshire, the Federalists were able to delay a final vote until individual opponents could be won over to their position. In the more important states the contests were bitterly fought and the final votes very close. In Virginia, ratification was carried by 89 to 79; in Massachusetts, by 187 to 168; in New Hampshire, by 57 to 47; in New York, by 30 to 27. North Carolina and Rhode Island did not ratify until after the Constitution had been installed as the law of the land. On April 30, 1789, George Washington took the oath of office at Federal Hall in Wall Street, New York City. The United States of America had its first President and its history as a national republic had begun.

4. THE HAMILTONIAN SYSTEM

Before Washington quit public office, Congress had accepted in its entirety Alexander Hamilton's program for the sound establishment of capitalist enterprising in America. The whole Continental debt was refunded at its face value and the revolutionary state debts were assumed: and thus was the confidence of moneylenders (past and future) in the new government assured. A national bank, chartered by the federal government, was created and vested with the right of note issue. A mint was set up. A tariff law was passed. The public lands were to be sold in large minimum lots, for the purpose of obtaining a revenue. A sinking fund was established. Excise taxes were imposed on the numerous small producers. Large property was now secure against any assaults by misguided sans-culotte legislators in the states; and its interests commanded the ever-watchful regard of the central government.

Hamilton's program, in large measure, was presented in a series of reports, which concerned themselves with the public debt, public revenues, the chartering of a national bank, and the encouragement of manufactures. In addition, he had much to do with the passage of tariff legislation and the writing of a land policy for the new government.

The "Report on Public Credit" came to grips at once with the problem that had concerned personally so many of the Founding Fathers: what was to be the status of the public debt of the central government and the states? Hamilton flatly argued for the funding of the Continental and Confederation debt and the assumption of the state debts. The outstanding debt with accrued interest, he conceded, was large: $11,700,000 represented foreign borrowings, $40,400,000 the domestic borrowings of the central government, and $25,000,000 the domestic borrowings of the states. But funding and assumption were necessary to put the public credit on a sound footing; in addition, these policies would consolidate popular support behind the federal government, on the one hand, and win the confidence of business interests, on the other, by creating a sorely needed credit medium. Over the opposition of agrarians, Hamilton carried the day, and the Funding Act of 1790 provided for a new issue of bonds to be exchanged for those of the old Continental debt and the Confederation domestic debt. Similarly, Congress voted assumption, the measure providing for an issue of $21,-500,000 in bonds; actually $18,000,000 on this account was paid out. The fact is, Hamilton drove a good bargain with the security holders, for four ninths of the new issues were to bear 6 per cent interest, another two ninths were to bear no interest for ten years and only thereafter 6 per cent, while three ninths were to bear only 3 per cent interest.

Also, a sinking fund was to be established for the redemption of the debt and for the support of the market of the so-called federal "stock." Certain revenues were to be earmarked to meet the interest; the proceeds of sales of western lands were to go toward redemption; while surpluses accruing to the federal government were to be placed in a special fund out of which open-market purchases of the bonds might be made if they should fall below par.

Meanwhile, Congress had already laid the basis for a federal revenue through the passage of the Tariff Act of 1789. The measure had mildly protective features: it placed an ad valorem duty of 5 per cent on "nonenumerated" articles; fixed specific duties coming to more than 5 per cent as a rule on hemp, cordage, nails, iron manufactures, and glass; and, to encourage the domestic merchant marine, offered a rebate of 10 per cent of the duties on all goods carried in American bottoms. Also, a tonnage tax of 50 cents a ton was put on foreign vessels in American ports. The leading thought was the raising of a revenue and to this Hamilton returned in his report on an excise. In March, 1791, Congress voted a tax of from 11 cents to 30 cents a gallon on rum and from 9 cents to 25 cents on whisky; these taxes were to be paid at the stills. The returns from this tax were disappointingly small, so that in 1794 the excise was expanded to include taxes on carriages, sugar, snuff, and auction sales.

The report on the bank received congressional approval also and in 1791 an act was passed establishing the United States Bank for twenty years. Hamilton had argued that such a bank would increase the active or productive capital of the country; that it would lend to the federal government in time of emergency; and that it would facilitate government collections and payments. His opponents, chief of whom was Jefferson, raised the cries of monopoly and unconstitutionality. But Washington listened to Hamilton and signed the bill.

The act authorized a capitalization of $10,000,000 in 25,000 shares. The government might subscribe to one fifth of these and was to name a similar proportion of directors. Private individuals could pay for their shares up to three fourths in the new 6 per cent federal "stock." A system of "regressive voting" was provided, the possessor of one share having one vote, three shares two votes, and so on up to twenty votes for one hundred shares. Foreign subscriptions were not barred but foreigners could not vote by proxy or serve on the board of directors of twenty-five members. The Bank's functions were to be the following: it could receive deposits; it could make loans to individuals, the states, and the federal government; and it had the right of note issue up to the amount of its capital and deposits. During the 1790's the Bank did realize many of Hamilton's hopes for it. It added something like $5,000,000 to the currency of the country; it extended credits to the federal government, so that in 1796 the federal indebtedness to the Bank was $6,000,000; and it handled deposits and disbursements for the Treasury. Beginning with 1796, the government began to sell its Bank stock and under Jefferson all holdings were disposed of. More and more the shares were bought up by foreign investors, so that, when the charter expired in 1811, 72 per cent of the stock was being held abroad.

Another Hamiltonian report was concerned with the establishment of an American system of coinage and a mint; and these Congress provided in the Mint Act of 1792. A bimetallic standard was created with the existing market ratio of fifteen to one for the silver dollar being accepted. The silver dollar was to contain 371 grains of silver, which was the content of the Spanish dollar. In the hope that Americans would bring foreign coins to the mint for refining, such an institution was created. But it was not until 1802 that foreign coins disappeared as legal tender.

The "Report on the Subject of Manufactures" of 1791 was perhaps the most famous of these state papers, for in time it became the textbook of all protectionists. Deploring the almost exclusive preoccupation of producers with agriculture, Hamilton called for greater support for domestic manufactures. He asked that the government encourage the immigration of foreign artisans; that aid be rendered inventors; that public authority give industry its fostering care by the imposition of protective duties and the granting of bounties; and that women and children be inducted into the factory system. Hamilton painted a roseate picture of the consequences to America. The establishment of manufactures would lead to a more efficient division of labor and therefore the greater production of goods. It would give "greater scope for the diversity of talents and dispositions, which discriminate men from each other." It would create, by providing employment for women and children and encouraging emigration from Europe, an expanding market for the products of American agriculture.

The report did not bear immediate fruit, for Congress did nothing, either through protective duties or bounties, to favor infant industry. The factory system, despite Hamilton's sanguine expectations, appeared only tardily in the United States. Indeed, as will be pointed out in detail later, industrial capitalism did not really begin to feel its oats until the late 1840's. Why was this? There was no dearth of either capital or a labor supply. It was simply that, in the face of English industrial competition, more lucrative avenues continued to exist for the investment of the savings and profits of American enterprisers. The period of the Napoleonic Wars particularly was the golden age for American commerce. Soon the China trade was to beckon. Also, the opening up of the West presented unexampled opportunities for capitalist activity in land speculation and the fur trade. As long as the characteristic undertakings of mercantile capitalism brought returns, there was little to tempt the American capitalist to change his status and put his fund into fixed plant.

Another Hamiltonian triumph was the dispatching of John

Jay to England to write a treaty with England in the interests of more settled diplomatic and commercial relations. Jay's Treaty of 1795 closed some of the outstanding disputes that had exacerbated feeling between both nations. On our part, we promised to pay back in sterling the bona fide private debts contracted by American planters and merchants before the Revolution. The English, on their part, agreed to evacuate western posts still held by their troops, pay damages for the seizure of American ships during the course of England's war on France, and finally establish a northeast boundary between the United States and Canada. Important commercial concessions were made. Commercial relations between the two countries were put on a nondiscriminatory basis; overland commerce between the United States and Canada was provided for; and American ships were to be permitted to trade with the British East Indies. The English were prepared to offer some concessions as regards the West Indian trade—the admission of American ships under 70 tons to these ports—but the demand of England that the United States consent not to carry characteristic West Indian products to Europe (molasses, sugar, coffee, cocoa, cotton) prompted the Senate to excide this article from the treaty.

The United States was compelled to recognize English control of the seas. But there can be no question that our economy profited immeasurably. To quote Samuel Flagg Bemis:

To balance against those great concessions to British sea power there was the assurance of continuing commercial prosperity, sound national finances, and the perpetuation of the newly consolidated American nationality. There was also the great achievement of redeeming the territorial integrity of the United States throughout the Northwest. . . . But the concessions to England were heavy. They were the price which the Federalists paid for peace, that peace with England so necessary for the maintenance of Hamilton's structure of national credit and with it of the new federal government under the constitution of 1787. It is not an exaggeration to believe that Jay's Treaty, which was really Hamilton's treaty, saved American nationality in an hour of crisis.

Nothing more completely demonstrated the farsightedness of the Hamiltonian program, as far as mercantile and banking capitalism was concerned, than the position of America in Europe's money markets. English and Dutch bankers were eager to extend commercial credits to our merchants, while the investors of these countries came to regard American "funds" (bank stock) and "stock" (federal bonds) as prime securities. By 1800, fully half of the federal "stock" and Bank of United States "funds" were held abroad; about one third of the capitalization of state banks was in European hands; and the shares of state-chartered insurance and turnpike companies were eagerly sought after. The fact is, almost one half of the public and private securities issued in America were in foreign portfolios; to this degree foreign capital was helping the young polity and economy establish itself.

The Hamiltonian program had the bitter hostility of the Anti-Federalists, led by Jefferson. They fought the chartering of the Bank, the assumption of state debts, the writing of protective tariffs, and Jay's Treaty. In the following wise later spoke a leading agrarian, John Taylor of Caroline, as regards protectionism:

. . . the policy of protecting duties to force manufacturing is of the same nature and will produce the same consequences as that of enriching a noble interest, a church interest, or a paper interest; because bounties to capital are taxes upon industry and a distribution of property by law and it is the worst mode of encouraging aristocracy, because to the evil of distributing wealth at home by law, is to be added the national loss arising from foreign retaliation upon our own exports.

The election of Jefferson, in 1800, marked the triumph of the Anti-Federalists; it is important to note, however, that the Hamiltonian pattern was not disarranged in any essential regard. Jefferson was clearheaded enough to understand that Hamilton's financial system was the foundation of the nation's stability; and that, even in other areas, as he said: "What is practicable must often control what is pure theory." The boundaries of action were thus limited. Jefferson cut down the national debt and taxes a little; he reduced public expenditures; he withdrew public funds from the Bank of the United States and put them into state banks. On the other hand, he entered upon new commitments with the purchase of Louisiana. In no case were any of his measures designed to fill the breasts of capitalists with alarm. The judgment of Witt Bowden is a harsh one, but there is much truth in it. He says:

To the Jeffersonians the propertied classes most worthy of power were the landed classes. To them the moneyed classes cherished by Hamiltonian policy were at first anathema. But . . . the Jeffersonian party came to terms with men of moneyed property. There was a reconciliation of the business men with the agrarian government on the basis of their acquiescence in "the reformed order of things"—which meant not a whole loaf as under Hamilton but a goodly portion.

Part III

—

THE VICTORY OF AMERICAN INDUSTRIAL CAPITALISM IN THE CIVIL WAR

CHAPTER FIFTEEN

The Role of the West

1. RENEWAL OF THE LEVELING SPIRIT

THE class oppressions, which seemed inevitable as a result of the victory of the big propertied groups in 1789, somehow miraculously were relaxed. For the open door of the western lands and the great increase in population due to immigration furnished bewildering opportunities for enterprise and advancement up the economic ladder to American small farmers, small traders, small producers, and even a few workers. The next fifty or so years constituted an age of extraordinary activity for American capitalism. But it was not the capitalism of industry but the capitalism of trade. In short, the period was comparable in its movement and variety to that which set in in western Europe with about the twelfth and thirteenth centuries. The extension of the horizons of enterprise, the great growth in the population, the vast reclamation and colonization projects that were inaugurated (in this sense, the opening up of the American West was, in its economic effects, exactly similar to the reclamation and colonization of France, the Low Countries, England, and eastern Germany in the twelfth to the fourteenth centuries): these provided the setting for the maturing of mercantile capitalism in the first half of nineteenth-century America.

The rise and decline of mercantile capitalism, therefore, constitute the history of the period and help to explain the events that unrolled. The initial opportunities for American mercantile capitalism were magnificent: in the development of the western lands; in the provision of means of communication into the American interior; in the expansion of the transatlantic and transpacific carrying trades; in the financing of speculative trading and manufacturing operations. For even industrial production—and this was one of the important characteristics of the period—was on a mercantile-capitalist basis. In the great proportion of the industries, the cottage and mill, instead of the factory, predominated as the unit of production. When mercantile capitalism—in land speculation, in trade, in the creation of means of transportation—had exhausted all the possibilities of further growth; and when it discovered, to its cost, that accumulation was not a constantly successful process in a free climate where too many chance factors operated: then the necessity for the conversion of mercantile capitalism into industrial capitalism became the order of the day.

From about 1843 on, this process visibly began to take place, stopping short of complete fulfillment because the rising industrial-capitalist class was not in possession of the instrumentalities of political power. In short, industrial capitalism, it became apparent by the late 1850's, was incapable of achieving full maturity unless it had control of the state. In these terms we are to read the meaning of the Civil War; for that conflict was a revolution in the sense that it represented a desperate struggle for political power between two classes each of which required control of the state to underwrite its own economic and social programs.

In an age marked by such great fluidity class lines could not harden altogether. Movement within the various layers of the middle class, at any rate, was indeed real. There is a remarkable passage in Hegel's *The Philosophy of History* (delivered in lecture form during the 1820's!) which shows that the true significance of the western lands was understood, even at the very moment when the processes of their conquest were being launched. Hegel wrote:

As to the political condition of North America, the general object of the existence of this state is not yet fixed and determined, and the necessity for a firm combination does not yet exist; for a real State and a real Government arise only after a distinction of classes has arisen, when wealth and poverty become extreme, and when such a condition of things presents itself that a large portion of the people can no longer satisfy its necessities in the way in which it has been accustomed so to do. But America is hitherto exempt from this pressure, for it has the outlet of colonization constantly and widely open, and multitudes are continually streaming into the plains of the Mississippi. By this means the chief source of discontent is removed, and the continuation of the existing civil condition is guaranteed.

This theory of the role of the American West was rediscovered and popularized by the American historian, Frederick Jackson Turner, in 1893. In his essay, "The Significance of the Frontier," he said:

Most important of all has been the fact that an area of free land has continually lain on the western border of the settled area of the United States. Whenever social conditions tended to crystallize in the East, whenever capital tended to press upon labor or political restraints to impede the freedom of the mass, there was this gate of escape to the free conditions of the frontier. . . . Men would not accept inferior wages and a permanent position of social subordination when this promised land of freedom and equality was theirs for the taking.

Indeed, pushing the doctrine much too far, historians of labor have even sought to explain the so-called backwardness of the organized American workers in the same terms. Thus John R. Commons:

The condition which seems to distinguish most clearly the history of labor in America from its history in other countries is the wide expanse of free land. As long as the poor and industrious can escape from the conditions which render them subject to other classes, so long do they refrain from that aggression on the property rights or political power of others, which is the symptom of a "labour movement."

A footnote to this too general position is necessary, and that is this. The western lands, as we shall see, were not in any real sense free, thus making it impossible for the completely dispossessed to pull themselves up by their own bootstraps simply by emigration. But the western lands did present economic opportunities for those underprivileged small farmers and traders who were falling behind in the race in the more settled communities of the East and in northern Europe. The western pioneers in large measure were farmers or the younger sons of farmers who were able to command enough capital or credit to finance their transplanting. It must be clearly had in mind that transportation costs, food and feed for human beings and work animals, and the possession of a team of oxen and a wagon required a sizable outlay before even the site of new settlement was reached. Even assuming that the cost of a farm was nominal, the erection of a home and farm buildings, the drainage, fencing, and plowing of the tough prairie sod (or the cutting out of a clearing in the river bottoms), the price of seed, and the upkeep of family and animals until the first crop was planted, harvested, and sold: all these demanded more funds. It is not difficult to assume that the typical pioneering family intent upon engagement in commercial agriculture required from $1000 to $1500 in the 1840's before it could consider itself secure in its new surroundings.

Industrial laborers in the East making on an average $1 a day when they worked, and the bitter victims of depression during 1837-43 and 1857-58, were incapable of shifting their status by transfer into a freeholding agricultural class—even assuming that functionally they were capable of a sudden change in occupation. The West really could attract only those whose experiences previously had been in agriculture or in related pursuits. In any case, there is ample evidence to indicate that the persons who went West were not industrial workers. Who then were the pioneers? It has already been pointed out that they must have been small farmers or their sons. In addition, small traders and, in time, small producers also were attracted into the newly opened regions. This modification of the crudely phrased theory of the West as a "safety valve," that is, that it acted as a stabilizer of potential social discontents and the corrector of a solidifying class society, nevertheless does no violence to the conception of the West's role as a leveling force.

Carter Goodrich and Sol Davison, whose studies have done much to compel the modification of the simple "safety-valve" theory, conclude very properly:

The analysis confirms . . . rather than questions the opinion that the abundance of western land drew away many thousands of *potential* wage-earners who might otherwise have crowded into the factories "from the hill towns of New England" and "from the exhausted farms of New York and Pennsylvania." Though here the "safety valve" was the farmer's rather than the worker's, we need not doubt that its operation tended to hold up the level of industrial wages.

Thus, the urban industrial workers wistfully regarded the West as a promised land, whose gates were really closed to them. But the small farmers of New England, the Middle States, and the backcountry South quit their impoverished holdings before they had exhausted all their capital resources. Their company was filled out by European immigrants with an agrarian background and heritage. The presence of the West prevented the too rapid induction of these men of small property into the army of the industrial reserve; and, in this sense, the proletarianization of the American agriculturist was delayed for a number of generations. It remained for the grandsons and great-grandsons of the original western settlers to take their places at those factory benches and machines from which their ancestors had found escape possible. In brief, the fluidity within the American society was largely confined to the middle class: petty-bourgeois property owners or the sons of such owners, who could hope for some assistance from their families, had real opportunities to improve their economic and social positions by movement upward. It is no accident at all that during the formative and progressive years of industrial capitalism in the United States the great majority of men of wealth came from this class. One finds difficulty in recording fortunes that originated in a proletarian background.

Before the Civil War, in this so-called Middle Period, the ideals and attitudes that we have come to associate with Jeffersonianism and Jacksonianism therefore held sway: the prevailing tone of American society was set by the small independent farmers and the petty-bourgeois traders and merchant-manufacturers who came from the ranks of the American yeomanry. Leveling doctrines once more raised their heads in the states and indeed triumphed ultimately in all the northern and eastern ones; and—for a time at any rate—the central government regarded with a benevolent eye assaults on privilege and where it could—as in the war on the Second Bank of the United States —aided them. Indeed, it is important to note that the Abolitionist movement arose and received its most devoted allegiance not in the New England urban areas, as is commonly supposed, but among this American petty bourgeoisie of independent farmers, small traders, and cottage-and-mill producers of the less densely settled regions of the North and Middle West. It was not until the late 1850's—when the twilight of mercantile capitalism had set in—that the leaders of northern capital seized upon the free-soil cause (no slavery in the territories) as the most likely cudgel with which to belabor the slave system. They made it their own, not, however, for the purposes of freeing the black men but to capture the central government from the hands of the planter capitalists.

Jefferson and Jackson were passionate egalitarians, but theirs, of course, was an egalitarianism of small-property rights and of individual and free producers. Jefferson hated and feared the capitalism of exploitation and of a factory proletariat; a certain amount of manufacturing, he later came to concede, was necessary but only to satisfy domestic needs. The manufacturing he was acquainted with was that of the cottage and mill; and plainly he had this form of organization in mind when, in 1805, he characterized American manufacturers as being "as much at their ease, as independent and moral as our agricultural inhabitants." Obviously this reservation did no violence to his essential program of economic equality. No one has more satisfactorily expressed Jefferson's ideal than Charles A. and Mary R. Beard. It was as follows:

In the course of time Jefferson worked out a fairly comprehensive scheme of social science: agriculture should be the economic basis of society; a mild and inexpensive government given to toleration and justice could easily maintain order; and equal division of inheritances and easy acquisition of land would make for a practical equality in status; universal education would afford talents for leadership . . . ; immigration should be limited to assimilable stocks and overpopulation avoided; slavery should be abolished and the slaves transported to a land of their own.

It was a creed all of whose essential particulars were acceptable to the small free farmers and the small industrial producers and mechanics who were not yet, of course, proletarians. We find it written on the banners of the Workingmen's parties of the late 1820's and of the reform movements of the 1830's and 1840's. Andrew Jackson took it over and popularized it; that is to say, he made it available to the "humble members of society" whom he addressed. Jackson, in the true sense, was a popular leader. He knew the aspirations of the people and had their hatred of wealth based on speculation and privilege, and therefore his utterances and his prejudices kept beat with the rhythm of the times.

While the Democratic party, in the 1840's and 1850's, passed into the hands of the slave lords and came—on the national stage, at any rate—to speak for a powerful vested interest exclusively, its tradition continued an active force in many of the Middle Atlantic, North Central, and Border States; and in these areas it served as an inspiration for the men of small means to carry on their struggles for equality. Nothing showed this more clearly, for example, than the leveling constitutions written in New York in 1846, in Ohio in 1850-51, and in Indiana in 1851.

It would be false to believe—as Turner has tried to prove—that this leveling spirit was the prevailing characteristic of a section. It was, rather, the guide of the class of petty-bourgeois producers, whether they were to be found in the East or in the West. Indeed, as the West came to be settled—as the young West, where Jacksonian ideals once had held complete sway, came to fill up—new leaders arose to speak for those who were pushing their way out of the status of the lower middle class. Such a man was Henry Clay. A westerner, his American System was a program designed to satisfy the demands of all big capitalists: a paternalist state program of protective tariffs for the growing industries of the East; a similar paternalist state program of public works, developed internal markets, and a free flow of immigrants for the expanding mercantile capitalism of the West. For the West, soon, came to be peopled not only with free farmers but with a pushing, energetic mercantile-capitalist class interested in land speculation, urban booms, canal and railroad building, and mineral and timber exploitation. Whiggery—and it should be remembered that the young Lincoln, for example, entered public life first as a Whig—had a firm foothold in western capitalist centers as much as in the eastern and southern. The Whig party spoke for the privilege of big property; while Jacksonianism spoke for the equality of small property when the possibilities of achieving a small-property position were still almost universal for those who had their origins in the petty bourgeoisie.

This leveling spirit, which fed at the streams of the economic opportunities opened up by the young America released by the forces of the Revolution, expressed itself in the states— old and new—in demands for political equality. In 1791 Vermont entered the Union with a constitution guaranteeing universal manhood suffrage; new western states did similarly; while in the older states—in Maryland in 1809, in Connecticut in 1818, in Massachusetts in 1820, in New York in 1821—pressure from beneath had to be yielded to. It was not until the 1850's that many of the southern states grudgingly bestowed the franchise upon all male adult whites. In Rhode Island, where big property had finally seized the agencies of government out of the hands of the sans-culottes who had held it during the Revolutionary period, resort to violence was necessary before even a partial leveling victory could be won.

In Rhode Island, as late as 1840, fully half the population of voting age was still disfranchised because of a property qualification. The old colonial charter contained no provisions for the assemblying of a constitutional convention; and the legislature refused to issue a call. A popular agitation, led by Thomas W. Dorr, was without effect: Dorr and his lower middle-class followers summoned an illegal convention which drew up a so-called People's Constitution. In 1841 this document was submitted to a referendum and obtained an overwhelming acceptance. It has been claimed by Dorr's defenders that, even if the votes of qualified voters alone were considered, these spoke for a majority of the whole electorate. The dominant propertied factions, afraid of the consequences of such an act, proceeded to draw up a new frame of government which embodied material concessions, notably the extension of the franchise to all native-born (but not foreign-born) citizens possessing two years' residence. This constitution, in turn, was rejected.

The Dorrites regarded this sequence of events as constituting a popular mandate and proceeded to hold an election in which Dorr was chosen governor. The conservatives did similarly, and in 1842 Rhode Island possessed two governments, each claiming power. The conservative government declared martial law; a troop of Dorrites armed themselves and marched against the state arsenal. Dorr was unsuccessful, his followers dispersed, and he himself fled only to return voluntarily and stand trial for high treason. Passions ran so high that the sentence imposed upon Dorr was a savage one. He was sentenced to solitary confinement at hard labor for life and he served a period of his term, an amnesty being granted only because of ill-health. The constitution, as finally accepted, did widen the base of the franchise, accord greater representation in the general assembly to the small rural communities, and extend the suffrage to non-property-holding native-born citizens. It was not until 1886, however, that foreign-born citizens who did not own property were permitted to vote.

A somewhat similar rising occurred in New York. Here, the thrust upward came from the urban egalitarians and the rural dispossessed. Under their combined leadership, a new constitution was written in 1846 which placed iron rings around corporate power, further popularized the government by making the judiciary elective, and finally put an end to what approximated copyhold land tenure on many of the great estates in the Hudson Valley. The tillers of the soil on these estates were tenants operating as leaseholders: they had nominal ownership and paid money rents; but they were also required to pay semifeudal dues, notably in association with the transfer of their holdings (i.e., alienation fines). The "sale" of a leasehold required the permission of the landlord, who sought to exact from one fourth to one third of the sale price; in any case, with transfer, improvements erected by the tenant reverted to the landlord. Where perpetual leases, or copyhold tenure, existed, a succession, or alienation, fine also had to be paid. Suffering from an inequitable distribution of the tax burden as well, many of these tenants had fallen into debt and arrears on their rent payments; many had been thrown into prison; all stood in danger of dispossession.

In the area, therefore, land riots were not infrequent. Such outbreaks took place in the 1820's, again in 1836, and once more in 1839 when the owners of the Van Rensselaer estate sought to collect $400,000 from their tenants. Writs of ejectment were secured. Sheriffs were stopped by armed farmers. State troops were called out. In other counties south of Albany "antirent parties" sprang up to demand legislative relief and constitutional reform. Yielding before popular pressure, the legislature passed laws abolishing seizure for debt and more equitably apportioning taxes between landlords and tenants. It remained for the constitution of 1846 to terminate all feudal vestiges: no leases, running for more than twelve years, were to be valid where any rents or services were reserved; and all fines, quarter sales, or other restraints on alienation, in leases made from then on, were to be considered void.

2. THE PUBLIC LAND POLICY

The push into the West, as has been said, afforded grand opportunities for the release and triumph of the leveling spirit; and for the creation of those new avenues of expansion for mercantile capitalism which the English Mercantile System had so effectively choked off. The land policy of the new central government was designed to serve both these needs.

Indeed, Hamilton, in laying down the general fiscal principles of the central government, when he came to the question of the disposition of the public domain, looked to the strengthening of a speculative landed interest as one of the sources of revenue for the state. From 1796, when the first general land act was written, up to 1862, when the Homestead Act was passed, the speculators rather than the small independent farmers were favored. There was no demand for the erection of an improvement, no limit put on sales nor on the transfer of titles, with the result that land engrossment quickly became the outstanding characteristic of the land operations of the period. The careful researches of Paul W. Gates clearly prove that land speculation and monopoly were the rule in the Military Tract of Illinois, the prairie sections of Indiana and Illinois, and the timber lands of Michigan, Wisconsin, and Minnesota. Agriculturists were at the mercy of the engrossers: they had to buy or borrow or settle as tenants. Indeed, the engrossing interest very frequently retarded the settling process because its refusal or inability to pay taxes held back public improvements and therefore the creation of those facilities that operating farmers required.

The liberalization of the land laws, after 1820, must not be regarded as much more than a pious gesture. Up to 1820, public lands were sold in large parcels (640 acres originally, later 160 acres being the minimum purchase) under the auction system and at generous credit terms. After 1820, the credit system was abolished, the minimum purchase was cut to 80 acres, then 40 acres, and the minimum knockdown price was put at $1.25 an acre. Yet it was under this dispensation that the land boom of 1833-37 took on all the aspects of a runaway speculation.

The little man without capital had no way of entering the public domain unless he bought from the land jobbers on credit and at high prices or unless he moved in as a squatter. This latter large numbers did and always in peril of ultimate eviction after they had made a clearing and erected an improvement. Such frontiersmen sought to protect their rights by combining with their fellow squatters in "claim associations"—whose function it was to frighten off the land-company agents at the auction sales. They also demanded congressional relief. Numerous special pre-emption laws for the protection of squatters were passed up to 1840, and finally in 1841 a general Pre-emption bill was carried which permitted a cashless squatter to locate 160 acres on the public domain and on a subsequent date acquire his holding at the minimum government price free from the dangers of the auction system. It should be observed, in passing, that the squatter was offered a legal title, but before he could complete it he had to turn to the usurious moneylenders for his capital. In such cases, interest rates of three and four per cent a month were not uncommon. Also, the Graduation Act of 1854, which, presumably in the interests of men of small means, permitted a scale of reductions in the minimum price of those lands that had remained unsold after being on the market for at least ten years, really played into the hands of the timber, mineral, and railroad companies.

The demand for free homesteads had long been a staple of the agitation of the Workingmen's parties and the labor movements. It was finally taken up in 1849 by Senator Stephen A. Douglas who appeared not so much as the friend of the small farmers but of those merchant-capitalist groups of the West whose urban land values and canal and railroad holdings were bound to profit from a faster settlement of the frontier regions. The House adopted a free-homestead bill in 1852 and again in 1854. The Senate did so in 1858 and 1859. Both houses passed a measure in 1860, only to see it vetoed by President Buchanan, whose stand mirrored the hostility of the southern slave lords to the quick settlement of the West. The Republican party, the party of the rising industrial-capitalist class, in 1860 championed the free-homestead program for political and economic reasons. It saw in this device a method for driving the wedge deeper between the agrarian South and the agrarian West; and it looked forward to the great expansion of the internal market by the homesteaders and therefore its own aggrandizement.

Throwing a lengthening shadow over the great public domain we are to see not the legendary pioneers so much as the land-speculating merchant capitalists. Indeed, land jobbing perhaps was the chief area of activity of American capital at certain periods: during 1816-19, again during 1833-37, and once more during 1854-57. During these years, whole townships passed under the control of speculating groups and companies so that single holdings of 5000 to 10,000 acres of unimproved land were common, and tracts of 50,000 to 100,000 were not unusual.

Even after industrial capitalism was beginning to raise its head, financial interests or individuals with surplus funds were more likely to acquire speculative land holdings than other forms of equities. In fact, it may be said that a characteristic of

mercantile capitalism was its tendency to speculate. Its necessity to keep its capital fund in a liquid form, its inability to tap
the resources of small savers, and its habituation to commerce
rather than industrial production naturally turned it to this
avenue of activity. In addition, special reasons made of speculation at certain intervals a necessity.

Oversea commerce, while its history was a glorious one, nevertheless did not present uninterrupted possibilities for expansion. The European trade was rich in opportunity until the
English orders in council and our own retaliatory embargo of
1807 and our Nonintercourse Act of 1809 cut its life short. The
Far Eastern trade was spectacular, until England opened the
Indian and Chinese markets to all her merchants. By the 1830's
our position in this commerce was declining. Similarly, domestic manufacturing was developing only on a small scale and its
promise was not great enough, before the 1850's, to attract large
aggregations of capital. But in the land and in those capitalist
activities associated with the land, notably canal and railroad
financing and building, there were to be found endless fields for
ready investment, quick turnovers, and large (at least, on paper)
profits. The role that the land played as an outlet for capital
manipulation is of the first importance, therefore, toward an
understanding of the Middle Period. Land speculation, as the
experiences of the panics of 1819, 1837, and—most important of
all—1857 showed, was too speculative, however: land jobbers
emerged poorer rather than richer men. After 1857, forward
enterprisers began to understand, capitalism's salvation lay in
industrial production aided and encouraged by a sympathetic
state.

A variety of forces contributed to make possible the development of a great speculative land interest. Even before the adoption of a general land policy, the central government had
employed the device of large grants to private companies for the
purpose of obtaining a revenue quickly. Every outstanding
capitalist of the first decade of the new nation's history was
involved in these companies, the greatest of them, Robert Morris, controlling 6,000,000 acres of land at one time. The program
of 1796-1854, as has been pointed out, continued to play into

the hands of the land speculators. A series of enactments, from
the end of the Revolution up to 1855, served the purpose of
turning over land warrants to returned soldiers and furnished
further opportunities for speculative enterprise. In this connection, after the Revolution, the Virginia Military Reserve in
Ohio and, after the war with Mexico, the state of Illinois
became the happy hunting grounds of land dealers. On good
authority we have the estimate that, from 1849 to 1857, 12,000,-
000 acres of the public domain in Illinois passed into the hands
of speculators, largely by the route of the military warrants.

Into the Middle West particularly poured the surplus funds
of New England, Middle States, and southern capitalists. In
fact, in northern Indiana, which was overrun by absentee landlordism, Yankee investors from New England were commonly
referred to as the "Yale Crowd." And of Illinois, Professor Paul
W. Gates writes:

> The role of the speculator has been one of profound importance
> in the history of Illinois. He preceded the settler, selected the choice
> locations, purchased them with land warrants or cash, surveyed and
> located them and then sought to turn immigration into his section.
> He was foremost in the advocacy of canals, railroads, plank roads
> and river improvements; to secure these his influence was exerted
> on the legislature, on county and city organizations and on Congress.
> As a factor in politics his influence cannot be overestimated.

Finally, we are to note the close links forged between finance
and the land-speculation interest. The Second Bank of the
United States was, during its whole history, deeply involved in
the financing of land schemes, and much of the hostility that it
engendered in the West was due to the fact that it pressed its
mortgagors closely and, in times of stress, chose to foreclose.
Indeed, the first American settlements in Texas in 1821 would
have been impossible had not Austin been backed by a New
Orleans banker who had waxed rich on land deals in the
Louisiana Territory. The pouring of Americans into the Spanish region and the subsequent Texas Republic became a mighty
flood precisely because the financing of Texas land associations
and of Texas state enterprises was gladly undertaken by specu-

lators, who, however, were quick to unload the shares and land scrip on gullible investing publics. Not least among the financial forces were the state banks, many of which were built upon dealings in land. Their paper issues furnished the means by which the speculations were continued.

Town jobbing in the newly opened-up regions of course was an important item in the land operations of the speculators. Starting as early as the activities of the great companies in Ohio immediately after the Revolution, speculation in town sites was to be found continuing up to the very end of the Middle Period. Insiders obtained the choicest sections on river and lake fronts; laid out, for example, the towns of Marietta, Cincinnati, and Cleveland; divided the paper communities into squares and lots; and waited for the settlers to come to provide them that unearned increment that was to become the basis of a few moderate American fortunes. Unhappy Kansas bled so profusely at every pore in the 1850's partly because the eastern land speculators saw in it a paradise of profits. Professor Arthur C. Cole records that the first governor of the territory, upon his arrival, bought town lots in some of the early communities and proceeded to lay out Pawnee City as his own private speculation. Lawrence and other free-state settlements were also the projects of eastern speculators. And Cole quotes a Kansas settler: "If it was not for land and town speculations, there would have been no trouble in Kansas."

The crisis of 1837, as has already been indicated, was one of the many series of crops of tares that land speculation sowed. In the years immediately preceding the panic, every public land office became an exchange thronged with milling dealers who bought pre-emption claims, soldier lands, and government sections and who often paid for them in the "rag money" of the wildcat banks. So, the American Land Company, organized in 1835 to speculate in southwestern lands and town sites, appeared with a capitalization of $1,000,000, four fifths of which was subscribed within a year. The significance of public land sales in furnishing outlets for capitalist activities may be seen from the fact that governmental receipts from this source mounted from $1,216,000 in 1825 to $25,167,000 in 1836, and fell to $7,000,000 in 1837.

The 1850's saw the speculative land mania reaching its final heights. There was one break in the trade following the recession of 1851; then in 1854 the fever chart began to mount again until, in 1857, it was estimated, more than $800,000,000 was invested in land deals. When the crash came in 1857—a crash that had world-wide repercussions—it shook not merely the jerry-built edifice of the speculators but the whole structure of mercantile capitalism as well. Vast paper fortunes were made in land speculation; and sizable real sums were lost in it. Many speculators, who had held on throughout the whole decade, paying interest, taxes, and agents' fees, were forced to sell at distress prices or were wiped out. They were replaced by landlords of a sterner breed; as Professor Gates reports the situation in northern Indiana:

The new owners were generally Hoosiers who lived in the prairie counties where they had already built up considerable fortunes from cattle trade, railroad construction, banking and the sale of town lots. They were a part of the community, had grown up with it and were now showing their confidence in it by investing their surplus at home. They were an aggressive group of men who had the capital and the driving force to make the prairies productive.

It is significant to note that no outstanding merchant-capitalist fortune emerged out of wild land speculation. By the late 1850's, American capitalism had learned this very important lesson.

CHAPTER SIXTEEN

The Exploitation of the Public Domain

1. THE FUR TRADE AND MINING

THE West furnished other opportunities for capitalist enterprise. Among these the most important in the trans-Mississippi West, certainly for the greater part of half a century, was the fur trade. Like the colonial fur trade, the trade of the Middle Period was organized not on an individual but on a capitalist basis. Stretching from the Mississippi to the far Pacific Coast was a vast virgin tract peopled by the wild creatures of the plain and the forest. The buffalo and the beaver were hunted and trapped by the nomadic Indians and their peltries and hides brought to the many stations that a few great fur companies had erected in the wilderness. The early companies, with monopoly concessions, were dominated by British capital. But in the first decade of the nineteenth century, the American John Jacob Astor arose to challenge the exclusive grip on the fur trade of these English concessionaires.

Astor's conception was as wide as that of the later western railroad king James J. Hill: he sought to link the occidental and oriental worlds over a bridge of trade. Looking to the erection of a vast number of posts throughout the trans-Mississippi West with their eastern terminus St. Louis and their western at the mouth of the Columbia River, Astor visualized a steady stream of goods from New York to St. Louis for the Indian trade and the collection of the peltries at the Columbia River for their export to China. With this plan in mind he organized the American Fur Company in New York at a capitalization of $1,000,-000 and began his attack upon the British and his other rivals. His methods were various. He bought into one of the British companies and thus made it his own. He succeeded in prevailing upon Congress, in 1816, to drive British capital in the fur business out of America. He had an end put to the public factories, or stations, on the Indian lands so that the hunters and trappers could do business only with the private traders. And he overcame and absorbed his native American rivals in the business by the customary devices of large-scale enterprise. By 1830 the American Fur Company, with its posts all over the backwoods Far West and its branch offices in every European country, was doing virtually all the buying and selling of American furs. But the business was to have only a brief life, as Astor was quick to understand. The impending exhaustion of all the beaver meadows and the change in men's fashions in hats began to show their effects in 1830. In 1834 Astor began to retire from the fur business. He moved his vast fortune into improved urban real estate and he and his heirs watched it multiply as New York City continued to grow into the great metropolis of the Western World and to pile up unearned increment for the Astor family. The Astors have remained great landlords into our very day.

Mining was another important center for capitalist enterprise in the West. In the Missouri country early pioneers found a rich natural reserve of silver, zinc, iron, black manganese—and particularly lead. Lead also was discovered in southwestern Wisconsin and in western Illinois: and large mercantile-capitalist fortunes began to be reared upon the smelting of and dealing in this humble mineral. Eastern capital flowed into Wisconsin in the 1820's and by 1828 more than 1,000,000 pounds of lead was being produced in this region. Indeed, in the case of the Illinois lead fields, located around Galena, one of the important reasons for the interest of eastern capital in the projected Illinois Central Railroad, in the late 1840's, was the creation of transportation facilities for this enterprise. The copper deposits of Michigan, too, in the 1840's and 1850's were attracting eastern capital and the fields began to be worked by miners moved over from the lead districts. One of the early great American fortunes, that of William E. Dodge, was built up largely in these far western copper fields.

The close linking of mining and mercantile pursuits is perhaps best illustrated in the character of the American capitalist interest in the Pacific Coast. Yankee traders had penetrated into the Spanish territory of California even before the turn of the century. They had begun to carry on a barter in otter skins for the China trade; they had developed whaling stations from which their ships hunted the whales in Pacific waters; they had branched out into the hide and tallow business, ranging as far north as the Russian possessions and south into deep Mexican territory. Later in the century the economy of the American settlers in the region partook of all the characteristics of the enterprise of the period. Thus, John A. Sutter, located in Sacramento Valley in the 1850's, herded cattle, ran a distillery, tannery, and a gristmill, and dealt in hides and peltries. The discovery of gold in California in 1848 and the beginning of the gold rush into the area the next year resulted in a great increase in the gold supply of the nation, of course; but it more particularly enriched the traders and merchants who were prepared to profit from the extraordinary increase in population. In 1848, California could boast of 10,000 souls; in 1850, its population had grown to 100,000.

The gold miners were not large-scale producers and, indeed, few single important mining fortunes were built in this initial era of far western gold digging. Upon the narrow base of gold mining, however, was reared a broad structure of trade and speculation. It was at this point that the mighty profits of mercantile capitalism were located. The provision of transportation facilities in the overland and oversea routes to California, the building up of San Francisco as the great entrepôt of the region, the supplying of food and furnishings for the prospectors engaged in the gold fields, the operation of stores, hotels, gambling hells, and the like: here were the places where accumulation took place and from which capital later flowed into railroading and timber and mineral lands. The promoters of the Central Pacific and the Southern Pacific Railroads were merchant princes whose fortunes were made possible by the appearance of the gold miners in California. Indeed, Charles Crocker, Leland Stanford, Collis P. Huntington, Mark Hopkins—great names in the early history of California—were not miners but peddlers, shopkeepers, and merchants who piled up large fortunes in mercantile pursuits and added to them from railroad building and land speculation.

2. THE EXPANSION OF THE PUBLIC DOMAIN

Capital thus led the way into the West in the Middle Period; and a governmental program of westward expansion furnished capital those rich opportunities for enterprise of which we have been speaking. At the formal close of the Revolution—by the Peace of Paris in 1783—the United States ruled over an area bounded on the south by the northern limits of Spanish Florida and on the west by the Mississippi River. At the opening of the decade of the 1850's, the continental domain stretched clear across to the Pacific Coast on the west, up to the forty-ninth parallel on the north, and lay across the Gulf of Mexico on the south. The continental possession was rounded out by purchase, conquest, and international agreement.

The early settlers of the trans-Allegheny West quickly found that their fortunes were linked with the Mississippi; and the presence of foreign and at times unfriendly powers at the mouth of the river was a source of irritation and economic danger. The early western staples of furs, hemp, grains, live-stock, timber, and tobacco were moved on its broad expanse into domestic and foreign commerce by way of New Orleans. The right of free deposit, at this entrepôt, therefore, became a topic of regular diplomatic exchanges with Spain, which had acquired the city in 1763. The right of deposit was granted for short intervals until 1798 and then terminated. After the city's acquisition by France in 1801 the port was opened again for a short time and then again closed. To put an end to this nuisance Jefferson authorized a group of American commissioners to enter into negotiations with Napoleon for the purchase of New Orleans and West Florida. They ended, in May, 1803, by signing a treaty for the acquisition of the whole vast French holding in America. By the Louisiana Purchase the United States gained possession of a territory 828,000,000 acres in extent which included, roughly, the regions watered by the Mississippi-Missouri Rivers system; and for it paid $11,250,000 in 6 per cent bonds and assumed the claims of American nationals against France for a total amount of $3,750,000.

That same western expansionist sentiment which had made the men of the western waters such bitter foes of Great Britain, and which had played such an important part in precipitating the War of 1812, regarded with resentment the presence of the Spaniard in Florida. Florida, also, constituted a missing piece in the economic plan of the trans-Allegheny Southeast. In its swamps were havens for runaway slaves; Indian relations—and Indian land titles—could never be satisfactorily adjusted until the weak Spanish grip on the territory had been loosened; also, into Florida ran a series of rivers the settlers of east Tennessee and of Mississippi territory needed to control in order to reach the sea. American patriots helped to foment uprisings in West Florida so that it was possible to annex the territory with a clear conscience during 1810-14. In 1819 East Florida was purchased from Spain for $5,000,000. None of this amount, it is interesting to note, reached Madrid, for all of it was required to settle American claims against Spain.

The possession of Texas and the Mexican territories clear to the Pacific came next. Americans had begun to press into Texas as early as 1821 on the basis of land grants received from the Spanish government and with the assistance of the capital furnished by American land companies. By 1830 there were some 20,000 American settlers in the region engaged in cattle raising and the cultivation of cotton. The Mexican government, concerned about its ability to absorb this alien population and to put a check on its hunger for land, sought to close the door to further immigration. Spurred on by southern fire-eaters, who saw in Texas a vast region for the expansion of the slave and plantation system, the Texans demanded autonomy and when this was refused they revolted. The Texas Republic was established in 1836 and efforts were begun for its annexation by the United States.

The pressure from the southern plantation interest, the cries for relief of the holders of the paper of Texas land companies and of the bonds and the land scrip of the Texas Republic, and the desire of American merchants in California to stabilize their position on the Pacific Coast: all these forces drove public policy in the direction of an armed attack on Mexico. For these reasons the short war with Mexico was a popular one; and as a result of its successful outcome Mexico lost an empire and the United States gained one. By the treaty of peace of 1848, Mexico recognized America's annexation of Texas, ceded New Mexico and California upon the payment of $15,000,000, and permitted the United States to assume the claims of American nationals against Mexico. In 1853 the southwest domain was rounded out when, for $10,000,000, the United States purchased a strip of land on the Mexican border which contained the lowest passes of the Rockies. This area was needed to facilitate the building of a Pacific railroad by a southern route.

The danger of strife with Great Britain over the fixing of the northwest boundary for a time actually threatened. Expansionists and economic interests in the area wanted to see the line put at 54°40′, which was deep into Canadian territory. But moderate counsels prevailed—obviously it would be difficult fighting the Mexicans and the British at the same time—with the result that in 1846 the frontier was run along the forty-ninth parallel. The continental expansion of the United States was now finished.

3. THE SETTLEMENT OF THE PUBLIC DOMAIN

The settlers of the West—settlers in the sense of permanent dwellers who cut out clearings from timber lands and river bottoms, who penetrated into the prairies to erect improvements, lay out communities, and provide social services—were agriculturists who came to grow wheat and fatten hogs and cattle in the northern section and to grow tobacco, hemp, sugar, and cotton in the southern. They were commercial farmers bringing capital along with them and requiring short- and long-term funds to permit them to produce for a market. Self-sufficing agriculture in the West was a brief and transitory phase in the American economy: the western settlers were caught in the tangled relations of the cash nexus quite from the very beginning.

The movement into the West was slow, hazardous, and costly. Using every conceivable conveyance and method of transportation, with household goods piled into the Conestoga wagons of the period, or heaped on canal and river boats; and walking, driving, carried by canal boat, river steamer, and later by train, the endless stream of settlers poured into the West year after year. The introduction of the steamboat on the western waters after 1812 and the opening up of the Erie Canal after 1825 created new arteries of travel; the connecting links of feeder canals and railroads permitted settlers to penetrate regions hitherto inaccessible to the white men. They came from the older communities of the East—notably from New England and the Middle Atlantic States and from the southern backcountry counties—and from Europe. They came as farmers to farm—and they filled up the vast, rich, empty void of continental America.

The waves of internal migration more or less synchronized with periods of business upturn in the settled areas in the East. That is to say, farming populations migrated westward not when the pinch of hard times, falling prices, and debt pressures made continuance under older dispensations undesirable or unendurable, as has been argued by many historians, but when good prices put cash in their pockets. The first great push into the West, immediately after the termination of the Revolution, brought a sizable population into the trans-Allegheny country and filled Kentucky and Tennessee with almost a quarter million of southern folk. Kentucky was admitted into the Union in 1792; Tennessee in 1796. The second movement took place at the turn of the century: Ohio was settled and became a state in 1803. The third movement—on a wider front and with greater volume this time, as a result of the addition of European immigrants to the host of settlers—began with the recovery following the hard times after the end of the Napoleonic Wars. The population of the West doubled and doubled again each decade from 1810 to 1830. In that interval the six new states of Louisiana (1812), Indiana (1816), Mississippi (1817), Illinois (1818), Alabama (1819), and Missouri (1821) were admitted into the Union. The fourth wave followed the end of the depression of 1837. Settlers, this time more heavily supported by contingents from Europe, pressed into the Northwest and Southwest to claim from the wilderness Michigan (admitted 1837), Iowa (1846), and Wisconsin (1848) in one section and Arkansas (1836) and Texas (1845) in the other. The movement westward reached flood tide in the decade of the 1850's due to European political disturbances and domestic prosperity. By 1860, there were more than 12,000,000 people in the American West, with the distribution between the two sections somewhat as follows: the Northwest had grown from 50,000 population in 1800 and 790,000 population in 1820 to 7,600,000 in 1860; the Southwest had grown from 335,000 population in 1800 and 1,345,000 population in 1820 to 4,730,000 in 1860.

4. EUROPEAN IMMIGRATION

Mention has been made of the fact that the human conquest of the West was assisted by the participation of European immigrants in the advance. All the new arrivals from Europe, of course, did not move westward: many European peasants could not because of their inability to command the necessary capital funds; and the urban dwellers obviously gravitated toward the cities to fill America's growing slums. Workers were needed on canals and railroads and in the mines and textile mills of the East. In this net many European immigrants from the British Isles and the Continent were caught and they never lived to see those wide rolling plains of the West whose magic had so fired their imaginations when they had taken ship for America. For the most part they hoarded in cities, watched their children grow up malnourished and stunted, and stood by dazed when the waves of prejudice beat about them.

The immigrant host began to pour in slowly. From 1789 to 1820, the average estimated number of aliens reaching America was not more than 7700 annually; during the 1820's, the annual average was 14,300; in the next decade it was 59,900; but in the 1840's, it was 171,300; and in the 1850's, 259,800. In the single year 1854, the number of new arrivals was 427,833. By 1860, 12.9 per cent of the total population of the country was made up of foreign born as against 14.4 per cent Negroes and 72.7 per cent native-born white. The immigrants came largely from the United Kingdom, Ireland, and Germany, and in each case the spur to flight was given by economic distress at home and the hope for economic improvement in the New World. Only in the case of a sizable company of German immigrants, following the unsuccessful revolutions of 1848, was the primary motive for migration of a political character; although many of these were members of a middle class whose opportunities for economic enterprise at home were being curbed by arbitrary, absolutist governments.

5. AGRICULTURE IN THE FREE STATES

As was to be expected—every period of expanding economy has told the same tale—agriculture in the free states enjoyed boom times. It was reorganized and integrated. Its efficiency was improved through partial mechanization. And it was put on a capitalist footing so that it might satisfy the constantly mounting requirements of both domestic and foreign markets. New transportation facilities, linking West and East, gave the American commercial farmer not a local but a national market; the industrialization and urbanization of western Europe and the throwing open of the English ports to American foodstuffs with the repeal of the Corn Laws gave him a great foreign one. During the Middle Period, therefore, American free agriculture grew to full maturity. Its speed of technical advance was not even, however, for about twenty-five years after the close of the Revolution there was little or no improvement over the still primitive methods of the Colonial Period. From 1810 to 1840, progress was surer but not very rapid. But from 1840 to 1860 changes for the better appeared with almost lightninglike speed.

Not only more wild lands, of course, but also more previously uncultivated land on farms were brought under the plow. Agricultural techniques were improved as crop rotation became a general practice. Natural and artificial fertilizer came to be employed. Hardier seed strains were introduced to overcome plant pests and diseases. As the area of extensive cultivation—particularly the production of small grains—slowly moved westward from the Connecticut River Valley across New York and Pennsylvania and even beyond Ohio and Indiana finally to rest on the prairies, intensive tillage appeared in the East. The demands of local markets for foodstuffs led to the appearance of truck farming, fruit culture, dairying, and the cultivation of artificial grasses in those regions where it had become too expensive to sow and harvest wheat, rye, and barley.

Beginning with the 1840's, wheat began to appear on the large prairie farms of Iowa and Nebraska; corn—as the great animal feed of hogs and cattle—crowded the fields of the East North Central States; while in Connecticut, New York, and eastern Pennsylvania farmers became husbandmen and experimented successfully with blooded Merino sheep and dairy cattle. One of the signs of the intensification of agricultural production in the East appeared exactly at this point: beginning as early as the 1800's for sheep and during the 1820's and 1830's for dairy stock, American agriculturists imported large quantities of foreign-bred animals which they crossed with native varieties in order to develop breeds which could thrive best under American conditions. They succeeded, and woolgrowing and the production of butter and cheese for domestic markets became significant agricultural activities.

The improvement of farm equipment and the partial mechanization of production, due on the one hand to a shortage of labor and on the other to the demands of the market, inevitably followed. Hand tools and wagons were better; plows first with iron moldboards and then with reversible moldboards (for use on hillsides) made their appearance; so did cultivators; the threshing machine came to replace the flail on commercial farms. In the 1840's a working mechanical reaper, perfected after many years of tinkering by Obed Hussey and Cyrus McCormick, at last made its appearance and the prairies were conquered. Iron and steel plows could turn up their tough sod; the horse-drawn reaper made possible the harvesting of vast stretches of ripened grain; the thresher quickly separated the grain from the chaff; and first sod and then wire fences were introduced to keep the livestock out of the fields of growing grain. Commercial farmers on the prairies were really operating factory farms.

The census of 1860 recognized the revolution in increased productivity that improved agricultural implements and machines had effected when it made the following comment:

By the improved plow, labor equivalent to that of one horse in three is saved. By means of drills two bushels of seed will go as far as three bushels scattered broadcast, while the yield is increased six to eight bushels per acre; the plants come up in rows and may be tended by horse-hoes. . . . The reaping machine is a saving of more than one-third the labor when it cuts and rakes. . . . The threshing machine is a saving of two-thirds on the old hand flail mode. . . . The saving in the labor of handling hay in the field and barn by means of horserakes and horsehayforks is equal to one-half.

Agricultural prices were good. Absolutely, farm prices rose higher than general commodity prices during the greater part of the Middle Period. Relatively, the price position of the commercial farmer in the free states was even better, thanks to the reduction of his unit costs through superior techniques and mechanization. The following other contributory factors are to be noted. The farmer possessed the advantage of competitive modes of transportation—monopolist railroad rings had not yet appeared to oppress him—to move his crops to market. His livestock he butchered himself or permitted local packers to handle for him instead of being compelled to send them to the few cash markets of the later monopolist packers. Crop failures in Europe during 1846, 1848, 1853, and 1854 and the widening English market gave him a superior international position. The American free farmer thus was prospering: his land values regularly mounted; the prices he received were more than good in terms of his purchasing power; and he bought, as a result, vast quantities of finished goods turned out by mills, forges, and factories.

By 1860, so rapidly did land use shift, the great area of wheat production was to be found in Ohio, Indiana, Illinois, Wisconsin, and Michigan, with Illinois the leading producer. The leading corn-growing states were Illinois, Ohio, and Missouri. The cattle-raising states were no longer those of the East, where barnyard feeding had been the rule, but Texas, Missouri, and Iowa, where beef animals grazed on the open plains. Yearlings were sent to Illinois, Ohio, and Indiana for fattening before being moved on to the stockyards. Sheep and swine were to be found throughout the United States, it is true, but principally in the states of the Middle West.

When the western states threw in their lot with the North, at the outbreak of the Civil War, it was not because farmer discontent made them restless. It was because northern agriculture, East and West, was rapidly becoming commercialized and its future destinies inevitably were linked with the expanding markets of capitalist production rather than with the contracted market of the slave and plantation system. One of the important reasons why the Republican party in 1860 was able to drive a wedge between the ranks of the country's agrarian host and win away many western agricultural regions from their old alliance with the southern Democracy was to be found in this crucial fact: western agriculture was soundly established during a period when the southern plantation economy was being shaken to its foundations.

CHAPTER SEVENTEEN

Internal Commerce and Mercantile Capitalism

1. WATERWAYS AND CANALS

IN PROVIDING internal transport facilities, early American capitalist enterprise discovered rich opportunities for expansion and accumulation. Indeed, it was at this point that there was to be found first that concentration and combination of capital resources which is so peculiarly the hallmark of our modern era. Roads and the improvement of interior waterways early attracted the attention of public authority. Canals were built with public funds raised by the flotation of issues sold in foreign money markets. Into the construction of the rails entered capital diverted from eastern mercantile enterprise, contributed by public bodies, and invested by foreign *rentiers*. As a result of such a concentration, it was no accident that when the first giant integrations emerged in the 1860's they should be in the field of railroading. It should be had in mind, however, that railroading, like industrial production, was really transformed in the fires of the Civil War. The investors in American rails in the Middle Period, notably those who put their funds into western rails, looked to obtain profits not from railroad operation so much as from the speculative rise in the land values of those sections of the public domain with which these companies were so richly dowered. In other words, even the building of the western railroads in the 1850's, when capital entered this field so heavily, was to a very real extent on a mercantile-capitalist basis.

Hard-surface road building was among the first interests that the released American capital turned to with the erection of the central government. Organizing into stock companies, enterprisers received franchises for the maintenance of private roads along which they might erect bridges and put up tollgates. The first such important road was built over a distance of sixty-two miles between the cities of Philadelphia and Lancaster, Pennsylvania; it cost almost a half million dollars and its immediate financial success encouraged imitation. Before long, most of the eastern states were chartering similar companies and, in fact, also investing public funds in them.

The necessity for reaching the West by overland routes forced the central government to inaugurate a program of public works in road building. In 1806 Congress finally yielded to pressure and authorized the building of that great Cumberland Road which preoccupied statesmen up to the 1850's. With its eastern terminus on the Potomac River, the road was pushed through the Alleghenies to the Ohio River and thence across Ohio, Indiana, and Illinois. The highway was of immeasurable assistance in the opening of the West. It presented opportunities for new forms of business in the creation of stagecoach and express companies, and it encouraged the states to accept the idea of road building as a customary social service. While, after the 1830's, as a result of President Jackson's decision, the central government stopped building highways, it continued to subsidize their construction indirectly by land grants for this purpose to the states.

The interior waterways of the country were opened up with the appearance of the steamboat on the western waters. Of course the great rivers of the western country had been used before the steamboat was invented: mention has been made of the part played by the Mississippi River in the acquisition of the Louisiana Territory. River navigation had decided advantage over land transport. There were no tolls to pay, no work animals to take care of, and no bad inns at which to put up. But floating goods down the rivers on keelboats and flatboats was a slow process and the return journeys were difficult. The development of the steamboat was a real boon to the farmers and merchants of the western states. That they quickly grasped its potentialities can be seen from the enormous increase in river traffic and the rise of the river towns.

Thanks to the steamboat, the Mississippi River during the 1830's and 1840's became the all-important artery of the whole great interior valley; and the number of such boats grew from 60 in 1820 to 1200 in 1848. Pittsburgh, Wheeling, and Cincinnati became important entrepôts and shipbuilding points; Louisville, Lexington, and St. Louis rose to eminence as key market towns. Into these communities capital readily flowed. And centered at New Orleans, the outlet to the sea of much of the produce of the West, there flourished a large company of merchant capitalists consisting of bankers, factors, warehousemen, and dealers who financed, speculated in, and handled tobacco, wheat, hemp, cotton, livestock, meat products, and the rest. At the beginning of the 1830's, the receipts of interior goods at New Orleans totaled $26,000,000 annually in value; by the early 1850's the total annual value of goods was $108,000,-000. New Orleans, nevertheless, was falling behind in the race with New York: for the fifties began to mark the declining significance of the river as feeder canals linked the interior northwest country with the Great Lakes and furnished the cereal and meat growers of the region an outlet to the sea via the Erie Canal and the Hudson River. In fact by 1846 the receipts of wheat and flour at Buffalo already surpassed those at New Orleans.

Canals had been built locally in America before the appearance of the Erie Canal. It was this great project, however, that launched the era of canal construction in the country and made this method of interior transport the most significant one until the maturity of railroading. Starting in 1817, and depending entirely upon its public credit (its bonds were taken up largely by English investors), New York State began the construction of a shallow ditch 360 miles long. In 1825 this watercourse from Albany to Buffalo was completed. The state had expended between $7,000,000 and $8,000,000 on the improvement; in less than ten years its capital cost had been met from toll charges. The canal was sensationally successful from a financial and an economic point of view. It reduced the time required for shipping freight from Buffalo to New York by two thirds, lowered costs from $100 to $10 a ton, and opened New York to the great raw-material products of the western country. Also, it forced the shift of New England agriculture from cereals and speeded the development of Cleveland, Detroit, and Chicago; and it prompted other states to emulate New York's example.

Canals began to crisscross Pennsylvania, New Jersey, Ohio, and Indiana. The fever touched legislators as far west as Illinois and Michigan. Almost all the southern states began to lay plans and raise funds for vast public improvement schemes with canal construction as the pivotal point. Of course, these plans also included road and bridge building and—after 1827, when Maryland had chartered the Baltimore and Ohio—the laying out of railways. Capital from every center of accumulation flowed into these projects. The federal government made land grants; private funds were invested in feeder railroads and guaranteed against loss by the states; the southern states chartered land banks under state patronage and these agencies issued bonds secured by private mortgage paper; others erected public banks; the English money market—lulled into security by the success of the Erie Canal—responded again and again to the call for funds.

The upshot was the piling up of a mountain of state debt. In 1820, the American states were free of obligations; in 1838, their indebtedness stood at $170,000,000; and in 1842, at $200,000,-000. Almost all these bonds had been purchased by foreign investors, largely the English. Most of the issues had been floated to make possible the launching of the great public-works program. Thus, in 1842, it has been estimated, $126,000,000 of the combined state debt was for the construction of canals, roads, and railroads; and another $56,000,000 was for state aid to banks, many of which also had financed public works. Boom times did not last very long in view of the fact that most of the canals and almost all of the railroads were far in advance of population and markets. They were, in short, purely of a speculative character: and when canals and railroads brought in no revenues and debt services could not be met, the whole towering edifice crashed in the panic of 1837. The overextension of credit to land companies, as we have seen, and the drop in the price of cotton abroad contributed to the same result.

As a result of the collapse, many American states took the

route of default and repudiation. In 1841 and 1842, nine states stopped paying interest. Michigan repudiated a portion of her obligations; while Mississippi and Florida invalidated all of theirs. The states defaulting were Indiana, Illinois, Louisiana, Arkansas, Pennsylvania, and Maryland. It has been estimated that foreign investors lost $40,000,000 through such repudiations and defaults. So badly were the English, notably, burned that (with the exception of the financing of the Illinois Central Railroad in 1850) fully a whole generation had to elapse before the oversea investor was prepared again to touch an American security.

2. THE COMING OF THE RAILS

By 1850, the processes of canal expansion were finished. The railroad had emerged on the horizon. Many of the technical difficulties it had presented—in connection with the right kind of rails, a uniform gauge, bridges—had been overcome; and it was beginning to attract public interest and private capital. The early railroads (the first one was open for use in 1830) were distinctly of a parochial character. Regarded only as feeders to waterways and canals, and laid down frequently for the purpose of deflecting local trade from one center to another, they were built from small subscriptions and in considerable measure as patriotic ventures. In New England, for example, where much of the initial construction took place, the lines were short north and south roads running down the river valleys to Long Island Sound; as late as 1850, their average length was but 36 miles; and it was not until this decade that New York and New Haven were linked. The greatest triumph of the rails was reached, in the late 1840's, when the traveler was able to journey from Buffalo to Albany over a dozen short lines with the attending inconveniences of car changes and waits. In all, by 1850, the total length of construction, after two decades of building, was but 9000 miles. The next decade saw more than 20,000 miles of road laid down; the value of the railroad net, by 1860, was $1,000,000,000.

The introduction of large capital funds into railroading accounts for its quick maturing. Although this is not generally known, public moneys really played the pioneering role. Thus, the Baltimore and Ohio, the first state-chartered railroad in America, received from Maryland $500,000 in 1828 and another $3,200,000 in 1836. This latter sum Maryland raised in the English money market. Similarly, the Western Railway of Massachusetts received from that state $4,300,000 in bonds, the funds also raised in England. States also gave lands to private companies, pledged their credit to help the financing, and even bought stock in the ventures. Municipalities erected terminals and made stock subscriptions. The federal government, beginning with 1850, made generous grants from the public domain to assist the railroad promoters in raising their funds. Private capital began to enter into the field, notably in conjunction with the building of the great western systems.

Indeed, it is at this point exactly that we begin to note the uncertainties and dilemmas of New England and New York mercantile capitalism in the 1850's. In the 1840's the possibilities of the New England fisheries, whaling industry, and carrying trade generally appear to have reached their outward limits of extension. Movement into more profitable fields was imperative. The railroads seemed promising, particularly the western roads, if the central government could be involved. Northern mercantile capital was ready to promote and to a certain extent underwrite construction of trunk lines in the western country if Congress was prepared to guarantee the investment. In short, huge grants from the public domain, along the rights of way, would protect the investments of the capitalists by making the railroad companies first and foremost land companies and only later, after the regions their lines penetrated had become settled, transportation organizations. The history of the Illinois Central Railroad adequately illustrates this whole tendency.

The state of Illinois had become, almost, a vast speculative arena during the 1830's and 1840's. Pushed by the agents of land companies and their politician, lawyer, and publisher friends, legislators had involved the commonwealth in a ruinously costly public-works program. At one time, the debt service on the state's outstanding obligations, incurred in the building of roads and canals, was in excess of its annual reve-

nues. But this program had borne little fruit. The state had not
filled up with eager agriculturists ready, by their toil and industry, to enhance the value of the unimproved rural lands of
the speculators and to make out of Cairo and Chicago busy
marts of commerce—to the profit of the lot jobbers who held the
choicest water-front and lake-shore sites. To protect these stakes
the dealers themselves and their political friends—Webster,
Douglas, Rantoul—thronged the lobbies of Congress and the
Illinois legislature in an effort to obtain more public works in
order to hasten settlement. Other pressures came from absentee
investors in the depreciated state bonds—who could hope to
realize on their securities only if Illinois' revenues were built
up via the route of an increased population—and from northern
merchant capitalists who were ready to move money into the
state if guarantees were adequate.

A variety of projects was considered. Originally there was
powerful support for the building of a railroad—through the
public domain and on the basis of generous land grants to the
promoters—from Cairo, at the confluence of the Ohio and Mississippi Rivers, to Galena, the center of the Illinois lead industry.
But a much more grandiose scheme emerged: nothing less than
a line from Chicago down the center of the continent with its
southern terminus at Mobile on the Gulf of Mexico. This
Congress approved in 1850, thanks to the tireless efforts of
Douglas, by turning over in trust to the states of Illinois, Mississippi, and Alabama alternate even sections (with provision for
indemnity lands) on each side for six miles along the railroad's
right of way. This regal domain in all came to include 2,500,000
acres of the richest land in America. It was to be the reward of
the railroad promoters upon the completion of the separate legs
of the railroad.

The struggle for a charter from the Illinois legislature to
build the Illinois Central was a prolonged one. Rantoul, representative of the Massachusetts capitalists, hastened to Springfield and, by all the devices familiar to modern-day lobbying
(newspapers were bought up and statesmen received "loans"
of money), finally obtained the charter for his principals. He
estimated its value then at $6,000,000. In the course of time the

Illinois Central realized $25,000,000 from the sale of the public lands which its promoters had received as a bonus for the building of the line.

The seven hundred miles of road were built in six years at a cost of $16,500,000. Much of the capital came from the East out of the shipping, fishing, whaling, and mercantile fortunes of the Griswolds, Morrises, Schuylers, Aspinwalls, and Neals of New York and Boston. The larger part came from English investors who bought the bonds (and got the stock thrown in) on the basis of their belief that the land values would rise. Indeed, Anthony Trollope, the English novelist, shrewdly observed: "They [the backers of the road] purchased land, looking to increase the value of it fivefold by the opening of the railroad. . . . It is in this way that the thousands of miles of railroad in America have been opened." During the first half decade of its operation the road was in financial difficulties; one of its loans sold as low as 70; and assessments were levied on the stock. But the war business of the government, beginning with 1862, put it on its feet; the post-Civil War colonization projects of the railroad brought the settlers in; and the English continued to hold on to their control of the Illinois Central until well into the twentieth century.

CHAPTER EIGHTEEN

Foreign Commerce and Mercantile Capitalism

1. THE UNCERTAIN COURSE OF THE CARRYING TRADE

THE carrying trade had furnished the elaborate network of connections through which the lifeblood of colonial capitalism had flowed: and merchants of the North had been compelled to enter the Revolution to release colonial capitalism from the hobbles imposed upon unlimited enterprise by the Mercantile System. But freedom had brought in its train other predicaments. Save for relatively short intervals (and with, perhaps, the exception of the port of New York), the oversea carrying trade never succeeded in offering completely adequate opportunities for the absorption of American capital accumulations. The uneven history of American commerce during the Middle Period, therefore, is one of the most significant indications we have of the nature of the cul-de-sac northern enterprisers were finding themselves in as the second half of the decade of the 1850's opened. It had become evident that both wild land speculation and all the activities associated with the sea could no longer be relied upon, even in measurable degree, as fields for continued exploitation.

The end of the Revolution had brought with it new disappointments. Merchants were free to trade with Europe and the Near and Far East, but they were shut out of the English home and colonial carrying trades. An early British order in council allowed the admission of American tobacco, pig and bar iron, and naval stores into England upon the payment of duties; but foodstuffs were barred. Similarly, Americans might sell lumber, live animals, rice, naval stores, and tobacco to the British West Indian islands; but not prepared meat and fish. Where the shoe pinched disagreeably, however, was in the fact that such goods as were allowed could not enter in American ships: and those great fleets which had left Boston and New York periodically on their regular Caribbean runs had to seek other areas of trade.

For a short time—from 1794 to about 1807—their owners and masters found them in the Far Eastern trade and in supplying the expanded necessaries of a war-torn Europe. Bold American ships, putting out of Boston, New York, Philadelphia, and Salem, began to press their way around Cape Horn into the Pacific Ocean, making stops at northwest trading stations to take on cargoes of furs, peltries, and whale oil. Thence they proceeded to the Hawaiian Islands to pick up sandalwood. And these freights they carried in the long transpacific passage to China. Others rounded the Cape of Good Hope and sailed across the Indian Ocean with holds filled with flour, timber, tobacco, candles, and whale products: and at Canton and in the crowded islands of the Malay Archipelago they exchanged their heavy raw materials for the glamorous products of the East—spices, teas, silks, nankeens, chinaware. Rich fortunes were made by bold captains and supercargoes to build for them stately mansions in the Boston Back Bay and on many of the islands that dotted the coast of Massachusetts; and to furnish the capital surpluses that flowed into early New England textiles and into western canals and railroads.

The outbreak of the Napoleonic Wars in Europe also helped to tide American mercantile capital over a bad period. The great demand for foodstuffs and raw materials by all the belligerents and the need for shipping furnished golden opportunities for American shipowners, commission men, and brokers. The laws of neutrality sometimes were observed and sometimes not; and whether by legitimate or illegitimate means the United States became the great carrying nation of the world. V. S. Clark records that from 1795 to 1801 the average net earnings annually of the American merchant marine totaled $32,000,000; that American merchant shipping—all built in American yards— grew from 200,000 tons in 1789 to 1,425,000 tons in 1810. Capital moved into shipping rather than into manufacturing during those two decades when native manufacturing might have been expanded; also, the returns on goods and shipping services sold abroad came not in terms of foreign capital investments but in foreign manufactured goods.

England, of course, was engaged in a life-and-death struggle with Napoleon. But England was not too engrossed to fail to cast an uneasy glance in the direction of the tremendous expansion of the American carrying fleet and the penetration of Americans into European markets. England's orders in council of 1804-06 (like the orders in council of 1914-16) struck both at the enemy and at the growing American mercantile rival. Napoleon's retaliatory decrees and Jefferson's embargo and Nonintercourse Act also contributed to the work of destruction: and America's engagement with England in the War of 1812-15 was the final blow necessary to drive American shipping from the high seas. The conclusion of the European wars ended America's chances of recapturing her supremacy; for the English mercantile fleets again appeared to queen the seas.

The China trade also was short-lived. The Pacific Coast hunters were exterminating the sea otters, eliminating one important return in this transpacific intercourse; English and French manufacturers began to appear in the American market with good and cheap imitations of Chinese willowware, silks, and nankeens; only China tea remained, and this by 1850 came to be supplanted by Brazilian coffee as the outstanding American nonalcoholic beverage. Slowly New England capital began to disappear from the traffic and the great mercantile centers of New England fell into a permanent decline. By 1840, Boston had yielded first place in the Far Eastern trade to New York; and Salem became a town of pleasant little homes of retired seafaring men—and memories. The experiences of J. M. Forbes, one of the greatest of these Chinese traders, were symptomatic. He retired in 1837 from the oriental centers, sadly confessing to a correspondent that "competition is so sharp here that money must be made either by the most penurious saving in fitting ships or storing goods, etc., etc., or by being constantly on the lookout and giving up body and soul to managing business"; and he took his own capital and that of his New England mercantile friends and put it into the purchase of the Michigan Central Railroad in 1846.

The period 1818-30 was a particularly bad one for the American commerce and carrying trade. Shipments and freights earned dropped off sharply in the Chinese, West Indian, and eastern European trades. There was a short half decade of recovery during 1830-36, thanks to the abandonment by England of the Mercantile System and the American reduction of tariff duties. The years 1837-43 saw another severe recession. How acute it was may be noted from the fact that the total burden of American ships engaged in foreign trade was but 943,000 tons in 1843, which was smaller than the tonnage owned in 1810. From 1843 to 1857, American importers and exporters once more were making sizable profits and the American flag was to be seen on great fleets thronging foreign harbors. In this period the tonnage of American ships in the oversea trade almost trebled: however, the gain was only in absolute figures but not in relative position; and the gain was based on wholly transitory causes. When, after the panic of 1857, American shipping entered into a decline it was to be a permanent one for more than a half century: this door to mercantile-capitalist expansion was finally and irrevocably closed.

We may note the following causes for expansion in the years 1843-57. Extraordinary and temporary demands were made on American shipping services as a result of the repeal of the English Corn Laws, the Irish famine, and the outbreak of the Crimean War. The discovery of gold in California in 1848 and in Australia in 1851 created new markets that America could reach more easily than her European rivals. The triumphant appearance of the American clipper ships—those speedy, slender craft with inward curving sides and crowded sail—gave us a short and final day of glory in the late 1840's and early 1850's. The opening up of China and Japan by Cushing, Perry, and Townsend Harris for a few years revived the Far Eastern trade.

2. THE DECLINE OF THE CARRYING TRADE

All this was really illusory. If the American merchant fleet was growing, those of her competitors in the American carrying trade were growing faster. In the first years of the republic, virtually the whole of the foreign trade was carried in American bottoms; in 1826, 92.5 per cent of the foreign trade entered and cleared in American ships. By 1860, only 66.5 per cent of the value of all American imports and exports was carried under the American flag. The role of freight earnings in the balance of international payments was revealing. During the period 1821-49, American ships, as an annual average, had earned in freights approximately $20,000,000 as against the annual average earnings of $1,000,000 by foreign ships serving us: the ratio was 20 to 1 in our favor. During the period 1850-73, which was one of relative and finally absolute decline of our carrying trade, the figures were: annual average earnings of American shipping, $28,000,000; of foreign freights earned, $20,000,000; a ratio of only 1.4 to 1 in our favor.

What had happened? America had developed the swift clipper ship, it is true, and it was the most perfect full-rigged sailing vessel ever conceived by man. But the clipper ship, being made of wood, simply could not expand in size indefinitely. In short, there was a natural limitation to its earning capacity. Granting all the clipper ship's advantages, it was, therefore, hopelessly left behind in the mercantile race when the English iron steamboat made its appearance on the high seas. While the American yards continued to lay down those handsome but not particularly trustworthy vessels of spars and sail, the English were fabricating ugly little iron boats with boilers and smokestacks. They belched forth great clouds of smoke and they rolled in heavy seas, but in the long run they were safer and faster and their charges were lower because hold space was not limited. That the English once more should recapture supremacy of the high seas through the introduction of the iron ship was only natural. Their wrought-iron and metallurgical industries were developed far in advance of ours, which were still suffering under the limitations of mercantile-capitalist organization. They found it necessary to expand their shipping services as a counterweight to the increased importation of foodstuffs after the repeal of the Corn Laws. And they made lavish use of governmental subsidies.

In fact, the English had begun to use subsidies to encourage regular packet service across the Indian and Atlantic Oceans as early as the 1830's. The American Congress had followed tardily in 1845 with a mail subvention scheme and in 1846— over the grumblings of southern legislators who wanted low freights and low taxes—had converted this into a program of straight subventions for new ship construction. New American services were laid out; but all this was unavailing because of the technological superiority of the English and the niggardliness of the American subsidies. The English Peninsular and Oriental came to dominate the Eastern trade and the Cunard and Pacific Steam Navigation Company snatched the laurels away from us in the transpacific and transatlantic services. Slender as the prop of subsidy was, in 1858 it was removed altogether by the action of southern representatives in Congress.

The depression following the crisis of 1857 hit most of the great mercantile centers with particular severity. Boston became a ghost city as prices collapsed and freights sank so low that, as Morison records it, it paid shipowners to let their vessels rot at their wharfs.

New York City's position was more certain than that of Boston, Philadelphia, and Baltimore, her great maritime rivals: so that, by 1860, New York was handling two thirds of the country's imports and one third of its exports. This was partially due to the fact that New York continued as the great outlet for the nation's surplus grains and meat products; partially, it was because New York was so closely linked with the economic life of the South. In the 1820's, New York became the great pivot of the famous "cotton triangle." Southern cotton and other products from the section were moved first to New York before being carried overseas to British and French ports; and, similarly, European goods bound for the South passed through the hands and countinghouses of New York merchants before transshipment to Charleston, Savannah, Mobile, and New Orleans was completed. The South needed credit for all its operations and purchases. And because New York merchants were prepared to carry southern planters on their books for a full year, growers of cotton and tobacco could not but submit—although they became increasingly restive. Indeed, it was generally being charged, the New York earnings from interest, commissions, freights, and insurance ate up forty cents out of every dollar obtained from cotton sales. By the late 1850's, southerners were beginning to sell their cotton direct to Liverpool; but they continued dependent upon New York for their textiles, ironware, notions, clothing, and house furnishings.

Nevertheless, mercantile fortunes at New York were not impressive. Robert G. Albion, in his *The Rise of New York Port*, notes the fact that in 1852 Carl Schurz was told that the possession of $150,000 represented real wealth. Professor Albion further points out that in 1855 there were to be found in the city twenty reputed millionaires. Says he of these fortunes:

Finance and industry accounted for relatively few, while shipbuilding was conspicuously absent. Commerce and real estate bulked most prominently and in many cases the fortunes, as in the case of Astor, represented a combination of the two. Land values in Manhattan were rising with extraordinary rapidity and Scoville claimed that Pelatiah Perit made more money from the casual purchase of some uptown lots than he did from his long and strenuous service as a Goodhue partner.

The astute New York merchant, despite the commanding position of the port, really ended up by being an urban landlord or a banker. For the race was a swift one and only the wiliest were able to survive as merchants pure and simple. Professor Albion cites a contemporary to the effect that bankruptcy sooner or later terminated the business histories of ninety-three out of every one hundred merchants in the city.

What was happening to shipping was happening to the fisheries and whaling. The fisheries continued to expand in northern waters, thanks to the maintenance of the federal bounty inaugurated in 1792; but relatively the industry declined as Europe developed new sources of supply and began to substitute meats for fish as the basic diet of its working populations. The whaling industry, which had preoccupied so much of New England mercantile capital in the Colonial Period and through the nineteenth century to the 1840's, also began to slip in

importance and by the time the Civil War was over very little
more than recollections of glamorous adventure and perils
were left. Nantucket and New London broke up their whaling
fleets in the late 1840's; by 1857, New Bedford, too, had given
up the unequal race as the schools of whales scattered and, more
significant, as coal oil and gas began to replace whale oil as
the outstanding illuminant. The whaling industry had been a
key one in the New England of the Middle Period, ranking
behind only those of cotton textiles and boots and shoes. Some
of its capital followed that of the China traders into railroading. Most of it waited for opportunities in industrial enterprise
—those opportunities that only the Civil War could release.

A word should be said of the character of American commerce. It changed markedly as the United States advanced from
the Colonial Period through the Middle Period. The old staples
of colonial commerce—leaf tobacco, fish, naval stores, indigo,
furs, and rice—dwindled in relative importance and some of
them virtually disappeared from our wharves entirely. The foreign lumber trade dropped out of sight for almost a half
century and it was not until the 1850's that signs of revival
showed themselves as American capital began to work the
forests of the Great Lakes country. Western flour, wheat, corn,
and meat products loomed up on the horizon to take the place
of the New England and middle colonies' foodstuffs in our
foreign trade and to be sent to European and, to a lesser extent,
oriental markets, in substitution for the old West Indian ones.
But it was cotton that ruled our export trade and provided our
ships with freights. At the end of the 1850's all the European
cotton textile centers depended upon American cotton receipts.
England took 2,000,000 bales annually; France 500,000 bales;
Belgium, Germany, and Italy lesser quantities. Indeed, in 1860
our cotton export reached the unprecedented total of 3,774,000
bales; and in that year the value of the cotton export was
considerably more than half of the total value of all our domestic
products sold abroad. It was small wonder that the seceding
South looked forward to victory confidently: cotton was going
to win the Civil War. In our export trade, manufactured goods
played an insignificant part: in 1860, the value of all American

manufactured goods moving into foreign trade was but $48,-
500,000, or just about 13 per cent of the value of domestic
products exported.

In return, we imported semimanufactured and manufactured
goods and agricultural commodities we were incapable of growing ourselves. In the first category (thanks to the lower tariff
rates of 1846 and the still further reductions of 1857) were to
be found large quantities of metals and manufactures of iron,
wool, cotton, leather, glass, paper, and wood; in the second
category, tea, coffee, sugar. How sharply our economy was
changed in a half century may be seen from the following
comparative figures, presenting annual average values of imports in specific classes:

AMERICAN IMPORTS BY CLASSES

PER CENT OF TOTAL IMPORTS, BY VALUE

Annual Average	Crude Materials for Use in Manufacture	Semiprocessed Manufactured Goods	Manufactured Goods Ready for Consumption
1850–59	8.55	13.08	51.85
1890–99	24.66	13.67	26.28

3. BALANCE OF INTERNATIONAL PAYMENTS

The balance of international payments indicated how completely the American economy was dominated by mercantile
capitalism. Thanks to the careful estimates compiled by Messrs.
Bullock, Williams, and Tucker, it is possible to make some
comparative analyses. From 1789 to 1820, American commodity
movements showed an excess of imports over exports, or an
unfavorable trade balance. Also, interest payments had to be
made to foreigners for their investments in United States bonds
and in the stocks of the First and Second Banks of the United
States and of state-chartered banks. Yet the period ended with an
increased stock of specie in the country, due to the fact that our
merchant marine was earning large sums in the carrying trade.
These not only balanced payments for goods but they also permitted the government to pay off its foreign creditors and the
First Bank of the United States to repurchase the stock holdings
of foreign investors. So good was our position that sterling
exchange was selling during the greater part of the period at a

discount here. One comes to an interesting conclusion: we probably occupied a creditor status, a position we were not to reachieve until a whole century later in the years of the World War. This early period was clearly the high water mark of mercantile capitalism in the United States.

From 1821 to 1837, the components of our situation changed sharply. Imports continued to exceed exports. Immigrants began to bring with them sizable capital funds, but this item was balanced by the expenditures of our tourists abroad. Capital from Europe began to flow into the country in impressive amounts to finance state-guaranteed public-works projects; therefore interest requirements were heavy. The earnings of our merchant marine continued large, but they were not adequate to offset the debit items. The period closed with the United States as a debtor nation—foreign investments here being in the neighborhood of $175,000,000. And sterling exchange was selling at a premium in the United States.

Following Bullock, Williams, and Tucker, our position during the years 1821-37 may be set out in the following balance sheet (figures in millions of dollars):

Items	Credits	Debits
Export of merchandise..................	1389	
Export of specie.......................	107.7	
Freights earned by our ships............	214	
Sale of ships..........................	8	
Immigrants brought in..................	11	
New capital invested by foreigners.......	125	
Total...........................	1854.7	
Import of merchandise..................		1574
Import of specie.......................		144.4
Undervaluation of pound sterling........		30
Freights paid to foreign ships............		8
Tourist expenditures abroad.............		11
Interest paid to foreign investors.........		60
Total...........................		1827.4

From 1838 to 1849, we obtained a slight favorable commodity balance for we were compelled to step up exports; and this was due to the facts that interest charges were heavy and our merchant marine was beginning to slip. Our status continued that of a debtor, the foreign stake in the United States at the end of the 1840's being in the neighborhood of $200,000,000. Europe sent more specie than we shipped, but this was due to the unusual conditions of the period 1845-47, when because of famine our cereal exports rose sharply.

The balance sheet for the years 1838-49 looked as follows (figures in millions of dollars):

Items	Credits	Debits
Export of merchandise..................	1392	
Export of specie......................	78.3	
Freights earned by our ships............	236	
Sale of ships........................	6.2	
Immigrants brought in.................	75	
New capital invested by foreigners.......	40	
Total...........................	1827.5	
Import of merchandise.................		1358
Import of specie......................		114.4
Freights paid to foreign ships...........		22
Immigrant remittances.................		15
Tourist expenditures abroad............		84.5
Mexican War and indemnity............		25
Interest paid to foreign investors........		144
Total...........................		1762.9

The next period for which the analysis has been made covers the years 1850-73. It was one of extraordinary significance in our history: for it bridged the Civil War and marked the transformation of our economy from an essentially mercantile to an essentially industrial one. The following characteristics of the period stand out. We had a very large adverse commodity balance (the last one, incidentally, in our history), imports exceeding exports for every year except 1858 and 1862. Our freight earnings dropped off sharply, absolutely and relatively. Indeed, for the first time in our history, during 1861-73, foreign ships earned more than American ships, marking another milestone. The foreign capital stake here increased greatly, necessitating large interest payments. Immigrants brought in sizable funds (because many of them came from the middle classes of Europe); but our tourist expenditures were even heavier.

How were we able to balance the heavy adverse trade? The answer is plain. New gold production in California was one of those amazingly fortuitous circumstances that from time to time have appeared; and with gold we helped pay Europeans for munitions and other commodities needed to continue the war effort and for raw materials and semiprocessed heavy goods to aid our industrialization after the war was over. During the years 1850-73, our gold exports amounted to $1,166,000,000!

And how did we pay interest on borrowings? Again, the answer is plain. We increased our capital indebtedness; in other words, foreigners reinvested earned interest in new capital ventures here, notably United States governments and rails. According to an estimate compiled by the Secretary of the Treasury, in 1853 foreign holdings here came to $222,200,000, of which $111,000,000 was in state bonds and $52,000,000 in railway stocks and bonds. Only $27,000,000 was in United States bonds. By 1869, according to David A. Wells, foreign holdings had risen to the very large total of $1,465,500,000, of which United States bonds came to $1,000,000,000, state bonds to $100,-000,000, and railway bonds and stocks to $243,000,000.

By the end of the 1860's, economists here and abroad were regarding our adverse commodity trade on the one hand and our heavy interest obligations on the other with uneasiness. We would have to step up our exports; and we would have to keep prices here down in order to make our market less attractive for foreign sellers of goods. Thus, Professor J. E. Cairnes wrote in 1873 with real vision:

. . . the present condition of the external trade of the United States is essentially abnormal and temporary. If that country is to continue to discharge her liabilities to foreigners, the relation which at present obtains between her exports and imports in her external trade must be inverted.

And as regards prices, Professor Cairnes predicted that a decline would have to come and that it probably would "come with a crash." The immediate future of the American trade was likely to be attended by "much disturbance and fluctuation, culminating, it is possible, from time to time, in commercial crises."

All this came to pass: the panic of 1873, continuing into long depression, and the gradual petering out of gold in California forced down prices in the United States. Imports fell off and in order to pay interest exports had to expand. And here emerged the historic role of our new western agriculture: with cereals and meat products we were able to establish favorable commodity balances. Agriculture was rescuing our advancing industrial capitalism!

The balance sheet for the years 1850-73 looked as follows (figures in millions of dollars):

Items	Credits	Debits
Export of merchandise.................	6585	
Export of specie.......................	1425	
Freights earned by our ships...........	643	
Sale of ships.........................	65	
Immigrants brought in.................	330	
New capital invested by foreigners.......	1000	
Total...........................	10,048	
Import of merchandise.................		8125
Import of specie......................		327.3
Freights paid to foreign ships...........		446
Tourist expenditures abroad............		576
Interest paid to foreign investors.........		904
Total...........................		10,378.3

CHAPTER NINETEEN

Manufactures

1. FROM MERCANTILE CAPITALISM TO INDUSTRIAL CAPITALISM

THE keys to the character of capitalist production and the class structure of the greater part of the Middle Period will continue to remain illusive unless we are prepared to visualize American society as, in large measure, based on mercantile-capitalist organization. Capital was being used in nonproductive enterprise: in land speculation, in speculative canal and railroad building, in the carrying trade. Even in the production of manufactured goods, always excepting the cotton textile industry, the organization was largely mercantile: the big enterpriser was not the producer so much as he was preeminently the financier and merchant. That is to say, he did not own the instrumentalities of production—the factories, equipment, and tools—but he bought the finished articles from small independent producers working in their own cottages and mills; sometimes he financed them and he moved these fabricated articles into the channels of commerce. Virtually up to the end of the Middle Period, in a number of the outstanding American industries—in boots and shoes, in meat packing, in considerable measure in woolen textiles, even in crude, or heavy, iron—the enterpriser was a merchant, or commission man. In brief, his status was that of the preindustrial capitalist of England and France of the early eighteenth century.

In the 1850's, the role of the typical capitalist began to change: more and more he was becoming interested in industrial production. The factors affecting this transformation may be summarized at this point. The creation of corporations, with state consent, was beginning to occur: so that the small accumulations of professional people, traders, and farmers could be tapped; as well as the accumulations of the newly appearing institutional savers—the savings banks and the insurance companies. Free agriculture was prospering, making it possible for farmers to stake their younger sons—on a low level, of course —in industry and trade. The social dislocations and upheavals in Europe (famine in Ireland, repeated crop failures as well as reactionary land systems in Central Europe, the abortive 1848 revolutions) sent pouring into the United States new immigrants driven off the land by engrossing, enclosure, and starvation; and also middle-class liberals thwarted in an effort to establish constitutional governments in Germany and Austria. The first group augmented our labor reserve and kept wages down. Just as in the sixteenth and seventeenth centuries in Europe, the gap between prices and wages was the point at which accumulation could take place. And the second group brought capital along with them to set up independent businesses. The prolonged depression of 1837-43 had had a purgative effect; and it had indicated that certain avenues for mercantile-capitalist exploitation were no longer remunerative. Also, the domestic market was expanding greatly, thanks to improved transportation and banking facilities. Perhaps most significant of all was the effect of the gold discoveries in California. Gold permitted the United States, for a decade, to enjoy the luxury of an unfavorable commodity balance: we could import more than we exported. With gold, therefore, we bought the foreign wares necessary to the establishment of an industrial-capitalist economy: railroad iron and machinery, as well as those raw materials we ourselves did not produce.

The so-called industrial revolution in America (by revolution, we are to understand the wholesale transformation of the role of the capitalist enterpriser and not simply the introduction of automatic devices in fabrication) therefore really did not have its beginnings until after the depression of 1837-43. In England, of course, the process had begun much earlier. Having its roots as far back as the sixteenth century, English industrial capitalism had come to flower in the period 1775-1815. A new class leadership then had emerged: a class leadership linked with neither landlordism nor commerce but with industry, and a class, incidentally, that did not have its origins in the older capitalist groupings. This was the epoch of the ironmasters, pottery lords, and textile barons. Thanks to the appearance of industrial inventions, but, more important, due to civil peace; a political and judicial apparatus capable of defending property rights; an augmented labor supply flowing out of the renewal and completion of the processes of enclosure; a widening domestic market being tapped by the new public-works construction of roads and canals; a growing foreign market in Europe and overseas made possible after the humbling of the French in the Seven Years' War: English industrial capitalism could advance on seven-league boots.

The period of the Napoleonic Wars presented unexampled opportunities to this class, just as did the Civil War in America to our native bourgeoisie, as we shall see. Armies and navies had to be supplied—at any cost. An extraordinary credit expansion could take place as a result of governmental wartime financing; for these public issues flowed into the banks which in turn used them to extend their lines of credit to business borrowers. As far as capitalism has been concerned, modern war (while it lasts) has been an unmixed blessing. And the grand effect was the triumphant emergence of the industrial capitalist. It was no accident that David Ricardo's defense of capitalism was published at this time; nor that the industrial leaders began to agitate for franchise reform and the complete dismantling of what was left of the Mercantile System.

I have said that these processes did not emerge in America until two whole generations later. And when they did appear, the potentialities of full and uninhibited maturation did not exist. For the state was in the hands of a hostile class—the planter capitalists of the South. The conquest of political power and the writing of a body of doctrine into the law and administration of the land were imperative to permit the unchecked advance of industrial capitalism in the United States.

There is a parallel between this situation in the United States and the period in France preceding the French Revolution. After the Seven Years' War, particularly, the French middle class continued to grow, in both trade and industrial production. But royal absolutism, operating in the interests of landlordism and the court bureaucracy, was erecting all sorts of barriers to stay the progress of a free bourgeoisie. It had to be got rid of: and this was the historic role of the French Revolution.

In the same way, a young and lusty American capitalism, its energies hampered by an older class occupying the citadels of power and privilege, and a capitalism, incidentally, whose nerves were frayed by the losses of the depression of 1857-58, was not prepared to be squeamish when the South resorted to the arbitrament of war. For wars can be made into revolutions; and that is exactly what the Civil War became.

This analysis leads to the following conclusions. American capitalism, at the end of the Middle Period, was not yet free of the restrictions of, and commitments to, mercantile capitalism. A large part of it was still preoccupied with the characteristic rounds of that earlier form: commerce, banking, land speculation, the speculative building of canals and railroads, cottage-and-mill manufacture rather than the factory system. During 1843-57, however, there was a rapid movement into industrial production. Nevertheless, restraints upon full expansion existed. The planter capitalists of the South, in control of the executive, legislative, and judicial apparatus of the central government (while their allies in the Democratic party manipulated power in many of the northern states), stood in the way of the following program. They opposed protectionism. They frowned on internal improvements. They fought the federal chartering of a Pacific railway system. They favored state banking and cheap money and were suspicious of federal supervision of banking corporations. They opposed homesteading. They would not encourage a governmental immigration plan. In the courts, "due process," assured under state constitutions, was given a strictly procedural rather than substantive interpretation: in other words, property rights could claim no protection from higher, or natural, law. On the other hand, all these were necessary to give state assistance and protection to a growing industrial capitalist class. They were obtained as a result of the Civil War.

And, as I have said, the circumstance of war itself hastened the process. A vastly expanded domestic market, created by the necessity of maintaining and supplying a gigantic military establishment, and the great increase in and circulation of the capital fund, due to governmental borrowing and spending, helped in the maturing of our industrial production, and, more particularly, our heavy industry, virtually overnight. By the end of the Civil War, the industries turning out boots and shoes, men's clothing, iron, machinery, dressed meats, and woolen textiles had reached full stature. The factory system now reigned in America.

2. MANUFACTURE UNDER MERCANTILE CAPITALISM

I have said that, in the greater part of the Middle Period, organization of production was still, in many key industries, under the leadership of the merchant capitalist. It must also be understood that, really up to the 1850's, the pre-Civil War worker was not a proletarian wage laborer. He did not sell his labor power to the industrialist and take up employment under the roof of a factory where production and management were planned and centralized. In short, he did not engage in social production. He labored in his own shop or in a rural mill, laid down his own conditions for employment, and worked only when his fancy or immediate necessity dictated. For in conjunction with his cottage or his labor in a mill he also ran a small subsistence farm as a rule. He was an independent producer economically and a petty bourgeois in terms of his class loyalties. Even in the New England cotton textile factories, the organization of the labor force, notably in conjunction with the so-called Waltham system of production, was really on a preindustrial capitalist basis. The operatives as a rule were young women who had been gathered from the countryside and inducted into the factories, but only for temporary periods. The average length of employment was not much in excess of two to four years, and then these female operatives returned with their small savings to the family farms to settle down as farmers' wives or to migrate west in the same capacity. They were not proletarians, therefore, in the modern sense: they were not completely dependent upon their wage labor for their livelihood.

And it was not until these young women were replaced by male immigrants, starting with the middle 1840's, that the proletarianization of the factory population in cotton textiles may be said to have begun.

The high hopes entertained by Alexander Hamilton for the development of manufactures in America, upon the establishment of the Republic, were blasted. The dumping of English finished goods in our markets, immediately after the termination of the Revolution, nipped in the bud those infant industries that had sprung up thanks to the fostering care of Revolutionary state governments; while the superior attractions offered to capital by land speculation, the creation of internal methods of transport, and the oversea carrying trade obviously could not be denied. The development of manufactures continued tardily.

The first transformation that took place was the conversion of household production into cottage-and-mill production. Notably in the cases of textiles and iron goods this movement began to take place and it continued from the end of the Revolution well into, and through, the whole Middle Period. Household production, as we have seen, was largely on a non-exchange basis in the capitalist sense. The colonial farm families had produced goods for home use and had entered small surpluses into their local markets only to create cash for the purchase of those necessaries they were incapable of fabricating themselves. After the Revolution, and as the domestic market expanded, it was natural that these household producers should become cottage workers for merchant-manufacturers, or merchant capitalists. Textiles (particularly those associated with the conversion of flax into linen cloth and the manufacture of hosiery and other knit goods out of wool), straw hats and bonnets, iron nails, boots and shoes: all those goods that did not require automatic machinery and where the processes of fabrication from raw materials into relatively crude finished goods were simple: these became the spheres of activity of the new capitalists. Production took place at the farm homes or in cottages erected as "ells" to the homes: the enterpriser, in large measure, was only a middleman. Thus V. S. Clark, in describing this early stage of the organization of production, writes:

Large vans circulated through New England and the Central States leaving at the farmhouses along the way bundles of straw plait to be sewed into hats and bonnets, and boot and shoe uppers to be closed and bound. . . . The making of garments was less an urban occupation than at present, and farmers' wives and daughters sewed and finished goods for city merchants.

It is not to be assumed that organization was always on this simple plane. Sometimes one process of production was already industrialized, as in the case of woolen textiles where the yarn warp and filling were made by power machinery and were then turned over to country weavers for final manufacture into cloth. Sometimes the cottage workers possessed only their workshops, laboring on raw materials and using equipment supplied by the merchant-manufacturer. Sometimes they worked in mills altogether, that is to say, even the workshops were owned by the enterprisers. But whatever the stage—whether it was complete cottage production, complete mill production, or a combination of the two—because the producers engaged in it were country-folk and the growers of their own immediate necessaries and the possessors of their own homes and because they had not yet been inducted into the round of social production, they were not yet a factory population. The compulsions of daily toil and the acceptance of a wage scale fixed by the employer did not exist.

Nowhere is this better illustrated than in the boot-and-shoe industry which was organized on a cottage basis until the demands of the Civil War for large quantities of ready-made shoes metamorphosed production overnight. The Middle Period enterpriser was a merchant—frequently the owner of the local grocery store. The producers therefore were paid in truck from the shelves of the shop, whose proprietor operated a central workroom and a storehouse either behind or above his mercantile establishment. He employed a few journeymen and other artisans on a piecework basis in the central workroom in order to prepare the leather for fabrication. A little later on, the in-workers also cut the soles and uppers. The actual sewing was performed by the outworkers in their cottages—as a rule in so-called ten-footers, or "ells" of that size, added to the farm homes. The merchant furnished the leather, binding, thread, and other materials; but not the tools. The semiprocessed leather and the finished boots and shoes were delivered and collected by carriers who received a percentage of the pay of the outworkers. As the merchant's activities expanded, with the growth of the market, particularly the western one, he surrendered his retail establishment, paid his outworkers in cash instead of truck, and concentrated on the operations of his office, warehouse, and packing and shipping departments.

It will be noted that under such a dispensation production was neither supervised nor continuous—two of the outstanding characteristics of the factory system. Indeed, the cottage outworkers were an independent and sturdy class of small producers. They were countrymen who were fond of their hunting, fishing, and small talk, and not an impoverished and beaten factory population: and these were the village artisans who prized their liberties, read and understood Emerson and Thoreau, and hated deeply the black slavery of the southern plantation economy. Notably in New England, the seat of the boot-and-shoe industry, these free yeomen-cottagers dominated production until well on into the 1840's; and it was not until automatic machinery and the demands of the war appeared that the ten-footers were abandoned and the producers became factory operatives.

Clark, again, may be quoted on this interesting situation. He is writing of the introducion of machinery in boots and shoes in connection with the operations of cutting and rolling the leather, pegging the soles, and finally sewing on the uppers.

Though at first these were operated by hand, their installation required capital and their maximum economy was derived from continuous operation. Such influences, assisted by a tendency to centralize already under way, and by the example of other industries, made it inevitable that these mechanical aids ultimately should be assembled in factory buildings. This result was not accomplished, however, until power was applied to shoe machinery, a development postponed until the outbreak of the Civil War.

What was true of boots and shoes was also in considerable

measure true of the great food industries, which, in terms of value of product, stood far in the van of the manufacturing activities of the Middle Period. Indeed, flour milling, baking, brewing, and meat slaughtering and packing were perhaps the last of the industries to quit the cottage-and-mill stage for the factory stage. Originally entirely household industries—for in an agricultural economy the creation of home necessaries is to be taken for granted—these were quickly caught into the domestic system as the growing market created outlets for their products. The role of the enterpriser in meat packing was characteristic. He was called a packer, but the term was used so loosely that in the 1840's and 1850's it included commission merchants, provision dealers, drovers, commercial farmers, and even stock raisers. Despite the existence of a number of packing centers in the West—notably Cincinnati (the "Porkopolis" of the 1840's), Louisville, St. Louis, Milwaukee, and, later, Chicago —a large part of the animals slaughtered and packed were handled by country butchers and at small rural and only temporary plants. Indeed, in the 1850's technical journals found it necessary to quote prices for something like two hundred and thirty-three different packing points scattered over nine states of the Middle West. Because of the inadequacy of transportation facilities, the dominant figure in those areas was the commission merchant who ranged up and down the countryside, picking up animals and packed provisions and moving them into commerce for farmer-butcher accounts.

The Civil War revolutionized the industry because it hastened its integration. The needs of the Union armies compelled the regularizing of the supply. Financed from government contracts, a body of men arose who proceeded to collect all the various functions of modern packing and slaughtering under a common roof. From being country butchers and commission merchants they became packers in the industrial sense. They set up their own stockyards (near receiving points); created a cash market; and slaughtered, packed, and erected plants for the utilization of the waste products. It was no accident that the men who obtained Civil War government contracts—Jacob Dold, Philip D. Armour, Nelson Morris—were to emerge by

1865 (when the Chicago Union Stockyards were established) as the packers of modern-day capitalist enterprise.

3. THE IRON AND TEXTILE INDUSTRIES

In iron and in the manufacture of woolens, the preponderant role of mercantile capitalism is not quite so clear; not because of overwhelming evidences to the contrary but because these industries were more scattered and it has been more difficult, as a result, to piece together a unified pattern of experience. Certainly, in the case of iron, mill production—in the sense that the term is used here to signify small country plants with a rural or village working population only partially dependent upon wage labor for its subsistence—continued to predominate right through the 1850's. Indeed, most of the blast furnaces, bloomeries, and forges—the plants converting the ore into the heavy iron of commerce—were located in the country because of the continued dependence of these works upon charcoal as their basic fuel. The millowner also ran a country store and paid his workers in truck: and the existence of truck payments is not only an evidence of highly organized integration (the company town of the 1920's) but also of cottage production. The semiprocessed iron was sold just as frequently to storekeepers for resale to cottage workers and local blacksmithies for rolling and slitting (hence the use of the term "merchant iron"), as it was to industrial rolling and slitting mills and to naileries.

It would be difficult to argue that even in the 1850's the iron industry was integrated to such a degree that it offered outlets for large-scale capital enterprise. Thus, industrially speaking, the production of crude iron was on such a primitive level that, despite the continued existence of a high tariff wall during the whole Middle Period—a barrier which at times reached as high as 100 per cent in ad valorem duties—not enough iron was being turned out to satisfy domestic requirements. Foreign stocks were constantly being imported; indeed, right up to the Civil War, our so-called railroad iron came largely from England. Also, the tardy growth of Pittsburgh, which, as soon as the Civil War was over, quickly came to dominate the industry, proves the point. In 1826, there were only seven rolling mills in the area and these did not consume much more than 6000 tons of blooms and pigs; in 1850, the number of rolling mills was fourteen and the consumption of heavy iron 59,000 tons. In 1857, the number of mills was twenty-one and the consumption of iron 132,600 tons. The Pittsburgh industry was constantly beset by difficulties. It could obtain capital only from local sources and in such small quantities that it was not until 1859 that the ironmongers of the area erected their own blast furnaces and began to free themselves from their dependence upon the uncertain supply of the country plants. The binding together of furnaces and mills was the first stage in the attainment of capitalist production.

The Civil War, of course, gave Pittsburgh its great opportunity. The Union government required armor plate, cannon, shot, shell, and rails; and Pittsburgh's constantly expanding mills, now linked with their own furnaces, turned all these out. By 1874, Pittsburgh's capacity for the production of pig iron had increased 600 per cent over the capacity of 1861.

The analysis presented here of the essentially preindustrial character of the iron industry before the Civil War is substantiated by L. C. Hunter in the following words:

[The year 1859 marked] the transition between two essentially different phases in the development of iron manufacturing in this country and at Pittsburgh. Of the period just closed it may be said that the manufacture of iron was controlled and conditioned by the needs and requirements of a pioneer agricultural population, which were met to a large extent by the forges and rolling mills without the mediation of manufactories of finished iron products. The principal function of the manufacturer of wrought iron was to supply the country iron workers, blacksmiths by profession or necessity, with bar iron to be shaped to meet the needs of farmer, wagoner and mill owner. . . . In the period which followed the iron manufacturer gradually ceased to serve the agricultural population directly. The demand for iron came increasingly from industries engaged in the production of finished iron goods and the machinery of industry and commerce. . . . The agricultural era gave way to what might be termed the *industrial era*.

The role of the pre-Civil War ironmaster was illuminatingly

revealed in a letter written in July 11, 1863, by Thaddeus Stevens to a military friend. Stevens was recounting the losses he suffered as the Confederate army swept northward into Pennsylvania; and he therefore wrote:

They then seized my bacon (about 4,000 lbs.), molasses and other contents of the store—took about $1,000 worth of corn in the mills, and a like quantity of other grain. On Friday, they burned the furnace, saw-mill, two forges and rolling mill. They slept in the office and store-room on that night, and burned them with books and all on Saturday morning.

They even hauled off my bar iron, being as they said convenient for shoeing horses, and wagons about $4,000 worth. They destroyed all my fences (I had just built a large quantity of post and rail fences, as I was clearing out a farm). My grass (about 80 tons) they destroyed; and broke in the windows of the dwelling houses where the workmen lived. They could not have done the job much cleaner. It is rather worse than I expected. All the bellows and bellow houses, and run out establishment are gone. . . . I know not what the poor families will do. I must provide for their present relief.

It is relatively easy to reconstruct the picture. Stevens, in conjunction with a group of farms, ran a sawmill and an ironworks. His workmen, in addition to being employed in the works, undoubtedly must have labored on the farms, for the eighty tons of hay destroyed was a sizable quantity. The whole establishment was located out in the country: for the workers' dwelling houses on Stevens' property and the "store" are to be noted. Of particular interest are the bacon and molasses seized—for these were the usual stock in trade of a truck-payment system. It is not difficult to draw the conclusion that Thaddeus Stevens, as an ironmaster, had closer links with the cottage-and-mill system of production of sixteenth- and seventeenth-century England than with the industrial Pittsburgh of the 1870's.

How significant a part cottage production played in the manufacture of woolens, by the time the Civil War opened, it is difficult to say. Woolens were less controlled by the style factor than other textiles, so that a sizable amount of stuffs must have entered local markets, particularly in the West, long after large plants operating automatic machinery had appeared in New England and New York. The role of the merchant-manufacturer was exactly similar in these backcountry regions of the America of the nineteenth century to that of the country clothier of sixteenth- and seventeenth-century England: he turned over to the cottagers the carded wool and yarn and bought back from them their woven cloth and knitted ware. A. H. Cole, the historian of the industry, declares that as late as 1830 household and domestic production was still exceeding factory production; and that even during the 1840's domestic production was significant. When we recall that the fabrication of woolens preeminently lends itself to farmhouse manufacture and that the constant growth of the country westward into areas not yet opened by adequate transportation facilities created a vast number of small local markets, we have every reason to assume that spheres of activity for cottage producers and merchant capitalists handling their products continued to flourish. Indeed, it was not until the 1870's that, according to Cole, domestic manufacture finally became a negligible feature of the industry.

The mixed character of the woolen industry is clearly indicated by Professor Cole in connection with his description of the organization of carpet manufacture. In New England, as early as the 1820's and 1830's, the factory system had already put in its appearance; in Philadelphia, on the other hand, the domestic system prevailed as late as the Civil War. So, Professor Cole writes:

. . . as late as 1860 we find published a complete description of the system as it existed in 1857. . . . Work was "distributed among a large number of workers" who were dependent upon the "manufacturers" for directing the industry. The "individual manufacturers," who numbered about 100, furnished employment to at least 1500 hand-loom weavers. . . . Seemingly, the relationship between employer and workers was that common to the putting-out system. The weavers owned their looms and tackle, and the employer furnished the material. . . .

Even in the case of cotton textiles, where the factory system appeared early, the organization of production was not at once

on an industrial-capitalist basis. Historians have permitted themselves to be impressed only too easily by the introduction of
automatic machinery in certain regions and have accepted the
existence of power spinning and looms as evidences of factory
manufacture. The factory system under capitalism does not
mean only the division of labor that the use of automatic machinery usually brings in its train. It also implies supervision
of work by the owner or his manager; continuous and rationalized, or social, production; the free utilization of capital for
both short-term and long-term needs; and the employment of a
working force wholly dependent upon wage labor. In this sense
industrial-capitalist production in manufactures—the factory
system—did not exist in the United States, as a prevailing tendency, until the Civil War quickly hastened its maturing. Even
in cotton textiles it was not really achieved until the middle
1840's. When Samuel Slater erected the first cotton textile plant
in America, at Pawtucket, R. I., in 1791, he was employing automatic machinery, it is true; but the factory system did not begin
here.

The Slater plant was really a mill, using automatic machinery
only for the manufacture of spun yarn. Weaving was done by
cottagers in their own homes—on the putting-out basis. The
Slater plant was owned by the mercantile firm of Almy and
Brown; the only capital it continued to utilize was the original
investment plus such profits as its owners were willing to plow
back. The labor force was also characteristic of this mixed organizational form: for Slater employed only children in his
spinning mill, while their parents, who were villagers and therefore also farmers, worked at hand looms in their own homes.
Also—and here again we notice the adherence to the type—wage
payments were in truck taken from the shelves of the Almy and
Brown store.

This Rhode Island type of cotton textile organization, as it
came to be called, continued to flourish well through the 1830's
not only in Rhode Island but also in Connecticut, southern Massachusetts, and the Middle Atlantic States generally. Its characteristics were everywhere the same: village or country plants
employing whole families presumably farm owners or laborers

with the children the mill spinners and the grownups the home weavers; payment in truck; and capital funds that rarely extended beyond the original financing and reinvested small profits. Miss Ware, the historian of the early industry, records the fact that in Rhode Island in the 1830's the average plant was capitalized at not much more than $30,000. It is also important to note that in Philadelphia, the principal rival of New England in the industry, production for a long time continued to take place in small hand-weaving shops where the yarn was supplied by merchant-manufacturers. The prevalence of this type of production in cotton and woolen textiles and of course the continuance of the mechanic or artisan in most of the customary urban trades help to account for the decidedly petty-bourgeois political and economic programs of the Philadelphia workers in the late 1820's and the 1830's.

In northern Massachusetts, in New Hampshire, and Maine, production in cotton textiles began to approximate the factory system, in its capitalist sense, more completely. Here sprang up, first around the river rapids of eastern and northern Massachusetts, starting with 1815, a group of industrial communities where automatic machinery in both spinning and weaving as well as complete factory organization was introduced. In the words of Clark:

Labor was specialized and workers were organized by departments. Wages were paid in cash, output standardized, cost accounting introduced and buying and selling systematized. In a word, the commercial, technical and operative elements of a factory were brought together in accordance with an intelligent plan and so co-ordinated as to make a more efficient producing unit than had hitherto existed in this country. Manufacturing was specialized completely and no longer retained even subordinate relations with household industry or general merchandizing. [For "household," read "domestic." L.M.H.]

Starting first at Waltham (hence the use of this city's name to express this type of organization) and quickly appearing in Lowell, Manchester, and Lawrence, large cotton textile factories arose to absorb sizable capital funds and to give employment to large numbers of workers. Thus, the Waltham Company, financed by a group of Boston merchants, started operations with

$300,000 paid-in capital which in less than a decade was doubled; the original capitalization of the mills established at Lowell ran from $600,000 to $1,000,000.

It has been pointed out that the working population was a factory population in its dependence upon wage labor; but not entirely so, for in the Waltham type of plants, up to the middle 1840's, the operatives were exclusively young women who were collected from their parental farm homes and permitted to return to them after the accumulation of small savings. In one sense, therefore, the "Waltham" operatives were not yet an urbanized proletariat. When these young women were supplanted first by immigrant male operatives and then by native-born men and women—their roots no longer in the countryside—the process of industrialization of the cotton textile manufacture was complete.

The "Waltham" cotton textile industrialists could continue to pose as philanthropists as long as their workers were these country girls: and through the 1830's, when the system was well established, they could point with pride to their benign rule. The young ladies were housed in model boardinghouses under the eagle eyes of matrons; the rooms in which they lived were neatly furnished with pictures and Biblical texts on the walls and flower boxes at the windows, the curfew bell rang at 10 P.M.; church attendance was required. In view of the fact that operatives were dismissed for straying from the paths of rectitude, it is to be presumed that the intention of the employers to return their youthful charges, after they had successfully hoarded up a dowry, to their country swains in no way blemished by their experiences in the mill towns was generally realized. This side of "Waltham" factory life had its attractions and the region became the mecca of approving English female travelers and American politicians. The reverse side of the shield told another story. Wages, after charges for board had been deducted, were $2 a week; the girls labored in the noisy and dusty and dangerous buildings (fires were frequent) 75 hours a week; within the silken glove of benevolence lay an iron despotic hand. The black list, as a means of weeding out the disaffected, was commonly employed; and industrialists combined to fix wages and hours.

By the middle 1840's, the young country girls were gone and urban male operatives, wage laborers in the full sense, had replaced them. But the despotism, now no longer benevolent, continued. The mill cities now were full company towns: churches, newspapers, local politicians were owned by the industrialists; the terror of the black list meant starvation and not simply banishment to the country. Said a workers' newspaper in 1846 of the factory system of modern capitalist enterprise:

That the factory system contains in itself the elements of slavery, we think no sound reasoning can deny, and every day continues to add power to its incorporate sovereignty, while the sovereignty of the working people decreases in the same ratio.

4. THE ORIGINS OF THE INDUSTRIAL-CAPITALIST CLASS

There can be no question that in some economic regions a direct transfer from mercantile capitalism to industrial capitalism took place. But because the shift occurred in cotton textiles historians have assumed too easily that this was the normal process on a universal scale. It is true that Almy and Brown, who financed Samuel Slater, were merchants; and that Lowell, Appleton, and Jackson, who turned to manufacturing after the disastrous decline of the carrying trade at the end of the Napoleonic Wars, were also merchant capitalists. The tapering off of the China trade in the 1830's caused another movement of mercantile capital into textiles; the end of the whaling industry in the 1840's also provided a source of capital for the building up of the industry. (In this connection, it is to be noted that New Bedford, a whaling port, in time became a textile center.)

But these were really exceptions. The old merchant-capitalist class, driven out of commerce—if it was able to salvage a sizable enough portion of its capital fund before it was too late—went into public-works promotion, real estate, insurance, banking, railroading. In short, these became "capitalists" in the sense that the term has popular currency today: the silent partners, rather than the industrial enterprisers, and the speculators, landlords, moneylenders, and investors. The old merchant families of New

England, for example, in the first quarter of the nineteenth century, founded the turnpike, canal, and river-improvement companies of the section; established its savings banks; became urban landlords; and built its great industry of fire and, later, life insurance. In the second quarter of the century, these old merchant families and their scions moved their activities, as absentee capitalists however, into the growing West: as land speculators, organizers of mortgage companies, and railroad promoters. J. M. Forbes, when he went into the Michigan Central Railroad in 1846, was backed by New England mercantile capital. So was Robert Rantoul, Jr., when he appeared in 1850 before the Illinois legislature and successfully pleaded for the charter to build the Illinois Central Railroad.

These people, naturally, controlled the instrumentalities of government. And because they were merchant capitalists by origin and outlook it was not until 1857 that a majority of the New England congressmen were ready to vote for high protective tariffs.

Where, then, did the industrial capitalists originate? As in eighteenth-century England, they came largely from the yeomanry, or the independent farmer class. All one has to do is compare the names of the great in commerce in the 1790's with the names of those who were becoming important in manufacturing in the 1850's and later in the 1870's: and it at once becomes apparent that next to no transfer took place. Sometimes farmers themselves, operating saw, grist, and fulling mills on swift streams, began to erect small textile plants on the same sites. Sometimes their sons did so. More frequently than not, country boys with a bent for tinkering worked over crude machines until they were ready to open machine shops; or, natively shrewd in the ways of small trading, hawked the wares of merchants or started off as bookkeepers until they could set themselves up as independent manufacturers. Before the Civil War, Eli Whitney, Cyrus McCormick, and Philip D. Armour came from such origins and had such humble beginnings. The same was notably true of that great company of industrial enterprisers whose exploits make our post-Civil War history such an astounding one. Andrew Carnegie's father was a country weaver.

John D. Rockefeller's father was an itinerant peddler living in small village communities. Henry Clay Frick's father was a farmer; so was John W. Gates'.

New talents were necessary to exploit the potentialities of industrial production in a growing United States; and the old merchant capitalists and their sons either were incapable of making the proper readjustments or had become both cautious and accustomed to extravagant living. In any event, pioneering in industrial capitalism—thanks to the existence of opportunities for enterprise and the absence of a pre-emptive foreign capitalist class—was the work of the children of America's petty bourgeoisie who came largely from small villages or the land directly.

CHAPTER TWENTY

Condition of the Workers

1. THE PREINDUSTRIAL WORKER

I N SUCH an atmosphere of flow and change: in an economy where production at one and the same time was being carried on by skilled urban artisans and mechanics working for small employers; by domestic workers in their rural cottages and in country forges and mills; by partially industrialized wage laborers; and by fully proletarianized factory workers: it was only natural that the role of the American worker should be a confused one. No clear impression emerges: as, indeed, it never has in periods of human history when constant movement forward is the characteristic of an age rather than the consolidation of gains already won. The dawn of the modern era, in fourteenth- and fifteenth-century Europe, was such an epoch. Men were rousing from the long sleep of feudalism, institutions were rapidly changing, there was a healthy stir and bustle in the air. Some achieved power and place; others were rapidly sinking into a permanently inferior status. The release of the energies of Americans from the confining restrictions of the Mercantile System had a similar effect. The history of the times, as regards the condition of the workers and their economic and political programs, is one of sharp antagonisms, impermanent organizational developments, and a misplaced confidence in not false but really hopelessly inadequate prophets. When the Civil War opened, the workers, after a half century of struggle and agitation, had made no advances as a class; but, at least, there was this gain: many had come to understand that they no longer were petty-bourgeois free producers but wage laborers who were caught inextricably in the meshes of the capitalist property relations.

The European urban guilds, by the time the British settlements in America were founded, had become authoritarian institutions. They were being used by a closed fraternity of master producers and merchants to check the aspirations of a vast body of underprivileged journeymen; and they had not been transported to America. How could they when so many English emigrants were fleeing from the mother country precisely because the guilds had become agencies of oppression? Urban production in the colonies, therefore—because production was still in the handicraft stage—was organized on a free associational basis, with the journeyman a wageworker, it is true, but with restrictions upon his movements into the master class only partially effective. In the larger cities, of course, the skilled mechanic, or artisan, having tired of working for a master cordwainer (early shoemaker) or printer or hatter or mason, when he sought to set himself up in his own shop, was compelled to purchase the freedom of the city, that is to say, make a sizable money payment. But he was not hounded at every turn by the monopolist and self-perpetuating corporations which the guilds of England and the Continent had become. And if he migrated to a smaller or newer community where artisans were sorely needed, or if he became an itinerant artisan—and there were many such—the possibilities of his becoming an independent small producer in time were certainly quite real.

These relations were carried over into the post-Revolutionary period—with a difference. As the population grew and the market widened, the organization of production had to be a more systematic one than the purely localized forms that enterprise could continue to tolerate under the Mercantile System. The merchant capitalist and merchant-manufacturer appeared, as he had in seventeenth- and eighteenth-century Europe, and with his greater command of liquid funds and his ability to buy raw materials cheap and sell dear in markets where dearth existed, he began to press hard the small independent producer. The journeyman, who worked for a master artisan until he gathered together his small horde preparatory to setting up for himself, began to see that his status was indeed becoming an inferior one. He was still a craftsman, commanding a highly developed set of technical skills; he directly performed all, or almost all,

the processes of fabrication himself; and when he worked in his
own cottage he still owned the instrumentalities of production.
But, as a worker, his wages were small, his hours long, and unemployment occurred frequently.

Nevertheless, psychologically and functionally, he was still a
petty-bourgeois producer; and when he joined with his fellows
for economic and political action it was not because he realized
that a yawning gap had appeared between his employer and
himself. A class consciousness on the part of the American
worker did not emerge really until the 1850's—and when it did
it could be felt only dimly and in a few isolated areas. Certain
evils had appeared to hamper his free movement: and these he
sought to shake off either by wringing concessions from his
employers or—vain hope!—by dreaming of fleeing from the
urban communities into a free West. Still possessing the petty-
bourgeois mentality, if he could not remain an independent
artisan or craftsman in the cities, he was prepared to become a
small independent farmer in the country.

2. EARLY ORGANIZATIONS

In the last decade of the eighteenth century and into the first
two decades of the nineteenth century in a number of the larger
cities, in Philadelphia, New York, Boston, Baltimore, Albany,
organizations of journeymen began to appear for the purpose of
combating the increasingly oppressive tactics of their employers,
many of whom had become merchant-manufacturers in addition to continuing as master craftsmen. The first such organization that we know of was that of the Philadelphia cordwainers
which emerged in the early 1790's to resist the growing strength
of the merchant-manufacturers in their industry. The journeymen cordwainers, the journeymen printers, the journeymen carpenters, the journeymen tailors, among others, formed local
societies, indeed, trade-unions, to protest against the extending
evil of apprenticeship with its lowering of standards, and to
demand a minimum wage and a ten-hour day. Strikes took
place; violence broke out; leaders were black-listed and compelled to flee from their communities.

These agitations were uniformly unsuccessful, not only because of the greater strength of the individual employers but because they also combined to fight the workers with both economic and legal weapons. Successfully invoking the common-law doctrine of conspiracy, the employers and their associations appeared in local courts and had these early trade-unions and the use of the strike weapon outlawed. This did not still the agitation, and between 1800 and 1820 the labor annals are filled with accounts of local organizational activity, strikes, repression: and, uniformly, failure.

The initial faltering steps forward were made in the late 1820's, when, again on a local basis but this time in combination, trade-unions of skilled artisans and urban domestic workers pooled their strength for both economic and political action. Thus, in Philadelphia in 1827 there appeared the Mechanics' Union of Trade Associations to agitate for the ten-hour day and to combat jointly the hostility of civil and judicial authority. Movement into the political realm—with a program that was a not too strange combination of industrial realism and petty-bourgeois idealism—was inevitable. A Workingmen's party sprang up in Philadelphia in 1828 and one made its appearance in New York in 1829: neither survived for more than a half decade, but their roles require analysis because of the brilliant light they throw on the still unformed working-class mind of the period.

The programs of these parties included: termination of imprisonment for debt, of the militia system, and of the conspiracy laws; the passage of mechanics' lien laws; and the establishment of free schools. Attacks were made on monopolies, notably the banks. This was an agitation directed by the small producers against the larger ones. Nothing indicates this more clearly than the position taken by Thomas Skidmore, one of the leaders of the New York party. A disciple of Tom Paine, and in direct line of descent of the English peasant revolters of 1386 and the English Diggers of 1649, he could see salvation only in a return to the land on the basis of its communal operation by the producers themselves. Specifically as regards New York, he called for the summoning of a constitutional convention to abolish all debts and all titles to property; equal redistribution then was to follow but with inheritance outlawed, so that ownership really would be social. Another faction, in the New York party, led by Robert Dale Owen, George H. Evans, and Frances Wright, placed all its confidence in free education. Thus, a broadside of theirs, published in 1829, said:

... a national system of education and guardianship which shall furnish to all children of the land equal food, clothing, and instruction at the public expense is the only effectual remedy for this and for almost every species of injustice.

The Workingmen's parties did not survive beyond 1833: their purposes were too confused; their leaders could be attacked viciously as Jacobins and Levelers, to frighten off the timid; and their reforming planks could be appropriated—and were—by the traditional political groups.

The next organizational activity, therefore, was only on the industrial level. Beginning with the early 1830's new local unions and new associations of local unions made their appearance to emerge in combination in 1834 in the National Trades' Union. This, a federation of local bodies from six urban centers, spoke again largely for the urban skilled mechanics and domestic workers and by 1836, when it was at the height of its power, claimed an affiliated membership of 300,000. At the same time, there were appearing the first crude forms of national craft organizations: among the cordwainers, combmakers, carpenters, printers, and (cottage) weavers.

Organization and agitation definitely took on mass characteristics. During the years 1834-38, local unions were formed all over the country; indeed, the movement into these craft groups was so heavy that in the large centers of Boston, New York, Philadelphia, and Baltimore there flourished one hundred and fifty such groups. Also, central bodies were to be found in New York, Baltimore, Philadelphia, Washington, Boston, Newark, Albany, Troy, Pittsburgh, Cincinnati, and Louisville. The agitational centers were increased wages, the ten-hour day, and the right to organize; and using the strike weapon constantly, fighting scabs, and bringing steady pressure to bear on politicians, these local embattled cordwainers, tailors, hatters, bakers, and building-trades workers met force with force—until the prolonged depression of 1837-43 destroyed their local unions and national bodies and reduced them once more to silence and impotence. In some areas the strikes, particularly for the achievement of the ten-hour day, were successful, notably in Philadelphia; in most of them, sometimes after prolonged bitter struggles, they were lost. One permanent victory, however, was achieved. In line with an earlier promise made by President Jackson, President Van Buren established the ten-hour day in the public service, but for artisans only; a few cities followed the federal government's example. Otherwise, there were no lasting gains.

Nothing reveals more clearly the continued petty-bourgeois orientation of leadership and following of these craft groups than their general demands. They endorsed producers' co-operation as the only escape from the jaws of the rapidly advancing wage system; they clamored for free entry into the public domain in an effort to recapture their disappearing independent status as small producers; and they endorsed free education.

3. THE LEADERSHIP OF THE UTOPIANS

During the 1840's and well into the 1850's, petty-bourgeois reformism and idealism held the stage completely. What was significant, as well, was that the earlier leadership from the small producers themselves had disappeared: the journeymen cordwainers, tailors, and building-trades artisans were silenced, as their status permanently became an inferior one due to the superior organization of the capitalist group; and the spokesmen for the underprivileged became the intellectuals of the period. This was not strange: the same thing was happening in England and on the Continent. In England Thomas Carlyle was crying out against the injustices of factory slavery and, alarmed by the violence of the Chartist agitation, began to retreat intellectually more and more into the haven of a never-existing past of freemen working under the sheltering wing of a noncapitalist guild system. In France Proudhon was preaching a utopian socialism of happy collaboration between the classes. Capitalists, themselves—as in the case of the French St. Simonians—believed that something could be done and busied themselves with schemes of social amelioration. This ferment of ideas, which expressed a vague discontent over growing inequalities and a hope that reason and justice could be made to prevail and hasten the establishment of free opportunity once more, naturally crossed the ocean.

The transcendentalism of New England, in all its fine and foolish manifestations, was an effort to recapture a fast-vanishing epoch: the day of those sturdy, free, and independent producers (whether on the land or in their own small workshops) who really were creators and masters of their own destinies. It is not necessary to examine in any detail the programs of the transcendentalists, humanitarians, and petty-bourgeois reformers generally, as they were applied to the economic scene of the 1840's and early 1850's. It is enough to know that the programs were doomed to failure not because of human stupidity but because they ran counter to historical reality. The movement of the times was forward. The small producer was being expropriated and driven increasingly into the ranks of the wage laborers; the merchant capitalist, haltingly, it is true, was being supplanted by the industrial capitalist. The shop, with its toiling and skillful handicraftsmen, was being gradually replaced by the factory with its automatic machinery, rationalization of operations and discipline, and its promise of a vast outpouring of standardized products. The road to freedom also lay forward and not back.

The Associationists, under the leadership of Albert Brisbane and Horace Greeley, offered to a changing society retirement into co-operative colonies (they were called "phalanxes"), where all sorts of talents were to be assembled for the production of immediate agricultural necessities and other goods on a handicraft basis. The scheme, which had been devised by the Frenchman Charles Fourier, did not call for the abolition of the capitalist, for capitalism was to participate and receive one third of the product; but the workers were to have stability and an opportunity to make use of their different individual aptitudes. Robert Owen founded a somewhat different school of Associationists under whose dispensation factory manufacture was to be accepted and the guidance was to be of a strongly paternalist character. A few such communities were established in America; they preoccupied themselves largely with agriculture; and they quickly vanished. The Associationists were important because they were articulate and because they captured the working-men's organizations of the 1840's.

The Land Reformers, who were a little more realistic and certainly more efficient in bringing mass pressure to bear on political leaders, preoccupied themselves with a varied program of agrarian reform. Their outstanding spokesman was the Englishman George Henry Evans, who came to America a follower of the radical Thomas Spence and with the message of equal property rights for all individuals. Evans' doctrine underwent a number of transformations. At first he preached the necessity for destroying industrialism and replacing it with "rural republican townships" where land would be held only by the actual cultivators and holdings would be inalienable; industrial production, on the basis of the handicrafts entirely, would be wholly for use. But, in time, Evans was compelled to bow before the inevitable and, seeking success for his efforts, watered down his program until it came to stand simply for free lands from the public domain for all real settlers. Greeley, who posed as the workingman's friend while he savagely attacked their trade-union activities and supported high protectionism, threw the columns of his New York *Daily Tribune* open to Evans. Workers of the 1840's began to read with some astonishment, no doubt, that if "the hoary iniquities of Norman land pirates" were abolished "capital could no longer grasp the largest share of the laborer's earnings, as a reward for not doing him all the injury the laws of feudal aristocracy authorize . . ."; while the way out—to those who were pauperized and lacking even in funds to make possible their movement westward—was free entry into the public lands. For then: "Tens of thousands, who are now languishing in hopeless poverty, will find a certain and speedy independence." For a time the workers were beguiled; but the only permanent effects of the movement

were on the later Republican party and its adoption of a homestead plank in its platform.

And finally, we are to note the revival of the co-operation
agitation, both on the consumer and producer sides, with the
real goal the latter. The consumer co-operative societies were
to hoard their savings and open small workshops to make possible escape from the wage-labor system. Small groups of workers listened to the earnest petty-bourgeois intellectuals and
formed such societies during the years 1847-52: iron molders
in Cincinnati, tailors in Boston and New York, printers in Philadelphia became co-operators; but all the societies quickly
failed.

4. HANDICRAFTSMAN INTO PROLETARIAN

Meanwhile, the workers themselves, during these decades,
were on the defensive. It has been pointed out that they had no
cohesiveness, no unity of purpose, because their status was a
changing one. Some were skilled craftsmen working in small
urban shops; some were the domestic small producers of cottage
and mill; some were becoming a factory proletariat. A working-
class organizational movement does not emerge—a movement
based upon a clear recognition of sharp and unbridgable class
differences between employers and wage laborers—until the factory system is fully matured. It is, again, no accident, therefore, that the labor movement, as we understand it today, should
appear in those industries and in those areas where a proletariat
had been created. They were a minority: and only for this
reason has the trade-union movement of the late 1850's no wide
repercussions.

The 1840's and the early 1850's had seen powerful currents
appearing to drag to still lower depths the workers of the country. In the New England textile factories, ownership had been
transformed. The original paternalist owners had been supplanted by the agents of absent corporations, who, in order to
obtain larger profits, had tightened up discipline, kept wages
low, and installed the speed-up and stretch-out. The young
female operatives, finding this too severe a regimen, had retired
to the parental rural roofs never to return. They were replaced

by sturdy adult immigrants, male and female, who, because they constituted a permanent factory population and were entirely dependent upon their wage labor for their subsistence, were less likely to complain. If they did, the black list was there to add terror to insecurity. And in place of the pretty little boardinghouses there mushroomed up the dismal tenements of milltown. No one has summed up the situation more clearly than Norman J. Ware:

> By 1850 . . . the white-gowned girls who marched to welcome Presidents, who talked so intelligently to foreign visitors, who wrote poetry and stories filled with classical allusions, were no longer found in the cotton mills. They had been driven out by a prolonged and fruitless struggle to protect their standards.

The period, also, was one of constantly growing immigration into the urban centers, from both Europe and the rapidly emptying New England countryside. The foreigners had appeared on the American shore originally to be employed on public works. Native country boys had been tempted into the cities with jobs as apprentices and hopes of climbing the ladder upward. Both groups had been turned loose with the completion of their original tasks and added to the labor reserves collecting in the larger cities. Mercantile capitalism did not provide the productive means by which all these workers might be absorbed into industry. They competed with one another in the city labor markets, lived crowded together in foul rookeries, and, when unemployed, were dependent upon an inadequate and uncertain poor relief. In 1845, it was declared, 80,000 persons in New York City, fully one fifth of its population, were requiring the ministrations of public and private charity. Nothing proves more clearly the inability of mercantile capitalism to organize production than this fact of mass unemployment in a period when the forces of the depression had already spent themselves.

The discovery of gold in California and the resulting rise in prices, while it brought rich profits to merchants and land jobbers, brought only misery and suffering to urban mechanics and milltown factory hands.

In consequence, as Professor Ware has so adequately indicated, the period was one of degradation for the American worker. The "aristocrats" of labor—the skilled cordwainers, printers, and hatters—during the middle 1840's were getting between $4 and $6 a week; while a pitifully inadequate budget, drawn up by the New York *Daily Tribune*, put the minimum weekly requirement for a family of five at $10.37! Day laborers in the cities were receiving 65 cents a day. Adult operatives in the milltowns were getting from $2.75 to $3.60 a week, laboring seventy-five hours and, as a result of the speed-up and stretch-out, were tending twice as many looms as the young females had covered. During the 1850's, money wages were slightly higher but real wages were even lower due to increased living costs resulting from the effects of the heavy production of gold upon prices.

The workers struck out blindly and, because they were without trained organizational guidance, they always met with defeat. The ten-hour demand was revived during the 1840's and 1850's and once again became the center of working-class agitation. Strikes were endemic during the whole period: against wage cuts, the black list, the speed-up, for the ten-hour day; and there are records of some of them lasting for as long as six months and involving 1300 workers in one city. Artisans struck in Cincinnati, Boston, Pittsburgh; coal miners struck in Pennsylvania; day laborers struck in New York; textile operatives struck in Fall River and Lowell. The strikes, with only rare exceptions, were lost. At the beginning of the Civil War, the average working day for the American laboring population was eleven and a half hours.

Out of all this there emerged a toughened labor movement; one that was to eschew political reform and concern itself only with day-to-day gains. And it frankly adopted a working-class psychology. Indeed, some of its own early spokesmen unburdened themselves with a hard-bitten realism that is curiously modern. Thus, the address of a newly formed national craft union, the National Typographical Society, in 1850, ran:

It is useless for us to disguise from ourselves the fact that, under the present arrangement of things, there exists a perpetual antagonism between Labor and Capital. . . . To remedy the many disastrous grievances arising from this disparity of power [between employer and employed] combinations for mutual agreement in determining rates of wages and for concert of action in maintaining them, has been resorted to in many trades and principally in our own. Indeed, while the present wage system continues in operation, as an immediate protection from calamities it is clearly the only effective means which labor can adopt. So far as it extends it destroys competition in the labor market, unites the working people and produces a sort of equilibrium in the power of the conflicting classes. . . . [We] regard such an organization not only as an agent of immediate relief but also as an essential to the ultimate destruction of those unnatural relations at present subsisting between the interests of the employing and employed classes.

The stonecutters in 1853, the hat finishers in 1854, and the iron molders and machinists in 1859 formed themselves similarly into national craft bodies with programs of business trade-unionism based upon the collective agreement.

This was maturity. Small wonder that the petty-bourgeois intellectuals found this fare of the closed shop, the boycott, and the aggressive strike backed by national craft bodies too much for them. The result was that the Associationists and Land Reformers retired either into the free-soil movement or, a little later, into the Republican party.

These class-conscious trade-unionists spoke, however, only for a small company of the workers of America of the late 1850's. The universal extension of the factory system was still necessary before the independent producer, with his visions of petty-bourgeois security, could be converted into the wage laborer, who was to learn that only through working-class solidarity could concessions be obtained from the employer class.

The reasons why the workers of America, as such, under their own captains and flying their own banners, did not participate in the Civil War, must now be plain: most of them were not yet proletarians, tried in the fires of the factory system, but skilled artisans or cottage-and-mill workers who had not yet been completely expropriated. The address of the national printers' craft union, in 1850, to such as these was in a strange tongue. When Abraham Lincoln, on the other hand, addressed his first message to Congress in December, 1861, he was speaking a petty-bourgeois language that was only then in process of losing its meaning:

. . . there is not, of necessity, any such thing as the free hired laborer being fixed to that condition for life. . . . The prudent, penniless beginner in the world labors for wages a while; saves a surplus with which to buy tools or land for himself, then labors on his own account another while, and at length hires another beginner to help him.

And in 1863 Lincoln was still saying:

The strongest bond of human sympathy, outside of the family relation, should be one uniting all working people, of all nations, and tongues, and kindreds. Nor should this lead to a war upon property, or the owners of property. Property is the fruit of labor; property is desirable; is a positive good in the world. That some should be rich shows that others may become rich, and hence is just encouragement to industry and enterprise. Let not him who is houseless pull down the house of another, but let him work diligently and build one for himself, thus by example assuring that his own shall be safe from violence when built.

CHAPTER TWENTY-ONE

Planter Capitalism

1. ITS GENERAL CHARACTERISTICS

SOUTHERN capitalism, unlike most of the northern capitalism of the Middle Period, had its roots deep in production; and its perplexities grew out of the peculiar nature of the type of organization it employed. It is not necessary again to emphasize that the plantation economy was not a unique social system so much as a form of capitalist enterprise made necessary by the fact that southern capital was invested largely in slaves rather than in land. The planter, therefore, was not a feudal lord producing in a natural economy but an enterpriser raising cash crops for sale in a money market. The factor that differentiated him from the industrial capitalist was that his capital fund had virtually no flexibility. He was committed—and doomed—to commercial and extensive agriculture because that was really the only thing his capital, that is his slave gang, was fitted for.

What was significant in the planter's position was the following set of circumstances. The price of cotton (fixed in a world market) fluctuated beyond his ability to control it and by the 1850's—when the crisis in southern capitalism emerged—prices received for southern staples were out of line with costs of production. It is true that there was no wide disparity between the prices of cotton and rice, on the one hand, and the prices for those necessaries planters required to maintain their farms and homes, on the other. But these latter were only one element in plantation costs: in addition, there were the freights, commissions, interest payments, and the capital costs of slaves; and these were steadily mounting. As a result of the toll taken by such fixed charges there can be no question that the value of the southern farm dollar was shrinking in a period that was witnessing an inflationary movement due to the heavy inflow of gold following the California discoveries.

We have seen that the agriculturists of the free states were able to adjust themselves to this situation by reducing their unit costs through mechanization and greater efficiency of production. The southern agriculturist could decrease his main fixed costs only at two points: lower rents (that is to say, constant movement from old regions into new) and lower costs for slaves. The first was regularly taking place: indeed, one of the characteristics of the whole Middle Period was the transfer of operations from already exploited areas into hitherto uncultivated ones. The most decided movement was into the Southwest; but southern planters were also constantly bringing under the plow land never before cultivated in old settled regions, that is, the opening up of the backcountry.

Up to the 1850's, this type of relief was enough to continue to insure in a measure the profitability of the plantation system. Indeed, it is a mistake to assume that one of the inescapable pressures on southern capitalist agriculture was its exhaustion of available lands for its particular type of exploitation. L. C. Gray, in his monumental history of southern agriculture, has clearly proved that the plantation system, rather than being confronted by land dearth, was, at the opening of the Civil War, faced by potential abundance with the promise of the throwing open of new regions by the railroads. The pinch came, however, when reduction of rent costs by transference to new areas of operations was not sufficient. For while prices of necessaries needed for farm and home were going up, and the price of cotton was fluctuating erratically, the price of prime field hands also was advancing. Why was this? It was due to the fact that superior methods of organization and their location in new planting regions made it possible for lower South farmers to tempt away the slaves from the interior, the Border States, and the tidewater. That is to say, by the late 1850's, with scarcity in the available unfree labor supply, slave prices were based on their productivity under ideal conditions. To a large company of southern planters, therefore, it was of the utmost importance that this form of capital costs also be reduced; and it could be done only by the legal reopening of the oversea slave traffic. The heart of the southern program was to be found at this point.

There was another area of disaffection. The inflexibility of southern capital has already been referred to: southern capital was concentrated in plantation operations. The result was, plantation owners were dependent upon outside funds—most of which came from the North—both for the maintenance of their homes and for all the processes associated with the planting, cultivating, harvesting, and marketing of their crops. The factors, bankers, brokers, shipowners, and warehousemen who served southern agriculture were merchant capitalists from without (New York City, in particular, was cast in this role), who monopolized these activities and drew their interest and profits from providing these services. For such services the South believed it was paying too high a price. Undoubtedly it was. The necessity for commanding capital funds to make possible the shifting of operations and with which to buy new slaves; and the constant need for intermediate credit to finance virtually everything the planter did: these put the southern economy completely at the mercy of the moneylender.

Thus, in the midst of the panic of 1857, when prices for southern staples continued good, southern publicists and political spokesmen were inveighing bitterly against the dominance over their economy by northern mercantile capital. This they characterized as "the unnatural and colonial dependency of our commercial community on New York." One may note that word "colonial"; southern leaders were projecting themselves back into an earlier period of revolutionary crisis in American annals and viewing their ills as springing once again from their exploitation at the hands of a superior and absentee economic power.

Here, therefore, was another series of costs which had to be reduced. How could this be accomplished? By a closer alliance with English capital which would help the South free itself of its unhappy connection with northern capital if the South were in a position to offer a *quid pro quo*: a system of free trade under which southern exports of plantation wares would be balanced by imports of English manufactured goods and English services and capital.

2. THE PLANTATION SYSTEM

The plantation system, as a method of agricultural organization, has been described earlier in connection with the southern colonial production of tobacco. When, after the Revolution, cotton became the basic cash crop of southern commercial farming, none of the essential characteristics of the plantation was changed. These were: a monoculture, which could employ labor for the greater part of the year; the use of an unfree labor force, which was able to produce surplus value over and above its own subsistence costs; extensive rather than intensive cultivation because of the necessity for extracting a maximum current money income from the capital, i.e., the slaves, invested; and dependence upon outside credit for much of the normal functioning of the whole structure.

In terms of such an order there existed many areas where weaknesses manifested themselves. Gray has described clearly the most significant of these:

It is probable that the characteristic tendency in commercial planting regions toward an economy that stressed maximum current money income was not favorable to the rapid accumulation of wealth over a long period. It involved the neglect of soil conservation and the numerous petty economies that contribute toward accumulation. The waste of the soil necessitated periodically heavy expenses in the purchase of land. The large money returns of fortunate years stimulated extravagance in the planting class, a tendency naturally promoted by the necessity of maintaining external evidences of superiority over economic and social inferiors. . . . That the South in general, and particularly the lower South, was continuously a debtor region was partly due to the requirements for new capital on account of the exigencies of expansion. But the relative poverty of the South, as compared with the North, was largely the result of a system of rural economy characterized by extravagance both in production and consumption, a system that concentrated a large proportion of the money income in the hands of a relatively small percentage of the population. A large proportion of the remaining white population were pushed into isolated regions where they pursued a largely self-sufficing economy. . . .

Thus, the plantation system was mining the soil of the older regions and also reducing them to impotence, productively, by draining off their available labor force. The plantation system had another serious social and economic consequence. Like the feudal system, at least in this particular, it had little use for an expanding population; while it was also compelled to assume a social responsibility toward the nonproductive groups in its own midst. Most of the whites were either plantation lords or yeomen farmers or the agents and overseers on the great plantations; opportunities for enterprise in the cities and for a free working population were relatively slight. The result was, immigrants did not move into the South and its own younger sons tended to migrate to other sections. Nothing is more revealing than the contrast between the dependent population of the South and that of the North. Considering dependents as falling in the age groups under fifteen years and over seventy years, in 1860 the South had 832 dependents (white and black) to 1000 population of working age as contrasted with the ratio in the northeastern states of 554 to 1000. The ratio of dependency to productivity was equally great for whites and blacks in the South. For whites, it was 815 to 1000; for blacks, 862 to 1000. The disproportionate numbers of young and old persons were obviously a very serious encumbrance upon the section's economy.

3. COTTON PRODUCTION

Cotton became a basic cash crop of the Middle Period for two reasons: the extraordinary increase in demand due to the rise of the cotton textile industry, which was closely linked with automatic machinery; and the ease with which it was possible to separate the seed from the lint, thanks to Eli Whitney's invention of the cotton gin. The first had preceded the second, for even before the Revolution England had begun to import cotton from the New World; but the cotton gin accounted for the amazing expansion of the planting area. The first important

regions of cultivation were in the upper South Carolina country
and in central Georgia, with cotton also being grown in Virginia, North Carolina, and Tennessee. As the zone of cultivation spread into the lower South the size of the crop increased,
not steadily, of course, for price was an important factor. Thus,
production stood at only 150,000 bales in 1815 and at 4,500,000
bales in 1859. Within that short space, production had doubled
from 1815 to 1820; it had doubled again by 1826; there was no
sharp increase up to 1830, and then from 1830 to 1837 it had
doubled again; there was little advance throughout the 1840's,
and then by 1851 the crop was twice that of 1837. In 1859, the
crop was double the size of 1849's.

The human movement into the lower South and Southwest
naturally went hand in hand with the increase in the cotton
crop. Notably during the 1830's and the 1850's, the flow of
younger sons, older planters themselves, and Negroes into the
rich alluvial lands along the Gulf, the Mississippi River, and the
tributaries emptying into the Mississippi River from the west
went on in an unending stream; and as these migrants quitted
Maryland, Virginia, and South Carolina to leave the old commonwealths for a time almost prostrate, they filled up Alabama,
Mississippi, Louisiana, and the eastern Texas and Arkansas
counties. Professor Carman records that by 1850 there were
388,000 Virginians and 128,000 Marylanders living in other
states. Alabama and Mississippi together grew from 40,000 population in 1810 to 1,660,000 in 1860.

Nothing reveals the shifting character of the area better than
the sources of supply of the cotton crop. In 1801 almost the
whole crop was raised in the old South, that is to say, in South
Carolina, Georgia, Virginia, and North Carolina; in 1826 more
than half of it was still being grown in this region; in 1834 only
one third; in 1859 considerably less than one fourth. In this
last year Mississippi alone was responsible for as much as the
four states of the old South.

The great outlet for American cotton was Europe, with England far and away the best customer and with France, Germany,
Austria, and Russia trailing in the rear. Indeed, England's consumption of American cotton was greater than our own, al-

though at the outbreak of the Civil War America's rate of consumption was increasing faster. Thus, comparing 1839-40 with 1859-60, England increased its use of American cotton 130 per cent; the United States, 184 per cent. By 1860, the United States was using 37 per cent as much cotton as did England. The role of cotton exports in American foreign trade has already been referred to: it is enough here to repeat that whereas in 1810 cotton exports had made up but 22 per cent of the country's total export, by value, in 1860 the proportion was 57 per cent.

Cotton prices, during the whole period, had changed rather sharply from time to time. According to Gray's figures, middling cotton was selling for 30 cents a pound at New Orleans in 1815; from thence on there had been a downward movement of prices, reaching a low in 1844, when cotton sold for 6 cents. In 1846 cotton was at 10.5 cents; in 1848 again at 6 cents; in 1850 at 12 cents; during 1852-54 at 9 cents. For the period 1855-60, the average price was in the neighborhood of 11 cents. This was well enough for a small company of new planters in the deep South; but it must have meant real distress for the plantations located in the interior and the tidewater states.

The handling of the cotton crop was not much unlike the marketing methods that had been developed in connection with colonial tobacco. Located at the great export ports were factoring houses which took the cotton from the plantations on consignment; into the bargain, the factor was the planter's banker in view of the southerner's great dependence upon credit. The costs of handling and financing obviously accumulated at an alarming rate: there was a charge of 2.5 per cent as commission; there was a charge of another 2.5 per cent for purchases made for the planter; interest had to be paid for long-term loans for land and slave purchases; and there were items arising from freight payments, warehousing, insurance, draying, weighing, and sampling. To cover all these costs the planter pledged his crop to the factor: he was committed to the system of single-cropping as soon as he had acquired a landed property and a labor force large enough to permit the seeding of a crop.

4. OTHER CASH CROPS

By the opening of the nineteenth century tobacco was lead-ing easily all the southern staples; that it should quickly fall behind in the race was only natural. Particularly after the Napoleonic Wars, Europeans turned to other sources of supply, while the need for an expanded public revenue encouraged foreign statesmen to impose sumptuary taxes on the leaf. Nor could tobacco growers compete with cotton planters for land use. Production stopped expanding during 1800-40, and it was not until the appearance of a new variety, which quickly gained popularity, that tobacco began once more to find favor with southern agriculturists. Rice similarly continued as an im-portant southern staple, but it too fell off in relative importance. It continued to be cultivated largely in the South Carolina and Georgia coastal plain. Sugar became a significant cash crop in the Middle Period. Confined, because of climatic factors, to southern Louisiana and southeastern Texas, and requiring addi-tional capital for grinding apparatus, its cultivation evidenced all the aspects of factory production. Concentration developed quickly so that before the Civil War one half of Louisiana's entire crop was made by about one hundred and sixty planters located along the Mississippi. The slave populations on these plantations were much larger than on cotton, production was more closely supervised, and returns were uniformly greater because price fluctuations were not so extreme.

5. THE SOUTHERN CLASS SOCIETY

The pyramidal form of southern white society in very con-siderable measure approximated that of feudal Europe in the fourteenth century. At the narrow apex, like the princes of feudal society, was perched a small group of powerful planting families whose economic and social methods and habits put their stamp on the whole economy. In the middle layer, like the sizable company of feudal knights, was to be found a larger group who possessed a few slaves but not enough to give them the economic status of great capitalist farmers. These small owners were as a rule tucked away in the backcountry and it was upon them that the pressures of the system, particularly in the 1850's, were most insistent. It was perfectly natural, therefore, that the hotheads of the section, who became the leaders in the clamor for secession, should come from this class. At the bottom of the pyramid, very much resembling the newly emancipated copyholders and free peasants of the late feudal age, was to be found a great company of nonslave-owning yeomen farmers some of whom produced occasionally for a cash market while some were almost entirely noncommercial agriculturists. In this class, also, were to be found the relatively few "poor whites" of the coastal plains and piney woods regions. (These last might be compared with the landless cotters.)

The sharply graded class divisions in southern society may be clearly indicated by the numbers of slaveholders in 1860. The following table is the compilation of Professors Kendrick and Arnett:

SLAVEHOLDING GROUPS ACCORDING TO PERSONS HELD IN 1860

No. of Slaves Held	No. of Holders	Per Cent of All Holders	No. of Persons in Holding Families	Per Cent of White Population in Families
100 and over......	2,292	.6	11,460	.2
20 and over......	46,274	12.1	231,370	2.9
10–19...........	61,682	15.8	308,410	3.9
5–9............	89,423	23.2	447,115	5.6
1–4............	186,256	48.5	931,280	11.8
Totals........	383,637	100.0	1,938,185	24.2

This reveals a startling situation. Only 24.2 per cent of the whole white population in the South was associated with slavery. Again, the small holders (possessing one to nine slaves), who were yeomen farmers working their own fields and who owned a handful of Negroes to assist them in the arduous rounds of planting, chopping, and picking cotton, made up nearly three fourths of the slave-owning population. In such a situation, concentration of ownership was to be expected: and the figures clearly prove it. Thus, in 1860, 7 per cent of the South's total white population of eight million persons belonged to families possessing ten or more slaves; and these 7 per cent of the whites owned 74.4 per cent of the enslaved blacks. Another 17.4

per cent of the whites belonged to families possessing nine
slaves or less; and these 17.4 per cent owned 25.6 per cent of the
slaves. As has already been said, the remaining 75.8 per cent of
the whites owned no slaves at all.

We are also to note regional differences. In the lower South,
one third of the white families were slaveholding as compared
with one fifth in the border South. Also, in the lower South,
two thirds of the whole population (white and black) were associated with the slave system as compared with but two fifths in
the border South. Again, in the lower South, 19.4 per cent of
the slaves were to be found on holdings of nine slaves or less;
while 14.2 per cent were to be found on holdings of one hundred slaves and over. In the Border States, 35.4 per cent were on
holdings of nine slaves or less; and only 3.4 per cent were on
holdings of one hundred slaves and over. Concentration of
ownership became even more marked in definite areas of the
lower South. L. C. Gray points out, for example, that in a number of counties in lower Mississippi the median number of
slaves on cotton plantations was around 117. This was capitalist
agriculture on a vast scale; and it was among this small company of slave lords that incomes ranged up to $50,000 annually.

Here were significant class divisions within a ruling group.
A handful of white owners represented concentration of ownership and, in the beginning at any rate, concentration of power.
A group, two and one half times its size, represented small
ownership which, in the beginning, was willing to accept the
political leadership of the great owners. But, by the 1850's, because the economic pressures on this middle group were becoming more and more exigent, *they* commenced to take the bit
in their teeth. Leadership in a shaping crisis more and more
fell into their hands. We may, at this point, summarize the
reasons why.

The small owners of slaves possessed the poorer lands usually
in the upcountry. They were distant from the means of communication, the market, and credit: in short, their costs of making, marketing, and financing their crops were higher. (To this
extent, therefore, it is to be noted that the practice of quoting
the price of cotton at New Orleans is deceptive. The upcountry

farmers received a considerably lower price on their farms; for they had to absorb the costs of transportation and handling to the distant market. Also, the big planters, who were near the markets, obviously could command better credit facilities.) The slaves they owned as a rule were only field hands: for they could not afford women and children. Thus, their capital could not tend to reproduce itself, as frequently happened in the case of the large plantation owners. Because of these factors the price-costs ratio of operations on these smaller farms tended more and more toward imbalance. It is in these terms that we can view the economic difficulties of the South, as the 1850's developed, and explain why there were divided counsels in the ranks of the ruling white group.

As has been said, at the bottom of the social scale were those independent white farmers who were not joined directly with the slave economy. Most of them were poor, of course, but only in the economic sense. They were the independent yeomen of the western counties of Virginia and North Carolina, the eastern counties of Tennessee, and the northern counties of Georgia, farming families who cultivated their steadily failing freeholds largely for the supplying of their own needs and for the raising of some cash crops. Here, the production of small grains, hay, and a little dairying took place; markets were local and the ties with the plantations were effected economically at this point. From this class also came the overseers of the great plantations and the white mechanics and artisans of the southern towns.

Not very distant from this group, in an economic sense, were the completely self-sufficing farmers of the highlands who worked their rough hillside farms with a wholly primitive technique and eked out a poverty-stricken existence by hunting, trapping, and fishing. Such highlanders were to be found in both the eastern Appalachians and the western Ozarks. They were a sturdy, independent group who jealously guarded their liberties from tax collectors and school authorities: from them later were to be recruited the hands of modern-day southern mill-towns and Ohio onion fields.

At the very base of this group were the relatively few "poor whites" of legend: the "sand-hillers," "crackers," and "clay eaters" of the eastern old South: those unfortunates who, because of poverty, had become isolated in nonproductive pine barrens and sandy coastal plains zones; who lived in a misery and squalor that has rarely had its equal in human history; and whose low physical and mental state was due to inadequate diets, malaria, hookworm, and constant inbreeding.

This analysis of the class structure of southern society has been in terms largely of a rural population. This does no violence to the facts, for even the businessmen and townspeople were caught inextricably in the social and economic relations of the slave system. Towns, as mercantile and productive centers, were few. Indeed, by 1860, there were only five southern communities with populations between 20,000 and 50,000 (Charleston, Richmond, Mobile, Memphis, and Savannah) and only one, New Orleans, with a population in excess of this upper limit (168,000 in 1860). The lower middle class in the southern towns was made up of the small independent producers and mechanics and artisans of an earlier day; for even mercantile capitalism had not yet entered the southern economy as far as industrial production was concerned.

As for a distinctly urban upper class, Professors Kendrick and Arnett point out that this did not constitute an independent bourgeoisie. The resident merchants, bankers, brokers, and professional men were more frequently than not planters themselves; and the persons who gave southern urban life its peculiar tone were as a rule planters living in their town houses during the winter and spring seasons.

We have seen that only a small proportion of the southern whites held slaves and were engaged in plantation agriculture. But slaveowner or not, virtually every southern white was committed to the slave system. There were economic reasons. Some of them employed slave labor directly; some were professional people, furnishing services to the slaveowners; some were the overseers; the great mass were the hewers of wood and drawers of water who in a thousand and one different ways were bound up with the economy.

There were social and psychological reasons. The presence

of a large number of unfree blacks gave the humblest white worker and farmer a sense of superiority: he, at least, was free to move and think as he pleased; he could sometimes vote and send members of his class to legislative halls. He belonged—so the apologists of the slave system told him—to a superior race destined to rule over an inferior one. Certain economic realities seemed to make no difference: that black slavery limited possibilities for economic advancement for enterprisers (the plantations were constantly swallowing up the farms of the independent yeomen); and that black slavery cut down the number of job opportunities for whites (slaves were to be found in mines, on railroads, in ironworks, in textile factories, and in the skilled crafts, thus constantly crowding the whites into narrowing spheres of activity). There is no question that the whites, particularly the poorer ones, accepted a low economic status because of the psychological compensations they were able to derive from the system whose supporters, and dupes also, they were. It is one of the great ironies of history that these were the men who freely thronged into the Confederate armies to give up their lives in defense of an institution which had victimized them so long.

A member of this class, Hinton R. Helper, in 1857 published a startling book, *The Impending Crisis of the South,* in which he sought to point out some of these things: the poorer whites would never be free, he said, until they were ready to escape from between the upper and lower millstones, by class war on the plantation "lords of the lash" and race war on their enslaved "black and bicolored caitiffs." But Helper's call for struggle was without avail, for the poorer whites were as much the prisoners of the system as were its chief beneficiaries. The Negro historian, W. E. B. Du Bois, wisely says:

But the poor whites and their leaders could not for a moment contemplate a fight of united white and black labor against the exploiters. Indeed, the natural leaders of the poor whites, the small farmer, the merchant, the professional man, the white mechanic and slave overseer, were bound to the planters and repelled from the slaves and even from the mass of the white laborers in two ways: first, they constituted the police patrol who could ride with planters and now and then exercise unlimited force upon the recalcitrant or runaway slaves; and then, too, there was always a chance that they themselves might also become planters by saving money, by investment, by the power of good luck. . . .

6. THE BLACKS

Of a little less than the four and a quarter million blacks living in the South in 1860, only a quarter million enjoyed the dubious privileges of freemen; the rest were slaves, the overwhelming majority field hands. The free Negroes, like the "poor whites," were the South's guilty reminders of the great injustices inherent in its mode of production. If the whites were racially a dominant group and the Negroes committed to slavery by anthropological, medical, and Biblical authority, then a free black capable of and successful in supporting himself and his family flew in the face of that "natural reason" that the medieval Schoolmen liked so much to appeal to. Every obstacle, therefore, was placed in the way of the achievement of such a pass. Whites refused to work side by side with free blacks; they were denied schooling; they were compelled to wear badges, post bonds, and register; quite frequently they were kidnaped and re-enslaved. And to prevent their numbers from growing, legislators hit upon the device of ordering the departure of emancipated blacks as soon as their manumission had been effected. There were a few free blacks who became so wealthy in the South, particularly as plantation lords, that they were accorded every legal protection in their property rights.

It has been said that the vast majority of unfree blacks were field hands. Nevertheless there did spring up a small group which, originally separated from agriculture only temporarily, and then later permanently, became identified with industrial activity. Of course, every large plantation had its own staff of slave handicraftsmen who performed the normal functions associated with the conduct of a plant as complex in its workings as must have been the factory farm—the blacksmiths, carpenters, wheelwrights, masons, harness makers, and cobblers. But, in addition, there came to exist a body of slaves who took the place of wage laborers in a wide range of industries. Their presence adequately disproves the often-heard contention that slavery, as such, was an inefficient system because the slaves themselves were incapable of mastering more than the crudest kinds of operations. Thus, slaves from the beginning had been successfully employed in the unskilled work connected with canal building and railroad construction; they labored in the mining and quarrying industries and in the South's lumber camps; and, when secondary manufacturing on a limited scale sprang up, slaves were put to work at forges, furnaces, factory benches, and textile looms. Gray shows that a considerable number of the South's cotton textile plants were run in whole or in part by slaves; that on the Cumberland River in Tennessee nearly 60 per cent of the workers in the local iron industry were slaves; and that in Richmond, Virginia, after 1845 the majority of the operatives in the ironworks were unfree blacks. It is significant to note, also, that in the antebellum South not only were railroad locomotives fired by slaves but not infrequently the important post of engineer was entrusted to an unfree black as well.

These were exceptions, of course; slaves were bred and bought and sold chiefly to toil on the plantations and farms of the capitalist agriculture of the South. Working in gangs on the large plantations and under the close supervision of overseers, the slaves performed all the operations connected with field labor. But because the plantation was not a simple organism, there existed as well a certain specialization of function. U. B. Phillips, the social historian of the slave system, notes the following slave composition of a large plantation on the James River in Virginia in 1854. On the domestic staff, there were 1 butler, 2 waitresses, 4 housemaids, 1 nurse, 1 laundress, 1 seamstress, 1 dairy maid, and 1 gardener. On the field staff, there were 8 plowmen, 22 hoe hands, 2 wagoners, 4 ox drivers, and 2 cooks. On the stable and pasture staffs, there were 1 carriage driver, 1 cowherd, and 1 hogsherd. In the crafts, there were 2 carpenters, 5 stonemasons, 1 miller, 2 blacksmiths, 2 shoemakers, 5 women spinners, and 1 woman weaver. In addition, there were 45 children and several superannuated blacks too old to work.

In 1810 the whole South had a slave population of 1,158,000; in 1860 of 3,950,000. By the Constitution, the oversea slave traffic had been outlawed in 1808 and, while a small illegal traffic continued up to 1860, the great increase in the slave population was due to natural causes. But in the old South, from 1810 to 1860, the Negro population had only doubled, while in the new and lower South it had increased tenfold in the same half century. Obviously, the great growth in the latter region was not due to natural reasons alone. The key to the riddle is a simple one: slaves were moved into the area on a commercial basis from a group of states which, in effect, became the breeding districts for the whole system. These states were principally Virginia, South Carolina, Kentucky, and Missouri.

It is a little difficult, perhaps, to prove that conscious breeding, as such, took place in the old and border South; but when slaves were being shifted from regions where they could not be employed productively any longer into others where the prices for them—after 1845—kept on mounting steadily, the end result was the same. During the period 1820-60, almost a million blacks were transferred from the old and border South to the lower South; it is safe to assume that the great majority of them did not move along with their migrating masters but in the coffles of the professional and commercial dealers. Put at an average price of $500 a head over the whole period, the value of the traffic to the rearing states must have been not far from half a billion dollars.

The traffic was competently organized and directed. The traders bought and sold for their own account or on commission; there were assembling centers in most of the southern towns at which were collected slaves picked up by field agents; and there were distributing points in the deep South from which the blacks were sent out into the plantation areas. When trading firms bought for their own account, they used the auction method to dispose of their human wares. Obviously, sentiment could play no part in the business: families were broken up, children being parted from their parents and husbands and wives separated as the demands of the buyers necessitated. There can be no question that much of the sexual looseness which so many sociologists assume is an innate characteristic of the Negro race was acquired during the years of the domestic slave trade in the South.

Here was a large servile population living, however, in a society which could not isolate itself from the rest of the world. Without, the climate was free; and reports of the struggle for freedom—in slave revolts in the Caribbean, revolutionary movements in Latin America, emancipation in the British possessions—were constantly beating upon its doors. The South sought to thrust these back. It built up the tradition of a patriarchal society and marshaled its intelligence to prove to the outside that the Negro was an inferior. All this, really, was unavailing. And as time went on, and as Negroes continued to rebel against their bondage either in flight or in sporadic conspiracies and plots and occasional outbreaks, force had to be resorted to.

During the history of slavery, tens of thousands of blacks fled from plantations to find refuge and live precariously in the swamps, mountains, and forests of the South. These so-called "maroons," as Herbert Aptheker points out, tried to establish sometimes a settled life; but more frequently, because they were being harried, they met violence with violence. "They offered havens for fugitives [says Mr. Aptheker], served as bases for marauding expeditions against near-by plantations and, at times, supplied the nucleus of leadership for planned uprisings."

The threatened and actual risings of Negroes in the South have been much more frequent than we have been led to assume. These movements were comparable to the outbreaks of the serfs in thirteenth- and fourteenth-century Europe. Unorganized and therefore rarely taking widespread forms; more often than not never getting much beyond incendiarism and murder; led by religious zealots frequently—they never really got out of hand. The whole slave period is filled with evidences of plots nipped in the bud, outbreaks which spread local terror until they were put down by the military, and conspiracies which did sometimes cover more than just an immediate neighborhood. Sometimes, stories of plots and revolts actually were able to escape out of the South—for undoubtedly there existed

a tacit censorship among southern editors and political spokesmen. The most important of these were Denmark Vesey's
abortive conspiracy in 1822 at Charleston, South Carolina, and
Nat Turner's revolt in 1831 at Southampton, Virginia. That
toward the end, in the decade of the 1850's, the South's career
was marked by a pervasive unrest among the slaves, evidences
of which were to be found all over the region, we are only now
beginning to understand. The fiction of the docile Negro living
contentedly in a "Greek democracy" and protected against his
own inadequacies has died hard.

The growing clamor of the Abolitionist crusade and the
uncertainties and perplexities which had the slave system in
their grip—coupled with the intensification of production in
the deep South—fed the flames of Negro unrest on the eve of
the Civil War. Plots and conspiracies everywhere were disclosed.
Occasional uprisings broke out, homes were burned, and slaveowners and overseers were killed—to the accompaniment of
shootings and hangings with or without legal formality.

The South, in fact, was constantly under arms. Says Mr.
Aptheker: "The carrying of some type of weapon was a universal
characteristic of southern white men. Well-trained militia companies and voluntary military units were numerous, patrols
were everywhere, armed overseers were on all plantations,
guards and standing armies . . . abounded in the cities." Legal
vigilance went hand in hand with military preparedness; and
every conceivable device was tested and used for the purpose
of preventing Negroes from consorting with each other or ex-
changing intelligence. Schools for Negroes were outlawed. The
activities of black ministers were closely scrutinized. Negroes
could not assemble without permission or supervision. They
could not move about without passes. They might not carry
weapons or resist whites. With the characteristic understatement
of almost all the commentators on this dark and secret side of
the slave institution, the historian Frederick J. Turner has remarked: "The principle of governing by fear gained supporters
in some states."

On the other hand, the civil status of the blacks under slavery
has been put this way by Professor Du Bois:

Slaves were not considered men. They had no right of petition. They were "devisable like any other chattel." They could own nothing; they could make no contracts; they could hold no property, nor traffic in property; they could not hire out; they could not legally marry nor constitute families; they could not control their children; they could not appeal from their master; they could be punished at will. They could not testify in court; they could be imprisoned by their owners, and the criminal offense of assault and battery could not be committed on the person of a slave. The "willful, malicious and deliberate murder" of a slave was punishable by death, but such a crime was practically impossible of proof. The slave owed to his master and all his family a respect "without bounds and an absolute obedience." This authority could be transmitted to others. A slave could not sue his master; had no right of redemption; no right to education or religion; a promise made to a slave by his master had no force nor validity. Children followed the condition of the slave mother. The slave could have no access to the judiciary. A slave might be condemned to death for striking any white person.

CHAPTER TWENTY-TWO

The Pressures on the Slave Economy

1. THE PLIGHT OF THE SOUTH

THE opening of the decade of the 1850's saw the contradictions at the heart of the slave system multiplying. An economy based upon slave labor utilized for the production of agricultural staples in a world market could not continue to develop evenly unless it was in a position to control all the economic factors entering into its costs structure. Under ideal conditions the slave plantation as a method of production was not inefficient; but such a status could be maintained only when the fixed charges of slave labor and the costs of interest and services could constantly be brought into line with the price that cotton commanded in the world market. Southern producers were hobbled by their dependence upon northern capital and the constitutional limitations imposed upon their slave supply: of those restraints it was imperative that they be free.

The immobility of southern capital has already been referred to. This was the heart of the slave-plantation problem. Capital was largely tied up in the securing of the slave supply; and because slave costs were great the southern planter was incapable of diverting his capital fund into such areas where he from time to time required relief. He was committed to planting. It is idle to assume that the South sought to become a wholly self-sufficing region engaged as well in a diversified manufacturing and agricultural economy. Sugar and rice cultivation, and frequently cotton cultivation, produced enormous profits and created a society entirely satisfactory to its outstanding beneficiaries. But the profits were great only when all costs were in line with the prices received in the markets for the South's basic crops. The question of rent was not so significant: there still remained a vast area of uncultivated land yet to be brought under the plow. Even the soils of old-settled regions could be reclaimed (as they have been in modern times) if labor costs were reduced sharply.

We must, in other words, see the dilemma of the planter as a problem in mounting costs. The cost of his slaves was increasing: this had to be cut. The costs of making and marketing a crop were high, due in part to heavy indirect government taxes. But this made the charges so high that something had to be done to cut them. About these problems clustered the agitation and demands of southerners. If the capital value of the slave property could be lowered, then a portion of the southern capital fund might be moved into transportation, warehousing, even banking. More particularly, if the prosperity of the planting economy could be assured, English capital, at a lower cost, might be attracted to displace northern capital with its high interest rates and unwarranted charges for services.

The upward movement of prices in the 1850's as a result of the gold discoveries; the high costs for short-term capital and services; most important of all, the alarming rise in the value of prime field hands: these events, in the face of an uncontrollable cotton market, precipitated the southern system into crisis exactly at the moment when northern industrial capitalism was beginning to sink its roots deep into the American economy. As far as the South was concerned, therefore, rejuvenation of its economy demanded the attainment of the following program. First, slave costs had to be cut, if necessary through the reopening of the African trade. Second, free trade had to be established in order to throw open the American market to English manufactured goods. Third, the South had to be freed of its dependence upon northern mercantile and banking capital for its shipping, brokerage, insurance, and credit. If the English could be permitted to sell more goods and services to the South than was the case, then English long-term capital would move into the region for the development of transportation facilities and, perhaps, banks. Fourth, it was imperative that every obstacle be placed in the way of the further strengthening of the economic alliance between New York and New England capital on the one hand and western enterprise on the other; for this reason the South was compelled to resist efforts to use public moneys to build northwestern railroads, to throw open north-western and far western public lands to homesteaders, and to lower the bars to unrestricted immigration. Finally, the move-ment into the western lands had to be checked to prevent the building up of the political power of the free states. If this program was impossible of maintenance, then secession and political independence constituted the inevitable alternative.

2. THE COST OF SLAVES

In the rising price of slaves, notably after the end of the de-pression of 1837-43, we find the Achilles heel of the plantation economy. It has generally been assumed that the price of prime field hands roughly followed the rise and fall of cotton prices: and that these two prime factors in the price-costs structure of the slave economy were therefore always in balance. But this was only generally true, for there were periods of sharp fluctuation in the costs of slaves; and, after 1846, the gap be-tween costs and prices tended steadily to widen.

The price of all types of slaves was based upon the value of the male prime field hand, that is to say, the male between the ages of eighteen and thirty years. And the price of the prime field hand was based upon the price of his hire. So, in general, the average price of slaves was about 40 to 50 per cent of the value of prime field hands, with infants being sold by the pound and boys and girls often being valued by their height and weight. On the other hand, the price of the prime field hand was put at six to eight times his annual rate of hire.

The elaborate investigations of Ulrich B. Phillips indicate that the following was the price movement of prime field hands.

For about twenty years following the outbreak of the Revolu-tion, there was a downward movement, which was checked temporarily just after the war by a sudden speculative rise. At the end of the eighteenth century, prices for prime field hands in South Carolina ranged between $300 and $350. Then, from the middle 1790's (following the invention of the cotton gin) to the outbreak of the War of 1812, there was a steady rise in price; and this in turn was followed by a drop of panic proportions due to the commercial difficulties with Great Britain. So, during 1808-10, at New Orleans, the maximum price stood at $900; two years later, it had dropped off $300.

Another period of speculative activity followed from the end of the war to 1819: and the price of prime field hands rose to as high as $900 at Charleston (in the old South) and $1100 at New Orleans (in the new South). Then there set in another period of low prices, lasting for upwards of a decade. From 1830 to 1837, the trend once more was upward, with prices between $1000 and $1200 for prime field hands. The depression of 1837-43 was reflected in a decline again which continued steadily until 1845. Then the price stood at $600.

The next rise was virtually unbroken until the outbreak of the Civil War. Professor Phillips has sought to read into this price movement the same speculative characteristics which undoubtedly were present in the sharp upturns of 1815-19 and 1830-37; but he is in error. This time, particularly in the 1850's, the upward climb was a reflection of growing dearth in the available slave supply rather than the market manipulations of traders at Charleston and New Orleans. The prices, then, mounted; so that prior to the Civil War, slaves of all ages in the Southwest probably were averaging $600. Prime field hands, by 1860, sold for from $1200 to $1800, with the average at $1500.

It has been said that during this last rise, the price of slaves was out of relation to the price of cotton. According to Professor Phillips, at New Orleans, the ratio of cents of cotton per pound to hundreds of dollars for the average slave stood as follows for various years: 1805, 4 to 1; 1819, 2 to 1; 1837, 1 to 1; 1860, 0.6 to 1.

By 1850, the demand for slave labor was intensified not only as a result of the superior bidding power of the southwestern plantations, but also because of the competition for slaves springing up from new economic regions. Notably in the Border States, the renewal of tobacco cultivation, railroad construction on a large scale, the opening of new ironworks, and the erection of cotton textile plants placed a mounting premium on the hiring-out value of slaves. In the South itself, pressure was also emerging from the following quarters: lumbering and turpentine production, particularly in the tidewater region; the mining of coal and iron in the southern Appalachian district; and public works, particularly river-improvement projects, everywhere.

The result was, the rates of hire mounted sharply. In 1797 laborers were hired out at $70 a year; and in 1837, the price was still around $80 to $90. But by 1857, male field hands were bringing $120 to $150 a year with board; and the owners of slave factory hands in the Southeast were receiving as much as $200. According to Professor Phillips, Virginia tobacco factories in 1860 were paying $225 a year. And in the Southwest, the hiring price the same year was between $300 and $360. In view of the fact, as has been said, that purchase price was based on hiring price, and that hiring prices were steadily climbing due to pressure from outside regions upon the available supply, it is a little difficult to accept Professor Phillips' supposition that the situation was an abnormal one. It was normal; there was dearth; and in this factor we find the greatest strain on the price-costs structure of the plantation economy.

It has already been pointed out that the stresses and strains were not equally felt. The chief victims of the imbalance were not the great planters of the southern alluvial gulf plain. Their plantations were operated on the gang system, so that productivity could be stepped up—and was. (It has been estimated that productivity on the huge factory plantations of the Southwest was two to four times as great as on the small farms of the old South.) Again, in part, the big planters could reproduce their own slave supply and so were not as completely dependent upon the market. But the small farmers, located usually in the up-country, felt the pressure keenly. They maintained only small slave establishments, as a rule without women and children. They had to hire in emergencies and buy when their field hands were no longer productive. The small farmers and their sons worked in the fields with the slaves: the gang system, with its intensified production, was therefore out of the question. And when we consider other disabilities under which those smaller farmers operated—poorer lands, distance from transportation and markets, inadequate credit and high prices for it—it is not difficult to see why discontent should flame up among this class.

The spokesmen of the smaller slaveowners became the intransigents and "fire-eaters" of the 1850's. To them, relief was necessary at the point of greatest pressure: the cost of slaves. To them, also, the answer was to be found in the reopening of the slave trade even at the price of secession. That the South divided on this question of the slave trade—as it did, indeed, on the more publicized question of the opening up of new slave territories—should therefore occasion no surprise. There were class differences and therefore special class interests among the planter capitalists, just as there were class differences among the capitalists of the North.

Notably with the beginning of the middle 1850's, the agitation for the revival of the African slave trade became intense. Every southern commercial convention of this period saw speeches made, resolutions presented, and committees appointed. The question was a difficult one and fraught with too many dangerous possibilities. The breeding states were obviously antagonistic: for an important capitalist interest was involved. During the 1850's alone, from 50,000 to 80,000 Negroes were moved from the Border States to the lower South; and the reopening of the African traffic would alienate this important region. Again, England was committed to the closing of the trade; and southern leaders hoped for the creation of closer economic links with Great Britain, a hope that would be dashed with the acceptance of such a program. Nor was the hostility of northern Abolitionism to be disregarded; for it must be had in mind that up to the very end the southern ruling class looked to the working out of a program of conciliation between the two sections. The small but vocal interest of Abolitionism would have fought bitterly any compromise that accepted the African slave trade.

But the southern "fire-eaters" cared for none of these subtleties. The class position of these people, in their own councils, was frankly revealed. Thus, at a convention in 1856, a Georgian declared: "The superabundance of Negroes in the South would make them cheaper and thus would allow all white men to own

slaves. A monopoly by the wealthy would thereby be prevented.
. . ." And in 1858, at another convention, a South Carolinian
argued for reopening on the following grounds: it would lower
the price of slaves and permit all whites to become slaveowners.
It would increase the labor supply and permit the expansion of
the South into economic regions other than planting. It would
widen the base of loyalty to the South's "peculiar institution"
by extending ownership.

By 1859, the die-hards had the bit in their teeth. At the last
of the southern commercial conventions, held in that year, the
economic program of the no-compromisers was carried. This
convention went on record as favoring free trade, direct taxation
only, the establishment of a direct line of ships between the
South and Europe, and the repeal of all federal and state statutes
outlawing the African slave trade. The South was trembling on
the verge of war; but the intransigents would not turn back.
One of them, a Georgian, speaking at the Democratic national
convention of 1860, frankly unburdened himself before an
audience that was bound to carry the report of his remarks into
all corners of the nation. Said he:

I would ask my friends of the South to come up in a proper spirit,
ask our northern friends to give us all our rights, and take off the
ruthless restrictions which cut off the supply of slaves from foreign
lands. As a matter of right and justice to the South, I would ask
the Democracy of the North to grant us this thing. . . . I tell you
that the slave-trading of Virginia is more immoral, more unchristian
in every possible point of view, than the African slave trade . . .
the great slavetrading state of Virginia . . . [is] opposed to the
African slave trade. . . . I am afraid that her error in this regard
lies in the promptings of the almighty dollar. It has been my fortune
to go into that noble and old state to buy a few darkies; and I
have had to pay from $1000 to $2000 a head, when I could go to
Africa and buy better Negroes for $50 a piece. . . . I advocate the
repeal of the laws prohibiting the African slave trade, because I
believe it to be the true Union movement. . . . I believe that, by
reopening this trade, and giving us Negroes to populate the territories, the equilibrium of the two sections will be maintained.

With secession, the Confederate government temporized on
the question, fearful of the unfriendly reactions of the Border

States and English public opinion. The constitution of the Confederacy spoke only of allowing importations from "the slaveholding states or territories of the United States." But the instructions given to Confederate ministers sent abroad warned them against writing commercial treaties with foreign countries with an eye to prohibiting the traffic; for while the Confederate government itself had no power to reopen the foreign slave trade, nothing in the constitution prevented the states themselves from doing so. Thus the Confederacy was compelled to carry water on both shoulders.

3. THE COSTS OF FREIGHTS, COMMISSIONS, CREDIT, AND NECESSARIES

There were other elements in the cost structure of the plantation economy which were unduly heavy, and this was largely because of the dependence of the southern planters upon the eastern mercantile centers. As has already been pointed out, cotton moved to England and the rest of Europe by way of New York, Boston, and Philadelphia, while on the third leg of the triangle the goods and services required by the South were returned from the East. For these needs the South obviously had to pay: in additional freights for the extra hauls, in commissions to merchants, in high interest for book credit, in charges to bankers handling "bills of domestic exchange." To cut these costs the South increasingly began to press for the establishment of direct routes of trade between southern ports and Europe. This agitation took on widespread proportions in the 1850's.

Most of the annual cotton crop was sold in New York or Liverpool through factors and commission merchants dealing with or representing the northern and English houses. Payments were made in the form of either four-month drafts on New York banks or sixty-day sterling bills. The drafts and bills were discounted by southern banks and sent on to New York, where they were used to pay the debts of southern merchants. Thus, New York became the narrow bottleneck through which flowed the greater part of the South's mercantile and financial transactions. If the New York money market was not in a position to buy the sterling bills or honor the New York drafts, then the planters were trapped.

R. R. Russel points out that this was precisely what happened in the panic of 1857. The South, having produced a short crop of cotton, seemed secure in its position, and there appeared·little danger that the repercussions of the depression, which hit so hard the speculative centers of America, would reach it. The local factors issued acceptances readily, for they had every confidence that the crop would meet all engagements. As Professor Russel describes what followed: "Cotton went on the market at 16½ cents, with sterling selling at 109¼ to 109½. On September 25 [1857], word came from New York that exchange was almost unsaleable. Money became tighter and tighter; sterling fell to 92½-97; and presently banks refused to take it at any price. Cotton buyers withdrew from the market. A large proportion of the cotton crop sold for several cents less than the promised price." The result was, planters were getting 10 cents for their cotton at New Orleans when cotton was bringing 19 cents at Liverpool.

Southern spokesmen could claim, as the result of New York's failure to support them, that their direct financial loss on that one season's transaction was enormous; one of them put the figure at $35,000,000. Professor Russel's comment is plain enough: "The moral was drawn that, had the South direct trade, there would have been a demand for sterling bills at home [to pay directly the South's obligations to England], and cotton would have gone forward without waiting for the recovery of New York."

To achieve their independence from New York capital and to forge closer links with English capital, the establishment of a system of free trade was imperative. It is scarcely necessary for our purpose to examine elaborately the intricacies of the tariff debate during the Middle Period. It is enough to note here that there did not exist in the country a powerful enough manufacturing interest to press the issue of protection so consistently as to make it a major public question. Indeed, after 1832, the problem of the tariff became a subordinate one and it did not re-emerge until after 1857, when the newly founded Republican party made it the heart of its economic program.

The tariff of 1789 was only mildly protective and its immediate successors were imposed largely for the purpose of raising a revenue. In the discussions over the tariff of 1816 for the first time an economic division manifested itself: and then representatives from the southern and New England sections opposed the bill; the first, because their region had already become wedded to the slave-plantation system, and the second, because their interests were mercantile and not industrial. The protectionists won, and a duty of 25 per cent was imposed on cotton and woolen textiles and sizable duties also were put on finished iron; the wall, however, was not high enough to bar English importations.

Henry Clay, as has been said, espoused the cause of protection; and, as a result of his American System, by which he bound the West, interested in public works, to the growing manufacturing activities of the East, a new tariff act was written in 1824. Rates were increased on most manufactured products and the western wool and hemp growers were given compensatory duties. Again the South and New England were in opposition. The high-water mark of protection was reached in 1828 when the wall was raised still higher to shut out foreign manufactured goods of cotton, wool, glass, wood, and iron, and raw and semiprocessed articles like wool, hemp, and bar iron. The South and New England once more voted against the bill; and so great was southern indignation, upon its passage, that southern spokesmen returned to their states to engage in formal protest. The act was amended in 1832, but relief was accorded only to the manufacturing interests by the lowering of duties on raw materials. Now the South moved into threats of nullification and, indeed, a South Carolina convention actually did pass a resolution to this effect. President Jackson met bluster with bluster and threatened force to compel southern compliance; but he did yield by demanding from Congress decreased duties. These the Act of 1833 provided by setting up a scale for gradual reductions over nine years.

In 1842, the Whigs once again, under the leadership of Clay

and Webster, restored the duties to the 1832 level; but the change was short-lived. In 1846 the southern planters with their northern mercantile allies, and with new support from the West, were firmly in power and enacted a low tariff law. It was not free trade, for the duties on iron, wool and woolens, and other articles still ranged around 30 per cent. In 1857, encouraged by a surplus in the federal treasury, the low-tariff bloc drove rates down even further and greatly extended the free list. But the panic of 1857 proved to northern industrial capitalism how precarious its footing was. It began to concentrate all its energies in an attack upon the southern tariff system and efforts were made to introduce new tariff bills in both sessions of the thirty-fifth Congress; but without avail. In 1859, a Republican plurality in the House forced through a protectionist measure with the voting now for the first time strictly on North and South lines; the Senate, still controlled by the planter interest, would not consider the bill. In 1860 the Republican party boldly announced its allegiance to protection, and the die was cast.

4. THE QUESTION OF SUBSIDIES

Another cause of southern disaffection was the continued existence of a governmental policy granting direct and indirect subsidies to the northern mercantile interests. On the one hand, through the expenditure of public funds, such a program increased taxes (whether they were direct or indirect) and therefore raised southern fixed charges; and on the other, it placed the South further at the mercy of northern capital. Thus, the South looked upon the monopoly grant of the coastal carrying trade to ships of American registry as indefensible and demanded the admission of ships flying foreign flags to the traffic. It sought the repeal of fishing bounties and, indeed, in 1858 the Senate did carry a bill to this effect which, however, failed of passage in the lower house. It successfully obtained revocation of ship-subsidy contracts in 1858. And it began to concentrate all its energies on the termination of governmental expenditures for internal improvements.

The South had not always opposed government support for

public works, particularly when this meant the modernization of southern harbors and work on river systems necessary to the maintenance of its internal transportation facilities. In fact, southern legislators had voted for the improvement of the Mississippi River system because this created close links between the western area and the lower South. Along the waters of the Mississippi and its tributaries had moved those vast stores of agricultural goods and raw materials—wheat, flour, work animals, provisions, lumber supplies—the South needed for the upkeep of its plantation establishments; and down the great river had come a bewildering variety of western products to be loaded on ships at New Orleans for shipment into foreign trade. For this reason, southern agricultural interests and western agrarians had seen eye to eye on most of the significant public questions of the first five decades of the century.

Indeed, as William E. Dodd has pointed out, up to 1850 the West was "peculiarly the child of the South." Its younger sons had moved up the rivers of the Mississippi system to fill out the southern counties of Iowa, Illinois, and Indiana; they had brought southern institutions and prejudices along with them. So much so that Negroes were regarded with hostility and while they were accorded the status of citizenship they were denied many of its rights: for they could not enter any of these states unless they had posted bonds first; they could not testify in court; nor could they serve on militias or send their children to the public schools.

But following the end of the depression of 1837-43, these western states increasingly were turning their face eastward. Economic ties were binding them with the East. And the new railroads were beginning to populate the northern counties of Indiana, Illinois, and Iowa and the southern counties of Wisconsin with a new people: small farmers from the East and small farmers and traders from Germany. These were indifferent to the slave institution; in fact, many were violent Abolitionists and did all in their power to thwart the territorial aspirations of the South and to give aid and comfort to the runaway bondsmen.

Attention has already been called to the fact that thanks to the extension of canal feeders to the Great Lakes, by the end of the 1840's the great entrepôt for western commodities was no longer New Orleans but New York. The extraordinary railroad-construction program of the 1850's only succeeded in making the supremacy of New York more secure. The 1850's were boom times for the West: and eastern capital poured in in a rich stream to exploit forests and mines, to prospect new railway lines, to buy great tracts of wild lands, and to build urban developments. The West began to fill up with promoters, commission men, and agents who looked first to Chicago and then to New York and Boston as their centers rather than to St. Louis, New Orleans, and Mobile.

Fast on the heels of the speculators and capitalists followed a mass movement of settlers: free farmers from the Middle States (and, farther back, from New England) and from northern Europe; and small shopkeepers, merchants, and manufacturers from Germany. In Illinois alone, according to Professor Dodd, between 1856 and 1860, almost a half-million newcomers arrived, a large part of whom were attracted into the new lands opened up by the Illinois Central Railroad. "The people who came [says he] to the state at this time were Germans, English, Scotch, and New Englanders, and they brought with them opinions and ideas hostile to slavery and to the South. . . ."

As in Illinois, so in Indiana and Iowa; and as on the question of slavery, so in the matter of political loyalties. Republicanism gained its first great accretions in this section. Toward the end of the 1850's, southern leaders were beginning to realize that the West was slipping from their grasp—if, indeed, it was not already lost economically. For this reason, the South began to oppose all further extensions of governmental policy which could only end in the strengthening of the enemy's foothold in the Northwest. The West was being populated if not by Abolitionists then by free-soilers; hence the South began to oppose further settlement with governmental aid. These are the reasons for southern opposition to the enactment of homestead legislation, to a freer immigration policy, and to the use of public credit for the building of a Pacific railway (particularly along the northern tier of states).

The South's successful opposition to the passage of a home-stead bill has already been commented on. It was equally successful in preventing the federal chartering of a Pacific railway. Southern representatives had yielded on the bill for the granting of public lands to build the Illinois Central Railroad in 1850; for they looked to direct benefits to their own section because the line was to run north and south from Chicago to Mobile. But the unhappy results in Illinois stiffened their opposition to similar legislation; and they steadfastly refused to authorize public assistance for the construction of an east-west line out to the Pacific Coast. The South was not averse to a transcontinental railway: but if one was to be built, it was to run not from Chicago but from Memphis or New Orleans; and not across the northern or central tier but along the thirty-second parallel by way of El Paso. Most important, the South was opposed to federal financing or assistance; so that the scheme it advocated was the creation of a corporation under the authority of the state and territorial legislatures, with contributions and subscriptions to be made by individuals and *state* (but not the *federal*) agencies.

The South's opposition to governmental subsidies and its fear of the settlement of the Northwest by an interest hostile to it were the basis of policy. Its leaders were thus on the horns of a dilemma. And from their perplexity the Republican party profited. The industrial capitalist interest of the East in effect formed an alliance with the free farming and speculative and small manufacturing interests of the Northwest: and this host entered the elections of 1860. The Northwest accepted the protectionism that was so vital to the progress of northern industrial capitalism; and the latter's representatives, in turn, pledged their support to homesteadism and the federal chartering of a Pacific road. This alliance of economic interest, on sectional lines, threatened to isolate planter capitalism.

5. THE CONFLICT OVER THE TERRITORIES

Meanwhile, the struggle for state power was being dramatized on another field: and this was in the debate over the opening up of the territories to slavery. Because, by the 1850's, the single and unchallenged control over the state was needed to the advancement of one or the other of the two contending interests —the badly beset planter capitalism of the South and the halted industrial capitalism of the North—the conflict over the territories was essentially a political and constitutional rather than an economic question. As far as the South was concerned, the movement of the plantation economy into the greater part of the western territories was really out of the question. Soil and climate were against it, and the pressures on the system would not have been relieved. But the South could have *colonized* the western territories and thus held them and used them *politically*. The success of such a program would have meant final victory in the contest for the possession of the state and the employment of political power to bring the price-costs structure of the southern system back into balance.

The admission of new states, under the leadership of planter capitalism, meant political power in the Senate, in the House (it will be remembered that slaves were partially counted for apportionment purposes), and in the electoral college. Through the presidency, it also meant control over the Supreme Court. And up to 1850, the South had been having its own way. Thanks to the Missouri Compromise of 1820, for more than two decades, and to the admission of Texas in 1845, for another half decade, the supremacy of the South had seemed secure enough. Operating through the Democratic party, the southern planting interest in the three decades from Jackson's election to that of Lincoln controlled the presidency and the Senate for twenty-four years, the House for twenty-two years, and the Supreme Court for twenty-six years.

But the country was changing too rapidly: a further attempt to achieve lasting security was imperative. This was the basis for the southern reopening of the territorial question in 1850 and the efforts on the part of some of the southern spokesmen to plunge the country into imperialist adventure in the Caribbean.

The issue of the disposition of the territories had been affected by the developments of the second half of the 1840's. The vast domain acquired from Mexico, the fierce debate precipitated by the Wilmot Proviso (calling for organization on a free basis of the whole Mexican cession) which had passed the House, and the insistent demand of California for admission as a free state were forcing matters. And when, in 1850, the exact balance between slave and free states seemed in danger of being destroyed (for there were fifteen states on each side and with California free there would be sixteen favoring free soil), then the time for the formulation of a new policy had come.

Clay's Compromise of 1850 settled only immediate questions. It provided for the admission of California as a free state; the passage of a fugitive-slave law with teeth in it; the organization of the new territories of the Southwest without the Wilmot Proviso; the abolition of the slave traffic in the District of Columbia; and the payment of compensation to Texas for lands added to the territory of New Mexico. But what of other regions for which a case for slavery could not be made out? Notably, what of Kansas, Nebraska, Colorado, Wyoming?

At this point, the formula of another great compromiser, that of Stephen A. Douglas, began to gain support. Douglas' doctrine of "popular sovereignty" we would today call local self-determination: that is to say, the territories themselves, once having been settled, should through the customary political processes decide for themselves whether they would enter the Union as slave or free. The motives of Douglas were undoubtedly mixed; for in part his formula grew out of a desire to see an orderly government established in Nebraska so that he and his friends (who were so heavily involved in Chicago real-estate operations) could push successfully their pet project of a Pacific railway through the northern or central tier of states with Chicago as its terminus. To achieve quickly the establishment of Nebraska as a territory, Douglas was prepared to bargain: hence the omnibus character of the Kansas-Nebraska bill.

In any case, the Kansas-Nebraska Act of 1854 settled, as far as the South was concerned, only another set of immediate questions. Kansas and Nebraska were to be set up as territories. The federal government, in line with the concept of popular sovereignty, was neither to establish slavery positively nor to prohibit it arbitrarily. When applying for admission as states, the territories were to be received with or without slavery, as their constitutions might provide. And the Missouri Compromise was declared to be "inoperative and void."

But Douglas failed as a result of what was considered a miserable surrender to the slavery interest: for the free-soil faction was completely alienated and decided to take its stand flatly on the demand of "no slavery in the territories." The old party groupings began to dissolve and after 1854 there emerged the new and original amalgam of Republicanism—which was free-soil. (It is important to note that it was not until 1858 that industrial capitalism's spokesmen began to be heard seriously in the councils of the Republican party; and, then, the retreat from the lofty idealism of the first few years was marked.)

This new amalgam is described by J. G. Randall in the following words:

Made up of old line Whigs, many of whom . . . preserved the southern conservative tradition, together with radical Abolitionists such as Sumner and Julian, Knownothings and free-soil Democrats such as Trumbull and Chase, the new party combined many diverse ingredients; the force that cemented them (at the outset) was common opposition to the further extension of slavery in the territories.

Feelings were further exacerbated by the events transpiring in Kansas and by the Dred Scott decision. Kansas was the testing ground in the contest for political supremacy. There was no orderly settlement here but colonizing, no calm debate but open warfare. Again quoting Professor Randall:

Artificially stimulated emigration, fanatical outside interference, campaigns of propaganda, frontier brawls, violence in Congress, frantic debates of press and platform, election frauds, and partisan efforts to make political capital out of the Kansas situation—such were the factors which mark the development of this turbulent territory. . . .

In the presidential campaign of 1856 the Republican party took advantage of the situation. Its platform and spokesmen attacked the repeal of the Missouri Compromise; opposed the extension of slavery into the territories; branded as unconstitutional the happenings in Kansas; called for its admission as a free state; and demanded that Congress stamp out slavery in the still unorganized regions. With an eye to gaining the support of the burgeoning capitalism of the Northwest, Republicans also advocated national aid for a Pacific railway and a federal program of public improvements. (Nothing, it will be noted, about protectionism or a generous immigration policy. These demands were added, significantly, in 1860—while the Abolitionism was heavily diluted.) In 1856, the Republicans carried Connecticut, Iowa, Maine, Massachusetts, Michigan, New Hampshire, New York, Ohio, Rhode Island, Vermont, and Wisconsin. They did not yet have, although they received large minority votes in, Illinois, Indiana, New Jersey, and Pennsylvania.

The Dred Scott decision of 1857 was a momentary triumph for the slave interest, however. Each of the justices issued a separate opinion. Six of them, headed by Chief Justice Roger B. Taney, a southerner, agreed on the following two crucial points. First, that a Negro "whose ancestors were sold as slaves" could not claim the rights of federal citizenship; and second, that the Missouri Compromise of 1820, prohibiting slavery in a part of the national territory, was unconstitutional. Taney argued, in view of the fact that Negroes were not citizens at the time of the writing of the Constitution, that "Dred Scott was not a citizen of Missouri within the meaning of the Constitution of the United States and not entitled as such to sue in its courts." On the second point, Taney insisted that slaves were property; that under the Fifth Amendment Congress could not take property without due process of law; and that the outlawing of slavery in the territories by Congress was the deprivation of the owners of slaves of property rights.

Nevertheless, all this was bound to be unavailing. In the 1850's, three new free states, California, Minnesota, and Oregon, had been admitted into the Union—and not a single slave state. And the West was already seating an expanding population of free farmers and petty-bourgeois enterprisers who, because their destinies were linked to northern capitalism, must sooner or later gain and keep the admission of their territories as free commonwealths. The Republicans understood this as 1860 approached, and they gave definite hostages to the rising northern industrial-capitalist interest. A new amalgam was formed.

When Abraham Lincoln was elected in 1860, he was a minority President in terms of his popular vote and the Republicans had not yet captured Congress. But it was only a question of time when the party and class which elected him (although he was not their leader) should be overwhelmingly in the ascendancy. The South's effort to control the state for the purpose of protecting and strengthening its special economic interest, planter capitalism, was doomed to failure. Secession was its only remaining choice.

6. WAS SLAVERY PROFITABLE?

The argument has been presented here that as the 1850's advanced the South's economy was increasingly being beset by difficulties. That does not mean it was confronted by complete collapse or that planters on a wholesale scale saw bankruptcy staring them in the face. There were many undoubtedly who, because of a favorable combination of circumstances—good lands and location, efficient plantation organization, close ties with credit institutions—not only continued solvent but received large annual returns from their operations. Indeed, in every critical situation in history there have always existed favored or fortunate beneficiaries who have been unaware of the desperate pass at which matters really stood for many of their fellow class members.

Nevertheless, this conclusion must be pressed: the economy within itself possessed no restorative or rejuvenating powers. Reference has been made repeatedly to the too great engagement of the South's capital fund in the maintenance of its labor supply. And when, in the 1850's, slave (i.e., capital) costs continued to climb out of all proportion to prices received, then the contradiction became even more sharply outlined.

L. C. Gray's conclusion to his great study makes this situation very clear. He says:

One of the most serious disadvantages of the slavery system was the slow accumulation of local capital. . . . Scarcity of capital retarded the adoption of labor-saving devices, and thereby intensified the scarcity of labor in the latter part of the period. On account of scarcity of labor in proportion to the supply of land, the land resources and the human resources of the section were inadequately or wastefully used. . . .

The practice of capitalizing so large a part of the labor of the country was also a source of profound disturbance to the economic life. In the case of free labor, the superior economic advantages of one industry or region as compared with another result in a more or less ready transfer of labor from less profitable industries to more profitable employments. In the case of slave labor, however, the difficulties of effecting this transfer were greatly intensified, for the high capital values represented by the capitalization of the future earnings of the slaves must also be transferred, and such transfers were further inhibited by sentiment against sale. Moreover, on account of the capitalization of the labor supply, the whole process of economic expansion was far more disastrous in its influence on the older southern regions than in the North. . . . This was a recognition of the fact that the process of expansion, rather than the institution of slavery, was mainly responsible for the industrial demoralization of the older regions. Slavery, however, retarded the developments of the compensatory conditions—immigration and industrial diversification—which in the North alleviated the "growing pains" of agricultural expansion. Hence we have the near-paradox of an economic institution completely effective under certain conditions, but essentially regressive in its influence on the socio-economic evolution of the section where it prevailed.

When to this basic fault in the internal structure of the economy we add the piling up of other elements of direct and indirect costs, the growing underprivileged position of a large proportion of the planter class itself (the smaller slaveowners), and the essential nonprofitability of operations as far as many planters were concerned, the reasons for regarding the end of the Middle Period as one of crisis are clearly revealed.

This factor of the profitability of cotton cultivation has not yet been studied in detail. But there are enough evidences at hand to raise at least this doubt: Could many of the planters, even when prices were good, be regarded as having been solvent?

R. B. Flanders presents the cases of two large planters in Georgia whose books show their financial condition. One of these, in 1849, recorded the worth of his investment (land, slaves, stock, tools, and equipment) as being $161,000. His operating costs for the year (including interest on his capital at 7 per cent, taxes, wages for overseers, medical attention for his slaves, the purchase of iron and clothing, molasses, tobacco, and salt for the Negroes) were $17,879. His cotton crop for the year sold for $19,868 and other produce brought in $2430, making total recipts of $22,298. This represented a profit of $4403, or 2.7 per cent on his investment. No allowance was made for depreciation.

The other, in 1851, represented his investment at $150,000. His costs came to $3130; his receipts totaled $4660. His net profit was $1530, or a return of 11¼ per cent. But he failed to include interest on his capital or a charge for depreciation of his property. Had he done so, he would have been hopelessly insolvent.

C. S. Sydnor presents the theoretical case of a typical large Mississippi planter of the 1850's in such detail that his analysis is worth repeating.

> The planter had 50 slaves, of whom probably 30 worked in the field on cotton. If these produced 5¾ bales each, there would be a total of 158 bales. At 10¢ a lb. this would be worth.... $6320
>
> Against this would have to be charged: Interest on the investment of 50 slaves averaging $600, or a total of $30,000. At 6% this would be... $1800
> Adding an equal amount for depreciation on the slave property from accidents, deaths, old age.........................   1800
> The average hand worked 12 acres, so that 600 acres would be ample for pasture, woodlot and fields. Allowing $10 an acre, the investment in land, at 6% interest, involved a yearly charge of...   360
> The land depreciated at the rate of 3% annually............   180
> The annual hire of an overseer was......................   300
> The purchase of clothes for Negroes and miscellaneous plantation supplies came to.................................   1000
> This made a total (without, however, including various miscellaneous expenditures such as the purchase of corn and pork, or taxes) of... $5440

The planter, therefore, received a profit of $880 on a capital worth of $36,000 as a minimum (for the author left out of his calculations stock, buildings, equipment, and the like), or about 2 per cent. Having made this admirable breakdown of plantation operations, Professor Sydnor then comes to the conclusion that his calculations were too optimistic in their results!

And he cites the case of an actual planter who, during 1851-52, with forty-nine slaves, obtained in net profits $2194.81, or 6 per cent on his investment. But this planter made no deductions for depreciation and his own wages as manager.

Professor Sydnor's observations are in point:

> Such figures as these explain why few cotton planters were able to follow Ingraham's advice [a contemporary] of buying Negroes and land on credit and paying for them in three years. While many tried, few succeeded. More stayed in debt, with crops mortgaged several years in advance, finally getting ahead with a good crop or in lean years losing part or all their Negroes. Even though successful, the planter was constantly tempted to enlarge his fields and increase his slave force on credit. Sheriffs' and trustees' sales, adverse balances on the books of New Orleans merchants, and debts to slave traders were all evidence that cotton plantations were not sure roads to wealth.

But, it will be argued, the large planter, at any rate, did not have to charge himself with interest on and depreciation of his slaves, for in addition to cotton he was also raising young Negroes. This was true enough: except that the mores of the South frowned on the indiscriminate sale of Negroes unless estates were being liquidated; and except that the factory plantations of the deep South were being run by overseers and managers who were interested only in the immediate returns extracted from their labor gangs. So that Professor Sydnor observes: "Especially in the regions of large and productive plantations, many slave owners . . . drove the Negroes too hard in making large cotton crops and thereby diminished the normal natural increase of their slaves."

Another point is worth mentioning. What did it cost to grow cotton on the farm? During the middle of the 1850's, with cotton selling at New Orleans at around 11 cents a pound, the big factory plantations could grow it at 5 cents. This left enough margin to pay transport, handling, and banking costs and return a profit. But what about less favored regions? In Georgia, the estimated cost on the farm was 8 cents a pound. The margin between profit and loss obviously was too thin for solvency for very long.

One is justified in suspecting that many planters, big and small and notably the small ones, were constantly tormented by their inability to balance their books. There is little cause for wonder, therefore, that a political program which held out the promise of relief from basic economic pressures should attract widespread support.

CHAPTER TWENTY-THREE

The Irrepressible Conflict

1. MERCANTILE CAPITALISM INTO INDUSTRIAL CAPITALISM

THERE is an interesting question that emerges at this point: Could capitalism in the North have bided its time and waited for the southern power to have been reduced to impotence as a result of its own internal contradictions? In other words, could mercantile capitalism have been converted into a full-grown industrial capitalism without the sudden and complete seizure of the state apparatus? One cannot give a certain answer. The following considerations, at any rate, afford the basis for a tentative reply.

In the first place, the examples of transfer from the lower to the higher level, particularly across the bridge of the Civil War years, from mercantile to industrial capitalism, were comparatively few. The argument has been presented here that the origins of the industrial-capitalist class were not to be found in either mercantile enterprise or landlordism. The different techniques and conditioning in operations, the ingrained attitudes toward consumption and extravagant living, notably the close links between mercantile capitalism and planter capitalism, were too high barriers to be overcome. The merchant capitalists had given too many hostages—close political, social, and economic associations—to the South to permit them to challenge planter capitalism's authority.

In the second place, exactly because these factors were absent as regards the new industrial capitalists, there was no need for temporizing. Just as the intransigents of the South kept on pushing their political leaders into advanced positions on the basis of which conciliation was impossible, so the intransigents of the North and Middle West were beginning to adopt similar tactics. The extremists, the minority group of the Abolitionists, of course could not be bought off. But neither could the spokesmen for the young and aggressive rising industrial-capitalist class who saw possibilities of arriving at maturity going aglimmering—and this was particularly so after the depression of 1857-58—unless they could have the support of protective tariffs, a sound banking system providing a uniform currency, a cheap and docile labor supply, and a compliant judiciary. In short, the challenging of the power of the old leaders of northern capitalism had already become too serious.

In the third place, and this is an interesting speculation, one may very properly wonder whether the merchant capitalists had the *economic* power by which to make the conversion into industrial capitalism. Incapable, through habit, of starting from humble beginnings as the rising industrial capitalists could, the merchant-capitalist class could make the bridge only if it could inaugurate large-scale industrial enterprise at once. This, in my belief, it could not do: for its strength was waning rather than waxing. Mercantile capitalism, toward the end of the 1850's (except, perhaps, in New York), was being confronted by a series of blind alleys. The carrying trade was slipping. Speculative activities in western lands and in the building of public works —and the depression of 1857-58 clearly demonstrated that— were ending disastrously. The cottage-and-mill organization of production was too inefficient to remain and grow. In short, there were no real points at which mercantile capitalism could accumulate a very large capital fund.

Even in New York City, as has been pointed out, after generations of striving, in the 1850's a respectable merchant-capitalist fortune was in the neighborhood of a few hundred thousands of dollars. Contrast this situation with the cases of the Carnegies, the Rockefellers, and the Fricks of the next epoch. Within their own lifetimes, these industrial enterprisers were able to build up fortunes that totaled into unnumbered millions!

But, it will be asked, where did the capital fund come from that made possible such extraordinary industrial advances during the Civil War, exactly at a time when the Union was engaging in a life-and-death struggle on the battlefield? The answer here is plain: the fund came out of the war itself. The federal government, through bond issues and greenbacks, added fully three billions of dollars to the basic credit resources of the nation; and the speed of turnover, due to wartime purchases, and the high profits made possible great accumulation. Government expenditures, war contracts, and wartime profiteering are the keys to this puzzle. It was no accident, therefore, that a young man like Andrew Carnegie, with an eye always to the main chance, could become a millionaire in five years!

In short, I am making the point that American mercantile capitalism—like earlier mercantile capitalisms—had not in all likelihood been sufficiently successful to make possible those accumulations which would have permitted its automatic transformation into industrial capitalism. One of the characteristics of mercantile capitalism, historically, had always been its wastefulness. Incapable of controlling all the forces under whose guidance it operated—at the mercy of public and private marauders constantly—the mercantile capitalism of the late Middle Ages and the early modern period had succeeded in piling up few sizable and permanent private fortunes. The rise and fall of Jacques Coeur and the Fuggers constitute typical examples of what was an inherent weakness in mercantile capitalism; for, not linked with production and incapable therefore of making permanent additions to capital, it was at the mercy of every parasitic group flourishing in an age of conspicuous consumption.

How then had the earlier transforming process taken place? Partly fortuitously; partly by bold class leadership. As has been pointed out, mercantile capitalism in Europe was standing still when the sixteenth century opened. Then, the discovery of the great silver mines of the New World provided that new blood so necessary for the revitalization of Europe's faltering economy. Because, in England notably, enclosures and rack-renting created an available labor reserve which could be driven into the characteristic pursuits of mercantile capitalism—the merchant fleets, the dock and warehouse activities, the cottage industries— the extraordinary rise in prices during the sixteenth and seventeenth centuries was not matched by a comparable rise in wages.

Within this growing gap, there was room for accumulation: such towering accumulation that not even the wastefulness and losses of mercantile capitalism could dry it all up.

In the second place, the oriental trade grew and flourished once more as a result of the ability of European merchants to balance their payments in the Eastern trading centers with gold and silver. But the East—as has already been said—hoarded and therefore sterilized its treasure: with the result that prices paid by European merchants in the East for Eastern wares did not rise nearly as spectacularly as did the prices these merchants received for the same commodities in the West. European merchants handling the goods of the Orient, therefore, were able to buy cheap and sell dear. Within this gap, also, there was room for capitalist accumulation. In the third place, the spoliation of subject peoples in the Caribbean, India, and the Far East and the unholy Negro traffic were at the basis of many great fortunes. And in the fourth place, the seizure of Church properties in England aided the processes of new accumulation.

Here were the capital funds that helped permit the transformation of mercantile capitalism into industrial capitalism in England—as early as the sixteenth and seventeenth centuries. One other step was necessary: the control of the state, in order to eliminate the greatest parasitic force of all, the absolutist crown. This was effected first in England in the Puritan Revolution, so that the Mercantile System perfected by the triumphant English middle class represented state power exercised in the interests of a single class. The movement into industrial capitalism thus occurred in England initially; this was only natural.

In America, in the first half of the nineteenth century, none of these conditions really existed. Accumulation had taken place, but too irregularly. It had been attended by too many chances and pitfalls to permit of the easy conversion. Fortunes were made—and as readily lost—in land and public-works speculation. The carrying trade, because of its occasional successes, tempted merchants to linger in it until it was too late and all or nearly all was lost. Americans were not able to profit fully from the California gold discoveries because an unfavorable balance of trade drained off a considerable part of the treasure into Europe. European investors wisely (in terms of their own interest) refused to build up American manufactures. American mercantile capitalism, in short, was too weak to pull itself up by its own bootstraps. And it had gone through a series of bloodlettings which had contributed little to its vitality.

2. BUSINESS CRISES AND MERCANTILE CAPITALISM

In view of its very real dependence upon speculative activity, northern mercantile capital was at the mercy of every chance wind that blew across the national and international horizons. Business was good from the turn of the nineteenth century until 1806 because the engagement of England and France in a sanguinary war created opportunities for American commercial enterprise in supplying the needs of the military powers and in those areas outside of Europe where the grip of the English Mercantile System had necessarily to be relaxed. And profits poured into the American shipbuilding industry, into land speculation, and into some manufacturing activity. From 1807 to 1809, domestic recession took place because of the blockade measures of the European belligerents and Jefferson's retaliatory devices. From the first quarter of 1809 to the middle of 1814, there was a mild revival. Then a depression once more set in as England turned her attention to the task of cutting down the growing stature of her oversea commercial rival in the carrying trade.

With the end of the Napoleonic Wars and the return of peace to Europe, America's recently achieved pre-eminence in the carrying trade and as a supplier of raw materials was seriously threatened. Too, England, devoting herself with increasing zeal to the development of her manufactures, was able to appear in our domestic markets to dump finished goods in our ports at much lower prices than our still unformed industrial production could compete with. Also, the end of the First Bank of the United States' charter meant the closing down of the only credit agency in the country operating on a national basis. The crisis was particularly severe in 1819; and American mercantile capitalism was badly hurt in its subordinate activities associated with land jobbing and the internal carrying trade.

The period 1821 to 1843 witnessed another series of advances in the American economy, which, however, was shaken from time to time by profound dislocations. The domestic market widened, thanks to the great growth of the population and the opening up of the interior regions by the steamboats and canal craft. Foreign capital poured into the country to make possible the construction of a vast public-works program. The movement westward of the cotton-planting area and the growing clamor of Europe for American cotton created unexampled opportunities for capital in the carrying trade and merchandizing. Profits from shipping were available for investment in land companies, the building of canals, and textile-manufacturing enterprise. The movement of credit continued unimpeded as a result of the ability of the Second Bank of the United States to tap English and American savings for the use of agriculturists, which was legitimate, and of land speculators, which was not. In terms of cyclical periods, business experiences ran somewhat as follows: from 1821 into 1825, revival and prosperity, followed by about a year of setback; from late 1826 into 1828, again good times, to be interrupted once more by a year of recession and depression; revival late in 1829, prosperity during 1830-33, and depression in 1834; and then a boom period which lasted until the collapse of 1837.

The whole edifice of northern mercantile capitalism came crashing in 1837 due to the overextension of speculative activity in land jobbing and public-works construction; as a result of the Jacksonian attacks on the Second Bank of the United States; and because of the contraction of spheres of activity associated with the sea, that is, shipbuilding, the carrying trade, the fisheries, and whaling. The China trade was virtually finished; American merchants were being pushed out of the Pacific; the fur business was disappearing; the remnants of the Mercantile System, in the form of the Corn Laws, still stood in the way of the export of American cereals to the growing English market. The crisis of 1837 was prolonged into deepening depression, a period of stagnation from which American mercantile capitalism did not emerge until 1843.

The period 1843-60 was not one of constant advance. Indeed, by the second half of the 1850's, it became increasingly evident that there were vital flaws in an economy that was based so heavily on the mercantile and speculative rather than on the productive side. Business picked up during 1843-45, declined during 1846-48, and enjoyed real prosperity in the years 1849-53. After a setback lasting from the middle of 1853 to the spring of 1855, revival and prosperity succeeded until 1857. As a whole, from 1843 to 1857, business was good, largely due to the following factors. The internal market was expanding once more, thanks to population growth and the further penetration into a West which was being opened up by the coming of the railroads and the introduction of steamboats on the Great Lakes. The heavy gold production in California permitted America to balance international payments abroad and also led to a rise in prices. Banking systems to a certain extent grew more secure as a result of the establishment of state agencies of supervision, notably in the East. Crop failures in Europe in 1846, 1848, 1853, and 1854 created a temporary rising market for American cereals and meat products; while the repeal of the English Corn Laws, completely after 1849, made for a permanent gain in this area. International disturbances—the war between England and China, the Crimean War, the Sepoy Rebellion in India—temporarily were to the advantage of American producers and shipowners.

New areas of enterprise—but more particularly of a speculative nature—tempted the accumulations of mercantile capitalism. Money therefore moved once more into the West in a growing flood: into the land offices; into the speculative buying of bankrupt railways; into the speculative development of timber and mineral properties. The difficulties that beset accumulation could not be concealed however. There was a premonitory tremor in the business world in late 1853; and a major panic in 1857 which lasted through 1858, although recovery was not complete even when the Civil War broke out. It was this calamity which proved the incapacity of mercantile capitalism to weather major disturbances and its inability to re-emerge with greater strength. The depression of 1857 and later really marked mercantile capitalism's permanent decline.

That depression proved at least four things. First, that speculation in wild lands and public works in undeveloped regions was the road to ruin. Second, that capitalism's continued life depended upon a sound banking system. Third, that mercantile capitalism's too close links with international trade made it the easy victim of European dislocations. (For the crisis of 1857 was both an international and a domestic one, and American mercantile capitalism suffered doubly because of its speculative ties with the West and its mercantile ties with Europe's industrial and commercial centers.) And fourth, the young industrial capitalism of textiles, iron, machinery, wood, and leather products was also shaken by the depression. It, in its turn, began to press for release from the limitations imposed by the inadequate economic organization of the nation under mercantile capitalism's leadership and the too great dependence upon Europe. It formulated its program: protectionism; a well-guarded banking system; an adequate labor supply; an expanding *domestic* market made possible by a federally supported public-works program. The implementation of this program necessitated the possession of the state: and the election of 1860, and the preliminary success of the Republican party, clearly proved that power was within the grasp of the industrial-capitalist class.

3. THE DEPRESSION OF 1857

Unfortunately, we do not yet know enough of the depression of 1857 and its aftereffects to set out its precise originating causes. But a number of conjectures may be made. Did it rise from an overexpansion of production, notably in the heavy industries? This is to be doubted. The developing heavy industries were the victims rather than the cause of the depression. The analysis presented here favors the position that the depression of 1857 was a commercial rather than an industrial crisis, in lesser part due to our excessively close dependence upon Europe, in greater part because of American mercantile capitalism's inability to free itself of its fatal dependence upon speculation.

To this extent, but only to this extent and not as an originating factor, the inadequate banking system of the country played a contributory role: for notably western wildcat banking fed the springs of speculation. The banks of the western states, chartered by state authority and only sketchily supervised, placed their capital and deposits behind speculation and thus their resources were not liquid. In the second place, their notes were inadequately secured. And in the third place, with the termination of the Second Bank of the United States, in 1836, there existed no centralizing control to regulate domestic exchange and to compel specie payments.

The First Bank of the United States, as has already been pointed out, was a part of the Hamiltonian program and it was chartered by the central government in 1791 for a life of twenty years. Its capital stock was to be $10,000,000 to which the government might subscribe for one fifth; the remainder was to be held by private individuals who were to be permitted to make part of their subscriptions in government bonds up to a total of $6,000,000. The Bank had the right of note issue up to the full amount of its capital and deposits; it might establish branches (ultimately eight were set up); and it was to act as a governmental depository and disbursing agency. The Bank used its capital resources in considerable measure to abet land speculation. Because of this and its refusal to accept the notes of state banks not on a specie basis; and because of the growth of influence by foreigners who came to own a majority of the stock and Jefferson's general suspicion of bankers, the central government began to retire from the Bank. In 1802 the United States government had sold all its stockholdings and was beginning to use state banks as depositories. When the charter expired in 1811 the state banks seemed to offer ample facilities for credit and the First Bank of the United States was not provided with a successor.

The unhappy experiences of the War of 1812, the setting in of business recession at its conclusion, and a currency inflation brought on by a policy of unregulated state bank-note issue furnished arguments for the revival of a centralized banking system. The result was the chartering of the Second Bank of the United States in 1816, again for twenty years. Once more the central government might acquire one fifth of the stock; and private subscriptions could be made in government bonds up to three fourths of the remainder. But this time the capitalization was put at $35,000,000. The customary functions for the government were included: the Bank was to handle governmental deposits and to serve as its collecting and disbursing agent; and, on the other hand, the government pledged itself to accept as legal tender only specie, treasury notes, notes of the Bank, and notes of such banks as were on a specie basis. The intention here was to force all banks to resume specie payments. As for its commercial functions, the Bank's debts (over and above deposits) were not to exceed its capitalization; it was not permitted to own land except that acquired in satisfaction of a debt; it could not charge more than 6 per cent interest on loans; it could not purchase state or municipal bonds; and it was forbidden to "trade in anything except bills of exchange, gold or silver bullion, or in the sale of goods really or truly pledged for money lent and not redeemed in due time, or goods which shall be the proceeds of its land."

The first five years of the Bank were not fortunate ones, the reasons being various. Governmental funds, formerly in state banks, were transferred to it only with difficulty. The branches, particularly those in the Southwest and West, embarked on a rapid career of expansion, lending on mortgages largely, so that the bulk of the Bank's capital was moving westward—really into speculation. There was also fraud in some of the eastern offices (Philadelphia and Baltimore). And when, in 1818, the Bank called on its western branches to settle their adverse balances in specie and when it also forbade the acceptance of the notes of state banks not maintaining specie payments, hostility became widespread. Some states sought to strike back by taxing the Bank's branches out of existence; only a Supreme Court decision, in 1819, saved them. Finally, during 1819-21, depression reigned in the South and West.

With the accession to its presidency in 1823 of Nicholas Biddle of Philadelphia, the Bank received a new lease of life. Note circulation was increased, this time on a sound basis, until, in 1832, the Bank's $21,000,000 in outstanding notes represented a large part of the country's legal-tender currency. (Indeed, it was declared that the Bank could at will contract the legal-tender currency by one third and re-expand it by one half.) More branches were opened. Initially, Biddle was suspicious of mortgage loans and loans secured by stock, and sought to expand commercial discounts. Also, increasingly, he used the Bank's own notes (instead of reissuing the notes of state banks), in this way forcing specie payments almost universally. Most important of all, the Bank came to play the part of a central bank, doing this through its ability to regulate domestic exchange.

The Bank's charter limited the charges it could make for discounts; and because this was so, local bankers were influenced in their rate adjustments. Again, the Bank, through its numerous branches, furnished exchange at rates which as a rule were not too heavy a tax on business enterprise; so that local bankers were compelled to follow suit. And finally, the Bank insisted upon the redemption of state bank notes and would not accept any for payment to the Treasury unless they were convertible into specie. Local bankers therefore could not inflate their issues. All this was to the good; but the Bank was too closely linked with eastern mercantile enterprise, on the one hand, while it overextended its western business as a result of the heavy dealing by the branches there in long-term domestic bills. When, in 1831 and 1832, Biddle tried to curb his southwestern and western branches and ordered cessation of expansion, he caused distress—and brought down the wrath of cotton planters and western land speculators upon his head. This action undoubtedly was the leading reason for the deep animosity toward the institution. The cry of monopoly could not be countered successfully.

Biddle also had earned the enmity of Andrew Jackson when in the election of 1828 he had thrown his powerful support to the Whig party, hoping in this way to assure the renewal of the Bank's charter. A truce, however, was patched up for a short time, Jackson promising to cease his campaign against the Bank upon the receipt of Biddle's word that he would not press for renewal until after the election of 1832. This pledge Biddle violated and a bill was introduced in Congress and passed. Jackson promptly vetoed the measure, throwing the issue into the presidential campaign of 1832. Jackson won and Biddle sought to terrorize Congress by ordering his branches to decrease their discounts, contract their exchange business, and collect debts from state banks in specie; the Southwest and the West were the areas feeling Biddle's heavy hand most. The administration retaliated by withdrawing its deposits from the Bank, introducing a bill for the creation of an Independent Treasury, and placing its funds in state banks. The Bank's charter was not renewed and the Second Bank of the United States became a state bank under Pennsylvania law in 1836.

From 1837 to 1863, state banking alone remained in the field. In New York and New England, carefully devised legislation and adequate supervision made the banking structure fairly sound. Not so in the West, notoriously, where the clamor for currency and the prevailing interest in land promotion opened the door wide for a crazily fabricated system. State supervision was so perfunctory that it was worthless; large numbers of banks receiving charters were banks of circulation only, their notes being based not on a specie cover but on stocks and on state bonds frequently selling at discounts; the note issues were over-inflated, or without real value or just plain fraudulent. Because many of the western banks were permitted to pay out the notes of any specie-paying bank anywhere in the United States—or even Canada!—obviously local notes were returned for redemption, leaving in circulation all the wildcat and "red-dog" issues of the remote, and sometimes nonexistent, institutions.

A contemporary of the period described the chaotic situation in this fashion:

In the West, the people have suffered for years from the issues of almost every state in the Union, much of which is so irredeemable, so insecure and so unpopular as to be known by opprobrious names. . . . There the frequently worthless issues of the State of Maine, the shinplasters of Michigan, the wildcats of Georgia, of Canada and

Pennsylvania, the red dogs of Indiana and Nebraska, the miserably engraved notes of North Carolina, Kentucky, Missouri and Virginia and the not-to-be-forgotten stumptails of Illinois and Wisconsin are mixed indiscriminately with the par currency of New York and Boston. . . .

These institutions worked hand-in-glove with the speculative interest of the West. Their capitalization frequently was simply the stock issues of promotional enterprises or, equally bad, the public issues of states which were involved as heavily in the speculative construction of public works. Their loans were not for commercial purposes so much as for the further financing of more speculative ventures.

It was small wonder that this pyramid came crashing in 1857. The first shock was felt in New York; it quickly spread throughout the whole West. The New York banks, their customers merchants, had been supporting a speculation in commodities because of good prices and steady European demand; also, wholesale merchants had overstocked their warehouses; and finally, merchants and banks had been taking heavy fliers in western rails, so that bank portfolios were in very considerable measure in illiquid form.

The panic started on August 24, 1857, with the failure of the New York branch of an Ohio bank. At the same time, commodity prices had begun to slip as a reaction to uncertain conditions in Europe. Whether they wished to or not, the New York banks could not protect their customers: for the state constitution of 1846 required that they maintain specie payments. The banks called their loans and began to demand daily settlements from country banks in specie. The round of deflation began, sweeping into its vortex New York and Philadelphia merchants and country banks throughout the whole West. Hoarding set in, prices dropped, and industrial producers were pinched.

The depression scarcely touched the South or California; and by the end of 1858, the eastern centers were rapidly emerging. Not so, however, a large part of the West, for late into 1859 Chicago and the far western country were still in the depths.

In such an environment of uncertainty it was only natural

that severe criticism should be directed against the nation's economic institutions. Legitimate enterprise was bedeviled by a fictitious currency: a national banking system was imperative. The low tariff of 1857, said the protectionists, had contributed toward the initial decline in prices. Heretofore, protectionists had been receiving little attention; but now industrial capitalists, particularly in Pennsylvania and New Jersey, began to prick up their ears. Perhaps Horace Greeley in New York and Henry C. Carey in Philadelphia—voices crying in the wilderness up to now—were really right? For Carey, in the midst of the depression, could say with telling effect: "At no period in the history of the Union has competition for the purchase of labor, accompanied by growing tendency toward improvement in the condition of the laborer, been so universal or so great as in 1815, 1834, and 1847, the closing years of the several periods in which the policy of the country was directed toward . . . protection." Industrial capitalists read such complaints as these and were convinced; and so did the wise directors of the new Republican party.

4. THE ELECTION OF 1860

With the country scarcely recovered from the effects of the depression and with the tempers of extremists on edge as a result of the Kansas struggle, the Dred Scott decision, and John Brown's raid, politicians began to prepare for the presidential election of 1860. The Democrats found their councils divided. Southern Democrats, who had followed Douglas in 1856, were now ready to part company with the doctrine of popular sovereignty. They took their stand foursquare on the following position, which naturally emerged out of Taney's opinion: Negroes were property and neither Congress nor any territory could abolish slavery; only a state might manumit and only within its own borders. Northern Democrats, on the other hand, adhered to the popular-sovereignty formula.

When the Democrats met at Charleston, South Carolina, in April, 1860, this conflict broke out at once in the resolutions committee and on the floor of the convention. The resolutions committee reported a majority plank underwriting the stand of the southern Democrats; and when the convention itself reversed the recommendation, the southerners walked out. At subsequent independent conventions, the southern Democrats nominated John C. Breckinridge and the northern Democrats named Stephen A. Douglas. To make confusion worse confounded, still a third party, calling itself the Constitutional Union, and nominating John Bell of Tennessee, appeared in the lists. The Unionists tried to avoid the burning issue of the day; they were simply for "the Constitution of the country, the union of the states, and the enforcement of the laws."

The Republicans had a heaven-sent opportunity, and they took advantage of it. Personal and sectional differences within the party were suppressed and a convention document was skillfully devised to catch every dissident vote. The platform paid its respects to the Declaration of Independence, without, however, naming the Negro. It approved of the Union. It attacked the sectional loyalties of the Democracy. It agreed that each state had the right to control its own domestic institutions. It regarded with abhorrence the work of the slavery men in Kansas. It reaffirmed the Wilmot Proviso. It insisted that neither Congress nor a territorial legislature could legalize slavery in the territories. It spoke up against the illegal reopening of the African slave trade. In other words, the Republican party was free-soil in the territories and not Abolitionist. Nor would it openly challenge the authority of the Supreme Court. Plainly, it was seeking to carry water on both shoulders. The Abolitionists had nowhere else to go; they had to stay with the Republicans.

The economic planks were wrought with equal skill. Industrial capitalists were offered a protective tariff, a more liberal immigration policy, governmental subsidies for internal improvements—all calculated to widen and defend the domestic market and lower production costs. The bait of free homesteads and a Pacific railway was held out to the westerners.

The nomination was given to Abraham Lincoln of Illinois, who was relatively unknown but no extremist on the slave question and complacent about the economic issues. The fact is, as his Abolitionist enemies within his own party were soon to learn, Lincoln did not believe in equality for the Negro or, indeed, in emancipation. There was to be no federal interference with the institution in the states; he favored the enforcement of the fugitive-slave law; and he was willing to approve of a constitutional amendment protecting slavery in those states where it already existed. The Abolitionists (who came to be called the Radical Republicans during the Civil War) were compelled to push him into advanced positions constantly. And it was not until the war was almost half over that an outstanding Abolitionist leader, Wendell Phillips, was able to declare: "Mr. Lincoln is a growing man; and why does he grow? Because we have watered him."

The Republican campaign spellbinders did their work well. They avoided as much as possible the troublesome Negro issue and talked homesteadism in the West and protectionism in the East; meanwhile Lincoln remained wisely silent in his home at Springfield.

Charles A. and Mary R. Beard describe the strategy of the campaign in this fashion:

In the West, a particular emphasis was placed on free homesteads and the Pacific railway. With a keen eye for competent strategy, Carl Schurz carried the campaign into Missouri where he protested with eloquence against the action of the slave power in denying "the laboring man the right to acquire property in the soil by his labor" and made a special plea for the German vote on the ground that free land was to be opened to aliens who declared their intention of becoming American citizens. Discovering that the homestead question was "the greatest issue in the West," Horace Greeley used it to win votes in the East. . . .

In Pennsylvania and New Jersey, protection for iron and steel was the great subject of discussion. Curtin, the Republican candidate for governor in the former state, said not a word about abolishing slavery in his ratification speech, but spoke with feeling on "the vast heavings of the heart of Pennsylvania whose sons are pining for protection to their labor and their dearest interests." Warming to his theme, he exclaimed: "This is a contest involving protection and the rights of labor. . . . If you desire to become vast and great, protect the manufactures of Philadelphia. . . ." In a fashion after Curtin's own heart, the editor of the Philadelphia *American and*

Gazette, surveying the canvass at the finish, repudiated the idea that "any sectional aspect of the slavery question" was up for decision and declared that the great issues were protection for industry, "economy in the conduct of the government, homesteads for settlers on the public domain, retrenchment and accountability in the public expenditures, appropriation for rivers and harbors, a Pacific railroad, the admission of Kansas, and a radical reform in the government."

Abraham Lincoln was elected, receiving a majority vote in the electoral college but only a plurality of the popular vote. Lincoln won the East from Douglas, carrying every free state except New Jersey. In the West, he won only narrowly. In the Border States, he stood at the bottom of the list of candidates; while in the ten states of the South he did not get a single popular vote. He was a minority candidate; and what would have been the outcome had the opposition concentrated on a fusion ticket is only a cause for speculation. In any event, he was to be faced by a hostile Congress. For the composition of the thirty-seventh Congress was to be made up as follows: in the Senate, 29 Republicans, 37 opposition; in the House, 108 Republicans, 129 opposition.

But the new President was to be spared at least this inconvenience; for even before his induction into office the southern states seceded. By February 4, 1861, secession had been declared in the six states of South Carolina, Georgia, Alabama, Mississippi, Louisiana, and Florida, and on that day a convention at Montgomery, Alabama, set up a provisional constitution for "The Confederate States of America." Texas quit the Union the same month; Arkansas, Virginia, North Carolina, and Tennessee did so in May and June. The attack on Fort Sumter, in Charleston harbor, on April 12, 1861, opened the Civil War.

CHAPTER TWENTY-FOUR

The Civil War

1. THE HISTORIC ROLE OF THE CIVIL WAR AND RECONSTRUCTION PERIODS

THE argument presented in my analysis may now be recapitulated. By 1860, a critical situation had arisen in American affairs. Because the southern planter capitalists were in control of the instrumentalities of the national state and, as a result, were thwarting the advance of the (too slowly) growing northern industrial capitalism, their claims to power had to be challenged. This the newly formed Republican party did. The partial success of the Republican party at the polls in 1860 drove the southern leaders—pushed on by extremists in their midst who were under heavy economic pressures—into secession. The Civil War broke out. The Union government, after the departure of the southern legislators, was now wholly possessed by the Republican party.

But what was to be the program of the Civil War—of this "Second American Revolution," as it has been correctly described by Charles A. and Mary R. Beard? Like all revolutionary hosts, the Republican party had a Radical and a Conservative wing. William H. Seward, the Secretary of State, was the leader of the Conservative wing. (Abraham Lincoln was associated with it and became, as the head of the government, its spokesman. One must say, however, that he was not consciously aware of the significance of the whole economic program of industrial capitalism. But without having personal or indeed emotional associations with that class, as did Seward, he accepted its position. The Mexican Rivera's portrait of him as a bemused man is an apt characterization.) Thaddeus Stevens in the House, Charles Sumner in the Senate, Horace Greeley in the press, and Wendell Phillips in the pulpit were the leaders of the Radical wing. The

339

Republican Conservatives wanted to end the war as quickly as possible without deranging the essential *political* and *social* patterns of the nation. They were neither Abolitionists nor egalitarians: the unequal status of Negroes and poor southern whites was of no interest to them. But, as spokesmen for industrial capitalism, the war furnished them the opportunity to round out the *economic* program of the class which they represented. Industrial capitalism was now in control of the state and they used it for the following purposes: 1. A vast extension of the credit base of the nation took place (as a result of bond flotations and greenback issues) and these resources were used to build up industrial capitalism via the route of war contracts. 2. The tax scheme was heavily weighted against the small consumers through a ramified program of indirect taxation, again aiding accumulation. 3. A protective tariff was written. 4. A national banking system was devised. 5. A Pacific railway was chartered which was not only given generous grants from the public domain but also lent federal funds. 6. A homestead law was passed. 7. Appropriations for internal improvements—river and harbor legislation—were made. 8. The admission of immigrant contract labor was authorized. 9. The military was employed to put down strikes.

The Republican Radicals—the so-called Radical Republicans—did not oppose this economic program in the interests of industrial capitalism. (To this extent, it is a mistake to assume that, like the Jacobins in the French Revolution, the Radical Republicans spoke for the petty bourgeois only. Thus, Stevens and Greeley were high protectionists; and Stevens was as eager as any mercenary despoiler of the public domain to lay his hands on mineral lands for his own aggrandizement. Nevertheless, while the Radical Republicans were not Jacobins in a class sense, they were akin to the Jacobins in their uncompromising and determined use of political power.) What, then, differentiated the leaders of the Radicals from the leaders of the Conservatives? We must understand that among the Radical Republicans there were two factions, which, however, did not part company until the Civil War itself was over. These we may call the Old Radicals and the New Radicals. Both were in agreement on this basic point: the war could be won only by the freeing and arming of the Negroes and the smashing of the economic and political power, once and for all, of southern planter capitalism. The Old Radicals were committed to this program for emotional reasons; the New Radicals from the point of view of expediency only.

Energetic, resourceful, embittered men (they had gone through the cruel fires of the Abolitionist controversy before the Civil War broke out), the Old Radicals pressed every advantage the revolutionary situation of the war afforded them: they voted to enthrone the industrial-capitalist class, for it was their class; but they also labored heroically in the interests of the establishment of Negro rights. Lincoln was opposed to the sudden and whole emancipation of the Negroes because he was not an egalitarian and because he feared to lose the support of the important Border States which had not seceded; and to this end he looked forward to compensating the slaveowners for the loss of their human chattels. But the Old Radicals (supported by the New Radicals) were ruthless. Over Lincoln's protests they passed through Congress the Confiscation Acts of 1861 and 1862. They drove Lincoln into issuing the Emancipation Proclamation. They established their own so-called Committee on the Conduct of the War (in Congress) and hounded the President until he got rid of weak generals and was ready to prosecute the struggle relentlessly. They clamored, until they were successful, for the arming of the Negroes and their use in the Union's armed forces. Indeed, in 1864, just when the Radical Republicans were on the point of dropping Lincoln, only military triumphs in the field made his renomination inevitable.

Thus the Old Radicals were revolutionists, in their use of political weapons, and egalitarians, for emotional reasons, as far as the Negroes were concerned. The New Radicals were revolutionists, too, but only in the political and economic senses. Wholeheartedly, these younger men in Congress—Conkling of New York, Blaine of Maine, Sherman and Garfield of Ohio—believed in the rising star of industrial capitalism; they completely accepted the tactic that the war had to be waged uncompromisingly. But they were too young themselves to have suffered in the Abolitionist struggle; and Negro emancipation, for them, was not a burning faith but a weapon. While the war raged, the New Radicals accepted the leadership of the Old Radicals. When it was over, they took over control of the Republican party.

Whatever the individual personal motives, then, we may say that the Radical Republicans, as a group, were deeply hostile to Lincoln and his tactic of conciliation. They were numerous on the floors of Congress, they had powerful support among the generals, some of them in fact served in both capacities, so that it was their prodding that compelled Lincoln slowly to move farther to the left. Lincoln made two important concessions, as has been said: he surrendered his program of gradual and compensated emancipation; and he consented to the enrollment of Negroes in the Union armies. But his intention to readmit the seceded states without guarantees, politically and economically, made the Radicals his implacable enemies. They were massing their strength against him as early as 1864. His assassination probably saved his reputation, though on this point one can only conjecture; for one must also keep in mind that Lincoln was an extraordinarily gifted politician and might have compromised with what had become the majority element in his own party.

Lincoln's successor, Johnson, had neither his political talents nor his detachment as far as the South was concerned: for Johnson came from Tennessee. Johnson was prepared to adopt the position of the Radical Republicans in 1864, but this was no longer enough. The Radicals did not want the readmission of the South—the South was to be treated as a "conquered province"—until their *political* and *social* program was now fully implemented. For three whole years (1867-70), therefore, we have the seizure of political power by Congress, controlled by the Radical Republicans.

The first phase of Reconstruction, then, had as its intention the debasement of the South, through a military rule under the guidance of Congress. For what purpose? *To grant and protect the civil rights of the now emancipated Negroes as citizens and voters so that these could assure the permanent victory of Republicanism in the South and therefore in the nation.* We must have in mind that the political program of industrial capitalism had been written during the Civil War years by a minority party operating in a series of rump Congresses. Power over the state had been seized by a *coup d'état*, in effect. With the war over, if the southern states were permitted to return to the Union unreconstructed, there was nothing to prevent southern and western agrarianism from joining once more, on the floors of Congress and in presidential elections; and thus wiping out the victory by making a successful attack on protectionism, the national banking system, and the rest. This then, was the grand scheme of Reconstruction, as it was devised by the Old Radicals: the South was to be captured for Republicanism through the instrument of the Negroes. And in this way the seizure of political power by industrial capitalism in the national arena would be made permanent.

But the Old Radical Republicans also had an Abolitionist heritage. Their agents in the South, through the Freedmen's Bureau and the establishment of Union League clubs, also labored to create social and economic as well as political equality for the Negroes. This dual intention was partially realized. Under the protection of Union soldiers, Negroes were given every encouragement to exercise the right of citizens and voters. There was also set up in the southern states a group of state governments which wrote enlightened state constitutions and enacted progressive legislation. These Reconstruction governments erected public-school systems. They democratized local and county units. They gave fair representation in state legislatures to the backcountry districts. They tried to free the judiciary from the executive. They established more equitable tax structures. They created public social services—eleemosynary institutions for the blind, insane, orphaned. With state funds they began to build railways.

But on the all-important question of land confiscation—a question to which from the very beginning the Old Radicals had committed themselves—their failure was complete. As early as 1861, men like Stevens, Sumner, and Julian had agitated for the confiscation of the great estates of the rebel leaders and their distribution among the landless Negroes. They had met with partial (but really hollow) victories in the Confiscation Acts of 1861 and 1862. When the war ended and Stevens and Sumner returned to the attack, Congress turned a deaf ear to their demand for full economic equality for the freedmen. In fact, as early as 1871, it was already becoming evident, Reconstruction in the southern states was doomed to failure.

What had happened? Had the victors become more merciful? Had the high idealism of the war years become spent as men returned to more mundane pursuits? Not at all. The New Radical faction had taken control away from the Old Radicals in the Republican party. They were not Abolitionists, as has already been pointed out. They wanted to maintain the South in vassalage, too, but not in a *political*, only in an *economic* dependent relationship. In short, as conscious and clear-eyed spokesmen for the triumphant industrial-capitalist class, they saw that the South was an important element in establishing a vast domestic market and a functioning capitalist economy. Southern products—cotton, tobacco, sugar, turpentine, lumber, hemp—were needed at home and to help balance international payments abroad. Southern raw materials—iron, coal—could be exploited by the investment of northern capital surpluses. Southern railroads could be built, factories erected, cities furnished with public utilities—always provided the section was prepared to co-operate with northern capital. To achieve this grand intention, political peace was imperative. The South was permitted to redeem itself, with the tacit consent of the New Radicals. It is significant to note that many of the redeemers, the so-called Bourbons, were not the old planter capitalists. A large company of them were the allies or agents of northern capitalism—railroad concessionaires, factory owners, mineral-land promoters. *But these redeemers were compelled to take over the southern states in the interests of the Democratic party.*

What, then, assured the triumph of Republicanism in the national political arena? The answer is plain. From 1870 on, after the Old Radicals were no longer in power, Reconstruction was continued until 1877 in a dwindling number of southern states: but not in the interests of the Negro. From 1870 to 1877, it may be said, the military was maintained in a number of southern states, purely as a temporary device, until the New Radicals could find allies for the support of industrial capitalism's program in the West. This they succeeded in doing. By admitting new states; by extending the benefits of protective-tariff legislation to western woolgrowers; by lavish grants of land to western railroads; by turning capitalists loose on the nation's rich timber and mineral resources; by pork-barrel river and harbor legislation: a large enough portion of the West was won away from its old agrarian and Democratic allegiances. When the Old Northwest and a goodly part of the new Far West began to vote Republican tickets in congressional and presidential elections, as they did after 1876, then the political design had been achieved.

Political control over the national state in the interests of industrial capitalism was now assured: the New Radicals could withdraw their military and judicial support from the Negroes in the South. At this point, that is to say, in 1877, when the final withdrawal took place, the Reconstruction era was formally ended. And industrial capitalism itself took up where the Freedmen's Bureau and the Union League clubs left off; so that there now began the peaceful penetration, industrially and financially, of the South with the assistance of the southern Bourbons.

2. THE CONDUCT OF THE WAR

In one way, Lincoln let constitutionality go by the board in the conduct of the war; but he stopped short of assuming full revolutionary powers. Until July 4, 1861, he acted without a congressional mandate; and when Congress was finally summoned it was confronted by a series of *faits accomplis*. These included the proclamation of a blockade of the seceding states, the expansion of the regular army, the suspension of the habeas corpus, and the entering into contractual relations with individuals for military supplies. Throughout his administrations the President pursued the same course; a good deal of his conduct had no legal or constitutional warrant, notably as regards the use of military power in civil matters, the arbitrary interference in state elections, and the persecution of the Copperheads (northern sympathizers of the Confederacy).

This was all very well as far as the prosecution of the war within the Union lines went; but it did not help win the war behind the Confederate lines. It was at this point that the Radical Republicans and Lincoln parted company from the very beginning; and throughout the entire conflict a struggle for political power went forward in Washington almost as sharp as the one on the battlefields. The Radical Republicans, too, gave the question of constitutionality short shrift. Unlike Lincoln, however, they declared openly that the act of secession had suspended the Constitution; that the people of the Confederacy, as well as its armed forces, were public enemies; and that every reprisal was permissible in order to crush the rebellion. As early as 1861, therefore, Thaddeus Stevens called for the forfeiture of the lives and property of "the traitors." And in 1862, throwing all caution to the winds, Stevens boldly declared on the floor of Congress that he "had grown sick of the talk about the Union as it was, and the Constitution as it is." It was small wonder that a contemporary referred to utterances such as these as "revolutionary incendiarism." Before very long, a company of similar spirits was following Stevens' lead. And by November, 1861, when the second session of the thirty-seventh Congress met, these so-called Radical Republicans were in open rebellion.

Lincoln himself recognized their existence when he pleaded for party unity in his message of December 3, 1861. This clearly revealed the theoretical and tactical differences between the two contending factions. Said Lincoln:

In considering the policy to be adopted in suppressing the insurrection, I have been anxious and careful that the inevitable conflict for this purpose shall not descend into a violent and remorseless revolutionary struggle. . . . The Union must be preserved; and hence all indisputable means must be employed. But we should not be in haste to determine that radical and extreme measures, which may reach the loyal as well as the disloyal, are indispensable.

What were these "radical and extreme measures" that the Radical Republicans were beginning to adumbrate? They included: the appointment of a congressional agency (as a sort of Committee of Safety) to supervise the activities of the executive, particularly as regards the military prosecution of the war; the confiscation of rebel properties and their division among the Negroes; the complete and immediate emancipation of the slaves; and their arming, so that the Negroes might join the Union forces and at the same time fight the Confederate host behind its own lines.

This, I have said, was the program of the Radicals. They made up a large body, and in his own Cabinet, on the floors of Congress, in the army, the press, and the pulpit they fought Lincoln relentlessly—until they won on almost every field. In the light of the subsequent careers of many, it will come as something of a surprise that many prominent Republicans started out by being revolutionaries. In the Cabinet, the Radicals included Chase, the Secretary of the Treasury, and Stanton, the Secretary of War. In the House, the outstanding Radicals were Stevens of Pennsylvania, Julian and Colfax of Indiana, Bingham and Riddle of Ohio, Lovejoy and Washburne of Illinois, Davis of Maryland, Conkling of New York, and Eliot of Massachusetts. The younger men, Blaine of Maine and Garfield of Ohio, also joined their caucuses. In the Senate, there were Sumner of Massachusetts, Hale of New Hampshire, Wade of Ohio, Chandler of Michigan, Trumbull of Illinois, and Grimes of Iowa. A large group of newspapers supported the Radical position, the outstanding being the New York *Daily Tribune* (Horace Greeley, editor), the New York *Evening Post* (Parke Godwin, editor), the Chicago *Tribune* (Joseph Medill, editor), as well as the *Missouri Democrat* and the Cincinnati *Gazette*. In the pulpit, the Radicals were represented by Wendell Phillips of Boston and Henry Ward Beecher of Brooklyn, New York.

The intransigence of Stevens and Sumner is well known; but it must not be assumed, as has frequently been the case, that these spoke for only an unruly and insignificant minority. The fact is, it was Lincoln who was in the opposition; and he was the one who yielded. The temper of these Radicals was that of the earlier French Jacobins.

Thus, George W. Julian of Indiana on the floor of the House on January 14, 1862:

. . . in such a contest we can spare no possible advantage. We want no "war conducted on peace principles." Every weapon within our reach must be grasped. Every arrow in our quiver must be sped towards the heart of a rebel. . . . I knew it was not the purpose at first of this Administration to abolish slavery, but only to save the Union and maintain the old order of things. . . . The crisis has assumed new features as the war has progressed. The policy of emancipation has been born of the circumstances of the rebellion. . . . I believe the popular demand now is, or soon will be, the total extirpation of slavery as the righteous purpose of the war and the only means of a lasting peace. . . . The nation is greater than the Constitution because it made the Constitution. The Constitution was made for the people, not the people for the Constitution. Cases may arise in which patriotism itself may demand that we trample under our feet some of the most vital principles of the Constitution under the exigencies of war.

And again, on February 7, 1865, when Julian paid his respects to Lincoln:

That this sickly policy of an inoffensive war has naturally prolonged the struggle and greatly augumented its cost no one can doubt. That it belongs, with its entire legacy of frightful results exclusively to the conservative element in our politics which at first ruled the administration is equally certain. The radical men saw at first as clearly as they see today the character and spirit of this revolt. . . . They knew that in struggling with such a foe we were shut up to one grand and inevitable necessity and duty, and that was entire and absolute subjugation.

And again, on February 8, 1865:

They [the people] expect that Congress will pass a bill for the confiscation of the fee of rebel landholders, and they expect the President will approve it. They expect that Congress will provide for the reconstruction of the rebel states, by systematic legislation, which shall guarantee republican governments to each of these states, and the complete enfranchisement of the Negro. . . . They expect that Congress will provide for parcelling out the forfeited and confiscated lands of the rebels in small homesteads, among the soldiers and seamen of the war, as a fit reward for their valor, and a security against the ruinous monopoly of the soil in the South.

And when General Frémont was removed from his Missouri command by Lincoln in November, 1861, partly because he had confiscated the property of rebels and liberated their slaves, a storm of indignation swept the Middle West. Thus wrote the editor of the Cincinnati *Gazette* to Chase, the Secretary of the Treasury:

Is it known to the Administration that the West is threatened with a revolution? Could you have been among the people yesterday, and witnessed the excitement; could you have seen sober citizens pulling from their walls and trampling underfoot the portrait of the President; and could you hear today the expressions of all classes of men . . . you would, I think, feel . . . alarmed. What meaneth this burning of the President in effigy . . . ? What meaneth these boisterous outbursts of indignation; and these low mutterings favorable to a Western Confederacy that we hear? Why this sudden check to enlistments? Why this rejection of Treasury notes by German citizens? . . . We are threatened with a revolution in the North.

Lincoln's tactic of conciliation—and its great weakness—was clearly understood by a distant observer following the progress of the war with breathless attention. Thus Karl Marx, on November 7, 1861, wrote in the Vienna *Presse*:

Anxiety to keep the "loyal" slave holders of the Border States in good humor; fear of throwing them into the arms of secession; in a word, tender regard for the interests, prejudices and sensibilities of these ambiguous allies, has smitten the Union government with incurable weakness since the beginning of the war, driven it to half measures, forced it to dissemble away the principle of the war and to spare the foe's most vulnerable spot, the root of the evil—*slavery itself*. . . .

The development of the Radical policy, which, in fact, was of major significance in the winning of the war, must now be examined in detail.

Committee on the Conduct of the War. Lincoln, in line with his program of winning the South back by suasion rather than conquest, sought to reassure slaveowners that he meant no harm to their "peculiar institution." He was going to take his stand on the Republican platform of 1860: that is, he had no designs on slavery in those states where it already existed. The pointing up of this position, by application to specific instances, only served to unleash the hostile forces at once. So, as early as May, 1861, General Butler, commanding the Union forces at Fortress Monroe, Virginia, sought to hold back three Negro refugees; he was ordered to surrender them to their owners. And in August, 1861, when General Frémont, in Missouri, had declared martial law and ordered the confiscation of the property of rebels and the freeing of their bondsmen, he was directed by Lincoln to modify his proclamation "to conform to existing law." Frémont's recalcitrance led to his removal. Similarly, when General Hunter, in May, 1862, freed Negroes in Georgia, Florida, and South Carolina, he was openly rebuked by the President.

Such temporizing, the continued presence of Democratic generals in the army, the inaction of McClellan, and the desire of the Radicals to control the military administration led Congress to establish the congressional Committee on the Conduct of the War in December, 1861. The committee was dominated openly by the Radicals, with Senator Wade of Ohio as its chairman and Julian of Indiana as the leading exponent of the Radical position from the House. The committee set itself a number of tasks, in all of which it was successful. Following the soldiers into the field, holding inquiries on the spot when military disasters took place, openly questioning and challenging the military policy of the Administration, it succeeded in getting rid of generals opposed to emancipation (the leading one being McClellan himself), in forcing the use of Negro soldiers, and in obtaining a full and uncompromising war effort. With Stanton as the Secretary of War, it may be said that the Radicals, through the Committee on the Conduct of the War, in time dominated the War Department.

The Confiscation Acts. In August, 1861, the Radicals pushed through Congress a confiscation act of limited scope. Applying only to property (including slaves) actually used for insurrectionary purposes, the law deprived owners of their use. Such property was to be seized and presumably was to be held in trust by federal officers. It was the intention of the second Confiscation Act, passed in July, 1862, to plug all the loopholes. Casting a wide net, the law defined the nature of treason against the United States, provided for its punishment, legislated for the confiscation of the property of persons in active rebellion, and ordered the liberation of their slaves.

Lincoln was fearful of the use of the weapon of expropriation and he vetoed the bill. The result was, Congress passed a joint resolution modifying its original intention and providing for only the sequestration of the life interest in real property of convicted offenders rather than the fee itself. Lincoln then proceeded to sign the original measure. It should be pointed out that Lincoln, in any case, refused to carry out the spirit of the act; for the Attorney General began very few proceedings. Thus, in all, not much more than $130,000 was paid into the Treasury under its terms.

Other forms of confiscation were resorted to, none of any importance. An act of June, 1862, called for the imposition of direct taxes in insurrectionary districts, with the sale of property for noncompliance. A total of $700,000 was collected in this way. Also, under an act of March, 1863, captured and abandoned property (for the most part cotton) was sold; in this case, the total amount realized was almost $30,000,000.

The Radicals were not content with such halfhearted measures. Julian in 1864, Stevens in 1865, and Stevens and Sumner in 1867 continued to press for confiscation, this time to be associated with the division of the estates among the Negroes. Julian in 1864 introduced a bill calling for further forfeiture and confiscation of the real property of rebels, the reversion of such lands to the public domain, and their parceling out "in small homesteads among the poor of the South, both white and black, who had aided in the military service of the North either as soldiers or laborers."

In his *Political Recollections* Julian justified his stand as follows:

The action of the President in dealing with rebel land owners was of the most serious character. It paralyzed one of the most potent means of putting down the Rebellion, prolonging the conflict and aggravating its cost, and at the same time left the owners of large estates in full possession of their lands at the end of the struggle, who naturally excluded from the ownership of the soil the freedmen and poor whites who had been friendly to the Union. . . .

In defending his bill, Julian was openly threatening. He called upon Congress to repeal the joint resolution of 1862 or the courts to interpret its provisions realistically. Said Julian:

Should both Congress and the courts stand in the way of the nation's life, then "the red lightning of the people's wrath" must consume the recreant men who refuse to execute the people's will. Our country, united and free, must be saved at whatever hazard or cost; and nothing, not even the Constitution, must be allowed to hold back the uplifted arm of the government in blasting the power of the rebels forever.

This southern homestead bill passed the House in May, 1864, by a vote of 75 to 64. Lincoln was unfriendly and the Republican platform of that year made no mention of the question. Stevens for the Radicals returned to the charge several times in 1865 and formally in 1867 when he introduced a bill in the House. In a speech in 1865 before his constituents he advocated the seizure of the real property of the Confederate leaders and its application to the payment of the war debt and the pensioning of Union soldiers. To further the reconstruction of southern society and prevent the return to power of the great landowners, Stevens also called for the breaking up of estates in excess of two hundred acres and the seating on them of small freeholders.

His bill of 1867 gave point to these ideas. The lands owned by the southern states themselves and private property liable under the Confiscation Act of 1862 were to be taken over by a commission with the rights of condemnation, sale, and division. The first claimants upon such properties were to be the new homesteaders, Negro heads of families, whether male or female, and all adult males, who were to receive forty acres each. Such

homesteads were to be inalienable for ten years and then absolute titles were to be granted. Other lands were to be sold
and from the proceeds homesteaders were to receive $50 for the
erection of improvements, while the sum of $500,000,000 was
to be set aside for pension payments.

Stevens envisioned a new South based upon egalitarian property rights. He was a vengeful man and fearful of the recapture
of political power by the old ruling class of the South. But he
was, as well, the honest friend of the Negro. Thus, he said in
defense of his bill:

> Nothing is so likely to make a man a good citizen as to make him
> a freeholder. Nothing will so multiply the products of the South as
> to divide it into small farms. Nothing will make men so industrious
> and moral as to let them feel that they are above want and are the
> owners of the soil which they till. It will also be of service to the
> white inhabitants. They will have constantly among them indus-
> trious laborers, anxious to work for fair wages.

It was too late, however: the strength of Abolitionism had
spent itself. The New Radicals, who had shouldered Stevens,
Sumner, and Julian aside, were not interested in the redevising
of the South to conform to leveling notions. Their only concern
was the defense of the new economic dispensation. Stevens was
given only polite attention and his measure never came to a
record vote. Stevens died in 1868, Julian retired from the House
in 1870, and Sumner from the Senate virtually in 1872. Thus
passed an old order.

Emancipation. In this sector, too, it was Congress that took
the lead. With an eye always on the Border States, Lincoln kept
on temporizing. Now he insisted his was not the right to free
the Negroes. Now he maintained that the extirpation of slavery
was only incidental to the conduct of the war and that the
preservation of the Union was its main purpose. Now he flirted
with ideas of gradual and voluntary emancipation by the states,
federal compensation, and the "deportation and colonization"
of the freedmen. But Lincoln gained no supporters among the
Border States; while the Radicals in Congress drove ahead step
by step to the achievement of their leading objectives: full

emancipation and the arming of the Negroes. In March, 1862, Congress forbade generals to return to their owners fugitive slaves who had taken refuge within the Union lines. In July, 1862, the slaves of rebellious southerners thus entering the Union lines were declared to be free. In April, 1862, slavery (with compensation) was abolished in the District of Columbia. In June, 1862, slavery (without compensation) was abolished in the territories. Thus Congress: without the President's approval, however, and without efforts on his part to enforce these enactments.

To the pleadings and threats of the Radicals Lincoln turned a deaf ear. In January, 1862, Stevens pointed out in a powerful speech that Lincoln's hesitancy armed the South: for while the white men fought, the black men behind the lines were "the mainstay of the war." But, said Stevens: "Let it be known that this government is fighting to carry out the great principles of the Declaration of Independence and the blood of every freeman would boil with enthusiasm."

Greeley's extraordinary open letter to the President of August 20, 1862, called "The Prayer of Twenty Millions," met with a reply but with no assurances. Lincoln was taken to task for not executing the Confiscation Act of 1862 and for his conciliatory attitude toward the Border States. "We complain," said Greeley, "that a large proportion of our regular army officers with many of the volunteers evince far more solicitude to uphold slavery than to put down the rebellion." And in the same month, Wendell Phillips' disgust was so great that he declared, after characterizing Lincoln as a "tortoise President": "The President, judged by both proclamations that have followed the late Confiscation Act of Congress, has no mind whatever. He has not uttered a word which gives even a twilight glimpse of an antislavery purpose."

Finally Lincoln's hand was forced: he no longer could remain insensitive to the waning war effort and the growing clamor abroad, particularly among the English workers. On September 22, 1862, after Lee had been stopped at Antietam, Lincoln issued his preliminary Emancipation Proclamation: after January 1, 1863, the slaves in the rebellious states were to be free. The

President continued to have his second thoughts; for in his December message to Congress he cast doubts on the constitutionality of his act and called for an amendment to the Constitution providing for federal compensation to the states and gradual emancipation over the next forty years. Certainly the definitive proclamation of January 1, 1863 was less than even half a loaf as far as the Radicals were concerned. Slaves everywhere were not freed. All the Union slave states were excluded. Tennessee was omitted. Those portions of Virginia and Louisiana already within the Union military lines were excepted. The Proclamation applied only to those areas under the Confederate control.

The Radicals accepted the proclamation for what it was worth; and they continued on guard. Through the Committee on the Conduct of the War they demanded that occupied southern territories be officered by emancipationists so that Negroes could be enlisted in the Union armies. And—so distrustful were they of Lincoln—in the Wade-Davis bill of 1864 (which was vetoed) they incorporated a provision to the effect that "all persons held in involuntary servitude . . . in the [seceded] states . . . are hereby emancipated and discharged therefrom."

But even partial emancipation had this effect: it hastened the arming of the Negroes and their use against the South.

The Arming of the Negroes. Even before emancipation was proclaimed, as has been pointed out, the Radicals demanded the fuller use of Negroes by the Union army. Sherman of Ohio bluntly declared that Negroes "made the best spies" and could relieve the Union soldiers of nonmilitary tasks. But, he pointed out bitterly: "The policy heretofore pursued by officers of the United States has been to repel this class of people from our lines, to refuse their services." To make possible at least the employment of Negroes in labor services, Congress passed an act to this effect in July, 1862.

Lincoln again hesitated. In the Emancipation Proclamation, he yielded a step before the pressure of the Radicals. He was prepared to promise that "such persons of suitable condition will be received into the armed service of the United States to garrison forts, positions, stations, and other places, and to man vessels of all sorts in said service." It will be noted that active duty in the fighting forces was excluded, by implication. But the Radicals could not be denied. Indeed, even before emancipation, General Hunter in April, 1862, had organized a regiment of Negro troops in the Department of the South. Lincoln had ordered its disbanding, but the step had revealed the unruly temper of the Radical generals. Finally, Stanton was permitted to go ahead and in January, 1863, a Massachusetts Negro regiment was enrolled; while—and this was far more important, for the act struck right at the heart of the South—in the same month four Louisiana Negro regiments were formed.

From then on events moved rapidly. In May, 1863, a special bureau of colored troops was set up in the War Department. In December of the same year, fully 100,000 Negroes were enrolled in the Union service, of whom actually half were bearing arms. Before the war was over, more than 200,000 Negroes had served in the northern armies and of these 125,000 had been recruited in the slave states. They occupied an underprivileged position, being officered by white men and receiving less pay (until January 1, 1864) and no enlistment bounties. The Negroes labored obscurely as workers, servants, and scouts and heroically as soldiers in the field,.running the risk of summary punishment when they fell into the hands of their former owners. For the Confederate generals refused to recognize as prisoners of war captured Negro soldiers who had fled from bondage; indeed, it was not until October, 1864, that captured free Negroes were accorded the formal rights of warfare.

In every way these fugitive slaves in uniform justified the confidence of the Radicals; and their presence in the Union armed forces confronted the South with the dread alternative of surrender to the North or surrender to the Negroes. The tactic toward which the Radicals steadily had been pointing was supremely successful.

3. THE CAMPAIGN OF 1864

There was another profound center of disagreement between Lincoln and the Radicals; and this had to do with the reconstruction of the seceded states once they fell into the hands of the

Union armies. Lincoln looked to the re-establishment of normal relations at the earliest possible moment; thus indicating his lack of understanding of the theory and results of the war—nay, revolution, as far as industrial capitalism was concerned. The Radicals saw the necessity for defending the revolution on two fronts: the protection of the civil rights of the freshly emancipated blacks and the consolidation of the economic gains of protectionism, and the rest. To the Radicals, therefore, reconstruction could be on the basis only of the "conquered province" theory: in other words, readmission into the Union after the furnishing of proper guarantees.

Lincoln moved first. In the autumn of 1863, after the five states of Virginia, Tennessee, North Carolina, Arkansas, and Louisiana had been possessed by the Union forces, the President appointed military governors. In December, 1863, he then proceeded to announce the conditions under which these states would be restored "to their proper relations" with the Union. They would have to give their allegiance to the Constitution of the United States and "the acts and proclamations promulgated during the war with reference to slavery." Everybody might take the oath of allegiance except certain high military and civil officials of the Confederacy; and all such would receive full amnesty and pardon.

At this point, Lincoln was prepared to be generous. As soon as 10 per cent of the 1860 qualified voters, ran on his proclamation, had taken the oath, they might set about to organize a loyal government; and with such an organization effected the President would recognize the state as having resumed its proper relations with the Union. Lincoln admitted that the election of congressmen and senators was a matter for Congress itself to decide.

Lincoln's strategy was apparent: he sought to create a hard nucleus of at least 10 per cent loyalists about whom those tired of the war might collect. But he was not even partially successful. During 1864 in only two states, Arkansas and Louisiana, were such governments erected, and even in these the loyal 10 per cent were recruited with difficulty—if, indeed, honestly. Their numbers were never added to. Not until the war was virtually over was such a loyal government organized in Tennessee under the leadership of Andrew Johnson.

The Radicals in Congress were incensed at the fact that the President had not consulted the legislative branch; at his mild terms; and at his easy surrender of the victory of the revolution. The upshot was, they took reconstruction into their own hands and passed the Wade-Davis bill in June, 1864. This was based flatly on Charles Sumner's thought that the seceded states had committed suicide: they were now only territories to be administered by the federal government until readmitted. The Wade-Davis bill set aside everything the President had already done in the matter of restoration as incompetent. It also abolished slavery in the rebellious states. It then imposed the following very severe conditions for readmission.

The eleven seceded states were to be regarded as territories over each of which the President was to appoint a provisional governor with summary powers. When rebellion had been put down, United States marshals were to be authorized to enroll all *white* male citizens of each state for the purpose of having them swear allegiance to the Union. A majority of the white citizens had to offer up loyalty first before the next step could be taken: the election of delegates to a constitutional convention for the purpose of erecting a new state government. Persons who had held any important military or civil office under the Confederacy were proscribed; and these could neither vote for delegates nor sit in the constitutional convention. The following minima were required of the new constitution: the abolition of slavery; the repudiation of the Confederate debt and the state debt incurred during the period of the Confederacy; the disqualification of Confederate officials from voting for or being elected to the governorship and legislature. Next, the Constitution was to be ratified by a majority of the voters. Only then might the President of the United States, with the consent of Congress, proclaim the establishment of the new state government.

Lincoln vetoed the Wade-Davis bill on July 4, 1864, after Congress had adjourned. He defended his course by what Professor Randall calls "a rather eccentric proclamation." Said the

President: It was fatal to admit that the states were out of the Union, as the bill did. Congress had no power to prescribe the abolition of slavery in the states. He was unwilling to set aside what had been accomplished in Louisiana and Arkansas or to commit himself to any one plan of reconstruction. And he ended with the astounding suggestion that the southern states might come back into the Union under the Wade-Davis plan if they chose!

Wade and Davis struck back almost at once. In a bitter manifesto, they challenged their party's leader, and this despite the fact that the presidential election was only three months off. Said they: "This rash and fatal act of the President is a blow at the friends of his administration, at the rights of humanity and the principles of republican government. . . . But he must understand that our support is of a cause and not a man; that the authority of Congress is paramount and must be respected; . . . he must confine himself to his executive duties— to obey and to execute, not to make the laws, and leave *political reorganization to Congress.*"

With such divided councils the Republican party prepared itself for the election of 1864. An earlier effort to sidetrack Lincoln and name Chase had failed; and Lincoln was renominated by the Republicans in June, although reluctantly. As Julian put it in his *Political Recollections*: ". . . of the more earnest and thoroughgoing Republicans in both Houses of Congress, probably not one in ten really favored it. It was not only very distasteful to a large majority of Congress but to many of the most prominent men of the party throughout the country."

But with Linoln's pocket veto of the Wade-Davis bill, his dismissal, really, of Chase, and with Grant's costly and ineffectual campaign against Richmond, the confidence in the administration sank to a low ebb. The Radicals discovered that they had popular support: and they began to conspire either to replace their party's candidate or to put another man in the field against him. Party to these conversations were Greeley, Wade, Davis, Whitelaw Reid, and others; and these Radicals went so far as to set a date and meeting—September 28, at Cincinnati—for their convention.

Davis expressed the thoughts of many when he wrote to a correspondent:

> There are hundreds of thousands who think that Mr. Lincoln cannot suppress the rebellion, and they are anxiously casting around their eyes, in this hour of deep agony, for a *man of mind and will* who is able to direct the national power to the *suppression* of the rebellion. . . .

The plot never was consummated. The antiwar declaration of the Democratic party (which had named General McClellan) and a series of decisive military victories—those of Sherman and Sheridan, in particular—led to a popular reaction; and the Radicals were compelled to acquiesce. They did not campaign for Lincoln; but they did not oppose him. Frémont, who had been named to head an independent ticket by his German admirers of the Middle West, also withdrew his candidacy. The road was open to Lincoln's re-election. With only the Union states participating, Lincoln obtained all the electoral votes except those of Kentucky, Delaware, and New Jersey. But there were large McClellan minorities in New York, Pennsylvania, Ohio, Indiana, and Illinois. Lincoln's popular majority over his rival did not exceed 400,000 votes.

The winter of 1864-65 saw the hopes of the Confederacy first waning and then approaching collapse. The Union forces were devastating Virginia north of the James River; Sherman, having taken Atlanta, was marching through the Carolinas; the armies were converging on Richmond. Lee evacuated his capital on April 2, 1865, but was quickly caught at Appomattox Court House where he surrendered to Grant on April 9. On April 14, while in attendance at the play, Lincoln was assassinated by the actor John Wilkes Booth. He died the next morning and Andrew Johnson of Tennessee succeeded to the presidency.

The Radical Republicans continued unrepentant to the very end, not even their antagonist's untimely death softening their rancor. Julian in his *Political Recollections* said:

. . . while everybody was shocked at his murder, the feeling was nearly universal that the accession of Johnson to the presidency would prove a godsend to the country. Aside from Mr. Lincoln's known policy of tenderness to the Rebels, which now so jarred upon the feelings of the hour, his well-known views on the subject of reconstruction were as distasteful as possible to Radical Republicans. ·

4. THE VICTORY OF INDUSTRIAL CAPITALISM

The war was being won on the floor of Congress in another way as well; for the progress of industrial capitalism was at last being rendered secure. The control of the state apparatus gave the Republican party the opportunity to carry out the economic program—and more—it had promised in its platform of 1860. At this point, it is important to note that no important questions of principle or tactics divided the two wings of Republicanism. Of course, there were individual differences: Stevens, for example, was a fiat-money man and believed Chase did not go far enough in freeing the country's currency from bullion; on the other hand, he was a good protectionist. Greeley cast ridicule on Stevens' financial heresies; but he gave the Pennsylvanian's protectionism stalwart support. Bingham made a series of eloquent pleas in defense of the civil rights of Negroes, but having represented railroads he was not unaware of the fact that corporations were running into difficulties because state courts were interpreting "the law of the land" or "due process" entirely in a procedural sense and therefore giving them no relief from oppressive taxation. In any case, perhaps by trading between sectional interests, industrial capitalism's requirements were satisfied. By the time the war was over Congress had taken a long step forward in placing the services of the state at the command of private enterprise. The devices by which this momentous change was effected must be now set forth.

The Financing of the Civil War. Salmon P. Chase, the Secretary of the Treasury, had two major methods for financing the war and both served excellently the purposes of a booming wartime industry: bond flotations and greenback issues. By an addition of $2,600,000,000 to the debt of the country before

the war was over and the printing of $450,000,000 in green-
backs, the nation's credit base was remarkably extended and
manufacturing now had its capital fund with which to build up
its plant.

The Treasury employed every effort to make its bond offer-
ings palatable. Interest rates were high (5 to 7.3 per cent). After
1863, they were sold at the market rather than at par. The new
national banks were virtually compelled to buy. And Jay Cooke
was made sole subscription agent and through him large quantities of the bonds were placed in Europe. Only in one way did
the Treasury protect itself: as a rule redemption was fixed at
indeterminate periods (5 to 20 years, 10 to 40 years), thus afford-
ing the opportunity of refunding at some future time.

In addition, on three separate occasions—by acts in February,
1862, July, 1862, and March, 1863—Congress authorized the
issuance of $450,000,000 in legal tender, or greenbacks. At the
end of 1861, too, the government suspended specie payments,
putting the nation on a paper basis. And up to the beginning
of the year 1864 (by Chase's direction) holders of greenbacks
of the first two issues could convert their paper into 6 per cent
government gold bonds. The later significance of this act lay in
this: the greenbacks had depreciated badly as confidence in the
Union government had waned so that the average value, in gold,
of a greenback dollar in 1864 was 64 cents; in fact, the low was
39 cents. Yet greenbacks could buy gold bonds. The inflationists
of the 1880's and 1890's were not far from wrong when they
contended that the Civil War had been financed with a 50-cent
dollar and was being paid back with a 100-cent dollar. The
rentiers, along with the war contractors, waxed rich as a result.

What role did taxes play in the war's financing? A very slight
one, so that industrial production was not heavily encumbered.
The high Civil War tariff acts were presumably fiscal devices,
but they brought in only some $305,306,000 in revenues. Ex-
cises gave the government an additional $291,760,000. Both of
these really were, for the most part, taxes on consumption. An
effort was made to raise a revenue from income taxes but during 1861-65 these brought in only $55,085,000.

As soon as the war was over, the slight penalties imposed on industry were quickly removed. In 1866, 1867, and 1868 the wartime excises on coal and pig-iron production, corporations, cotton, advertisements, and manufactured goods generally were repealed; internal revenues were reduced from $309,200,000 in 1866 to $184,300,000 in 1870. In 1872 the inadequate income tax went. In 1883, Congress cut the duty on tobacco in half and abolished the taxes on friction matches, patent medicines, bank checks, commercial and savings-bank deposits, and bank capital; so that, in 1885, internal revenues brought in only $112,-500,000.

By the 1890's, the government's fiscal program was made up of tariff duties and excises on tobacco and liquors: all taxes on the nation's consumers. Industrial capitalism was in that idyllic state where it could have its cake and also eat it. The government gave it a protected market, a railroad net, a cheap labor supply, a sound currency—and shunted the costs onto the backs of the workers and farmers.

Protectionism. Morrill of Vermont had fathered a tariff bill during the congressional session of 1859-60, and the House had passed it; but the Senate, still dominated by the Democrats, had refused to act. The bill had offered to go back merely to the rates of 1846, though the iron and wool duties pointed clearly in the direction of protection. With the southerners gone from Washington, the lame-duck session of Congress early in 1861 passed the bill and President Buchanan (who was a Pennsylvanian) signed it on March 2. The march had begun.

Every session of Congress, from 1861 to the middle of 1864, saw new bills, pushing rates upward, introduced and passed. Always the defenses were the same: new revenues were needed to support the war effort; and domestic manufacturers had to be compensated for the heavy excises they were being compelled to pay. But in the Act of June 30, 1864, all pretense was discarded: this was protectionism undisguised and unashamed. Morrill and Stevens rushed the bill through the House in two days; the Senate halved that time. At the end of the Civil War the average rate on dutiable goods stood at about 47 per cent as compared with the 18.8 per cent at its beginning.

During the war, as has been said, there was much talk of the high duties as offsets to the high excises. The excises were quickly removed as soon as the war ended; but the high duties remained on. It was being estimated that the protected industries profited by fully a 20 per cent price rise the duties afforded them.

Tariff tinkering continued during the whole Reconstruction period. In 1867, the wool and woolen interests (this time their causes furthered by powerful lobbying associations) got new rates; in 1869, the duty on copper was raised sixfold; in 1870, steel rails were taken under Congress' wing and the rate was so high that English rails were virtually shut out of the American market. Now began boom times for the American steel industry and not even the depression of 1873-79 could really hurt it.

In 1870, frightened by western clamor and embarrassed by a Treasury surplus, the House Ways and Means Committee brought in a bill which proposed to cut duties on iron, wool, coal, and lumber. This was to be done by the general device of a horizontal reduction of 20 per cent. The Senate refused to yield and, aided by Speaker Blaine, rapidly coming to the fore as the leader of the New Radicals, forced the House reformers to accept a bill which halved the reductions. The horizontal cut of 10 per cent affected manufactures largely; but many raw materials were put on the free list (thus really not hurting the protected interests). The only tangible result was a shrinkage of $53,000,000 in federal revenues. In 1875, because of the depression and the resulting decline in governmental income, the 10 per cent reduction was quietly restored, while the free list remained untouched. The result was, cotton goods, woolens, iron and steel, paper, glass, leather, and wood were better off than ever before. The rate structure was not touched again until 1883.

The protective tariff was here to stay: and not even the eastern Democrats sought seriously to disturb it. The heavy revenues that poured into the Treasury as a result were a source of embarrassment, for they led to surpluses. Except for the single year 1874, when there was a slight deficit, there continued to be an average annual surplus of almost $100,000,000 up to the year

1890. The Treasury redeemed as much of its outstanding obligations as it dared—but without avail. Generous appropriations for rivers and harbors, post offices, and the modernization of the navy (after 1883) could not dry up the rich stream quickly enough: until the Republican party hit upon a brilliant expedient. Why not give the surpluses away (and thus defend the protective system at the same time!) to the returned soldiers? Pension act followed pension act until in 1890 a service-pension measure pure and simple was passed. The Grand Army of the Republic—the veterans' organization—every election marched to the polls to vote in Republican tickets out of gratitude; and protectionism was secure.

A National Banking System. The uncertain conditions attending the outbreak of the war; the fact that the country had not fully recovered from the effects of the depression of 1857-58; the heavy involvement of many mercantile centers in southern financial relations; and the suspension of specie payments first in New York and then officially at the end of the year: all these affected banking seriously. There was a heavy toll of banking failure particularly in the Middle West and in the Border States. Then a sharp inflationary movement set in, as war orders and bonds began to pour from Washington. Bank-note issues multiplied, new banks sprang up, and the old threats once more put in their appearance: an unsound paper currency, inadequately secured, and the absence of reserve mobilizations. Some idea of the expansion of the paper currency may be obtained from the fact that in the Middle Atlantic States alone, in two years, the increase in bank notes was 50 per cent. By 1863, there were 1600 banks of issue with about 12,000 different kinds of notes in circulation. Counterfeiting, too, was general.

The Treasury took two important steps to stabilize banking, having an eye to the future, when the abnormal wartime needs would be over, as well as to its own current requirements. One of the immediate considerations for national banking reform was the creation of financial agencies that would facilitate the absorption of Union bonds; the long-term consideration was the creation of a sound system, under national control, that would help enterprise weather storms like the depressions of 1837-43 and 1857-58. The result was the passage of the National Banking Act of 1863 (rewritten in 1864), which created a nationally supervised system; and the virtual outlawing, in March, 1865, of state bank notes by imposing an annual tax of 10 per cent on them.

The outstanding provisions of the banking act follow. First, as to capitalization and the right of note issue. Commercial banking institutions might be incorporated under federal charter—which meant they would have to accept federal supervision exclusively. A minimum capital of $50,000 was fixed for institutions in communities with less than 6000 population; of $100,000 for larger cities. (Obviously, this imposed a serious disability on the agricultural regions.) Half of the authorized capital was to be paid in before the bank could open its doors. These banks were to have the right of note issue, but only against United States bonds, which were to be deposited with the Treasury. In the first place, such bonds were to be equal to at least one third of the bank's capital and not less than $30,000 (wildcat banking was being aimed at here) and, in the second place, notes could be issued only up to 90 per cent of the market value of the bonds. (Bank capital and notes were being tied to the government debt. But in exchange, bankers were assured a two-way return: the interest from their bonds and the interest from commercial loans financed through note issues.) The maximum national bank-note issue was set at $300,000,000.

Second, as to reserve requirements. Specie and lawful money reserves had to equal at least 15 per cent of deposits and note issues. The leading financial centers of the country were designated "reserve" cities. In these cities, national banks were required to maintain 25 per cent reserves, although they could deposit with New York banks part of their reserves up to one half of the requirement. As for country banks, they could deposit up to three fifths of their reserve requirement in banks located in "reserve" cities. New York, in effect, became the nerve center of the whole system and in time fully two fifths of the reserves of the country's national banks were concentrated there. Indeed, nine so-called "superbanks" held two thirds of these bankers' deposits, fulfilling, in a loose and unofficial way, the function of a national central bank.

The grand intentions were the contraction of state banking and the mobilization of reserves, as has been said. The first was realized almost at once; the second never achieved real success. So, from the 1880's on, there was a constant preoccupation with banking reform. In any case, however, the immediate demands of industrial capitalism were satisfied: wildcat banking was a thing of the past. Between 1863 and 1865, the number of state banks fell from 1466 to 297; and the number of national banks rose to 1634. The value of their bank-note issues mounted to $276,000,000 by the end of the year.

Some of the defects of the national banking system—as they became evident in time—have already been hinted at. For one, rural districts were being discriminated against, because of high capital requirements for establishment. It was no accident, therefore, that the Populists of the 1890's became the bitter foes of the national banking system. Second, the currency issued by the banks—because it was tied to the federal debt—had an inverted elasticity. In periods of business depression, the premiums on bonds would induce the banks to sell their holdings, and this succeeded in accentuating the deflationary movement. In periods of business revival, low bond prices would induce banks to buy, thus making possible the financing of too-speculative enterprise. Into the bargain, the government's retirement program for the debt contracted as a whole the base for note issue. In time, of course, the use of checks (but more particularly only in the industrial and commercial centers) helped the banks get around this difficulty.

In the third place, the reserve system did not exactly work out. True, concentration in large part took place in New York; the trouble was, however, the commercial banks here used a sizable proportion of reserve deposits to put out at brokers' loans. There was no machinery to direct the reserves for the relief of distressed areas. The result was, in periods of emergency, when reserves were called home, they left unsupported the security markets and depression therefore spread out in widening circles.

This was precisely what happened in the 1873 depression. When the panic broke, country banks had on deposit with reserve agents, mainly in New York City, $64,000,000. Between September 12 and October 13, these banks withdrew $38,000,-000 of these deposits and reduced their deposits with other banks another $20,000,000. At the same time, the country banks began to contract their loans—by about 5 per cent. But the reserve agents were compelled to contract their loans even more sharply—in the case of New York, by 10 per cent. The drains on New York for cash ended with the reduction of the reserves of the New York banks in this same month from $49,000,000 to $21,000,000. At the same time the plugs were being pulled out of the stock market. It was not until 1913, by the Federal Reserve Act, that some of these shortcomings were finally conquered.

Disposal of the Public Domain. Various interests dictated the passage of the Homestead Act in May, 1862. Undoubtedly, the desire to hold the West in political alliance with the East was paramount. But one must not lose sight of other considerations: homesteads would make possible the quick settlement of the public domain and thus develop the national market for domestic manufactured ware. They would also build up a great home agricultural industry whose surpluses of cereals and meat products could be poured into the world market to right our very unstable international position. The crying desideratum of our economy was a favorable commodity balance to permit interest payments on foreign borrowings, and it was this service that western agriculture performed with amazing success. Nor is one to forget the idealistic motive of an egalitarian like Julian, who was the ever-watchful friend of the homesteader. To Julian, in his daughter's words: "Should it [the Homestead bill] become a law, the poor white laborers of the South as well as the North would flock to the territories, where labor would be respectable, our democratic theory of equality would be put in practice, closely associated communities could be established as well as a system of common schools offering to all equal educational opportunities."

The Homestead Act, which Lincoln signed in May, 1862,

gave to heads of families or individuals twenty-one years of age or over, who were citizens or declarants, a quarter section (160 acres) of land. Final title could be entered after a five-year residence and the erection of an improvement. A homesteader was allowed, at any time after his location, to commute his quarter section into a pre-emption and thus buy his farm outright at the regular knockdown price of $1.25 an acre. He could also buy an additional quarter section on the same terms.

This was not the only device created for throwing open the public domain to settlement—and exploitation. Great tracts of land were turned over to the railroads—as we shall soon see— and these were quickly placed on the market to attract commercial farmers who saw the necessity of locating near transportation. Land could also be purchased from the states. As has already been pointed out, as far back as the beginnings of the American nation, the federal government had begun the practice of making grants from the public domain to individual states to encourage internal improvements and the establishment of common schools. In 1862, these state holdings had been enormously increased through the passage of the Morrill Agricultural College Act, which gave every state establishing a public agricultural college 30,000 acres for each representative that it had in Congress.

Other statutes were placed on the books in the same period: and whatever their motives, the end result, as we shall see, was land engrossment. The push into the West continued, but the average settler was compelled to buy his freehold if he intended to farm or raise stock for the market. The Republican party obviously kept an eye open for the capitalist possibilities of the western lands. In their own interest and those of their financial friends, the following other laws were written: In 1864, the pre-emption of coal lands was made the subject of a special law. The Timber Culture Act of 1873 gave homesteaders, or others, title to quarter sections if they agreed to plant part of their property in trees. The Desert Land Act of 1877 gave away whole sections presumably of arid land on condition that irrigation be employed. And the Timber and Stone Act of 1878 permitted the land-office authorities to sell quarter sections unsuited for agriculture but capable of being worked for timber and minerals for $2.50 an acre.

The whole system of land disposal soon became honeycombed with fraud. There was fraud in the filing of homestead entries and in the purchase of land under the Pre-emption Act. There was open theft of the public domain through illegal enclosing, particularly by cattle men. Timber and mineral lands were illegally pre-empted. The land-grant railroads were notoriously culpable: they sought to maintain possession of their sections without troubling to comply with the terms of the awards, and, even after they had laid down their tracks, many continued to hold out the choicest sections for their speculative values. The Republican party got the West settled and an agricultural interest, raising commercial crops for the world market, seated on the land. But through its land program it also laid the foundations for some great land, timber, and mineral fortunes.

Pacific Railways. With southern opposition gone, the Republicans could proceed to the realization of a project so close to the hearts of industrial capitalism: the spanning of the continent by at least one Pacific railway. In July, 1862, two federal corporations were chartered, the Union Pacific which was empowered to build west out of Omaha to the eastern boundary of California, and the Central Pacific which was to build eastward from the Pacific coast for the purpose of effecting a juncture with the Union Pacific. The Republicans were more generous than simply authorizing the laying down of the lines. The rights of way were guaranteed; the Indian titles were extinguished; military protection was promised against marauding bands; and the builders were given free use of timber, earth, and stone from the public lands.

These were only the lesser beneficences. Following the precedent established in the Illinois Central Railroad charter of 1850, the government voted the Pacific railroads huge land grants, to wit, twenty sections (in alternate plots on each side of the right of way) for every mile of track laid down. Nor was this all. The federal government also pledged its credit for the assistance of the builders. Originally taking a first mortgage, then making its claim a junior lien, the government promised to lend the companies $16,000 for every mile built in level country, $32,000 for every mile built in the foothills, and $48,000 for every mile built in the mountains. The Union Pacific was not really begun until 1866; in May, 1869, both lines were finished when a juncture was achieved at Promontory Point, Utah.

The fraud attending building was on a gargantuan scale. Through dummy construction companies, insiders got most of the government bonds. The promoters of the Central Pacific— Leland Stanford, Collis P. Huntington, Charles Crocker, and Mark Hopkins—were more astute than their eastern confreres and their profits were much greater. Subsequent inquiry divulged the fact that Crocker and Company received $121,000,-000 for the construction work; the most favorable estimate of the worth of the property was $58,000,000. The difference went to the four partners.

In all, during this period of war and reconstruction, the Republican Congresses chartered four Pacific railways and each received land grants. These were: the Union Pacific-Central Pacific in 1862; the Northern Pacific in 1864 (to run from the head of Lake Superior to Puget Sound); the Atlantic and Pacific in 1866 (to run along the thirty-fifth parallel—later this road became part of the Santa Fe system); and the Texas Pacific in 1871 (later absorbed by the Southern Pacific). From 1850 to 1873, when a stop was put to the practice, 158,000,000 acres of land were voted by Congress to land-grant railroads; and of this amount, 116,000,000 acres were certified and finally patented. The money loans came to a very large sum. The Union Pacific got $27,200,000 in federal bonds; the Central Pacific got $25,-800,000; four lesser companies received $11,500,000. These railways quickly defaulted in their interest payments so that by 1890 accrued interest came to the gigantic total of $50,000,000. Only the threat of foreclosure proceedings in 1897 compelled the railroads to settle with the government; and then they agreed to pay the principals of the loans but only a small part of the long-overdue interest.

Immigration and Labor. The Republican party had promised a federal immigration policy: and this pledge Republican congressmen proceeded to fulfill when in 1864 an Immigration Bureau was set up in Washington. In the same year Congress legalized the entry of contract laborers from Europe and China. For four years the latter law stood on the statute books; but until 1885, and then only as a result of the pressure of the Knights of Labor, nothing was done to bar such laborers from entering. Despite the Civil War, the immigrant tide beat upon our shores and European workers moved here to take advantage of the (only relatively) higher wages while European farmers bought freeholds in the trans-Mississippi West. In the 1850's immigration had accounted for an addition of 2,600,000 to our population; in the 1860's the immigration total was 2,314,000 (of which about 600,000 came during the war years); in the 1870's, it was 2,812,000. In 1870, there were 56,000 Chinese in America, almost all of them residing west of the Rocky Mountains.

Most of these new accretions were added to the labor reserve of the nation, chiefly as unskilled workers. And their presence tended to make the organizational problem only the more difficult. Unionism continued at a low ebb (at least, on national organizational lines) during the greater part of the conflict; the result was, labor received an unequal share of the expanding national income. By 1865, the general average of money wages stood 43 per cent higher than in 1861; but the greater increase in living costs pushed real wages down to about two thirds of the 1861 level.

Some of the skilled workers were able to take advantage of their wartime opportunities and through unionization raised wage scales. But on the whole, labor fared poorly, having less than government support. In fact, governmental policy was openly hostile. To quote Professor Shannon: ". . . the unions were fought savagely, union rules were abrogated wherever employers found it possible, and the federal government openly encouraged the importation of foreign contract labor to break strikes. Union generals sometimes dispersed strikers by military force, while elsewhere legal permission was obtained to employ prison labor at wages as low as 20 cents a day."

And this brings us to an interesting theoretical question:

Why did not the workers participate—as workers—in the Civil War? The whole problem still remains to be illuminated. But, in general, these facts seem valid. The workers of America did not appear in the Civil War, which was a revolutionary event, as an independent party with class demands. They did not even have representation within the ranks of the Republican party and we find no fraction here comparable, for example, to the Hébertists among the Jacobins of the French Revolution. Also, rather than actively championing the war, they opposed it at the beginning, gave it only a sullen support throughout, and rejected its idealistic purposes. They fought conscription; they refused to re-enlist; they would not buy war loans; they deserted in large numbers. And in 1863 they engaged in savage riots against the war in many American cities because of war weariness, wage exploitation, and their hatred of Negro strikebreakers.

This conclusion seems inescapable and it fits in with the earlier analysis already presented here: industrial production was not yet mature enough, and the workers were not yet proletarianized sufficiently to realize that a revolutionary situation presents opportunities for the advance of *every* underprivileged class.

The American Civil War turned out to be a revolution indeed. But its striking achievement was the triumph of industrial capitalism. The industrial capitalists, through their political spokesmen, the Republicans, had succeeded in capturing the state and using it as an instrument to strengthen their economic position. It was no accident, therefore, that while the war was waged on the field and through Negro emancipation, in Congress' halls the victory was made secure by the passage of tariff, banking, public-land, railroad, and contract-labor legislation.

CHAPTER TWENTY-FIVE

The Reconstruction Period

1. CONGRESSIONAL RECONSTRUCTION

THE presidency of Andrew Johnson the Radicals were prepared to regard with complacency: he had been a stanch Union man; he had been unfriendly to the slave interest in his own state of Tennessee; he favored the Wade-Davis program for Reconstruction. But before 1865 was over the Radicals were Johnson's implacable enemies and they not only succeeded in destroying his authority but they almost drove him out of office. Why was this? It was because it was soon revealed that between the President and the Radicals on the two questions of principle on which the Radicals (that is to say, the Old Radicals) could not, nay, dared not, compromise, a wide chasm yawned: the enfranchisement of the Negro in order to hold the South loyal to Republicanism and the maintenance in power of industrial capitalism.

Johnson's opposition to the Radical position sprang out of his own heritage and class loyalties. Johnson had originated in the South's lower middle class—that class that Helper had seen as one of the leading victims of the slave institution—and through a hard young manhood had learned to place his confidence in the free white yeomanry of his section. He was, in short, a petty bourgeois in his political and economic orientations; and he sought to redeem the South for neither the old planter capitalists nor the Negroes but for the small white farmers. Negro suffrage, therefore, he would not accept as a basis for Reconstruction, fearing that the competition of the free Negro would drive down standards. At the same time he looked on the victory of the revolution with a jaundiced eye. There are two revealing passages among his utterances that light up his position and indicate why men like Stevens and Sumner had

374

to try to hound him out of office. For Johnson meant to turn the clock back to an era of Jeffersonian white democracy and egalitarian small property. Said Johnson in his first congressional message:

Monopolies, perpetuities, and class legislation are contrary to the genius of free government. . . . Wherever monopoly attains a foothold, it is sure to be a source of danger, discord, and trouble. . . . The government is subordinate to the people; but, as the agent and representative of the people, it must be held superior to monopolies; which in themselves ought never to be granted and which, where they exist, must be subordinate and yield to the government.

And in 1867 he declared:

To the people, the national debt is to be paid; but to the aristocracy of bonds and national securities it is a property of more than $2,500,000,000, from which a revenue of $180,000,000 a year is to be received into their pockets. So we now find that an aristocracy of the South, based on $3,000,000,000 in Negroes, who were a productive class, has disappeared and their place in political control of the country is assumed by an aristocracy based on nearly $3,000,000,000 of national debt. . . .

The war of finance is the next war we have to fight. . . . The manufacturers and men of capital in the eastern states and the states along the Atlantic seaboard . . . these are in favor of high protective and, in fact, prohibitory tariffs, and also favor a contraction of currency.

That Johnson meant to wage this fight against the new masters of the nation unrelentingly he showed when in June, 1866, he vetoed a land-grab bill giving the New York and Montana Iron Mining and Manufacturing Company (in which Stevens and Wade were interested) 12,800 acres of the public domain rich in minerals and timber for $1.25 an acre.

As for Reconstruction, the southern states were to be readmitted in the interests of the establishment to power of the small white farmers. The President was prepared to be clement toward all common men: and in May, 1865, he offered a general amnesty to all who had participated in the rebellion upon their taking an oath of allegiance to the United States. The leaders of the Confederacy as well as all those who owned taxable property in excess of $20,000, however, had to apply individually to the President for pardon.

Meanwhile, loyal state governments once more were to be erected. Arkansas, Louisiana, Tennessee, and Virginia, Johnson recognized at once. In the other seven, during May-July, 1865, Johnson appointed provisional governors and directed them to summon constitutional conventions in which could participate all whites who had taken the oath of allegiance or had received the President's special pardons. *He did not extend the franchise to the Negroes.* Once having met, as a condition precedent to readmission, the conventions were to repeal the ordinances of secession, repudiate that part of the state debts contracted in furtherance of the war, and abolish slavery. These demands the southern states satisfied; so that by the time Congress assembled, in December, 1865, they were all (except Texas) back in the Union as, presumably, sovereign commonwealths. The Thirteenth Amendment, freeing the Negroes, was ratified by these states (as well as a sufficient number of loyal states) with the result that in December, 1865, it was proclaimed a part of the Constitution. But what Johnson had wrought soon became apparent to the horrified eyes of the Radicals: for southern legislatures, dominated by the white yeomen, began to enact so-called "Black Codes" for the purpose of maintaining the Negroes in an unequal civil and economic status.

To save these two positions—political control over the southern states and the security of industrial capitalism—the war had to be fought again. This was, in effect, the meaning of congressional, as opposed to presidential, Reconstruction. Stevens openly revealed the high purpose of the Old Radicals when he uttered the following warning to the House, in January, 1867:

I am now confining my argument to Negro suffrage in the rebel states. . . . The white Union men are in a great minority in each of those states. With them the blacks would act in a body; and it is believed that in each of said states, except one, the two united would form a majority, control the states and protect themselves. . . . *It would assure the ascendancy of the Union [Republican] party.* Do you avow the party purpose? exclaims some horror-stricken demagogue. I do. For I believe, on my conscience, that on the continued ascendancy of that party depends the safety of this great nation. If impartial suffrage is excluded in the rebel states then every one of them is sure to send a solid rebel representative delegation to Congress, and cast a solid rebel electoral vote. They, with their kindred Copperheads of the North, would always elect the President and control Congress. . . . Now you must divide them between loyalists, without regard to color, and disloyalists, or *you will be the perpetual vassals of the free-trade, irritated, revengeful South.* (My italics. L.M.H.)

It is not necessary, for our purpose here, to detail the processes by which congressional Reconstruction was attempted. It is enough to say that after a number of preliminary maneuvers, during which the status of the southern states remained uncertain while Congress renewed the Freedmen's Bureau, put Negro civil rights under the protection of the federal courts, and passed the Fourteenth Amendment, the Radicals undid all of Johnson's work. In March, 1867, they passed the First Reconstruction Act as a result of which ten of the southern state governments which Johnson had helped to erect were superseded. The South was now really a conquered province. The Reconstruction Act was thoroughgoing. It demanded universal Negro suffrage; it placed the states under military rule; and it called for the summoning of new conventions from whose elections and deliberations were to be excluded all persons high in the military and civil councils of the Confederacy. New state legislatures, after the conventions had done their work, were to enfranchise the Negroes and ratify the Fourteenth Amendment; and only after Congress had approved the constitutions and after the Fourteenth Amendment had been adopted were the military governments to be removed and the South's senators and congressmen reinstated in their seats. Other acts, supplemental to the first, were passed during 1867 and 1868 for the guidance of the military in charge.

As a result of such measures, when the federal troops completed their rolls of the eligible voters, it was seen that the Negro electors were in the majority in six of the ten states, although in but two of them did they constitute an actual majority of the population. In the other four states, namely Virginia, Arkansas, Texas, and North Carolina, the whites made up the larger part of the registered voters. It is to be noted, however, that in each of these there was a sizable party of whites, particularly in the mountain sections, who had bitterly resented secession and who therefore tended to act with the Republicans against their old antagonists, the former large slave-owners. These were the "scalawags." This circumstance, together with the fact that the election officials appointed by the military were all men who could take the "ironclad oath" (to the effect that they had never voluntarily given aid or comfort to the rebellion), insured Republican control of all the conventions except that of Virginia.

Participating also in the work of the conventions were the "carpetbaggers," thus dubbed by southerners because presumably they had appeared in the South after the war with all their worldly goods packed in a single carpetbag. Some of these persons were outright adventurers; some had been Freedmen's Bureau agents, members of the Union armies, or federal Treasury officials; some were honest and zealous social workers; many were little capitalists who came to invest in agricultural properties or set up small industrial plants. These forces were responsible for the establishment of new state governments in the South during the years 1868-70.

The southern constitutions gave the Radicals what they wanted: universal manhood (including Negro) suffrage and the disfranchisement of the leaders of the Confederacy. But they were much more than this: for, as a result of the combination of Negroes and white scalawags and carpetbaggers, they established the supremacy of petty-bourgeois enterprise in the South. They were, in short, leveling documents which sought to defend the civil and economic rights of men of small property, both white and black. And, interestingly enough, because they were so satisfactory to the majority of *whites* in the South, they were maintained long after the southern Reconstruction governments were overthrown. Thus, the Florida constitution, written in 1868, was kept on until 1885; the Virginia constitution survived from 1870 to 1902; the South Carolina constitution from

1868 to 1895; and the Mississippi constitution from 1868 to 1890.

Only at one point did the southern egalitarians of the Reconstruction period fail, and this, as has been pointed out, was due to congressional indifference: they did not succeed in obtaining the partition of the estates of the large, disloyal landowners. Be it noted, the body of reforms incorporated in most of these constitutions made up a notable achievement. Some, and frequently all of them, contained the following provisions. Negroes were enfranchised and were granted full equal civil rights. The property rights of women were protected. A system of free and mixed education was set up. Local governments were reorganized and granted a greater measure of self-rule on the basis of popular election. The judiciary was placed under popular control. Imprisonment for debt was abolished. Property qualifications for voting and holding office were done away with. New tax systems were devised based upon uniform rates of assessment on all types of property. Charitable institutions—orphanages, asylums, homes for the blind and deaf—were created.

On the whole, these governments, considering the inexperience and lack of leadership of the great mass, worked well. There was inefficiency and there was corruption but not any more or less however than characterized most of the government of the period. These Reconstruction governments left the southern states with a heavy burden of debt. But it must not be forgotten that a goodly portion of this indebtedness was due to the fact that in their zeal to hasten the building of public improvements, the Reconstructionists fell into the hands of dishonest promoters. Particularly was this true of railroad construction, in connection with which southern states guaranteed the principle and interest of private bond issues. Notably South Carolina, North Carolina, Florida, Georgia, and Louisiana suffered as a result of the sharp practices of northern financiers and concessionaires. Also, as Professor Du Bois points out, a part of the swelled public debt of the states was due to the fact that they had to sell their bonds at large discounts in northern money markets.

Professor Du Bois discusses the question of Reconstruction corruption, in connection with the South Carolina situation, in the following fashion:

This brings us to the center of the corruption charge, which was in fact that poor men were ruling and taxing rich men. And this was the chief reason that ridicule and scorn and crazy anger were poured upon the government. . . . The wilder charges have all the stigmata of propaganda and are in some respects intrinsically unbelievable. It is impossible to be convinced that the people who gave South Carolina so excellent a constitution, who founded good social legislation, a new system of public schools, and who were orderly and earnest in their general demeanor, could at the same time in all cases be stealing, carousing, and breaking every law of decency.

In any case, all efforts to evaluate the success or failure of the Reconstruction governments in terms of their fiscal policies are wide of the mark. A contemporary white southern historian, Francis B. Simkins, with a courage and candor that does him great credit, makes the following keen observation:

A reinterpretation of the tax policies of the Radical regimes suggests a new explanation of the odious reputations possessed by these governments. . . . It seems that the worst crime of which they have been adjudged guilty was the violation of the American caste system. The crime of crimes was to encourage Negroes in voting, officeholding, and other functions of social equality. This supposedly criminal encouragement of the Negro is execrated ever more savagely as with the passing years race prejudices continue to mount. . . . Attempts to make the Reconstruction governments reputable and honest have been treated with scorn, and the efforts of Negroes to approach the white man's standards of civilization are adjudged more reprehensible than the behavior of the more ignorant and corrupt. Social equality and Negroism have not a chance to be respectable.

The end result was failure of congressional Reconstruction. The reason here is simple enough: Congress after 1870—now dominated by the New Radicals—was not interested in supporting the Negroes and their white egalitarian allies in the South. As has been said: there was an emotional letdown after the war; and the New Radicals had never been brought up under the stern and Calvinist discipline of the Abolitionists. Of equal importance was the necessity for pacifying the South to make possible the quick penetration of northern capital.

In consequence, the southern redemptionists had a relatively easy time of it; and before 1877 was over they were reinstalled in the seats of political authority in the southern states. These redemptionists (we call them the Bourbons) were more than the old planter class: they represented a combination of landlordism and the new capitalism allied with northern financial, railway, and mineral interests. They were nonegalitarians; and they were fearful lest the poorer southern whites in time would be won over to the support of the Reconstruction governments which, in fact, were in their interest as well as that of the Negroes. To divide the leveling host, therefore, it was necessary to separate the underprivileged whites from the Negroes. This is what the Bourbons did. Playing upon racial suspicions and fears, conjuring up horrendous images of miscegenation and racial impurity, the Bourbons gained their goal. The poorer whites went over to the side of the minority landlords and southern capitalists: and redemption was achieved openly and cynically through the tactics of intimidation, violence, fraud, and willful murder. The Ku Klux Klan, which flourished in the South during 1868-71, the traditional view holds, was the southerner's answer to the Union League clubs and Negro militias. A more realistic study would show that the Klan was the dupe of the southern middle class seeking the recapture of political and economic power.

The analysis presented here of the essentially class nature of southern redemption is strikingly confirmed in a still-unpublished paper recently written by another white southern historian, Professor Howard K. Beale of the University of North Carolina. Professor Beale says:

And what of the poorer white man? Were his interests really opposed to those of the Negro or is this just another shibboleth encouraged by men whose interests were opposed to both Negroes and small white farmers? Bourbon supremacy embodied the conservative swinging back of the pendulum that frequently has followed the excesses of revolution. Planters shared the new aristocracy with men of business and were often dominated by them. In overthrowing the Radicals, the Bourbons fastened upon the South a government that served badly the interests of poorer white men who had for a time appeared freed by the Civil War from aristocratic control. It took the Populists years to win back some of the democratic privileges lost in Bourbon restoration. In many cases the Bourbons maintained control over a majority of white men by raising fear of the Negro and at the same time using Negro voters in black counties to overbalance white majorities.

Professor Randall describes the less violent processes of intimidation in some sections of South Carolina as follows. The redemptionists formed rifle clubs and

. . . armed usually with pistols they would invade Republican political meetings, heckle the speakers, and insist on their own speakers being heard. In the course of the meeting, they would move about in the crowd, persuading Negroes and white Radicals that the healthy course would be to vote Democratic. If forced to disb..nd they would reorganize as missionary societies and dancing clubs and carry on as before. . . . By such means Negroes in large numbers, and a great many white Republicans as well, were induced, usually without actual violence, to "cross Jordan" (i.e., shift to the Democratic party).

The first states to be redeemed were Tennessee, Virginia, North Carolina, and Georgia. Later came Mississippi, Alabama, Texas, and Arkansas. And finally, in 1877, as a result of a deal made following the contested presidential election of 1876, federal troops were withdrawn from South Carolina, Florida, and Louisiana. The Bourbons took over, the Negroes and white Radicals were driven out of power, and congressional Reconstruction was ended.

2. NORTHERN RECONSTRUCTION

It was really in the Old Northwest that the processes of Reconstruction were completed; for with the establishment of Republican power in states like Ohio, Indiana, Illinois, Michigan, and Wisconsin the dogs of war could be called off. The serious threat of a combination once more of southern and western agrarians was stayed: and the economic program of the revolution was secure.

The Republican politicians who succeeded the Old Radicals were therefore ordinary timeservers. They cultivated every important capitalist interest that would keep their party in power—the iron-and-steel masters of Pennsylvania, the wool-growers of Ohio, the woolen manufacturers of Massachusetts, the lumber kings of Wisconsin, the metal-mine operators of the Far West—and they cynically exploited the officeholders, shook down the lobbyists, and themselves fed at the public trough. The period 1870-96 marked the nadir of American political life; for it was characterized by open corruption, personal betrayal, and unprincipled public conduct. The achievements, theoretically and actually, of all the men at the control of affairs were negligible.

Why was this? It was due to the fact, simply, that the road for the advance of industrial capitalism was opened up during the years of the Civil War and the Reconstruction periods; for it was during 1861-75, as we have seen, that the nation was committed fully to the protective system, a national banking structure, homesteads, government aid to Pacific railways. During the same period, as will be pointed out, too, the national government adopted a "sound"-money program. By 1875, virtually, the task was done; and it remained merely for the later politicians (Republicans and, indeed, eastern Democrats) to act in the capacity of the train-wrecking crew in order to keep the tracks free of obstructions.

It was possible notably for the new leaders of Republicanism —the Blaines, Conklings, Garfields, Shermans, McKinleys—to fulfill this function without let or hindrance (and in this we have the explanation of the personal excesses of many of these men) because the Civil War had done its work only too well. It had destroyed a *political* opposition based upon a class interest. In this connection, a study of comparative politics is fruitful: for in England and Germany the Liberal (industrial capitalist) parties had constantly to guard themselves against the criticism of the Conservative (landlord plus *rentier*) parties; and they had to walk in the path of rectitude. In France, where

the intrigues following the establishment of the Third Republic had discredited the opposition, the political spokesmen for
the industrial-capitalist class were as venal as in the United
States.

In the United States, devotion to the cause of industrial capitalism received its reward: the politicians were permitted to line
their own pockets; their party chests were periodically filled
by the protectionists; and none said them nay when they attached the whole Grand Army of the Republic to the destinies
of the Republican party through the passage of pension legislation. An inexpensive device to make the Old Northwest, in
particular, safe for Republicanism was river and harbor legislation. Early appropriations were modest enough: in 1866,
$300,000; in 1870, $3,500,000; and in 1890, $11,700,000. But
the money was spent frankly in those regions where it did the
party the most good.

In a still-unpublished essay, Miss Helen M. Jenson clearly
establishes the link between Republican triumph and public
improvements in the state of Wisconsin. Uninterested in the
fate of the Negro, indifferent to the processes of southern Reconstruction, personally hostile to Stevens and Sumner, Wisconsin Republican politicians could "deliver" their state because they brought back to their constituents ship canals to
help the lumbering industry, river and harbor improvements
for the farmers and merchants, and land grants for railways
and wagon roads. Wisconsin congressmen voted Stevens' Reconstruction Act in 1867 because they got pork-barrel legislation;
and they voted for protectionism in 1870 for the same reason.
And Miss Jenson quotes a Republican newspaper of Wisconsin
which in the campaign of 1868 could say with refreshing
candor:

. . . the American people owe a debt of gratitude to the Republican
Union party for constructing a highway to the Pacific, for giving
homesteads to the helpless, and freedom to the slave. And the
people of this congressional district are especially indebted to a
Republican Congress for the liberal appropriations and for the improvement of their harbors. . . .

It was not an easy victory for Republicanism in the Old North-west, for agrarianism in this region was justly suspicious of protection, "sound" money, and national banks—but in time it was won by appropriations and, sometimes, the open buying of elections. The presidential contests were close enough. In 1872, Grant carried Indiana by only 22,000 votes, Ohio by 37,000 votes, and Wisconsin by 18,000 votes. In 1876, Hayes carried Illinois by only 20,000 votes, Michigan by 20,000 votes, Ohio by 7000 votes, and Wisconsin by 7000 votes; he lost Indiana by 5000 votes. In 1880, Garfield's pluralities were a little larger: Illinois went Republican by 20,000 votes, Indiana by 7000 votes, Michigan by 54,000 votes, Ohio by 35,000 votes, and Wisconsin by 30,000 votes.

The following figures show Republican successes in the con-gressional elections in this region during the crucial years 1870-80. It was a hard fight, but by 1880 Republicanism was victorious.

ELECTIONS TO LOWER HOUSE OF CONGRESS, 1870–80

States	1870	1872	1874	1876	1878	1880
Illinois	7 R.	14 R.	8 R.	11 R.	13 R.	13 R.
	6 D.	5 D.	11 D.*	8 D.	6 D.	6 D.
Indiana	6 R.	10 R.	5 R.	9 R.	6 R.	8 R.
	5 D.	3 D.	8 D.	4 D.	7 D.	5 D.
Michigan	4 R.	9 R.	6 R.	8 R.	9 R.	9 R.
	1 D.	0 D.	3 D.	1 D.	0 D.	0 D.
Ohio	14 R.	13 R.	8 R.	12 R.	9 R.	15 R.
	5 D.	7 D.	12 D.	8 D.	11 D.	5 D.
Wisconsin	4 R.	6 R.	5 R.	5 R.	5 R.	6 R.
	2 D.	2 D.	3 D.	3 D.	3 D.	2 D.
Total R	35	52	32	45	42	52
Total D	19	17	37	24	27	18

(*Note:* R. = Republicans; D. = Democrats. D.* includes Democrats and third-party men.)

3. CAPITALIST CONSTRUCTION

The processes of making capitalism's house secure went on during the Reconstruction period. Some of these achievements of Republicanism we must now pass in review.

The War Bonds and "Sound" Money. The Civil War bonds had been bought in considerable measure with a paper cur-rency; and Secretary Chase, concerned about precipitating a controversy, had been judiciously vague about redemption.

Some of the war bonds, therefore, had promised to pay principal and interest in gold; some had specified "coin"; and some had been entirely noncommittal. In 1869, a triumph was achieved by the men who talked of the necessity for defending the honor and credit of the nation; and Congress voted to make payments in "coin." This was an initial trial of strength between inflationists and contractionists, for the cheap-money interest had prevailed upon the Democratic party in 1868 to promise redemption in paper; and the Democracy had lost.

A second trial of strength was over the number of greenbacks to remain in circulation. The inflationists wanted as many as possible; the contractionists none at all, if possible. The inflationists were the debtors generally and the farmers in particular, who sought more money to maintain high crop prices and to make their debt burden as light as possible. The contractionists were usually the bondholders (of course, they called themselves "sound"-money men), who had paid for their bonds in paper and hoped to see their holdings appreciate through contraction. After considerable juggling, Congress, finally in 1878, determined that the amount of greenbacks then outstanding, $346,681,000, should remain a permanent part of the country's currency system.

The bonds were to be redeemed in "coin" said the legislation of 1869. And what was "coin"? In 1873, Congress decided that "coin" was only gold and simply failed to provide for the minting of silver in a new and involved act it passed called: "An act revising and amending the laws relating to the mints and the assay offices and the coinage of the United States." Whether this was by design or oversight one can only speculate: in any case, silver was demonetized.

The "sound"-money interest won its crowning achievement in 1875 and capital was safe from assault at the hands of inflationists: for in this year legislation was passed ordering the resumption of specie payments on January 1, 1879. America's *rentiers* could now rest assured that their investments in farm mortgages, railroad bonds, and state and municipal securities would, if anything, increase in value through the maintenance of a dear dollar. The problem of building up a cover for the greenbacks was not so simple, but as a result of a series of circumstances, some fortuitous, the Treasury obtained a large enough reserve to make possible specie payments on the stipulated date. These were the swinging of the commodity balance to our favor after 1875, crop failure in Europe, so that European countries bought cereals with gold, and the return of European capital to the United States for long-term investments. In consequence, the gold stock in the country mounted from $121,000,000 in 1875 to $246,000,000 at the beginning of 1879 —and the premium on gold disappeared.

The Fourteenth Amendment and Due Process. The Fourteenth Amendment had been drawn up by a congressional Joint Committee of Fifteen, which the Radicals dominated, and was passed by both houses in 1866. Unlike all other amendments to the Constitution, the Fourteenth contained more than one proposition. Section 1 included the heart of an earlier Civil Rights bill and also declared the Negro to be a citizen of the United States—something the Supreme Court had denied in the Dred Scott decision. The other sections were of a punitive character as regards the southern states and former Confederate leaders. It will be recalled that under congressional Reconstruction the southern states were compelled to ratify the Amendment; while their readmission depended upon the incorporation of the Amendment into the Constitution. The Amendment was formally proclaimed in 1868.

The Fourteenth Amendment was presumably designed to protect the liberties of the newly emancipated Negroes—and this undoubtedly was the chief intention of the Radicals who wrote it. But they may very well have had something else in mind also: the defense of private-property rights against attack at the hands of state legislatures. And this, whether or not the leading design of its framers, in time became the great significance of this charter: that property could not be taken by the states without due process. In fact, unwittingly or not, this was the greatest achievement wrought by the Radicals in defense of the revolution.

Section 1 of the Amendment read:

All persons born or naturalized in the United States, and subject to the jurisdiction thereof, are citizens of the United States and of the states wherein they reside. No state shall make or enforce any law which shall abridge the privileges or immunities of citizens of the United States; nor shall any state deprive any *person* of life, liberty or property without *due process* of law; nor deny any *person* within its jurisdiction the *equal protection* of the laws. (My italics. L. M. H.)

About the precise wording of this section a great historical controversy has raged, due to the statements made by Roscoe Conkling (one of the members of the Joint Committee) before the Supreme Court in the argument on a tax case involving the Southern Pacific Railway. Conkling's story ran as follows: The Joint Committee of Fifteen had set out to labor not only in the interests of Negro rights; it was seeking to protect property rights, as well, against the encroachments of state legislatures. It had therefore advisedly written the word "person" into the "due process" and "equal protection" clauses of the Amendment, because it meant more than "citizen"; the committee had in mind the use of the word "person" in its ordinary juristic meaning of corporation, too. In short, said Conkling, corporations as well as Negroes were to be protected in their rights to life, liberty, and property according to due process of law and the equal protection of the laws. And Conkling, to impress the Court, made frequent references to the journal of the Joint Committee, which he held in his hand.

The Court, when it decided on this particular suit, took no cognizance of Conkling's argument and based its findings on other points of law. But in 1886, in a similar tax case, the Court accepted Conkling's assertions as to the wider meaning of "person" and "due process." From then on, the Supreme Court increasingly relied on the "due process" clause to protect corporate rights.

How much credence are we to give to Conkling's statements? Very little, certainly, as far as his argument was based on the journal of the Joint Committee. Also, as Howard Jay Graham has so convincingly demonstrated, while one of the framers of the Amendment (John A. Bingham of Ohio) "as early as 1856 had employed due process of law as a substantive restraint upon the legislatures, no indication was found that Bingham in these early usages ever employed the guarantee to protect other than rights of 'natural persons.'" There was no conspiracy, then; but Mr. Graham is of the belief that by 1866 even Bingham, while he as an Old Radical was preoccupied essentially with the defense of Negro rights, must have realized that there was in existence already a wider interpretation of due process. And this included both natural and corporate persons.

In other words, due process was beginning, if only shadowily, to have a different usage than the currently accepted legal one, in the minds of some of the committee members. Heretofore, due process had had a *procedural* meaning to the courts; that is to say, persons were receiving due process at the hands of government if their procedural rights were being adequately safeguarded. If persons were tried for crimes by proper judicial procedure (i.e., "the law of the land"); if property rights were adjudicated in the same way; if the state's powers of eminent domain or taxation were exercised with due deference to statute or custom: then due process, in a procedural sense, had been observed. Up to the 1860's certainly, no serious effort had been made to use the concept in a *substantive* sense, that is, as a limitation upon government or the *substance* of legislation, as a result of which the Lockian natural and inalienable rights of the person to life, liberty, and property could not be abridged.

To anticipate our story a little bit: it was this latter substantive conception of due process that was accepted by our courts after 1886. And, in consequence, due process became one of the bulwarks of the American doctrine of the judicial review of legislation—and also of private-property rights. As Justice Holmes put it in his dissenting opinion in Truax v. Corrigan (1921), the concept of due process has frequently been so applied as to "prevent the making of social experiments that are an important part of community desires, in the insulated chambers afforded by the several states. . . ."

Because the subject has a contemporaneous interest, a further digression here may be permitted. Since his appointment to the Court by President Franklin D. Roosevelt, Justice Black has been laboring to reduce the concept of due process once more to a strictly procedural reading. His opinion in the Chambers, *et al.* v. Florida case (involving four Negroes who had been sentenced to death by Florida courts) is a masterly summary of his position as well as an eloquent defense of due process from a procedural viewpoint. The opinion, in which a unanimous Court concurred, was handed down on February 12, 1940. A portion of the decision may be cited:

. . . in view of its historical setting and the wrongs which called it into being, the due process provision of the Fourteenth Amendment . . . has led few to doubt that it was intended to guarantee procedural standards adequate and appropriate, then and thereafter.

To protect, at all times, people charged with or suspected of crime by those holding positions of power and authority. Tyrannical governments had immemorially utilized dictatorial criminal procedure and punishment to make scapegoats of the weak or of helpless political, religious, or racial minorities and those who differed, who would not conform, and who resisted tyranny. . . .

From the popular hatred and abhorrence of illegal confinement, torture, and extortion of confessions . . . evolved the fundamental idea that no man's life, liberty, or property could be forfeited as criminal punishment for violation of that law until there had been a charge fairly made and fairly tried in a public tribunal free of prejudice, passion, excitement, and tyrannical power.

Thus, as assurance against ancient evils, our country, in order to preserve "the blessings of liberty," wrote into its basic law the requirement, among others, that the forfeiture of the lives, liberties, or property of people accused of crime can only follow if procedural safeguards of due process have been obeyed.

To follow now Mr. Graham's argument:

1. Bingham, in 1856, as an Abolitionist, had first hit upon the possibilities of due process in a substantive meaning when he was casting about for devices to defend Negro rights. Under such a natural-rights conception Negroes were not only "persons" but also "citizens" and, into the bargain, "citizens of the

United States"; and, as such, they were entitled to protection in the enjoyment of their rights to life, liberty, and property.

2. In the 1850's, corporations (life-insurance companies, railways) coming under the fire of state legislatures, which raised license fees and premium taxes and repealed franchises, had appealed to the courts for relief under the denial of due process, among other reasons. Now, Bingham was a lawyer and, to boot, a railway lawyer. It is hard to believe that as such he was unaware of this use of due process in the arguments on behalf of corporations before state courts.

3. The state courts were uniformly finding against corporations and denying the *substantive* conception. It was small wonder that lawyers, interested in defending corporate rights, as soon as they learned that Congress was at work on an Amendment, began to petition it for *federal* protection. The facts bear out Conkling's statement in 1882 before the Court, to wit:

At the time the Fourteenth Amendment was ratified [Conkling obviously meant *drafted*, i.e., early in 1866], as the records of the two houses will show, individuals and joint stock companies were appealing for congressional and administrative protection against invidious and discriminating state and local taxes. One instance was that of an express company, whose stock was owned largely by citizens of the State of New York who came with petitions and bills seeking acts of Congress to aid them in resisting what they deemed oppressive taxation in two states, and oppressive and ruinous rules of damages applied under state laws.

Mr. Graham has found that there were at least two hundred such petitions for relief, notably from insurance companies, and he draws the following conclusion:

It cannot be inferred that the Amendment was deliberately or consciously framed to assist the insurance companies or other corporations, but everything about the petitions . . . suggests that they would have been likely to raise the question of corporate status while the framers [of the Amendment] were at work.

4. At the same time that these insurance-company petitions were converging on Congress, there came the prayer from the Cleveland and Mahoning Railroad, an Ohio corporation whose

franchise to operate a part of its road in Pennsylvania had been repealed by the Pennsylvania legislature in the interests of the Pennsylvania Railroad's monopoly of transportation in the district in question. These pleas, like those of the insurance companies, were "suffused with due process of law." But, more important even, were these facts: Reverdy Johnson of the Joint Committee had been the lawyer for the Cleveland and Mahoning Railroad in its cases in the federal courts. And the federal courts had found the repeal of the franchises illegal on the ground that the Ohio corporation had been denied the "due course of law" guaranteed by the Pennsylvania constitution. Says Mr. Graham: "It therefore seems likely that Reverdy Johnson, at least, must have understood that to add a due process clause to the Federal Constitution as an express restraint upon the states was to add a source of valuable protection to corporate interests."

Nor was Johnson the only member of the Joint Committee involved. In May, 1866, Stevens, another member of the committee, introduced a bill for the relief of the Ohio railway company and its affiliates. During the debate, the federal opinion, referring to the voiding of due process in Pennsylvania, was read into the record. And voting for the bill in the House, along with Stevens, were also Conkling and Bingham.

One may infer as little or as much as one wishes from these facts as regards the intention of the framers of the Amendment. But this, at least, is clear: Bingham, Johnson, Conkling, and Stevens, if no others, knew of the wider significance of the word "person" and the new meaning of the concept "due process" that corporation lawyers were trying to write into the law of the land. The result, in time, was the use of these instruments in the interests of big property.

The Establishment of Monopolists on the Public Domain. In the same way, the quick disposition of the public domain by the Civil War and Reconstruction Congresses ended in the firm establishment of monopolists on the land—whether as landlords, great cattle barons, timber dealers, or mineral exploiters.

It has been a common misconception that the Homestead Act of 1862 opened the public domain to free settlement and that a

numerous agricultural interest, made up of freeholders, benefited from the governmental (i.e., Republican party) largess.
Exactly the reverse seems to have been the case. Not only were
the homesteaders the least favored of the groups attracted into
the western lands (by 1890, for example, only 372,659 entries
had been perfected, for a total of 48,225,736 acres, as contrasted
with the more than four times as much land received by the
land-grant railroad companies); but the public land system
continued to encourage speculation, monopolization, and fraud.
Homesteaders, in fact, settled on the least desirable lands, most
of the freeholders were compelled to purchase, and tenancy
quickly appeared on the public domain. Throughout the whole
period of disposal—at any rate, until the 1890's—there runs the
ugly vein of land-office inefficiency and collusion. So that Professor Gates concludes: "The palpable frauds committed and the
large areas transferred under these acts [the acts of 1862-78,
above referred to] and their interference with the homestead
principle lead one to suspect that their enactment and retention
were the results of political pressure by interested groups."

In addition, as in the pre-Civil War period, government policy of disposition played into the hands of the land speculators
and monopolists. The vast tracts given to the railroads and the
states were sold, and the choicest regions were acquired not by
settlers but by companies. The cash-sale system was maintained
throughout the period and in the trans-Mississippi and Far West
notably (Kansas, Nebraska, Colorado, California, Washington,
Oregon) huge estates and factory farms were built up that operated on the basis of tenancy or the migratory labor system.
Indian land rights were extinguished and these territories more
frequently than not also became the possession of a speculative
land interest. Here, policy was obviously devised—by disposition
in large blocks—to help the engrossers. The upshot was concentration of holdings and sale of land to settlers rather than
free disposal. Professor Gates' conclusion is a startling one:

With over 125,000,000 acres of railroad lands, 140,000,000 acres
of state lands, 100,000,000 acres of Indian lands, and 100,000,000
acres of federal lands in large or small blocks, and with the opportunities for evasion of the Homestead and Pre-emption laws . . .

it is obvious that there were few obstacles in the way of speculation and land monopolization after 1862. As before, it was still possible for foresighted speculators to precede settlers into the frontier, purchase the best lands, and hold them for the anticipated increase in value which the succeeding wave of settlers would give to them.

Professor Gates therefore is able to record case after case of the establishment of immense properties in agricultural and timber lands. For example: William Scully and Ira Davenport, two of the greatest landlords of the period, purchased 41,421 acres and 16,949 acres respectively in single districts in Nebraska. Four Rhode Island speculators entered with cash 96,000 acres in one district in this same state. Indeed, between 1862 and 1873 (during the Civil War and Reconstruction periods!), according to Gates, twenty-seven other persons obtained title to a total of 250,000 acres in Nebraska. What was true of one state was equally true of Illinois, Iowa, Minnesota, and Missouri—part of the richest agricultural region of the country. The same tale is encountered in the case of the pre-emption of the timber lands in the Lake States, the Gulf States, and the Pacific Coast States. Ezra Cornell, the New York lumber dealer, located more than half a million acres of rich lumber lands in the Northwest with New York Agricultural College scrip. (Small wonder that he became a benefactor of his native state!) There were many others like him. In the South, the story was repeated. Lumber men, frequently northern capitalists (thus establishing the connection with the political Reconstruction program of the New Radicals), between 1880 and 1888 acquired five and one half million acres of the wealthiest timber properties in five southern states.

This, then, was what the land policy of the Republican party achieved, as part of the program and fruits of the revolution: Concentration of agricultural and timber holdings in the hands of land companies, engrossers, and speculators, frequently built up through fraud and the collusion of public officials. Sale, rather than free disposal, as the basis for the establishment of freeholds. The almost immediate appearance of tenancy, even in frontier regions, where cash could not be commanded to permit the purchase of a farm and equipment for it (so, as early as 1880, in Kansas and Nebraska—particularly the happy hunting grounds of the monopolists—16 per cent and 18 per cent respectively of farm operators were tenants). And the creation of great factory wheat farms—in the New Northwest and on the Pacific Coast—where a casual, migratory labor force was employed to toil in the harvest fields.

The Role of Agriculture. Within this capitalist framework American agriculture flourished mightily. Thanks to a growing domestic and foreign market, the opening up of the West by the railroad net, the governmental program of quick disposal of the public domain, public assistance to farmers by executive agencies, and also to the support of science: agriculture expanded and the number of farms, amount of land in cultivation, and the capital value of plant increased many times over. The farmer prospered, certainly until the late 1880's; and thus lulled into a sense of security, he gave tacit approval to the political and economic program of Republicanism.

Even when Grangerism for a short time raised its head in the Middle and immediate trans-Mississippi West in the middle 1870's and farmer parties obtained control of state legislatures, this was not radicalism. The embattled farmers were not fighting to break the property relations of the capitalist system; and such occasional alliances as they effected with the workers were neither thoroughgoing nor lasting. The owning farmer of America was a capitalist just as much as was the industrial enterpriser: he bought and sold in a market, owned a plant and equipment, used credit, and looked forward to the time when he might retire to live from the productive labors of others, either as landlord or *rentier.* He was meeting with oppression at the hands of the contractionists (so that the sudden drop in prices made debts burdensome), the railroad pools and manipulators, the warehouse men, and the land engrossers. His political revolt of the 1870's ended unsuccessfully; for even the state railway-control legislation he wrote during this period was either repealed or rendered nugatory by the courts. And then the price curve swung upward, so that he retired from independent politics for another fifteen years.

The objective conditions for agricultural expansion existed.

What, however, was there in the specific American situation that made such expansion profitable? The answer is to be found in two series of facts: the growing dependence of England upon the outside world for foodstuffs; and the requirement of our balance-of-international-payments situation that we develop a favorable commodity balance. At this latter point, American westward expansion and industrial growth were linked in an irrefragable chain of cause and effect. American industrial capitalism could stabilize its position at home if it kept out foreign manufactured ware (through tariffs), had the advantage of an expanding domestic market (through railway building, partially financed by foreign capital), and was in a position to obtain necessary raw materials and heavy goods we did not in the beginning produce. In short, industrial capitalism needed to *import* capital on the one hand and tin, nickel, crude chemicals, rubber, silk, manganese, machinery, and fine tools on the other. To pay interest charges and meet bills for goods we had to develop our *exports* vastly. The foodstuffs of the American West from the end of the Civil War and once again cotton from the South after 1878 fulfilled this function.

The state of England was the second series of links in the chain. By the middle of the nineteenth century English agriculture was heavily weighed down with the characteristic burdens of an agrarian economy in decline—high rents, impoverished soils, inelastic fixed charges; its abandonment was necessary. This is exactly what the industrial-capitalist masters of England achieved when they decided to put an end to the Corn Laws— those tariff duties and import restrictions that had been protecting the English growers of grains since the days of the Tudors. The repeal of the Corn Laws in 1846 (wholly effective in 1849) really marked the triumphal culmination of the English liberal-capitalist revolution; and the fifty-odd years that followed saw the middle-class masters of England astride the world. Wages for skilled workers were high, trade-unionism became reformist and made no independent bid for political power, and the social services were developed and extended. Thus the aristocracy of English labor was enlisted in the cause of English imperialism. American rails, Argentinian and Australian meat-packing plants, Indian jute mills, Chinese and South African rails—these received their capital (often in the form of credits for the purchase of English capital goods) from the London money market. By the end of the nineteenth century English *rentiers* and enterprisers were drawing perhaps as much as a half-billion dollars in interest and profits annually from their capital stake abroad.

If England's life line fed the world with a golden stream, America's life line of foodstuffs in turn fed England, beginning particularly with the 1870's. It is interesting to observe that the world of those years was not unaware of this intricate connection. Thus, S. S. Cox, a New York congressman, writing in 1879, declared: "By the repeal of the Corn Laws, England enlarged the area of her agricultural resources. Free interchange annexed the food-growing acres of other nations. . . . The United States became practically a part of England." And Dr. Alexander Peez, an Austrian observer, gave it as his opinion that "hereafter England's wheat fields will lie in America." In commenting on the flood of American foodstuffs into the European markets, Dr. Peez remarked:

In the sixteenth century American competition ruined the mining industries of Europe, changed the direction of world commerce, brought about by the increased amount of precious metals a revolution in prices, transformed the social conditions, and prepared the terrible civil war of the seventeenth century—the Thirty Years' War. May the competition of America in the nineteenth century lead to more happy results. No doubt it is the greatest economic event of modern times.

Thus, the American grower of cash crops in effect became the cat's-paw for our industrial capitalism: he was encouraged to push out his horizons endlessly, to put more and more virgin acres under the plow, to engage in greater and more magnificent livestocks enterprises; so that the railroad manipulators, the steelmasters, and the factory lords could bring their industrial plans to maturity without molestation from foreign competition. Such was the part performed by historical necessity. It was a kind of, perhaps only dimly felt, economic compulsion, but

whether understood or not its role was played out without inter-
ruption. The expansion of American agriculture, during the
long period we were a debtor nation, permitted industrial capitalism to triumph.

I have said that our great agricultural surpluses helped in the
righting of our unbalanced international position and permitted a sharp shift in the nature of our imports. Some figures
will illuminate these very significant changes. The following
table presents American exports of foodstuffs for selected years:

AMERICAN EXPORTS OF FOODSTUFFS, 1852–81
(SELECTED YEARS)

Annual Averages	Wheat and Wheat Flour (*1000* bu.)	Corn and Corn Meal (*1000* bu.)	Beef: Cured, Salted, Pickled (*1000* lbs.)	Beef: Fresh (*1000* lbs.)	Pork and Its Products (*1000 lbs.*)	Cattle (Number)
1852–56......	19,172	7,123	25,980	......	103,903	1,431
1862–66......	40,183	12,059	27,662	......	252,485	6,531
1872–76......	66,036	38,560	35,826	......	568,029	45,672
1877–81......	133,262	88,190	40,174	69,601	1,075,793	127,045

What relative part did agricultural exports play in total
exports? A very large one. Thus, in 1875, total exports were
worth $539,000,000; and of this, agricultural exports repre-
sented a value of $389,000,000 (72.2 per cent). In 1881, total
exports were worth $919,000,000; and of this, agricultural
exports represented a value of $738,000,000 (80.3 per cent).
Some notion of the comparative positions of foodstuffs as against
cotton in these two years may be obtained from the following
figures:

VALUE OF SELECTED AGRICULTURAL EXPORTS, 1875 AND 1881
VALUES IN MILLIONS OF DOLLARS

Commodities	1875 Value	1875 Per Cent of Value of All Agricultural Exports	1881 Value	1881 Per Cent of Value of All Agricultural Exports
Wheat and wheat flour........	82	21.1	213	28.8
Meat and meat products......	68	17.4	134	18.1
Cotton.....................	191	49.0	248	33.6

The following figures show the sharp shift in imports in the
years under consideration. The table gives percentages of the

values of crude materials for use in manufacturing, semi-processed manufactured goods, and finished manufactured goods, in terms of values of total imports. In the first class are ores, crude chemicals, fibers, hides and skins, silk, wool, rubber. In the second class are copper, heavy iron and steel, heavy leather, vegetable oils. The third class is self-explanatory. It is at once apparent how both the first two classes mount at the expense of the third.

AMERICAN IMPORTS BY CLASSES, 1850–79

PER CENT OF TOTAL IMPORTS, BY VALUE

Annual Averages	Crude Materials for Use in Manufacture	Semiprocessed Manufactured Goods	Manufactured Goods Ready for Consumption
1850–59	8.55	13.08	51.85
1860–69	12.54	13.41	41.50
1870–79	14.55	12.39	33.76

The position of agriculture in our balance of international payments is thus revealed. We may now present the figures for the years here discussed, again using the estimates compiled by Messrs. Bullock, Williams, and Tucker and referred to earlier in this book. The period covered is from 1874 to 1895. The outstanding characteristics of the period follow. There was a large favorable commodity balance. The heavy outflow of gold tapered off by almost half that of the previous period (1850-73); the inflow of gold was very sizable and almost balanced the outflow (this being due to gold shipments for agricultural goods during years of European dearth). Our merchant marine was almost finished, and we were paying on balance for carrying services. There was a resumption of capital borrowings by the United States, so that at the end of this period the foreign stake here was in excess of $3,000,000,000. And on this, heavy interest payments had to be made.

Stress must be given once again to the fact that we were a debtor nation. But our enterprisers were beginning to invest small amounts overseas, almost entirely in the form of direct investments (branch manufacturing plants, mines, oil-distributing agencies, agricultural properties, sales organizations) in Canada, Mexico, and the Caribbean. But this foreign stake of ours was very small: according to Cleona Lewis, in 1897 it stood

400 The Triumph of American Capitalism

at only $684,500,000. So tardy was our development as a *rentier* nation that not until 1897 was the first foreign dollar loan floated in the American money market.

The balance sheet for the years 1874-95 looks as follows (figures in millions of dollars):

Items	Credits	Debits
Export of merchandise and silver........	17,231.1	
Export of gold.......................	809.5	
Freights earned by our ships...........	148	
Immigrants brought in................	180	
New capital invested by foreigners......	1,000	
Total...........................	19,368.6	
Import of merchandise and silver.......		14,738.3
Import of gold......................		697.6
Freights paid to foreign ships..........		708
Tourist expenditures abroad...........		770
Immigrant remittances and miscellaneous items............................		440
Interest paid to foreign investors........		1,870
Total...........................		19,223.9

CHAPTER TWENTY-SIX

Triumphant American Capitalism

1. INDUSTRY'S ADVANCE

UNDER the leadership of the new and vital force released by the Civil War and Reconstruction measures, American industry strode ahead on seven-league boots. The ranks of the industrial-capitalist host were filled with shrewd, energetic, personally frugal (in the beginning) young men who originated for the most part in the petty bourgeoisie, who were distrustful of finance, who managed their own concerns, and who carefully watched and tended their businesses, expanding them by the plowing back of profits. Their personal psychologies were curious: having come up from the ranks they were hard-bitten and dangerous antagonists, who never yielded an inch to competitors or workers; adepts at in-fighting, they took advantage of every opening, corrupting government officials and rivals' employees according to the rules (or rather, no-rules) of rough-and-tumble combat; born, largely, into Calvinistic households, they never parted company with the stern training of early boyhoods and were truly devoted to their churches and their creeds. Thus, their attitude toward the poor was characteristically petty bourgeois and Puritan: the poor were the unsuccessful in an aggressive, competitive race where victory went to the swift and resourceful. The poor therefore had to be taken care of through personal benefactions; and a tithe also went to the church.

From the Civil War up to the 1890's, certainly everything favored this capable, hard-working, and hard-fighting company. Tariffs protected a domestic market. The domestic market grew vastly, thanks to the completion of the railway net and the inpouring of great numbers of immigrants. An expanding agriculture fed the native population and also produced surpluses to pay for imports of raw materials and semiprocessed goods and to make possible the meeting of interest charges on foreign borrowings. Never did nature itself dower a land with a greater abundance and variety of natural resources. The enterprisers had ready at hand lumber, iron, coal, petroleum, lead, copper, and silver. Accumulation could continue and did, because of these factors and because profits could mount at the expense of labor. Wages were low, the sweating of women and children was the rule, and the workers really continued unorganized until the 1890's.

The end of the Civil War left American capitalism ready for new advances. With the capital plant and the profits originating in that period, the enterprisers resumed railway building and building construction; and the heavy-goods industries were strengthened and expanded. The manufactures of iron, lumber, brick, petroleum products, and glass were stimulated; so were those of machinery generally, mechanical transportation equipment, and agricultural implements; markets and ready capital gave spur to invention, new processes, and new plants. While there are some evidences to indicate a rise in real wages from 1867 to 1872, thus giving a lift to the consumer-goods industries (meat products, boots and shoes, clothing), the boom was in the heavy-goods sectors. Leadership was taken by iron (and later steel) and by the foundry and machine-shop industries so that mechanization proceeded apace, leading to mass production on the one hand and the greater productivity of labor on the other. According to a Bureau of Labor report of 1886, over the previous "fifteen or twenty years," productivity had increased 50 to 70 per cent in agricultural implements, 80 per cent in boots and shoes, 65 per cent in carriages, 40 per cent in machines and machinery, 50 per cent in silk manufactures. In Appendix A will be found a group of tables, based upon census figures, which indicate the nature of America's industrial progress during the thirty years 1850-80. The extraordinary growth of heavy industry (iron, machinery, agricultural implements, lumber, clay products) is clearly revealed.

New inventions and new processes further stimulated the two great capital-goods leaders of iron and steel and machinery. According to David A. Wells, writing in the 1880's, the following "inventions, discoveries, and applications" were already developed and in use:

The mechanical reapers, mowing and seeding machines, the steam-plow and most other eminently labor-saving agricultural devices; the Bessemer process and the steel rail (1857); the submarine and transoceanic telegraph cables (1866); photography and all its adjuncts; electroplating and the electrotype; the steamhammer, repeating and breech-loading firearms and rifled and steel cannon; gun-cotton and dynamite; the industrial use of India-rubber and gutta-percha; the steam excavator and steam-drill; the sewing machine; the practical use of the electric light; the application of dynamic electricity as a motor for machinery; the steam fire-engine; the telephone, microphone, spectroscope, and the process of spectral analysis; the polariscope; the compound steam-engine; the centrifugal process of refining sugar; the rotary printing press; hydraulic lifts, cranes and elevators; the "regenerative" furnace, iron and steel ships, pressed glass, wire rope, petroleum and its derivatives and analine dyes; the industrial use of the metal nickel, cotton-seed oil, artificial butter, stearine-candles, natural gas, cheap postage and the postage stamp. Electricity which a very few years ago was regarded as something wholly immaterial, has now acquired a sufficiently objective existence to admit of being manufactured and sold the same as pig iron or leather.

There was advance; but there was depression, too, because frontiers were pushed out too hastily. A downturn took place following the end of the Civil War but it was due to the inevitable adjustments required by the conversion of wartime production into peacetime uses. From 1868 to 1872 the forward pace was once more swift. Railroad construction (employing most of the capital-goods industries) showed the way. In 1868, 2979 miles of new track were laid down, increasing to 7379 miles in 1871. The next year, a decided tapering off took place (to 5878 miles), again involving the capital-goods industries. In 1873, the drop was even sharper. The depression that followed, beginning with panic in September, 1873, was undoubtedly caused in large part by this slowing down of the heavy industries dependent upon construction.

But there were other causes, chief among them the continued

close connection between European finance and the American money centers. In the spring of the year, panics had hit many of the European Continental cities; in England, money had suddenly become tight. Europeans holding American rails had begun to liquidate; balances here were being withdrawn. And because we were a debtor nation, at the same time having a sizable unfavorable commodity balance, we needed Europe's confidence more than ever. This was no longer forthcoming: and the American banking houses closely tied to European finance could not stand the strain. Speculation also played its part here so that bank reserves, as we have seen, were out at call supporting the security markets. With the withdrawal of reserves by country banks the plugs were pulled out and security values collapsed. Railroading, too, had been extended speculatively. Promoters continued to build, hoping that soon the opening up of wheat lands, coal fields, and iron deposits would permit the meeting of obligations. Debts piled up; but as long as Dutchmen, Bavarians, and Swiss were ready to buy rails from Jay Cooke and others there was no cause for concern. In 1872, out of three hundred and sixty-four listed rail securities, only one hundred and four were paying dividends. They moved into insolvency when hard-pressed foreign investors wanted cash.

It was no accident that the American banking house most closely linked with European capital—Jay Cooke and Company of Philadelphia and New York—should crack first. Its New York office closed its doors in September, 1873, and brokerage houses began to tumble. Railroad bankruptcies followed, the exchanges shut down, and commercial failures mounted sharply. Before 1873 was over, 5000 such failures were reported, involving liabilities of $228,000,000. As for the rails, eighty-nine were in default on bond issues worth $400,000,000. The depression continued for six years: railroad building virtually stopped; the unemployed reached at one time 3,000,000; immigration slowed up; prices dropped by 30 per cent below the level of 1870-73; there were widespread vagrancy and serious industrial conflict.

A purged capitalism emerged out of the depression—and so did a minority left-wing labor movement. For the deflationary process permitted capitalism to resume its forward career once more after 1879—thanks to liquidation, a favorable commodity balance, and European crop failures (in 1879, 1880, 1881), so that foreign gold poured in. Railroad construction was resumed (new building in 1879 totaled 4817 miles). Farmers with more purchasing power as a result of better prices bought new equipment. The iron industry began to build new furnaces for the making of steel: and the capital-goods industries once more were experiencing revival. By 1883, when the boom was again in full swing, new railroad construction came to 11,569 miles. The railroads were all beginning to put in steel rails and to buy heavier locomotives and cars. Industrial capitalism was developing into its full strength. And, on the other hand, a proletarianized labor movement was emerging.

2. THE MATURING OF THE LABOR MOVEMENT

The Civil War brought no lasting gains for the workers of the country. A few tentative organizations sprang up and some strikes took place as a result of the sharp rise in living costs. But the results of these were not cumulative: so much so that leadership again fell back on the characteristic petty-bourgeois and reformist programs of the pre-Civil War period—producers' cooperatives and a free-land agitation. Indeed, except for the minority left-wing organizations, until 1881 (when the Federation of Organized Trades and Labor Unions of the United States and Canada, the precursor of the American Federation of Labor, was formed), national labor leadership was rarely in touch with the problems of the rank and file. The workers were confronted by the rapid inroads being made into the handicrafts by the machine; wages were low, housing was vile, hours were long; the employers resisted improved industrial relations through the use of the black lists and conspiracy suits in the courts. There were national unions and national bodies forming; but these had neither the realistic direction nor the structural solidity to start strikes properly and win them.

A series of national unions emerged during this period. In 1861, a miners' union appeared; in 1862, a union of ironworkers; in 1863, the locomotive engineers were organized; in 1864, the cigarmakers; in 1865, the carpenters, bricklayers, painters, heaters, tailors, coachmakers; in 1866, the silk-and-fur-hat finishers; in 1867, the spinners; in 1868, the shoemakers and railroad conductors; in 1869, the wool-hat finishers; in 1870, the coopers and telegraphers; in 1872, the woodworkers and iron-and-steel heaters; in 1873, the furniture workers, miners, railroad firemen, German printers. In all, there were by 1872 some thirty-two such national bodies with a claimed membership of 300,000.

But there were significant functional weaknesses. The national unions were decentralized with the result that the locals were isolated; as yet no real machinery had appeared to make for successful collective bargaining; there was no realistic planning in terms of the building up of strike funds and the establishment of friendly benefits. The spokesmen for labor constantly gravitated toward politics. So, even in the boom years 1868-72, strikes as a rule were lost and more and more arbitration was being accepted as basic policy. With such internal faults, it was small wonder that these early national unions suffered mortally during the depression of 1873-79. At the close of this decade, there were about half a dozen national unions surviving with a membership of less than 50,000.

This tale of unsuccessful organization was repeated as regards national confederation. The short-lived International Industrial Assembly appeared in 1864. During 1866-72 it was replaced by the National Labor Union. Presumably basing its strength on the new national unions (although trade-union tactics received only a perfunctory support), this body in reality was dominated not by labor men but by politicians and social reformers. The strike weapon was discarded. And the agitational centers became the eight-hour movement, land reform, and cheap money. Professor Ware characterizes its role in this fashion: "It was a typical American politico-reform organization, led by labor leaders without organizations, politicians without parties, women without husbands, and cranks, visionaries, and agitators without jobs."

Political action was the inevitable decision of such a grouping. In 1873 an Industrial Congress was called for the purpose of welding trade-unionists together into an effective political force. Also, the National Labor and Reform party was organized. Both efforts quickly collapsed. Under reformist direction another effort was made in 1874 when the National Greenback party was founded. In the presidential election of 1876 Peter Cooper was nominated and received 100,000 votes. The long depression and the vague and fumbling programs of such organizations had the inevitable effects: survival was impossible.

Meanwhile, in still another sector, an effort was being made to unite the workers of the country together for economic and legislative action and mutual aid. This was the Noble Order of the Knights of Labor. Beginning in 1869, at Philadelphia, as a secret society made up of a handful of garment cutters of whom the leader was Uriah S. Stephens, the order set about to organize workers into craft bodies on local lines. The intention was a tightly centralized national society operating through local and district assemblies with control of policy from the top. The first local assemblies were trade groups and it was not until considerably later, when the Knights began to penetrate into small towns, that mixed assemblies appeared. Into these were admitted not only all workers but all persons associated with productive activity; the only exceptions were saloonkeepers, lawyers, and bankers. Put simply, the leading characteristic of the order, in organizational terms, was one-big-unionism.

The order grew slowly. Not until 1872 was a second assembly formed—that of ship carpenters and calkers in Philadelphia. The first district assembly, that of Philadelphia, appeared the next year; the second, at Camden, in 1874; the third, at Pittsburgh, in 1875. In 1877, local and district bodies were to be found throughout Pennsylvania and also in West Virginia, Ohio, Indiana, and Illinois. But the membership at this time totaled not much more than 9000.

In these early years the Knights of Labor, its strength weakened by the depression and the bold attacks of the organized employers, was dominated by pure-and-simple trade-unionism. It adhered to secrecy because of necessity; it engaged in strikes; it eschewed politics and grandiose programs of reform. In 1878, however, it was metamorphosed: and the Knights of Labor, captured by an ambitious leadership, took on the characteristic habiliments of petty-bourgeois reformism. To this extent, it did not differ markedly from the utopianism of the 1840's and the National Labor Union of the late 1860's.

In 1878, a general assembly was formed, secrecy was abandoned, and under the direction of a new "grand master workman," Terence V. Powderly, magnificent proclamations were issued. The preamble of the order's constitution and its declaration of principles stormed the heavens. Thus, the preamble read:

The alarming development and aggressiveness of great capitalists and corporations, unless checked, will inevitably lead to the pauperization and hopeless degradation of the toiling masses. It is imperative, if we desire to enjoy the full blessings of life, that a check be placed upon unjust accumulation and the power for evil of aggregated wealth. This much-desired object can be accomplished only by the united efforts of those who obey the divine injunction: "In the sweat of thy face thou shalt eat bread."

And the following were to be the order's aims:

To make industrial worth, not wealth, the true standard of individual and national greatness.

To secure for the workers the full enjoyment of the wealth they create; sufficient leisure in which to develop their intellectual, moral, and social faculties. . . .

This was all very well; but a militant rank and file wanted support for its day-to-day struggles against miserably low wages and long hours. Reluctantly—for the leadership was committed to reformism—this demand was acceded to and a national fund was built up. Before long, however, the fund was being dipped into increasingly to further the co-operation and education (i.e., political agitation) in which the top directors were interested.

The order, from 1880 to 1886, grew by leaps and bounds. At the end of 1883, it claimed a membership of 52,000; in 1886, 730,000 members. The depression was over and workers once more were interested in organization. The Knights made an especial appeal to the unorganized and, because they were willing to set up mixed assemblies in disregard of craft lines, they could sign up workers on a mass basis. The outbreak of a series of great strikes (although as a rule they were lost) attracted national attention to the body. And, in the beginning, the reformist program was meeting with some success. This detracted attention from the fact that at the top the Knights frowned on strikes and more and more emphasized arbitration. Nor would they tolerate the appearance of national trade-unions, autonomously controlled.

Reformism moved on two wings: the establishment of producers' co-operatives and participation in local and national independent political activity. In connection with the first the order sought to establish national co-operative societies and also encouraged the formation of local bodies. In fact, some two hundred such groups, based on the ideas of self-employment and profit sharing appeared; in time, however, they all foundered. The political programs evidenced the confusion of intention. On the one hand there were demands for safety and public-health codes, weekly-pay and mechanics'-lien laws, the abolition of child and convict labor, and the prohibition of the entrance of immigrant contract labor. On the other hand the Knights called for the reservation of public lands for settlers only, the abolition of national banks, the issuance of legal tenders (or paper money) by the federal government, the establishment of postal-savings banks, and government ownership of railroads.

But there were two events of the period that made the more realistic, hard-bitten trade-unionists of the great industrial centers indifferent to the order. These were the great railroad strikes of 1877 and the appearance of the eight-hour agitation of the early 1880's. And because the bureaucracy of the Knights supported more particularly the second movement only hesitantly, the proletarianized workers turned away from the organization.

Like all the strikes of the depression years, the railroad strikes grew out of the desperation of the workers. Repeated wage reductions, irregular employment, and the introduction of doubleheader freight trains (thus causing displacement of engineers) led to the outbreak of rank-and-file strikes without adequate organizational preparation. Starting on the Baltimore and Ohio, the strike movement spread from the Atlantic seaboard to St. Louis, involving most of the great trunk lines of the region. Because union leadership was a faltering one, the men could not be held in line and when state executives called out militias, violence broke out. At the request of the governor of Maryland, President Hayes ordered the dispatching of federal troops into that state—the first appearance of federal soldiers in an industrial dispute. Troops were also sent into Pennsylvania.

The bitterest center of controversy was Pittsburgh, where a complete tie-up of traffic on the Pennsylvania Railroad lines was effected. The local authorities were impotent in the face of the organized strength of the strikers and their sympathizers, with the result that a call was sent to Harrisburg (the state capital) for the militia. What followed is told by Philip A. Slaner:

Major General Brinton . . . arrived July 21 at Pittsburgh with his contingent of Philadelphia militia with the intention of dispersing the strikers and opening the railroad to traffic. He found that they were supported by striking miners from Wilkensburg and by the unemployed of the city; they had even the sympathy of merchants and businessmen of Pittsburgh. . . .

The attempt of the militia to arrest the leaders of the strike was resisted, and their advance was met with groans, hoots and hisses. At 28th Street, Brinton ordered the troops to fire; twenty persons were killed (including women and children) and twenty-nine wounded. According to [General] Latta, Brinton ordered the troops to fire before any resistance was offered, but other observers stated that the troops were met with a volley of stones and lost their heads.

These killings inflamed the workers of the city, who resolved to drive the troops out of Pittsburgh. The militia, stationed in the roundhouse of the depot on the evening of July 21, attempted to defend themselves against the attacks of an aroused citizenry who were seeking to avenge what they considered wanton murder. The workers attempted to cannonade the roundhouse, and after some time the building burst into flames. . . .

The small contingent of police and the three thousand members of the militia could not, of course, prevent the firing of the Union

Depot at Pittsburgh and the terminals of the Pennsylvania Railroad. The railroad tracks and buildings were fired. Some workers broke into the freight cars which had been stalled for the last few days and marched off with food and other provisions.

The strikes everywhere failed and the men obtained no redress. But the movement brought home certain lessons to the American people. More and more the frightening realization was appearing that American society was becoming polarized. In the words of Professor Ware: "The old master–journeyman relationship was gone forever. Great corporations owning mines and railroads, employing private police and semi-private detectives, calling vainly for state but more successfully for federal protection, influencing if not controlling courts and legislatures, were set over against labor masses, ignorant and unorganized, daily losing their one possession, their craft skill, and aroused to futile action only as a result of long depression."

And the already radicalized workers saw their grim prophecy realized: that the capitalist property relations led to class warfare. Radicalism (in its modern sense of Marxian socialism and anarcho-syndicalism) had made its appearance in the United States in the late 1860's and the 1870's: and it had been brought into the country by the class-conscious German workers. The early socialist movement here had followed the leads of both Karl Marx and Ferdinand Lassalle and indeed these two factions (despite bitter enmity between them in Germany) had coalesced, forming the Workingmen's party in 1876. A year later the name was changed to the Socialist Labor party.

While the Workingmen's party played no part in the calling of the railroad strikes, it seized the opportunity to broadcast the ideas of socialism. Great meetings were held in Chicago, St. Louis, and New York; and in the fall elections of 1877 the party met with substantial successes in local elections. The return of prosperity and the outbreak of doctrinal controversies among the members kept the organization small; but a seed had been sown.

The anarchism of Michael Bakunin was also having a following in America. Formally launched in 1883 at Pittsburgh as the

International Working People's Association, this group, at first receiving its support from recently arrived immigrants, quickly established centers in the industrial cities of the Middle West and began to attract small numbers of radical American workers. The western anarchists, while they subscribed to the basic tenet of the movement for the seizure of power through the "propaganda of the deed" (i.e., violence against the capitalist class, the state, and the church), began to adumbrate the characteristic tactic of later anarcho-syndicalism: action through revolutionary trade-union organization. Said Albert R. Parsons, one of the American leaders of the Chicago anarchists, of this program: "The International recognizes in the trade-union the embryonic group of the future 'free society.' Every trade-union is, *nolens volens,* an autonomous commune in the process of incubation. The trade-union is a necessity of capitalistic production, and will yet take its place by superseding it under the system of universal free co-operation." Thus the trade-union movement was penetrated in Chicago and St. Louis by radicals who brought with them a coloration of anarchist ideas.

The tardy support of the eight-hour agitation by the Knights of Labor leadership also antagonized the more advanced workers. The Federation of Organized Trades and Labor Unions (chiefly made up of skilled immigrant workers), at its fourth convention in 1884, had inscribed this demand on its banners; and it called for a general strike on May 1, 1886 to force compliance from employers. The socialists and anarchists helped in the formation of Eight-Hour Day Associations and the winning over of central-trades bodies to the demonstration. Ironically enough, Powderly of the Knights of Labor was hostile and issued a secret order against participation; but the great mass of semiskilled and unskilled workers of the country identified the Knights with the agitation and flocked into the order.

The general strike of May 1, 1886 led to an outpouring of more than 200,000 workers throughout the country. Its effects were both wide-sweeping and momentous. Many workers (the skilled, largely) won the eight-hour day. The shootings and the bomb outrage in Haymarket Square, Chicago, on May 4 in part rose out of it. The Knights of Labor rapidly disintegrated and the order was replaced by the American Federation of Labor. With 1886, America's organized workers, under the leadership of skilled craft unionists, many of whom were permeated by socialist ideas and with none beguiled by petty-bourgeois notions, began to move in the direction of effective economic action. This was the other side of the shield of industrial capitalism's maturing.

3. ANDREW CARNEGIE, INDUSTRIAL CAPITALIST

In 1853, when he was eighteen years old and without any formal schooling to speak of, Andrew Carnegie obtained a new position. For a salary of $35 a month he became a telegraph clerk in the office of Thomas A. Scott, superintendent of the Pittsburgh division of the rapidly growing Pennsylvania Railroad. Carnegie's father had been a hand-loom weaver, or cottage worker, in his native Scotland and the whole family had been compelled to flee before the advance of machine production. The father was incapable of making a proper adjustment in the new world of America; and all the members of the family were compelled to work, Andrew beginning his vocational career at the age of thirteen.

At the Pennsylvania, the young man cultivated his employer and his opportunities: he moved up to become Scott's general assistant, he learned the railroading industry, and he became acquainted with (and perhaps did favors for) the road's important shippers. One may only conjecture as to the nature of Carnegie's business acquaintances at this time; in any case, he did accumulate a little money over and above the immediate needs of himself and his family. In 1859, he succeeded Scott as superintendent of the Pennsylvania's western division at a monthly salary of $125; and at the same time he was beginning to invest in small enterprises and a number of speculations.

The first outstanding interest of this sort was a one-eighth share in the Woodruff Sleeping Car Company, the initial enterprise of its kind. Carnegie put up no money for his stock subscription, receiving a bank loan without interest to permit him to make the first payment; and subsequent installments came from dividends. Again, it is easy to see why fortune smiled on our young capitalist. Woodruff had a new idea to sell to the railroads; Carnegie, on his part, as chief of the most important division of an outstanding railway organization, had great influence, particularly with Thomas A. Scott, who was now vice-president of the whole road. Obviously, too, a local banker would be pleased to be of help. In any case, the Woodruff Company obtained a contract to build sleeping cars for the Pennsylvania and the Woodruff Company therefore prospered. When he was twenty-five years old, in 1860, Carnegie was earning $5000 a year in dividends on a stock that hadn't cost him a penny.

The Civil War presented new chances for a young man with talent, influential friends, and a small store of liquid capital. Carnegie went to Washington with his patron, Scott, who was chosen to co-ordinate the railway and telegraph services of the War Department. Carnegie, once again, was Scott's assistant; apparently, however, he was only on leave from the Pennsylvania, for he did not formally resign from the road until 1865, when he was thirty years old. At that time, his salary was $200 a month.

The war, it would seem, did not absorb all his time, or his emotions, for that matter: like his contemporaries, J. P. Morgan, J. D. Rockefeller, and William Vanderbilt, he perhaps may have felt that he had a greater usefulness on the home front. Nor did the Pennsylvania Railroad, his employer, have his undivided attention. A young man with energy—and friends—could watch other pots. We know that he became interested in a sutler's business which was supplying the soldiers' camps, in a horse-trading concern designed to sell cavalry mounts to the Union government, and in a construction company. Also, he had acquired stock in a Pittsburgh bank and a local street railway company. In any case, in 1863, in a private memorandum that he must have prepared with a good deal of justifiable self-satisfaction, Carnegie recorded that his income was $47,860.67! It will be observed, once more, that his basic salary was $2400.

This memorandum merits breakdown. It ran as follows (I have rearranged the items somewhat):

Columbia dividends..	$17,868.67
Sales 40 shares "Cola" @ $100; cost $10........................	3,600.00

(The Columbia Oil Company was a company which for $40,000 purchased a farm in the Pennsylvania oil fields. In a short time, oil having been struck, the property was worth $5,000,000; and the field brought in oil for 25 years. Carnegie had been able to finance his stock subscription out of his earnings from the sleeping-car company.)

Central Transportation Company dividends......................	3,050.00
Extra dividend, Central Transportation Company................	2,000.00

(This was the sleeping-car company under a new name.)

T. M. C. from Kloman...	4,250.00

("T. M. C." were the initials of Carnegie's brother. "Kloman" was the name of an iron mill into which Carnegie had bought as a secret partner. This was his initial entrance into the iron business, and it was as a capitalist. He had appeared in it in 1861, with a small investment. The enormous profit came from the war business in which the company was engaged.)

Piper and S[hiffler]...	7,500.00

(This was another iron firm which Carnegie had helped to organize and again he was a secret partner. The firm manufactured railway bridges. Later it was reorganized as the Keystone Bridge Company; and it became one of the basic properties of the Carnegie Company.)

Salary..	2,400.00

(From the Pennsylvania Railroad)

Adams Express Company...	1,440.00
J. V..	4,000.00
Insurance..	120.00
Sales, 50 shares of stock from E. C............................	750.00
Union Line...	450.00
Freedom Iron Company..	250.00
Western Union..	182.00

(These last seven items were income from earnings from old investments, speculative fliers, and the like.)

Total...	$47,860.67

In 1865, as has been said, Carnegie quit the Pennsylvania and spent the next few years organizing a series of iron concerns in and about Pittsburgh. He was no plant manager and no technician: but he chose his aids wisely (his brother Thomas and Henry Phipps), while he furnished a part of the capital, the connections, and the business policy. This series of companies included the following; it will be observed that all were in heavy iron and not steel.

The Superior Rail Mill—for the manufacture of iron rails.

The Union Iron Mills—for the manufacture of railway axles and structural iron. The old Kloman works became a part of this property. In 1865 it was capitalized at $500,000.

The Keystone Bridge Company—for the manufacture of railway bridges. This was the old Piper and Shiffler firm. In 1865 it was capitalized at $300,000.

The Pittsburgh Locomotive Works.

Then, in 1867, Carnegie moved permanently to New York City where he set up office as a bond broker; but again the connection was with railroading, for his activities largely centered in the handling and distribution of new railway securities in the New York and more particularly in the London money markets. Later Carnegie claimed that between 1868 and 1873—the great years of early railroad construction in the United States—he sold $30,000,000 worth of bonds in London. John K. Winkler, one of Carnegie's few irreverent biographers, describes, perhaps a bit imaginatively, the bond operations in this way:

He would obtain an order, say, for a bridge construction for the Keystone Bridge Company. This, in turn, would throw work to the Union Iron Mills. Then Carnegie would offer to market bonds for the bridge construction company. In the majority of these operations, he worked hand in glove with his old bosses of the Pennsylvania Railroad, J. Edgar Thomson and Col. Thomas A. Scott. Carnegie was the go-between for these distinguished gentlemen in deals in which they did not wish to appear publicly. There was undoubtedly a private profit-splitting arrangement.

In 1868, Carnegie was still reporting the income of a millionaire. His private memorandum (again rearranged a little) showed the following sources from which his mounting fortune was being derived; it will be observed how his iron properties contributed the lion's share.

Keystone Bridge Company	$15,000
Union Iron Mills	20,000
Rail Mill	6,000
Central Transportation Company	6,000
Columbia Oil Company	2,000
Southern	300
Union Pacific	3,000
Lochiel	400
Bitner	2,000
Third Bank	300
Union Line	360
Empire	450
Surplus	300
	$56,110

It was iron, however, that was Carnegie's first, and always real, love. In 1870, to supply his ironworks, he began the construction of his first blast furnace, the Lucy Furnace; and in 1877, in the midst of depression, the second Lucy Furnace was erected. Finally, in 1873, the Carnegie group turned its attention to the making of steel and for this purpose Carnegie, McCandless and Company was organized with a capitalization of $700,000 of which Carnegie held $250,000. Work was undertaken at once on the building of a steel furnace on the Monongahela River and was pushed until 1875, when the Edgar Thomson Steel Company (named after the president of the Pennsylvania Railroad) began operations. The furnace was the only producer of steel rails in the Pittsburgh region and, because of this as well as its intimate connections with one of the greatest railroads in the country, its position was secure.

Carnegie had shown his characteristic energy and confidence here. He had begun to build against the advice of his partners; he had disregarded the depression; he had obtained liquid assets wherever he could—by disposal of his sleeping-car, bank, and street-railway stocks—to put, as he later boasted, "all his eggs into one basket." And he had been right. For the steel business had weathered the depression, although in the process Carnegie had lost some of his old partners. They were the casualties of the earlier speculative mania; and he gave their plight only a passing thought as he proceeded to buy them out. In 1878, the Carnegie Company was recapitalized at $1,250,000 and this time Carnegie held 59 per cent of the outstanding stock. He never relinquished majority control.

The rise of the Carnegie steel business was meteoric in the next two decades. Of course, steel grew with the country—with its railways, its bridges, and its lofty buildings beginning to use structural steel. But that was less than the whole story. Carnegie was the demoniac force that pushed steel's achievement to greater and greater heights. These were some of the secrets behind the Carnegie success.

1. Carnegie never entered the money market for funds. His company was an association of partners with his interest representing the majority of stock on the books. The result was, he never had to give hostages to bankers or to bow before the

clamor of stockholders for the distribution of earnings. Profits were kept as liquid reserves and used to buy out competitors, acquire raw materials, and transport; and, more particularly, to construct new plant and constantly modernize equipment. Also, with financial power, he could fight organized labor successfully. For example, using his own financial resources entirely, in the eleven years 1889-1900, Carnegie was able to increase annual steel production from 322,000 tons to 3,000,000 tons.

2. In another sense, Carnegie's great achievement—although he was no plant manager, as has been said, or indeed, steelmaster in the technical sense, for he maintained his office in New York—was his ability to drive costs of production down constantly. He was able to do this with the might of the company's earnings which he controlled. With these surpluses at his command, he could ceaselessly experiment in an effort to achieve greater productivity and therefore lower costs. Some examples will prove the point. The so-called First Furnace, in 1880, had to use 2736 pounds of coke to make a ton of pig iron; the so-called Fourth Furnace, in 1890, was using only 1847 pounds of coke for the same ton of iron. And as for costs and prices, here are some typical experiences:

In 1875, the average monthly *cost* of making steel rails was $57 per ton; the *price* received at the works was $66.50.

In 1878, the average monthly *cost* was $38; the *price* received was $42.50.

In 1883, the average monthly *cost* was $34; the *price* received was $37.50.

In 1888, the average monthly *cost* was in the neighborhood of $28; the *price* received was $29.83.

The Carnegie message to industrial capitalism he phrased in these words in an essay he wrote in 1900, after he had virtually retired from steelmaking:

If there be in human society one truth clearer and more indisputable than another it is that the cheapening of articles . . . insures their general distribution. . . . Now the cheapening of all these good things . . . is rendered possible only through the operation of the law, which may be stated thus: Cheapness is in proportion to the scale of production.

3. The Carnegie Company was made up of an association of partners, as has been said. All these associates worked for the firm as heads of departments. Not only did Carnegie reward merit by permitting young men to acquire partnerships—paying for their shares out of earnings—but he forbade the sale of shares outside of the organization of active enterprisers. Thus, in 1887, all the partners were compelled to sign a so-called "Ironclad Agreement" under which, as a result of retirement, disagreement, or death, the shares of individuals reverted to the company. Payment was to be made on the basis of the existing book value of the stock and in installments. Thus Carnegie could reward devotion and enterprise—it was said that by 1900 he had succeeded in making forty millionaires in the Pittsburgh area— and at the same time control policy without danger of surprises, cabals, and conspiracies. Among the men who grew up with Carnegie, in addition to Phipps and Frick, were George Lauder, Charles M. Schwab, Henry M. Curry, William H. Singer, Laurence C. Phipps, and Alexander R. Peacock.

4. Carnegie himself handled the sales through the New York office. His close contacts with railroading, his knowledge of the business, and his native wit and shrewdness placed him far in the forefront of his competitors.

5. Also, his close associations with railroad men made it possible for him to get rebates from the railroads—not only constantly but perhaps even larger rebates than his competitors might command.

6. Carnegie was never averse to entering steel pools; but he did this not to protect his own organization—for he could always undersell his rivals—but to get a larger proportion of production in the industry. Nor did he hesitate to violate pooling agreements when such a course served his purpose. In any case, he participated in pools for fully twenty-five years.

7. Carnegie was always an individualist in labor relations. He fought unions when he thought he could obtain an advantage, recognized them (and compelled his competitors to do so) when

he wanted to see a uniform wage scale established, and broke them when his costs were in jeopardy. In an early labor dispute, in 1867, he crushed a strike of puddlers by getting contract laborers in Europe to replace his American workmen. In 1875, he compelled a group of recalcitrant workers at one of his works, whom he locked out, to sign a "yellow-dog agreement," under which they promised not to unionize. In 1884, he challenged the authority of the powerful Amalgamated Association of Iron and Steel Workers; and he won. In 1888 he won another strike and re-established the twelve-hour day at the Edgar Thomson plant. And then, in 1889, he came to terms with the Amalgamated, as a result of which a wage agreement for three years was signed and shop-grievance committees were established. Carnegie's determination, in 1892, not to renew, to cut the wage scale, to reduce the labor force, and to eliminate the grievance committees led to the bloody Homestead episode of 1892—and the destruction of the Amalgamated.

8. Of course, Carnegie, along with other steel men, demanded high tariffs and got them. But protection played only a minor role in the advance of his business. The driving forces were ingenuity, enterprise, a hardheaded and shrewd management, and, perhaps most important of all, the Calvinistic virtue of thrift. Profits were made; they were plowed back into plant expansion and efficient production; an integrated industry began to be built up; and costs—as well as prices—were regularly being lowered. This was the triumph of industrial capitalism in the heyday of its glory; and before the finance capitalist took over.

Here are some tangible evidences of Carnegie's victories. In 1876, at the height of the depression, the Edgar Thomson Steel Company recorded a profit of $181,000. In 1877, in the midst of the great railway strikes when disorganization in transportation spread as far west as St. Louis, the profit in steel was $190,000. In 1878, still a depression year, it was $401,800. In 1880, the steelworks were making one seventh of all the Bessemer steel produced in the country, were selling rails at $85 a ton, and were clearing a profit of $1,625,000. The iron furnaces and mills also made a profit of $446,000. Profits were used to expand the old blast furnace and to erect a new one.

In 1881, there was another reorganization with most of the iron properties and the steelworks being combined into a single company. It took the name Carnegie Brothers and Company, Ltd. (although there were only seven partners of whom Carnegie himself, his brother, and Phipps were the important ones). The capitalization was now $5,000,000; and of this Carnegie held $2,738,000.

In 1881, the profits were $2,000,000. In 1882, they were $2,100,000. In this year, Carnegie began his long and successful process of integration. Henry C. Frick, who controlled vast coal deposits and the greatest unit of coking ovens in the country, was prevailed upon to form the H. C. Frick Coke Company; and into this the Carnegie group bought shares. By the next year, 1833, Carnegie himself was the largest single stockholder in the Frick Company and it passed under the actual, although not the legal, control of Carnegie Brothers and Company, Ltd. In 1883, the profits were $1,000,000; and Carnegie bought the Homestead plant, erected by competitors, which he proceeded to modernize. During the depression years 1884 and 1885, the Carnegie Company made profits of $1,300,000 and $1,200,000 respectively. In 1886, Homestead was now in full operation—and the profits jumped to $2,900,000. In 1887, they were $3,400,000.

In 1889, Frick, whose worth Carnegie recognized, was made a partner in the firm, though he was permitted to buy only a 2 per cent interest. Nevertheless, Frick was made chairman. In 1890, having gained his spurs, he was sold an 11 per cent interest; and it never exceeded that. Under Frick's active management, the profits in 1889 were $3,500,000 and in 1890, $5,400,000.

In short, here was a business which, in 1873, was capitalized at $700,000; and in twenty years (1873-92) it had earned $40,000,000. Carnegie continued to undercapitalize it, seeking to control the undistributed surpluses for the expansion of plant. In 1892, the firm owned furnaces and mills at Duquesne, Pittsburgh, Homestead, and Beaver Falls; it had its own coke ovens some coal deposits, and some iron mines. Now another reorganization took place; the name Carnegie Steel Company, Ltd., was adopted; and the book value of the stock was placed at $25,000,000 with Carnegie continuing to own more than half. The number of partners had grown to twenty-three; and the two outstanding minority ones were Phipps (with 11 per cent of the stock) and Frick (with a similar amount).

Once more, in the depression of 1893-96, Carnegie was able to take advantage of the distress of competitors, raw-material producers, and transportation companies. He bought properties widely: iron deposits in the Mesabi Range, ore ships on the Great Lakes, ports and docks and warehouses, and railroad lines to link his coal, coke, limestone, and furnaces and mills into a single chain. The end of the depression saw him dominating the heavy-steel field, the controller of a complete vertical integration, and the fixer of prices for the finished-steel manufacturers. He had weathered Homestead and the collapse of the railway business, and he was prepared to meet aggressively in the heavy-steel field new rivals created by finance capitalism.

But his own house was not in order. Frick, a remarkable manager who had, however, become involved in outside speculative interests, and who was listening to the new calls being piped by the rising finance capitalists (consolidations, expanding corporate activities, communities of interest), kept on pressing for a distribution of earnings on the basis of real value instead of book value. Carnegie, who was hostile to Frick's really dangerous notions and who continued ever suspicious of investment bankers and security markets (Frick had become friendly with Morgan and Rockefeller), was unyielding. Frick could go if he wished—but only on the basis of the terms of the "Ironclad Agreement." A lawsuit was begun but never finished, and Carnegie yielded.

In 1900, the Carnegie Company was established, made up of the properties of Carnegie Steel and Frick Coke; it was capitalized at $320,000,000 (half in stock and half in bonds). Carnegie kept $174,000,000 of the new value and paid off Frick with $31,000,000 in the securities. This new capitalization was about the real worth of the properties. As a result of the bargains picked up during 1893-96 and the modernization and expansion program made necessary in the next four years to catch up with the recent rivals financed by the banking houses of J. P. Morgan of New York and Moore Brothers of Chicago, the Carnegie properties had grown to five hundred times the worth of the original investment in 1873, less than thirty years previously! From 1890 to 1900, annual profits had increased from $5,400,-000 to $40,000,000; and annual steel production from 322,000 tons to 3,000,000 tons.

When the United States Steel Corporation was formed, in 1901, Carnegie retired from the steel business. Carnegie drove a shrewd bargain but the price he received was not excessive in the light of the integration he had created and the productivity of his works. The Carnegie Company received $492,000,000 in bonds and stocks from the new organization for all its assets. And Carnegie, distrustful of Morgan and not too sanguine about the success of the country's first giant corporation, took his share—$225,000,000—in the 5 per cent gold bonds he compelled Morgan to issue.

This was the business saga of the greatest, although a typical, industrial capitalist produced by America. Well might he contemplate the fruits of his labors and find them good. In 1886, Carnegie, out of gratitude to his adopted land, had published an ecstatic book hymning its glories. He had called his book *Triumphant Democracy;* two typical passages indicated how firmly he believed that the United States was the land of opportunity for the petty bourgeoisie.

The Republic today is, as it ever was, a nation of workers. The idlers are few—much fewer than in any other great nation. A continent lies before the American, awaiting development. The rewards of labor are high and prizes are to be won in every pursuit. The family which strikes out boldly for the west, settles upon the soil and expends its labor upon it, may confidently look forward to reach independent circumstances long before old age. The mechanic with skill and energy rises first to foremanship and ultimately to a partnership or business of his own. As the country fills, these prizes naturally become more and more difficult to secure, but the very knowledge of this acts as an additional incentive, and impells men to "make hay while the sun shines."

America, blessed land of peace, is inundating the world not only with her products but with her gospel of the equality of man as man, and the old-time nations will soon be forced to divert their energies from war to peaceful work.

In the light of his successes, there was small wonder that Carnegie should phrase the dedication of *Triumphant Democracy* as he did. It ran:

TO THE

BELOVED REPUBLIC

UNDER WHOSE EQUAL LAWS I AM

MADE THE PEER OF ANY MAN, ALTHOUGH DENIED

POLITICAL EQUALITY BY MY NATIVE LAND,

I DEDICATE THIS BOOK

WITH AN INTENSITY OF GRATITUDE

AND ADMIRATION WHICH THE NATIVE-BORN CITIZEN

CAN NEITHER FEEL NOR UNDERSTAND

ANDREW CARNEGIE

Conclusion

—

END AND NEW BEGINNING?

CHAPTER TWENTY-SEVEN

Was American Capitalism a Success?

U NDER the bold leadership of industrial capitalism, the processes of exploration, conquest, and settlement of the American scene went on: but for a shorter interval than we have been
led to assume. By the end of the nineteenth century, really, the
grand design was completed. The continental domain was settled, so that the frontier (at least, in a physical sense) was gone.
The great heavy industry of the nation, railroad planning and
building, was drawing toward its end. Steel had reached maturity: it was integrated organizationally and functionally and
was being operated so efficiently that American steelmasters
could lay down rails in foreign markets in competition with
the English and German producers. The potentialities of electricity already were being understood. Mechanization of agriculture—at least on great factory wheat farms in the New Northwest—was a reality. Enormous cities, built of steel and stone,
their sprawling areas bound together by rapid transit, telephonic
communication, systems of water supply and waste disposal,
had already become the nerve centers of the nation. Producer
goods, of course, but increasingly consumer goods—factories
were being manned by disciplined wageworkers (who, more
frequently than not, were antagonistic to each other because of
racial, religious, and cultural barriers)—were being turned out
in an endless stream. The national wealth—as farm lands were
being improved, forests were being leveled and converted into
boards and wood pulp, mines were being opened, water power
was being harnessed, factories were being erected, homes were
being built—jumped by leaps and bounds. So, naturally, did the
national income. The real wages of labor, despite the great horde
of immigrants from southern and eastern Europe every year in
greater numbers pressing through our gates, were increasing.

Industrial capitalism, its energies released by the victory of the Civil War, had done all this—and in less than two generations. Not, of course, without aches and pains. The commercial agriculture of the West and South, in the face of a constantly growing foreign market for its cotton, tobacco, wheat, and meat-stuffs, began to drop behind in the late 1880's as its price-costs structure once more was being unbalanced. From 1873 on, prices had begun to decline; nevertheless, for a decade and a half costs also had been reduced, because of mechanization and the farmers' ability to command competitive transportation facilities. At the end of the 1880's, the farmers' reciprocal advantages had melted away. Land values had steadily moved upward, as engrossment of available lands had become more complete. Credit—for long-term and intermediate needs—was hard to obtain and costly. The railroads were no longer struggling desperately among themselves for business, but were now combined in "pools" to fix rates and prorate freight. The protective tariff system—by 1890 its rates were the highest in American history until that time—placed the farmers at the complete mercy of a native manufacturing interest. Monopolistic "pools" (in agricultural implements, wire, twine, other farming necessaries) had already begun to rear their ugly heads.

The agrarians of the West and South—as they had, successfully, before 1850—once more joined hands for the purpose of seeking to capture political power. Under the leadership of Populism (which also penetrated deeply into the political thinking of the far western and southern states themselves, and which again invoked the American doctrine of egalitarianism), the farmers inscribed on their banners three basic demands. They wanted a People's Land, a People's Money, and a People's Transportation. But the alliance had come too late. By 1896, when the challenge for power was made, industrial capitalism was too well organized. And there now existed in the factory towns of the East and Middle West a vast throng of foreign-born workers who were cold to the petty-bourgeois strivings of the aroused American agriculturists. William Jennings Bryan lost; and the threat of an agricultural revolution was now and for all time checked. The farmers had become permanently a mi-

nority interest who could only bargain with the controllers of
the nation's policy but never command.

Labor, too, particularly unorganized and unskilled labor, was
restive. The American Federation of Labor, fully launched
upon its career in the late 1880's, was quietly and successfully
making progress among the crafts. Skilled workers, because of
their command of strategic areas of production, were organizing under their own leaders in powerful national unions, were
building up their strike and friendly-benefit funds, were writing
collective-bargaining agreements with employers, and were raising wages and lowering working hours for themselves. The
skilled workers had become pure-and-simple craft unionists:
they had no working-class psychology or politics; they felt no
obligation toward (indeed, did not sense the ultimate threat to
their own stability in the existence of) the great army of unskilled laborers. Occasionally, bold leaders appeared to gal-
vanize into activity this latter group. The metal miners and
casual harvest hands of the Far West, the woodworkers of the
New Northwest, the seamen: these came to be organized, upon
anarchosyndicalist lines, and to talk a curiously American language of revolution. There were violent strikes, bitter legal and
illegal reprisals, property destruction, and wholesale jailings;
yet very little, if any, permanent gain.

Thus the general scene: outwardly placid, except for occasional and temporary dislocations; and characterized by confidence, security, no little smugness, and endless material advance. Small enterprisers—a great number Puritan in their
heritage and outlook—worked hard at their businesses, stinted
and saved, and built with their own hands big things from little
beginnings. In this fashion, America grew—up to the end of the
nineteenth century.

I have said that the scene, outwardly, was a placid one. However, underneath ran swift currents that were to change its
aspects markedly before another American generation was to
complete the race. For even before the World War was to break
out, the leadership of industrial capitalism was to be shouldered
aside and the new directors of enterprise were to become the
finance capitalists.

The enterprisers of the industrial-capitalist epoch had been interested in profits, naturally: but they had also been goaded on by the instinct of workmanship. To turn out great profusions of goods, to lower costs constantly, to defeat their competitors in trials of strength: this was as much a creative effort as the long and solitary toiling over his bench of the original skilled handicraftsman. The finance capitalists, operating out of their banks, frequently completely alien to the processes of production, every transaction a bookkeeping one rather than involving men, machines, raw materials, and fabricated ware, were interested only in profits. The impersonalization of capitalism—and the beginnings of its decline—had begun. Profits were to be made at all costs: by monopoly controls, first and foremost; and also by limiting production, withholding invention, fixing and keeping inelastic prices, rigging the security markets, manipulating and vulgarizing the judicial processes, and encouraging paid management (itself insecure) to fight labor mercilessly. Finance capitalism operated through the device of monopoly: and monopoly killed the expansive and progressive characteristics of free industrial enterprise.

It is true that efforts at monopoly had made their appearance before the finance capitalist pre-empted the stage. The late 1880's had seen a veritable plague of "pools" and "trusts" descending upon industrial America. But, the fact is, these had not been too successful. Made up, usually, of equal producers, who sought to curb the excesses of cutthroat competition, the formers of "pools" and "trusts" had got together to allocate production and fix prices; sooner or later, however, most such arrangements ended in failure because one or another participant violated the agreements drawn up. The large corporation had to appear first, based on vertical or horizontal integration, before monopoly could seriously threaten.

The Standard Oil Company had been such an example of an horizontal integration: for its preoccupation had been not with the production of crude petroleum (this was to be made available to it in a free producers' market), but with refining, transport, and—later—marketing. The Carnegie Company had been an example of vertical integration: for it had built up its commanding place in steel on the basis of its ownership of its coal, coking, iron, limestone, transport, furnace, and mill requirements. Nevertheless, the Carnegie Company made only heavy steel, which it sold to the manufacturers of light steel.

But with integration achieved in some areas, the investment bankers could move in. They had moved in first in the case of railroading, in the late 1880's, and more particularly as a result of the disastrous collapse of the railroading industry during the depression of 1893-96; and, due to these triumphs, they were fully panoplied. The finance capitalists had come more and more to control the agencies of savings—the insurance companies, the trust companies, the savings banks—and they had European allies. With these funds they could threaten, cajole, and tempt the industrial capitalists. They offered reorganizations—with heavy write-ups of capitalizations—to tempt enterprisers to surrender their businesses and live off the returns of equities for the rest of their natural lives. They threatened competition to already existing and sound concerns by putting up rival plants and engaging in savage and disorderly price wars. They manipulated the railroad-rate structure and credit agencies to bludgeon the recalcitrant into compliance; and the stock markets to prove they could make or break the hesitant.

With the end of the 1893-96 depression, an era of giant-corporation creation set in in the United States, the leadership being taken by the finance capitalists. Attention has already been called to how Carnegie was compelled to incorporate because his outstanding partner, Frick, had thrown in his lot with the great finance capitalists of the day, the Houses of Morgan and Rockefeller. And the pressure of Morgan, who began to erect a competitive heavy-steel company and to combine the light-steel manufacturers against Carnegie, forced Carnegie's surrender. The appearance of the United States Steel Corporation was a symbol: it was a monopoly and it was controlled by finance. As in steel, so also in metal mining, machinery, agricultural implements, building materials, oceanic transport, municipal rapid transit, electrical equipment, hydroelectric power, telephonic and telegraphic communication, meatpacking, woolens.

Before the epoch of finance capitalism, the accumulations of American enterprise had been used at home to build up America's productive plant. Under the aegis of finance capitalism, monopoly profits—no longer interested in rationalization of plant and, therefore, lower costs—poured out of the United States. From 1900 to 1914, American accumulations embarked on economic imperialist adventure. In 1897, our capital stake abroad (American ownership of foreign securities and direct investments in foreign lands) had been only $685,000,000. By the end of 1908, this sum had climbed to $2,525,000,000, and by the middle of 1914—when the World War broke out—to $3,514,000,000. Not only had we advanced our position absolutely, but relatively as well. For, at the end of 1908, our net liabilities to foreigners on capital account (after our foreign investments were subtracted from the investments foreigners held in the United States) was $3,875,000,000; by the middle of 1914, these net liabilities had declined to $3,686,000,000. The extraordinary profits of monopoly and their investment beyond the confines of continental United States were converting us into a creditor nation.

By 1914, our investment bankers had sold American *rentiers* (whether individual, institutional, or corporate) more than $400,000,000 in foreign dollar loans. And, under their prompting, American enterprise had sunk heavy sums in Caribbean sugar and other plantation wares, Mexican mines and cattle lands, Canadian forests and nickel deposits; and in railroad construction, public utilities, branch factories, petroleum production and distribution, sales organizations, and banks and urban real estate all over the world. We were heavily involved in Canada, Mexico, and Cuba, as was to be expected; but our stake was also to be found in almost all the Latin American and European countries and in Asia.

So the processes of monopolization and imperialist penetration continued, aided and abetted by the inflated profits derived from the World War. The prosperity of the 1920's was a false one: agriculture entered into final decline as early as 1921; during the whole decade there existed a permanently disemployed group of 2,000,000 workers; we were a creditor nation and also a nation possessing a favorable commodity balance in its foreign trade—so that many foreign purchasers of our exports perforce had to be financed by our dollar loans. Worst of all, a sizable part of annual national income, incapable of finding opportunities for savings in productive enterprise at home, was driven to engage in security speculation.

As a result of the long depression setting in with 1930, a new epoch in capitalism's history in America appeared. To halt large-scale business and banking failure, to prevent agricultural bankruptcy, to take in the slack created by the decline of foreign markets, and to alleviate human distress, protect small-property ownership, create work, and guarantee social security to unemployables, the New Deal launched on its way state capitalism in the United States. Private enterprise had sold its heritage (its tough-mindedness, its creativeness) for a mess of pottage (security and monopoly prices). It was no longer capable, apparently, of fabricating goods cheaply and in this way devising work. And just as finance capitalism had moved in a generation previously, now the state was moving in.

For the state was complementing, supplementing, and increasingly superseding private enterprise. It was borrowing money; however, no longer only to finance war, as had been the case previously. It was now borrowing to buy and sell commodities, process goods, create electric power and light, conserve the natural resources of the land, deal in real estate, engage in warehousing, the banking business, the operation of ships and railroads, foreign trade. It was borrowing; but this time to stimulate production and distribution, so that national income might be raised from the depths. Then, ran the program of the New Deal, taxation, imposed on excessive incomes and earnings, would in time balance the federal budget. And it was using the organizational forms of private enterprise: corporations and corporate agencies which possessed assets of their own, reported earnings, and had great rolls of employees as well as complex hierarchical structures—so that responsibility to Congress was becoming more and more indirect and obscured.

Such was the social-service state of our present day: social service because its *economics* was based on welfare. It was also in danger of becoming the bureaucratic state: so that its *politics* someday might threaten to be linked with the self-perpetuation, that is to say, the power, of its functionaries. This is what had happened in the case of the institutionalized Catholic Church after the tenth century; and also in the case of the Mercantile State of seventeenth-century England and eighteenth-century France.

This was the journey America had traveled over a long and involved road in the space of three centuries. Capitalism had been its guide. Private enterprise, first the mercantile capitalism of the Colonial Period and then the rising industrial capitalism of the late Middle Period, had been twice in danger. And in both instances it had beaten off its attackers. It had in the one century of its greatest triumphs, the nineteenth century, created the potentialities of physical abundance and left behind the legacy of political freedom.

If Joseph Wood Krutch will forgive my paraphrasing his thoughtful query about Europe, I should like to conclude these observations with a similar query. Was American Capitalism a Success? In the light of the analysis I have pursued through these pages, it seems to me that to raise the question is to answer it. The capitalism that settled America in terms of the active faith of Protestant Puritanism; that defied the authority of the English Mercantile State; that penetrated the western wilderness and established in it free enterprise and the free man who knew how to put the public official in his place; that overthrew the economic and political pretensions of the slave power; that conquered (wastefully, it is true) and harnessed the natural resources of a great land, and filled that land with efficient agencies for turning out consumer goods in a vast flood: that capitalism was a success.

The capitalism I have described gave us the physical means of achieving abundance; and, it seems to me, Americans will never accept, under any dispensation or false ideology, dearth as their portion. The capitalism I have described gave us even a richer heritage: for it wove the idea of egalitarianism into the warp and woof of our tradition. What have been these leveling notions of which I have sought to make so much? They have been the following. The natural rights of the individual to his life, liberty, and the pursuit of his happiness. Representative, republican government. The separation of the church and state. The public school. Universal suffrage. A free associational life. Equality before the law. The hatred of a privileged caste. The right to challenge oppressive public authority. Notably and always the last.

Is any tradition, any idea, strong enough to withstand physical might? Without question; perhaps this has been man's only armor. That is why, at bottom, I am really not fearful of American state capitalism. It is here to stay—and we shall use it as a servant and not as a sovereign. That is why, too, as I pointed out at the beginning, the analogy between the old mercantile capitalism and our present-day state capitalism is not too apt. The Mercantile State forswore abundance; our new state heralds it. And intervening between the day of the absolutist Mercantile State, with its cynical contempt for the individual, and our own, there stands the tradition of the Enlightenment, the American Revolution, Jeffersonianism, Old Radical Republicanism, Populism. This is the American tradition: and I firmly believe it will make us economically secure and keep us politically free.

Growth of Manufactures in the United States, 1850–80

1. GROWTH OF MANUFACTURES IN THE UNITED STATES

(FIGURES OF VALUE IN MILLIONS OF DOLLARS; WAGE EARNERS IN THOUSANDS)

Items	1850	1860	1870*	1880
Capital invested..................	533.2	1009.9	1694.6	2790.3
Value of products................	1019.	1885.	3386.	5369.6
Value added by manufacturing......	463.9	854.2	1395.1	1972.8
Wages paid out...................	236.8	378.9	620.5	947.9
Number of wage earners...........	958.1	1311.2	2054.	2732.6

2. PER CENT INCREASES

Items	1850–60	1860–70*	1870–80*	1850–80
Capital invested..................	89.4	67.8	64.7	423.5
Value of products................	85.	79.5	58.6	426.9
Value added by manufacturing......	84.4	63.3	41.4	325.2
Wages paid out...................	60.	63.8	52.8	300.4
Number of wage earners...........	36.9	56.6	33.	185.2

3. VALUE OF PRODUCTS OF SELECTED LIGHT INDUSTRIES

(FIGURES IN MILLIONS OF DOLLARS)

Industries	1850	1860	1870*	1880
Cotton manufactures..............	61.9	115.7	142.	192.1
Woolen manufactures..............	48.6	73.5	159.4	238.1
Boots and shoes..................	54.	91.9	145.3	196.9
Men's ready-made clothing.........	48.3	80.8	118.9	209.5

4. PER CENT INCREASES

Industries	1850–60	1860–70*	1870–80*	1850–80
Cotton manufactures..............	87.	22.7	35.3	210.5
Woolen manufactures..............	51.1	117.	49.4	389.8
Boots and shoes..................	70.3	58.1	35.5	264.9
Men's ready-made clothing.........	67.3	47.1	76.2	333.7

5. VALUE OF PRODUCTS OF SELECTED HEAVY INDUSTRIES

(FIGURES IN MILLIONS OF DOLLARS)

Industries	1850	1860	1870*	1880
Pig iron.........................	12.7	20.9	55.7	89.3
Agricultural implements...........	6.8	20.8	41.7	68.6
Machinery.......................	28.	51.9	110.8	214.4
Lumber.........................	60.4	96.7	168.1	233.3
Clay products....................	8.2	14.	29.1	41.8

6. PER CENT INCREASES

Industries	1850–60	1860–70*	1870–80*	1850–80
Pig iron	63.7	166.9	60.3	600.6
Agricultural implements	204.5	99.9	64.8	903.2
Machinery	85.3	113.6	93.5	665.6
Lumber	60.1	73.8	38.7	286.1
Clay products	70.8	108.0	43.8	410.6

* When the census of 1870 was taken, there was a premium on gold of 25 per cent because specie payments had not yet been resumed. In order to make the figures comparable, the values recorded in the census of 1870 have been converted into gold dollars by reducing each item by 20 per cent.

A number of obvious generalizations may be made from an examination of these tables. Tables 1 and 2 indicate very clearly the extraordinary development of manufactures in the United States during the decades 1850–80. Over the thirty years, the capital invested in manufacturing enterprise and the value of products turned out increased more than 400 per cent. Wages increased 300 per cent; but the number of wage earners (due to greater mechanization and more efficient production) increased less than 200 per cent.

It will be observed that when the country's record generally is considered, the increases over the decade 1850–60 were superior to those over the decade 1860–70; and that the decade 1870–80 marked a further slowing down of the process. But if we examine the performance of the selected *heavy* industries as compared with those of the selected *light* industries (tables 3–6) the conclusion is the reverse. In other words, *heavy* industry achieved greater gains by far than did *light* industry for the whole thirty-year period. Again, *heavy* industry continued to advance at an accelerating tempo during the decade 1860–70. Finally, *heavy* industry's recovery from the long depression of 1873–79 was very rapid.

These interesting observations may be presented in another way. Taking the value of manufacturing products for the country as a whole, for the years 1850–80 the per cent increase was 426.9. Of the four outstanding *light* industries analyzed, none showed gains that approximated the general figure. On the other hand, among the five *heavy* industries analyzed, there were three whose performances were vastly superior and one whose record came within striking distance of the general average. The remaining one (lumber) was off considerably; but this was due to the fact that lumbering was still in large part a southern industry and the South had not yet recovered from the Civil War.

This, then, substantiates the position taken in the text that industrial capitalism (more particularly, *heavy* industry) benefited from the Civil War and it continued to make great forward strides (despite a severe depression) after the political victory was firmly secured.

Authorities Cited in the Text

CHAPTER I

P. 12. Trotsky, L. D., *The History of the Russian Revolution,* 3 vols. (New York, Simon and Schuster, 1932), vol. 1, p. 10.

CHAPTER II

P. 18. Sombart, Werner, *Der moderne Kapitalismus,* 3 vols. in 6 parts (Munich and Leipzig, Duncker and Humblot, 1921-28), vol. 2, p. 23-173.

CHAPTER IV

P. 49. Tawney, R. H., *Religion and the Rise of Capitalism* (New York, Harcourt Brace, 1926), p. 240.

P. 50. Tawney, *op. cit.,* p. 230.

CHAPTER V

P. 59. Keynes, J. M., *A Treatise on Money,* 2 vols. (New York, Harcourt Brace, 1930), vol. 2, p. 154-56, 159.

P. 60. Nef, J. U., "The Progress of Technology and the Growth of Large-Scale Industry in Great Britain, 1540-1640" in *The Economic History Review,* vol. v (1934), p. 3-24; "A Comparison of Industrial Growth in France and England from 1540 to 1640" in *The Journal of Political Economy,* vol. xliv (1936), p. 289-317, 505-33, 643-66; "Prices and Industrial Capitalism in France and England, 1540-1640" in *The Economic History Review,* vol. vii (1937), p. 155-85.

CHAPTER VI

P. 65. Nef, J. U., "The Progress of Technology and the Growth of Large-Scale Industry in Great Britain, 1540-1640," *op. cit.*

P. 74. Price, W. H., *The English Patents of Monopoly* (Cambridge, Harvard University Press, 1913).

CHAPTER VII

P. 79. Levy, Hermann, *Economic Liberalism* (London, Macmillan, 1913), p. 89.
P. 80. Scott, W. R., *Records of a Scottish Cloth Manufactory, 1681-1703* (Edinburgh, University Press, 1905), p. 21.
P. 80. Hill, Christopher, book review in *Science and Society*, vol. iii (1939), p. 261-63.
P. 81. Levy, Hermann, *op. cit.*, p. 43.
P. 86. Andrews, C. M., *The Colonial Period of American History*, 4 vols. (New Haven, Yale University Press, 1934-38), vol. 4, p. 108.
P. 87. Andrews, C. M., *op. cit.*, vol. 4, p. 114-15.

CHAPTER IX

P. 110. Dodd, W. E., "Emergence of the First Social Order in the United States" in *The American Historical Review*, vol. xl (1935), p. 217-31.

CHAPTER X

P. 132. Harrell, I. S., *Loyalism in Virginia* (Durham, North Carolina, Duke University Press, 1926), p. 26.
P. 138. Mantoux, Paul, *The Industrial Revolution in the Eighteenth Century* (New York, Harcourt Brace, 1927), p. 65.
P. 140. Dickerson, O. M., *American Colonial Government, 1696-1765* (Cleveland, Arthur H. Clark, 1912), p. 25.
P. 143. Russell, E. B., *The Review of American Colonial Legislation by the King in Council* (New York, Columbia University Press, 1915), p. 118.
P. 143. Swank, J. M., *The History of the Manufacture of Iron in All Ages* (Philadelphia, American Iron and Steel Association, 2nd edition, 1892), p. 479.

CHAPTER XI

P. 149. Nettels, C. P., *The Money Supply of the American Colonies Before 1720* (*University of Wisconsin Studies in Social Sciences and History*, no. 2, 1934).
P. 150. Andrews, C. M., "Anglo-French Colonial Rivalry, 1700-1750: The Western Phase" in *The American Historical Review*, vol. xx (1915), p. 539-56, 761-80; "Colonial Commerce" in *The American Historical Review*, vol. xx (1915), p. 43-63.

P. 153. Weeden, W. D., *Economic and Social History of New England, 1620-1789*, 2 vols. (Boston, Houghton Mifflin, 1890), vol. 2, p. 468.

P. 159. Nettels, C. P., "The Place of Markets in the Old Colonial System" in *The New England Quarterly*, vol. vi (1933), p. 491-512; "The Menace of Colonial Manufacturing" in *The New England Quarterly*, vol. iv (1931), p. 230-69.

P. 160. Beer, G. L., *The Origins of the British Colonial System, 1578-1660* (New York, Macmillan, 1908); *The Old Colonial System, 1660-1754*, 2 vols. (New York, Macmillan, 1912); *British Colonial Policy, 1754-1765* (New York, Macmillan, 1907).

P. 163. Schlesinger, A. M., *The Colonial Merchants and the American Revolution, 1763-1776* (New York, Columbia University Press, 1917), p. 268-69.

P. 164. Nettels, C. P., *The Roots of American Civilization* (New York, Crofts, 1938), p. 610.

CHAPTER XIII

P. 173. Fisher, S. G., *The Struggle for American Independence*, 2 vols. (Philadelphia, Lippincott, 1908), vol. 1, p. 261.

P. 175. East, R. A., *Business Enterprise in the American Revolutionary Era* (New York, Columbia University Press, 1938).

P. 175. Beard, C. A., *An Economic Interpretation of the Constitution of the United States* (New York, Macmillan, 1913).

P. 176. East, R. A., *op. cit.*, p. 209.

CHAPTER XIV

P. 178. East, R. A., *op. cit.*, p. 242.

P. 181. East, R. A., *op. cit.*, p. 261-62.

P. 182. Nettels, C. P., *The Roots of American Civilization, op. cit.*, p. 676.

P. 193. Bemis, S. F., *A Diplomatic History of the United States* (New York, Holt, 1936), p. 103.

P. 195. Bowden, Witt, *Industrial History of the United States* (New York, Adelphi Publishers, 1930), p. 231-32.

CHAPTER XV

P. 201. Turner, F. J., *The Frontier in American History* (New York, Holt, 1920), p. 259.

P. 201. Commons, J. R. and Associates, *History of Labour in the*

United States, 2 vols. (New York, Macmillan, 1918), vol. 1, p. 4.

P. 202. Goodrich, Carter and Davison, Sol, "The Wage-Earner in the Westward Movement" in *Political Science Quarterly,* vol. l (1935), p. 161-85 and vol. li (1936), p. 61-116.

P. 204. Beard, C. A. and M. R., *The Rise of American Civilization,* 2 vols. (New York, Macmillan, 1927), vol. 1, p. 457.

P. 212. Gates, P. W., *The Illinois Central Railroad and Its Colonization Work* (Cambridge, Harvard University Press, 1934), p. 119.

P. 213. Cole, A. C., *The Irrepressible Conflict* (New York, Macmillan, 1934), p. 113.

P. 214. Gates, P. W., "Land Policy and Tenancy in the Prairie Counties of Indiana" in *Indiana Magazine of History,* vol. xxxv (1939), p. 1-26.

CHAPTER XVIII

P. 237. Hughes, S. F., editor, *Letters and Recollections of James Murray Forbes,* 2 vols. (Boston, Houghton Mifflin, 1899), vol. 1, p. 116.

P. 240. Morison, S. E., *Maritime History of Massachusetts, 1783-1860* (Boston, Houghton Mifflin, 1921).

P. 241. Albion, R. G., *The Rise of New York Port, 1815-1860* (New York, Scribners, 1939), p. 259, 286.

P. 243. Bullock, C. J., Williams, J. H., and Tucker, R. S., "The Balance of Trade of the United States" in *The Review of Economic Statistics,* preliminary vol. 1 (1919), p. 215-32.

P. 246. Cairnes, J. E., *Some Leading Principles of Political Economy Newly Expounded* (New York, Harpers, 1878), p. 370.

CHAPTER XIX

P. 254. Clark, V. S., *History of Manufactures in the United States,* 3 vols. (New York, McGraw-Hill, 1929 edition), vol. 1, p. 441.

P. 255. Clark, V. S., *op. cit.,* vol. 1, p. 445.

P. 258. Hunter, L. C., "Influence of the Market Upon Techniques in the Iron Industry in Western Pennsylvania to 1860" in *Journal of Economic and Business History,* vol. i (1929), p. 241-81.

P. 260. Cole, A. H., *The American Wool Manufacture,* 2 vols. (Cambridge, Harvard University Press, 1926).

P. 260. Cole, A. H., "American Carpet Manufacture" in *Facts and Figures in American Economic History* (Cambridge, Harvard University Press, 1932), p. 386-87.

P. 262. Ware, Caroline, *The Early New England Cotton Manufacture* (Boston, Houghton Mifflin, 1931).

P. 262. Clark, V. S., *op. cit.*, vol. 1, p. 450.

CHAPTER XX

P. 276. Ware, N. J., *The Industrial Worker, 1840-1860* (Boston, Houghton Mifflin, 1924), p. 153.

CHAPTER XXI

P. 283. Gray, L. C., *History of Agriculture in Southern United States to 1860*, 2 vols. (Washington, Carnegie Institution, 1933), vol. 1, p. 459-60.

P. 285. Carmen, H. J., *Social and Economic History of the United States, 1500-1875*, 2 vols. (New York, Heath, 1930-34).

P. 288. Kendrick, B. B. and Arnett, A. M., *The South Looks at Its Past* (Chapel Hill, University of North Carolina Press, 1935), p. 42.

P. 292. Du Bois, W. E. B., *Black Reconstruction, 1860-1880* (New York, Harcourt Brace, 1935), p. 27.

P. 294. Phillips, U. B., *American Negro Slavery* (New York, Appleton, 1918).

P. 295. Aptheker, Herbert, "Maroons Within the Present Limits of the United States," in *The Journal of Negro History*, vol. xxiv (1939), p. 167-84.

P. 297. Aptheker, Herbert, *Negro Slave Revolts in the United States, 1526-1860* (New York, International Publishers, 1936), p. 62.

P. 297. Turner, F. J., *The United States, 1830-1850* (New York, Holt, 1935), p. 159.

P. 297. Du Bois, W. E. B., *op. cit.*, p. 10.

CHAPTER XXII

P. 301. Phillips, U. B., *Life and Labor in the Old South* (Boston, Little, Brown, 1929).

P. 307. Russel, R. R., *Economic Aspects of Southern Sectionalism, 1840-61 (University of Illinois Studies in Social Science*, vol. xi, 1922), p. 102-103.

P. 310. Dodd, W. E., "The Fight for the Northwest, 1860" in *The American Historical Review*, vol. xvi (1911), p. 774-88.

P. 315. Randall, J. G., *Civil War and Reconstruction* (New York, Heath, 1937), p. 134, 135.

P. 317. Gray, L. C., *op. cit.*, vol. 2, p. 941-42.

P. 318. Flanders, R. B., *Plantation Slavery in Georgia* (Chapel Hill, University of North Carolina Press, 1933), p. 221-23.

P. 319. Sydnor, C. S., *Slavery in Mississippi* (New York, Appleton-Century, 1933), p. 196-97.

P. 320. Sydnor, C. S., *op. cit.*, p. 198.

CHAPTER XXIII

P. 337. Beard, C. A. and M. R., *The Rise of American Civilization,* 2 vols. (New York, Macmillan, 1927), vol. 2, p. 34-35.

CHAPTER XXIV

P. 349. Marx, Karl and Engels, Frederick, *The Civil War in the United States* (New York, International Publishers, 1937), p. 81-82.

P. 351. Julian, G. W., *Political Recollections, 1840 to 1872* (Chicago, Jansen McClurg, 1884), p. 238.

P. 352. Julian, G. W., *op. cit.*, p. 243-44.

P. 360. Julian, G. W., *op. cit.*, p. 255-56.

P. 368. Clarke, G. G., *George W. Julian* (Indianapolis, Indiana Historical Commission, 1923), p. 113.

P. 372. Shannon, F. A., *Economic History of the People of the United States* (New York, Macmillan, 1934), p. 392.

CHAPTER XXV

P. 380. Du Bois, W. E. B., *op. cit.*, p. 419-20.

P. 380. Simkins, F. B., "New Viewpoints of Southern Reconstruction" in *The Journal of Southern History,* vol. v (1939), p. 49-61.

P. 382. Randall, J. G., *op. cit.*, p. 866.

P. 388. Graham, H. J., "The 'Conspiracy Theory' of the Fourteenth Amendment" in *The Yale Law Journal,* vol. xlvii (1938), p. 371-403 and vol. xlviii (1938), p. 171-94.

P. 391. Conkling quoted in Graham, H. J., *op. cit.*

P. 391. Graham, H. J., *op. cit.*

P. 393. Gates, P. W., "The Homestead Law in an Incongruous Land System" in *The American Historical Review,* vol. xli (1936), p. 652-82.

P. 399. Lewis, Cleona, *America's Stake in International Investments* (Washington, Brookings Institution, 1938).

P. 399. Bullock, C. J., Williams, J. H., and Tucker, R. S., *op. cit.*

CHAPTER XXVI

P. 402. Wells, D. A., *Recent Economic Changes* (New York, Appleton, 1889), p. 64-65.

P. 406. Ware, N. J., *The Labor Movement in the United States, 1860-1895* (New York, Appleton, 1929).

P. 410. Slaner, P. A., "The Railroad Strikes of 1877" in *Marxist Quarterly*, vol. i (1937), p. 214-36.

P. 411. Ware, N. J., *op. cit.*, p. 50.

P. 416. Winkler, J. K., *Incredible Carnegie, the Life of Andrew Carnegie (1835-1919)* (New York, Vanguard, 1931), p. 106.

P. 423. Carnegie, Andrew, *Triumphant Democracy* (New York, Scribners, 1886), p. 116-17, 232.

CHAPTER XXVII

P. 434. Krutch, J. W., *Was Europe a Success?* (New York, Farrar & Rinehart, 1934).

Note: All the selections quoted in the text are reprinted by the permission of the separate publishers, whose courtesies are herewith acknowledged. I am indebted to my student Richard G. Birnberg for his generous assistance in checking the facts and bibliography in this book and in helping with the preparation of the Index.

L. M. H.

Index

About the Author

Louis M. Hacker, one of our younger historians, has already established a secure reputation as a writer and teacher. He studied at Columbia University where he now teaches economic history. He has also taught at the University of Wisconsin and Ohio State University. In 1932, in collaboration with B. B. Kendrick, he published *The United States Since 1865*, a standard history now in its third edition. He has also written *The Farmer Is Doomed, A Short History of the New Deal, The United States: A Graphic History,* and *American Problems of Today*. He has contributed a great many articles and reviews to most of the outstanding magazines and journals. His discussions of agriculture and naval policies and his analyses of the New Deal theory and program have also attracted wide attention.

A Representative Selection of Publications
from the Inner Sanctum of
Simon and Schuster

THE BIBLE DESIGNED TO BE READ AS LIVING LITERATURE
edited by ERNEST SUTHERLAND BATES

MEN OF MATHEMATICS *by* E. T. BELL

MEN OF MUSIC *by* WALLACE BROCKWAY *and* HERBERT WEINSTOCK

MEN OF ART *and* MODERN ART *by* THOMAS CRAVEN

A TREASURY OF AMERICAN PRINTS *and* A TREASURY OF ART MASTERPIECES
edited by THOMAS CRAVEN

THE ART OF THINKING *by* ABBÉ ERNEST DIMNET

THE STORY OF PHILOSOPHY, OUR ORIENTAL HERITAGE,
and THE LIFE OF GREECE *by* WILL DURANT

THE EVOLUTION OF PHYSICS *by* ALBERT EINSTEIN *and* LEOPOLD INFELD

WITH MALICE TOWARD SOME *by* MARGARET HALSEY

I BELIEVE: THE PERSONAL PHILOSOPHIES OF CERTAIN EMINENT
MEN AND WOMEN OF OUR TIME *edited by* CLIFTON FADIMAN

NOW IN NOVEMBER *by* JOSEPHINE JOHNSON

A TREASURY OF THE THEATRE *by* BURNS MANTLE *and* JOHN GASSNER

NIJINSKY *by* ROMOLA NIJINSKY

WOLF SOLENT *and* OTHER NOVELS *by* JOHN COWPER POWYS

EYES ON THE WORLD: A PHOTOGRAPHIC RECORD OF HISTORY
IN THE MAKING *by* M. LINCOLN SCHUSTER

THE FIRST WORLD WAR: A PHOTOGRAPHIC HISTORY
edited by LAURENCE STALLINGS

HISTORY OF THE RUSSIAN REVOLUTION *by* LEON TROTSKY

VAN LOON'S GEOGRAPHY *and* THE ARTS
by HENDRIK WILLEM VAN LOON

THIS is a book about the meaning of American history. It is not a record of dates, battles, and political campaigns. It doesn't interpret America in terms of outstanding personalities. It isn't another story of the American people. It is wholly concerned with the underlying forces, economic and political, that have made American history.

The Triumph of American Capitalism does not come down to the present day. It ends at the turn of this century. But up to that point it presents a rounded, comprehensive, and intelligible picture of American history as a whole.

Louis Hacker's book begins where America began—in Europe. He then shows how Europe established itself in the New World, and why the thirteen colonies revolted from British rule. This revolt he represents as the successful overthrow of British merchant capitalists by the combined forces of the merchants and planters of the colonies. But during the so-called Middle Period the slave system of agriculture in the South prevented the rising northern capitalists from making the most of their independence. It took the Civil War and the Reconstruction period to put American industrial capitalism firmly in the saddle.

Mr. Hacker tells how the British overlords of the thirteen colonies and the plantation owners of the Old South came to grief, and why the American capitalist came into his own. His story is expanded at those points where crises and political conflicts in our history emerged. In fact, his pervasive theme may be characterized